What Works for Working Children

JO BOYDEN

BIRGITTA LING

WILLIAM MYERS

What Works for

Working

Children

United Nations Children's Fund
INTERNATIONAL CHILD DEVELOPMENT CENTRE
Florence · Italy

MEMBER OF THE INTERNATIONAL
SAVE THE CHILDREN ALLIANCE

Save the Children

Save the Children Sweden works for children and young people on the basis of the UN Convention on the Rights of the Child. We fight child abuse and exploitation and work for the protection of children in Sweden and all over the world. We provide assistance to these children and amass experience through practical action. We influence public opinion, values and attitudes in society through information and education.

Save the Children Sweden publishes books for people who work with children in order to disseminate knowledge concerning the situation of children and provide guidance and impulses for new ideas and discussions.

UNICEF

The UNICEF International Child Development Centre (ICDC), established in Florence, Italy in 1988, works in cooperation with other parts of UNICEF for the effective implementation of the Convention on the Rights of the Child (CRC) in both developing and industrialized countries.

Its three main areas of activity are:
- Information management: filtering existing information and its own research results to produce key findings, policy studies and case materials on critical children's rights concerns;
- Research: carried out to promote the understanding, development and monitoring of children's rights;
- Capacity building: transforming the information management and research activities into training programmes for UNICEF staff and other partners on CRC-related issues.

The Centre disseminates the results of its activities through publications targeted at executive decision-makers, programme-managers and other practitioners in child-related fields both inside and outside UNICEF.

The opinions expressed in this publication are those of the authors and do not necessarily reflect the policies or views of UNICEF or Save the Children.

ISBN 91-88726-13-4

Production management: Vibeke Jörgensen
Editing: James Hurst Company
Graphic design and Cover: Ateljén Arne Öström
First edition: 1
Printed by Fälth & Hässler, Smedjebacken, Sweden 1998

Foreword

In recent years an important international debate on child labour has emerged. At times that debate appears to shed more heat than light on this complex subject. The main issue has been how to eliminate child work through, for example, minimum age legislation, compulsory schooling, and trade policy.

Some of the arguments for the elimination of child work are based on concepts of childhood and child development that have been formed largely in western industrialized countries. The values expressed in the debate are drawn from various international human rights declarations and conventions, some of which are still the subject of considerable controversy, including along a 'NorthSouth' dividing-line. Linking the child work issue to the subject of 'social clauses' in trade agreements, conditioning trade benefits on a country's employment practices, has intensified the conflicts. Increasingly, the debate about working children is also linked to the notion that low-income countries will not be able to increase their competitiveness in the global marketplace through the exploitation of children while neglecting the challenge of making basic education more relevant and affordable for all children on the basis of equal opportunity.

In our view, however, a major problem with the policy discussions to date is that they rarely take the reality of working children, or more generally the 'best interests of the child', as a starting point. The child's own perceptions of his or her situation and developmental needs have yet to be recognized. It is our firm belief that an approach based importantly on the actual situation of working children and children at risk of exploitation, including these children's own views, is urgently needed.

As the authors have documented in this book, more and more knowledge about working children is now being compiled, not least from these children's own organizations. Slowly but surely, our understanding is growing of the positive and negative roles that work may play in the lives of children. The knowledge the children are bringing us is also widening our understanding of the complexity of the issue of child work and the need for much more comprehensive and child-centred policies and programme responses to this problem.

By ratifying the 1989 Convention on the Rights of the Child, States Parties have committed themselves to make a reality of these rights. One of the basic principles expressed in that Convention is the child's right to dignity and respect and to be heard. Children have finally acquired a right to be listened to and to be able to influence decisions regarding their own future. As evidenced in recent debates on children's right to participate in international conferences dealing with issues that concern them, there is still an enormous gap between high principles and actual practice.

A child who works is not only a working child. He or she has the right to be considered a human being with a full range of rights, needs, responsibilities, and expectations. Working children's rights and needs for education, rest, play, and sound relations with adults must not be underestimated or neglected in the policy debates.

We firmly believe that addressing the issue of child work from the child's own perspective is a precondition for finding lasting solutions to the numerous problems that are caused by the economic exploitation of children in today's increasingly competitive world.

Rädda Barnen and UNICEF both seek to support effective strategies and policies to address these difficult problems. It is our hope that this book will be a substantive contribution to that process.

Görel Thurdin
Chair
Save the Children
Sweden

Paolo Basurto
Director
UNICEF International
Child Development Centre

Contents

Introduction

Recent years have witnessed a worldwide explosion of interest in the work of children. In both industrialized and developing countries, the matter often has come to public attention largely through media stories that have seemed at once both shocking and puzzling. On the one hand, for example, graphic television and print denunciations of developing country children working long hours to help manufacture products sold in rich countries have stirred up protective sentiment among consumer groups, organized labour, religious institutions, and the general public. Reports of young children missing out on school and play while working day after day for a few pence have especially outraged industrialized countries, where many governments and civil society groups have called for the global 'elimination of child labour'. They take it for granted that children released from the drudgery and exploitation of factory work will be able to enjoy a proper childhood devoted to school and play and unburdened by excessive work responsibilities.

On the other hand, there are equally persistent reports that saving children from having to work can leave them worse off than before. Indeed, industrialized country groups pressing for new trade laws, consumer boycotts or other actions to prohibit the importation of goods produced with the involvement of children sometimes have been surprised and puzzled when highly respected child advocacy and welfare groups have opposed their campaigns as not in the best interests of the children involved. Moreover, children turned out of shops and factories where they made clothing, sports equipment, carpets or other goods, have often complained bitterly, seemingly not one bit happy to be rescued from their hard work. Worse, follow-up reports sometimes have showed that children removed from such work did not return to study or play, but instead drifted into even more harmful and oppressive forms of work. Looking beyond the currently fashionable interest in factories producing consumer items for export, the picture is similar. Media reports from various developing countries have alerted the world to widespread violence against working children, in many types of work, not only by unscrupulous employers, but also by police and other government authorities who should instead be protecting them. Not least among surprises, large numbers of children, while complaining of such problems, still insist that they want to work and that work is beneficial for them. Some even have complained in national and international meetings that they are being victimized by the very people who are trying to save them from 'child labour'. This strikes many as bizarre.

What is going on here? How are such seemingly inexplicable contradictions possible? Why do some working children protest against the enforcement of labour laws intended to protect them, and how can it be that prestigious organizations devoted to the protection of children condemn actions that would rescue children from the recognized evils of 'child labour'? And, given the widespread media reporting of the violence and exploitation often suffered by working children, why do many children insist that work is good for them and that they should be allowed to engage in it? Do these children speak with representative voices, or is there a great 'silent majority' of children who think differently? Is it really possible that what so many adult professionals and organizations promote as best for children might in fact be harmful to them? Or is the problem just one of miscommunication and misunderstanding? Could it be that when rich countries and developing countries discuss the work of children they do not have the same realities in mind? How can we make sense of all these surprises and contradictions? Even more importantly, how can we be sure that what we do to protect children against abuse in the workplace will in fact be good for them? Are there rules or principles that can guide us? How can we know what works for working children?

Why this book is needed and what it tries to do

This book provides a framework within which apparently baffling contradictions may become understandable, and questions about how to best help children can eventually be resolved in practice. It devotes particular attention to the conceptual issues, the ways in which the world thinks about children's work, and the options for dealing with it. That is because we, the authors, have concluded from our experience and research that the most vexing problems of dealing with child work in practice spring from serious conceptual errors. Starting out with wrong ideas prejudices all that follows. In our view, the practical impasses now faced by so many trying to address the workplace abuse of children will become resolvable only through the reorientation of much popular thinking about the nature and causes of children's work, the basic dynamics of child development, the relationship between the work of children and their development, and the ways in which different interventions protect children against workplace abuse. Accordingly, we not only criticize the false assumptions and faulty analysis that condemn much action to failure even before it starts, but we go on to suggest some principles that we think will be helpful in mounting practical action that effectively protects children.

Trying to keep this book focused and practical for policy-makers, programme-planners and children's advocates, we have centred the discussion on certain selected issues that seem to us to constitute particularly serious impediments to successful action. Space limitations prohibit doing otherwise. The book is therefore neither a comprehensive review of the child work literature and experience nor a manual for designing policies and activities. Even the issues it does include are discussed more superficially than we would like; subjects that we cover in a single chapter merit an entire book on their own. Other limitations are also inescapable. One of them is a contradiction inherent in focusing the book on a single aspect of children's lives — their work — while insisting, as we do throughout, on the need for a holistic perspective that takes the child's full context and activities into account. Every reader will recognize that the development of children is affected by many aspects of their lives — including play, family relationships, and peer friendships — and not merely by school and work, as our necessarily disciplined focus on the book's topic could sometimes seem to imply. In the chapters that follow we will show that the experience of working is far more important in the development of children, especially in the poorer regions of the world, than either policy-makers or child development researchers generally realize. But that is not to claim that the influence of work predominates over all other aspects of life. Despite such limitations, we have tried to provide key information, conceptual frameworks, and references that can equip interested practitioners to successfully tackle difficult child work problems that so far have resisted traditional modes of thinking.

We focus primarily on two lines of action — research and policy and programme-planning — which largely determine the relevance of interventions and which are, in our view, the source of most error that has crippled past attempts to prevent or reverse the workplace abuse of children. Our emphasis on studies may be unpopular; we know it runs against the grain of current institutional biases that tend to dismiss research as mostly inessential and a waste of time and resources. However, we do not agree with the commonplace assertion that enough is now known to put a stop to the exploitation of children if only there were sufficient political will. The chapters that follow will seek to demonstrate that current understanding of child work and its impact is in fact so precarious that it is a major obstacle to policy and programme success. We will recommend much more research rather than less, all of it addressing key policy and programme needs, and we will indicate topics meriting priority attention.

We also reopen the issue of what values and objectives should drive interventions in the work of children, casting doubt on some of those hallowed by history and proposing others that might be more fitting in today's world. We also question the validity of old assumptions that underlie some of the most common intervention strategies, and we cite evidence suggesting that different approaches now receiving less attention may be more productive. Readers planning action or advocacy against abuse of children's work should consider the issues we address with some care, whether or not they agree with our conclusions, for we contend throughout the book that ignorance, misconceptions, and sloppy thinking frequently neutralize even the best-intentioned and most lavishly supported child protection efforts.

We ask readers to reconsider even some things that they now think they know for certain. A good opportunity for such reconsideration has been raised by recent changes in the context within which the work of children is today being conceived and discussed. Contemporary thinking about child work and child workers has been much affected by the fact that the period of life up to the age of 18 now has a special status in international law and popular understanding. This is due in part to the nearly universal ratification of the 1989 United Nations Convention on the Rights of the Child, the CRC (to be described in a later chapter), which among its child protection provisions includes an article specifically dedicated to guarding children against work that is detrimental to their health and development. The inclusion of child work in the CRC has drastically expanded public and governmental attention to the issue. As recently as 1997, for example, two major international conferences and several regional ones focused exclusively on the subject of 'child labour', and the International Labour Office is expected to discuss, and will probably adopt, a new convention on the subject during its 1998 and 1999 policy-making sessions. Indeed, global discussion on this topic has not been so intense and widespread since the early decades of this century, if then.

Expanded attention to the subject has generated a veritable flood of new studies, ideas, and experiences, with the result that information becoming available in the 1990s quickly overwhelms and outdates what has been thought, written, and disseminated earlier. It has become virtually impossible for a single person to discover and keep up with even the most significant new information on the topic. This means that even the most dedicated child rights activists, government officials and legislators, and NGO programme managers are unlikely to have ready access to important concepts and information which would be useful in improving the reach and quality of their efforts to protect children in the workplace. There is need for updated review of critical issues and approaches which traces the various lines of thinking and experience, analyzes their implications for concrete action and identifies areas where knowledge is still lacking and research is needed. This book attempts to help meet that need.

We also take a very particular perspective on the problem, considering the questions of child work, and interventions in it, from the standpoint of what is best for the children involved. We think that this is the only really moral position, although this is not to say that other social considerations should not also be taken into account. Our view is very much that of the most fundamental principle of the Convention on the Rights of the Child, which holds that "the best interests of the child" should be a primary consideration in all deliberations regarding its welfare and protection. The implicit question underlying this book is: How would we approach the issues of children's work if the children involved really mattered most? We have been surprised and saddened by the discovery of how few studies and programmes have approached the subject of children's work from a rigorous and explicit concern for the best interests of children. In fact, what is best for the children is often considered last, or not at all. We would like to reverse the priorities, approaching children's work from the premiss that what is best for children should be the first and most important consideration of all.

However, this raises the question of how one is to define what is best for children. What criteria should be used? This is a big question, but one logical solution is to approach the issue from the standpoint of what is known about child growth and development. What promotes the development of children can be considered to be in their best interests, whereas that which impedes their development would be considered harmful to children's interests. Additional criteria might of course be added, but the developmental factors seem to provide a very good place to start. We therefore open with a rather extensive discussion of child development as it relates to children's work, deriving a series of child development principles which we suggest should help orientate the planning of both studies and activities addressing the work of children.

What is best for children should be the first and most important consideration.

The chapters that follow apply these principles as a lens through which we examine essential policy and programme areas such as research and statistics, legislation and enforcement, social mobilization, education, and economic incentives. During our research and writing, we found that looking at these important issues from a child-centred viewpoint sometimes so changes their long-familiar shape and configuration that we ourselves felt slightly disorientated at times, rather as one is made dizzy by peering at the world through someone else's spectacles. Some of what we have to say will sound unfamiliar, and perhaps controversial. We would only point out that such is not so much caused by personal idiosyncrasies than by the simple fact that not many others have yet explored the subject of child work from a child-centred perspective, so we have but limited precedents upon which to draw. Moreover, we have tried to carry the more important of our observations to what seem to be their logical implications for action, and this occasionally generates unconventional views. On the other hand, we note that new technical consensus about child work seems to be forming along the lines of our main arguments. As we prepare this text to go to press, for example, we have received the report of the child labour section of a conference on urban children, held in Trondheim, Norway, in June 1997, in which two of us participated. The parallels between the workshop observations and our chapters that follow are striking, although cross-influences among the participants have not been great. Political consensus, however, appears to be trailing far behind technical thinking.

We do not attempt to present here a new 'child-centred' model for thinking about the subject. That would be both presumptuous and premature, although we think that such a model would be useful, and we hope this book makes progress towards one. It is enough for us to outline certain important issues, indicating where feasible some practical policy and programme implications of addressing them from the standpoint of what is best for the children involved. We also note important voids where further research is needed, indicating those we believe to be of high priority. We expect that others will soon address these issues, and that our exploratory contribution will before long be supplanted by more definitive findings.

It is above all our hope that this book can help draw more attention to working children themselves. We want to put them and their best interests back into the centre of the picture, which sometimes seems to have been taken over by abstract economic and political discussion of 'child labour', not to mention the self-interest of many national and international organizations involved in the issue.

Special sources

Most of the following discussion is based upon published or unpublished literature readily available to researchers dealing with the subject of children's work, and which is duly recorded in the notes and bibliography. However, we also rely on certain important new sources not yet published at the time of writing. The most important of these are a series of field studies and a literature review commissioned by Rädda Barnen (Swedish Save the Children) and which will in due course be published in their own right. The first of these is a postal survey of organizations and individuals considered to have substantive experience in regard to children's work issues. Respondents included animators, teachers, and other practitioners, administrators, project staff and managers from international and local non-governmental organizations (NGOs) and governmental and inter-governmental organizations, as well as researchers. The purpose of this survey was to obtain a sense of how organizations and individuals working in this area conceive and think about certain key questions. The questionnaire included both multiple-choice and open-ended 'essay' questions. From 600 questionnaires sent out and a response rate of nearly 40 per cent, 199 replies were found to be sufficiently complete and usable, and are the basis of the discussion. The reader should remember, however, that while the distribution of answers among those who replied can be considered interesting, the sample was not representative, and therefore cannot be interpreted as statistically significant. It represents only those who chose to answer from the selection of organizations Rädda Barnen knew how to contact, and there will certainly be biases.

A second Rädda Barnen study, much cited in the following chapters, interviewed working children in five areas (Bangladesh, Ethiopia, Philippines, and three Central American countries) to ascertain how they see their work in the context of their overall lives, especially in relation to school and family life. A secondary purpose of this study was to develop a practical methodology which can be utilized by Rädda Barnen field offices and other organizations to obtain such information in a reliable and comparable manner. A third study assessed the impact of different intervention approaches on working children. It examined in some depth the thinking, activities, and effects of selected Rädda Barnen projects in five parts of the world — Bangladesh, Ethiopia, Senegal, Peru, and El Salvador. In addition to being appraised by outside evaluators, as per the usual practice, these programmes also were systematically criticized by children having contact with them, thus providing a multi-faceted picture of their ideas, operations, and impact. The fourth specially commissioned study was a review of the child development literature and a theoretical discussion of the implications of modern child development thinking for addressing child work issues. This piece is virtually unique as a knowledgeable reflection on the importance of child work in and for child development thinking, and is therefore much cited in the first two chapters of this book.

Another non-standard source is the professional experience of the authors, all of whom have for some years been deeply involved in international child work issues, primarily in connection with either non-governmental organizations or United Nations agencies. Since there is little or no suitable literature regarding some of the questions we raise, we have occasionally drawn upon our own experience as a primary source. We try to alert the reader when we are serving as our own source. The reader also should realize that some deep concerns arising from our experience have motivated us to write this book. First of all, we have been impressed by the many working children we have met and learned from. It has always been clear that these often complex, shrewd, responsible and resilient children did not generally match the 'passive victim', 'juvenile delinquent' or other stereotypes by which adults tended to label them. Yet adults have always made important decisions about these youngsters, with no idea of what the children were really like, without listening to their frequently poignant observations and creative ideas, and without the slightest notion of what it feels like to be a working child. That is sad, because it is evident that working children, who often seem more articulate and worldly-wise than their non-working peers, have much of value to share and which adults need to know. We cannot by ourselves bridge this gap between children and adults, but we do seek in this book to bring at least some voices of children into the subjects we consider. We also suggest ways in which working children can be brought more fully into activities intended for their protection and advancement, not only as beneficiaries, but also as participants.

A second factor motivating this book is our broad observation that some of the most traditional and widely prescribed measures for protecting child workers from exploitation and abuse do not work well; at least for the children who most need protection. They tend to be coercive measures and, on the rare occasions when they are not easily evaded, they miscarry, sometimes making victims of the people they are supposed to help. Everybody in the poor communities affected — children, parents, community and religious leaders, employers, low-level local government officials — seem to know that. Who often appear not to know it, or at least to recognize it, are those who have the power and responsibility to make the social rules — especially government policy-makers and administrators. Supposed protection programmes that end up actually oppressing or otherwise endangering working children are extremely common. For example, the extensive literature on street children is rife with descriptions of how police and court authorities in many parts of the world regularly detain, beat, imprison, kill or otherwise mistreat young street workers under the pretext of protective policies and statutes. We also have had experience with well-intentioned 'rescue' operations — such as the sudden removal of children from the sex trade or bonded labour — in which the 'saved' children protested that they were cut off from their only means of support without being offered viable alternatives. Similarly, we have seen young street workers unjustly labelled as abandoned and removed from their families into institutional care. It is widely recognized by field workers that many 'rescued' children will revert to the situations they were 'saved' from, or something equally bad, but this highly indelicate fact is almost never put into writing. And, of course, it is very widely observed among those living close to the situation that enforcement of child labour laws in poor communities or countries tends to drive child exploitation problems further underground and exacerbate them. This book goes beyond condemning what does not work for children to suggest principles and lines of action that do.

A third concern stems from our observation that national and international policies governing the work of children tend to be strangely divorced from the practical realities faced by poor developing country families and their children. This problem is exacerbated by current trends toward universalizing both concepts of 'child labour' and strategies for dealing with it. Countries increasingly are asked to pull their definitions, objectives and actions regarding children's work into line with global policies established through international conventions. Generally speaking, the people who frame such policies have had little or no contact with working children, their families, or organizations who directly assist them. Their ideas about the nature, causes, and effects of children's work frequently seem unrelated to the context within which countless children and their parents eke out their daily survival. The powerful and the powerless exist in such different worlds that they tend to talk past one another, each uncomprehending of the other, even on those rare occasions when they attempt to communicate. Such a radical divergence of perspectives poses a formidable obstacle to achieving sensible polices regarding child work that even the poor will accept as legitimate, and which therefore can be successfully implemented. This book addresses some of the important issues attending the unfortunate division between high-flown rhetoric and more down-to-earth facts. It especially homes in on questions of what can fairly be universalized and what must respond to the particulars of circumstance.

Our experience also generates a fourth concern much reflected in the chapters that follow. That is a tendency by the public, including many people and organizations who should know better, to grossly oversimplify the issues surrounding child work and then to single-mindedly promote that false view and actions based on it. When it is self-serving, this insistent ignorance can be as exploitative of children as are the workplace abuses it criticizes. We hope that this book will encourage and help readers to address child work issues in their proper complexity without being intimidated. To start with, it needs to be noted that there are three different categories of working children, and they live in dissimilar situations, merit distinct concerns, and require diverse forms of protection and advancement. The first group is comprised of children in occupations or working conditions that are clearly hazardous or seriously detrimental to their well-being and development. This group is sometimes referred to as engaged in 'intolerable' forms of child work, and it merits very high concern. Children in forms of slavery and prostitution are invariably mentioned among those classified this way. A second group includes children who are in a 'grey' area of less objectionable work that may or may not contain potentially detrimental aspects, or who are at substantial risk of falling into detrimental work. This category probably is much larger than the first, and deserves a level of attention less intense. The third group is made up of children whose work is in no way harmful to their well-being or development and might even be beneficial. Apart from some routine vigilance, this group may not merit either worry or intervention. The chapters that follow will help clarify these distinctions.

Why we discuss child work instead of child labour

The venerable term 'child labour' has over the years lost its original connotation of regular, toilsome, low-skilled paid work, and is now so thoroughly confused with the broader notion of child work that it is no longer useful in precise discussion. It is not uncommon for three or four participants in a conversation about 'child labour' to use the same term, each having in mind a different phenomenon. In discussing what should be done to control the workplace abuse of children, for instance, imagine the confusion if a trade union representative thinks of child work primarily in terms of full-time factory jobs, an urban social welfare worker conceives of it as mostly the part-time child street traders so common in many cities, and a government policy-maker has in mind the large majority of rural child workers who work seasonally in agriculture. The problems and remedies vary enormously between these situations and, without identifying exactly the work and young workers under discussion, agreement on action may be difficult.

In addition, the distinctions properly separating 'labour' from 'work' in English do not translate into other important languages such as French and Spanish, leading to considerable awkwardness in documents produced in multiple tongues. Despite these disadvantages, 'child labour' continues to be used even in serious technical discussions, probably because of tradition and for ease of expression, even by some authors having misgivings about the term.

Another important reason to avoid the term 'child labour' is that it is used by many to describe specifically those kinds of children's work that are harmful to children, and our chosen subject is far broader. We wish to consider work that is harmless or beneficial for children, as well as that which is detrimental to them. Regarding the broad topic of children's work too exclusively from a narrow 'child labour' orientation not only eliminates some forms of work we wish to discuss, but also completely misses many of the most important child growth and development questions. It also distorts the issues by tending to place *a priori* negative connotations even on activities more likely to be beneficial than dangerous for children.

For all of the above reasons, we will speak primarily of children's work, intending the term to be free of any previous judgement about its value or effect on children unless we indicate otherwise through the discussion context or modifiers such as 'detrimental', 'exploitative', 'harmless' or 'beneficial'. 'Child labour' will from this point be reserved for historical references, quotes, and other limited uses in which the context of the word is plain.

However, this focus raises another problem, which is to define just what constitutes 'work'. Because this is a fundamental issue, it is important that the reader should understand rather well what is involved in it before launching into the chapters that follow. The matter is thornier and more tedious than might be expected because so many possible definitions are available. The ample literature on the nature of work provides a bewildering choice of concepts ranging from a narrow economic focus on paid employment (a 'job') to a broader meaning that has to do with shaping one's life and environment (a 'life's work'). Some of the many definitions are precise and intended for official use. The International Labour Organization, for example, defines work as economic activity — which means any activity that contributes to the Gross Domestic Product (GDP) of a country according to criteria established under the international System of National Accounts (SNA). But the SNA criteria can look very strange when applied to typical poor people and households, and they are not always clear even to experts, let alone to lay persons. But let us consider them, since they generate the definition of 'work' which the ILO has generally applied to children as well as adults, and which is especially influential in international conventions and debate about the work of children.

To start with, let us imagine a young African girl living in a rural area who, typically, would help her family in a number of different tasks. When she gets up an hour before sunrise to help clean the house, fetch water, and make breakfast, she is not working, according to official definitions. That is because these activities are not considered to contribute to the national economy. But when she goes outside to help her mother tend the garden from which they sell products in the local market, she now begins to work, as indeed she still does when they go together to the market to sell some produce. However, when she takes vegetables from the same garden inside and prepares the midday meal from them, she is no longer working. Later she goes out to fetch firewood, which is heavy to carry and must be brought from over a mile away, but she is not working. Then she goes back out to gather fodder to feed the farm animals which are used for traction, and is now working again. She is also officially working when she helps her family in the fields. When she goes back inside to clean up in the kitchen and to help bed down her younger brother and sister, singing them to sleep long after sundown, she is not working. And, of course, she was not working during the three hours she spent in school. According to the way governments usually define work for purposes of statistics about work and workers, she worked only a minor part of the day. In common parlance, however, most of us would agree she was a very busy little girl who in fact worked a long day with little or no time for rest and play. To confuse the matter even further, she would in many places not be counted as working at all. The reason is that she goes to school. Official statistical systems often will not record children as working if they are enrolled in school, even if they have a paid job for more hours than they study. That is because a child who attends school is, in many systems, presumed unavailable for work, no matter what the reality of the situation. In many places, work by school children outside class hours is automatically excluded, which of course would make it appear in the statistics that work and school are mutually exclusive.

Then there is the issue of full versus part-time work. A child who is not in school, but is involved in at least sporadic economic activities, might be counted in national statistics as a worker without reference to the number of hours or days per month actually spent working. But, all around the world, people who hear the terms 'child worker' or 'child labour' tend to think immediately in terms of a full-time regular job. While many children do indeed work full-time, available evidence suggests that the large majority do not. To confuse things even more, many countries do not even bother to collect data on children below the legal minimum age for work — usually somewhere between 12 and 15 — since they are not supposed to be working. Another complicating factor is the period during which work is noted. Some systems count as workers only people who are working near the time of the survey (for example, during the week prior) while other studies may include those who worked, say, anytime during the last year. This makes an important difference, since huge numbers of children work only seasonally or intermittently. Large numbers of children who work only during the harvest season, for example, would be counted as workers in one system but not in another. The reader will by now understand why even experts conversing about children's work sometimes discover that they are not considering the same phenomenon. It is necessary to be precise about what work is being considered.

For the purposes of this book, we use 'work' in its popular rather than official sense, which means we include time spent in home maintenance chores as well as in money-making activities inside or outside the home. To us, the hypothetical African girl described above worked all day. By our criteria, it does not matter whether children work for recompense or not, which allows us to include the vast number of children who work a significant amount of time in family undertakings without receiving any pay. We also encompass part-time work, although we mostly have in mind that which goes beyond occasional light chores to occupy signifi- cant time — for instance ten or more hours per week. We certainly count school children who work such hours out of school to be workers. We would also consider as part-time workers those children who work inten- sively during particular seasons but do little work in between; for exam- ple, industrialized-country rural children who work hard in agriculture during the summer holiday but do relatively little work during the rest of the year when they are in school.

The above discussion ignores, of course, how children themselves would define work. As many a parent knows, younger children especially some- times tend to consider any assigned task they dislike doing as 'work', while even rigorous economic activities may be viewed as a form of pleasure and recreation by children who enjoy doing them. This calls attention to big sub- jective and cultural elements in defining what is and is not work.

Even if we cannot clearly delineate what is and is not work, surely we can define who is a child ... or can we? Well, not easily, it seems. As the first chapter will present in some detail, this apparently simple question is anything but that, and it is hardly capable of a single answer, especially on the basis of age. For purposes of this book, we will for simplicity's sake generally think of 'child work' as any work performed by children up to middle adolescence: roughly 15 years of age. It needs to be recog- nized, however, that the Convention on the Rights of the Child considers young persons to be children up to the age of 18. But when one thinks specifically of child work, there are major differences between younger and older children, not the least of which is that one can in most countries become a legal worker with full workers' rights by about 14 or 15 years of age. Even though much of our discussion is about children younger than late adolescents, it must be remembered that the concern for protecting children against hazards to their well-being and develop- ment continues up to the age of 18.

A brief summary of child work in the world today

In view of the above discussion of the problems of enumerating child workers, it should be easy to see why nobody knows how many children in the world really work, how much they work, or whether their work is detrimental to them. Because of intense public and government demand for global quantitative information, the International Labour Organization — the leading United Nations agency on child labour matters — from time to time feels obliged to release an estimate of how many children work; the most recent version at the time of writing is 250 million. Such estimates are cited in the média and elsewhere as though they were authoritative. They are not, by any stretch of the imagination, even though the ILO goes to considerable trouble to make its 'guesstimates' as intelligently as possible. The unvarnished fact is that, the ILO's best efforts notwithstanding, nobody has a credible notion of how many children in the world 'work', and cannot possibly know until some important changes are made in the way countries collect and analyze their data. All published global estimates of the number of children working are not only inaccurate, but probably misleading. However, some vague orders of magnitude and a very general child worker distribution profile can be tentatively deduced from the more useful country data that are available.

In all parts of the world, children work, but the work they most commonly do, the reasons why they work, and the conditions under which they work differ greatly according to region, especially between industrialized and developing countries. From a global perspective, the vast majority of working children are in developing countries, and well over half of those are in Asia — which reflects the fact that this is where most of the human race lives. There is some indication that the proportion of all children who work may be highest in sub-Saharan Africa, which is also the poorest of the developing regions. In all regions, adolescents and older children are much more likely to be in the job market than are younger children. Many children and adolescents in Europe and North America also work, and the percentage who work may in some cases not differ very much from many developing countries. For example, recent studies from Britain showed that roughly half of school children over 11 years old engage in work during the school year. However, their reasons for working and their working hours and conditions differ greatly from those of working children in developing countries. Few industrialized-country children or adolescents are driven to the job market by grinding poverty — in the USA, middle-class children are more likely to work than are poorer children — or must put up with 60-hour weeks under noxious or dangerous conditions. Also, rich-country children seldom begin to work as young as do children in developing regions. Even though the industrialized-country studies indicate that, in some places, the majority of young workers work in violation of child labour regulations — such as those limiting how late children may work at night — there is no question that developing-country children are far more likely to work in seriously adverse conditions that can seriously jeopardize their health or development. Child work is not unique to developing countries, but it is there more likely to be seriously exploitative or dangerous, and for that reason we agree that developing regions merit the big share of global attention and concern.

The vast majority of children who work are in rural areas, and most of these are unpaid help to their families, mostly in agriculture. In some societies, girls do more agricultural work than do boys, and everywhere they do more housework than boys. There is considerable evidence that girls in most places work longer hours than do boys. Where education facilities are adequate, it appears that rural children typically receive some schooling, but they are less likely to enrol in school or finish primary education than are urban children. Therefore, rural children are more likely to be working essentially full-time at an earlier age. That work sometimes may have a strong skills-training component but, contrary to the romanticized suppositions of people not familiar with rural life, much agricultural work is unsafe or unhealthy for children, and therefore its huge scope and significant risks would seem to make it the most logical focus of concern by 'child labour' activists. But life is not always logical, and the rural child workers who should be at the very centre of world concern about 'child labour' are largely ignored. It is worth noting, however, that the percentage of urban child workers grows as the whole world becomes more urban. Even though the developing countries are expected to become over half urban sometime during the first quarter of the next century, it will take considerably longer before most child work is urban. The reason is that the percentage of city children who work is significantly lower than that of rural children, and this differential seems to hold up even when rural families migrate to the cities.

Another extremely large group of child workers — perhaps equal in size to that of children working in agriculture — are full-time housekeepers and baby-minders either tending to their own homes or employed as domestic workers in the homes of others. They are overwhelmingly girls. Because children who work unpaid in their own or in others' homes usually are not counted as workers in conventional definitions used to collect national statistics, vast numbers of working girls are excluded from official view, which makes child work wrongly appear to be pre-dominantly male. It is now thought that, if children in domestic service or working full-time in their own homes are counted as workers, in many or most countries child workers would be seen to be mostly female. Such studies as exist on child domestics suggest that they are massively exploited and subject to serious physical, mental, and sexual abuse. It is very dangerous work for children, especially when they must live in the homes of their employers, cut off from family and friends. Until recently, these child workers were almost completely ignored but international organizations and NGOs now have begun to take an interest in their plight and to explore ways of reaching them with effective protection.

A third very large group of working children is found in small shops, stores, ambulatory vending, small construction and other economic undertakings which, being unregistered and unregulated, are vaguely known as the 'informal sector'. This sector, which employs huge numbers of the poor, commonly makes up from one- to two-thirds of a developing country economy. In urban areas, most child employment may well be found in the myriad small businesses and independent activities typical of the informal sector. The highly visible 'street children' shining shoes, selling flowers and other small items, parking cars or cleaning windscreens are but a relatively small part of this group of largely urban child workers. Street-trading children are so visible and have been the focus of so much attention that many assume they constitute the majority of urban working children. In fact, they are almost always a small minority of working children, and may not be among the worst off. It is common to find children working in back-alley shops where they are exposed to toxic chemicals and particulate matter, dangerous machinery, uninsulated electrical wiring, and so forth. Many informal sector occupations and working conditions are seriously hazardous not only to children, but to adults as well.

Only a small minority of child workers are found in the comparatively modern, larger, and more established industrial and commercial establishments that make up the formal sector. An even smaller portion — almost certainly well under five per cent — works in the production of goods entering international trade. The relative unimportance of carpet, clothing, sporting goods, and other export industries in the overall child work picture may come as a surprise to the public in rich countries, for most industrialized-country 'child labour' publicity in recent years has focused on the involvement of children in producing goods exported to the North. This, plus a tendency to think of child work and workers in primarily industrial terms (a hangover from the history of the 'child labour' struggle in Europe and North America) has led to a serious distortion in how child work is perceived and the priorities for action decided. A fashionable fixation on the small minority of children who work in the formal sector, in export industries or on city streets has effectively obscured the vast majority of working children — including those most imperilled by their work — from public view.

The challenge now is to call attention back to the large mass of working children who need to be seen, to identify those who are most in need of protective assistance, and to reach them with help that promotes their best interests, as the Convention on the Rights of the Child demands. In practice, this means finding how best to guarantee their safety and their physical, mental, and social development. This book hopes to make a useful step in that direction.

CHAPTER ONE

Perceptions of Child Development

The best way to approach a discussion of child work is to consider it within the context of what is known about childhood and the processes of child development. Debate regarding the work of children has, in both industrialized and developing countries, been informed largely by conceptions of childhood and child development devised some time ago by developmental psychologists and educationalists in Europe and North America. This has presented some problems, especially in relation to the application of northern understandings and definitions of childhood to other cultures where very different norms prevail. Also, the tenets of conventional developmentalist thinking are now seriously disputed within the field of developmental psychology. The implications of these opposing ideas for the generation of policies and programmes for working children will be discussed at length in this chapter. Because it must reduce a large amount of fairly technical research material into a single chapter, this discussion will be unavoidably dense. However, because it forms the basis of the rest of this book, we ask the reader to persevere.

Since the eighteenth century, northern childhood has been progressively structured as a period of "extended economic dependency and protected innocence, a period of rapid learning regulated by natural growth processes and enhanced through universal schooling, which is largely separated off from economic and community life".[1] It was in this context that child development theory flourished; the core thesis being that child development is a unitary process marked by a series of transformations or stages, each preceding stage being a necessary condition for the subsequent one, the overall trend entailing evolution from simple to complex behaviours, an immature child to mature adult, and dependent childhood to autonomous adulthood. Major theorists in this approach were Jean Piaget, whose work focused on cognitive development, and Eric Erikson, whose special concern was the socio-emotional development of adolescents.

This model has left a powerful theoretical legacy whose influence has been expressed internationally in five main ways. Firstly, the view that all children everywhere pass through the same stages of development legitimates the idea that childhood is a natural and universal phase of the human life cycle in which biological and psychological factors have a stronger role to play than social or cultural forces. Secondly, the idea that children progress according to a linear pattern of growth and change raises the possibility that children whose development does not conform to this pattern are in some way at risk or in trouble. Because the norm is based on school children in the North, this supports the belief that working children are either deviants or victims. Thirdly, the notion of a pre-set path of development provides the basis for thinking of children as passive in the face of compelling biological and psychological forces. This provides a foundation for excluding children from the adult world of work and containing them in school, where their socialization and development can be institutionalized and controlled.

Fourthly, the view of childhood as an extended period of dependence leads to the conclusion that work is not a significant contributor to childhood experience. Hence, having been devised with non-working, northern children in mind, contemporary social science thinking contributes very little to the debate on the developmental effects of work. Fifthly, an explicit research focus on infancy and early childhood has become virtually exclusive, leading to neglect of middle childhood in research and theoretical discussion. This neglect is based largely on the premiss (what Erica Burman calls the "developmental fallacy"[2]) that early behaviours and experiences are causally related to subsequent developmental achievements or psychological states and adaptability in adulthood. Squeezed in between infancy and puberty, two periods of rapid growth and change, middle childhood is treated as a period of latency in developmental terms, the observation being that children of this age cease to develop new basic functions and instead "integrate, practice, and refine the previously learned functions".[3]

A universalist theory of child development containing many of these ingredients has now assumed credibility globally and underpins important international instruments like the ILO Minimum Age Convention and the UN Convention on the Rights of the Child, which conventions are described in Chapter Five. This theory is built on the belief that it is in the best interest of all children to be economically dependent, at least until a specified minimum age; school being a more appropriate context

for growth and development than work. Thus, while work
potential threat to development, it is not envisaged that scho
negative impact. This is made explicit in the Convention on
the Child, in a juxtaposition between Article 32, which ass
part of children's rights to be prevented from certain kinds
work, and Article 28, which states with equal certainty that all children
should be required to attend primary school.[4] The degree of international
penetration of this model of childhood is illustrated in the postal survey
conducted by Rädda Barnen.[5] An overwhelming 80 per cent of respondents affirmed that childhood should be dedicated primarily to play and
school and not to work. Several added that childhood should be a joyful,
stress-free time.

The results of this survey raise an interesting question. Does the substantial penetration of an originally European ideal of childhood into non-
European contexts justify the claim that this model is, or should be, universal? Is universality equivalent to popularity? In the argument to be
developed below, this chapter will suggest a more nuanced approach to
thinking about what is general about the development of children and
what is specific to particular social contexts, especially as concerns child
work. It is based primarily on a review of anthropological and psychological literature describing the processes through which children develop, with special attention to how these apply to thinking about children's work.

At a very general level, some important dimensions of child well-being
and development that can be either imperilled or fostered by child work
are:
- Physical development, including overall health, co-ordination,
  strength, vision, and hearing needed to survive and contribute into
  adulthood;
- Cognitive development, including literacy, numeracy, basic cultural
  knowledge, vocational skills, and other knowledge required to live a
  reasonably successful life;
- Emotional development, including adequate self-esteem, family attachment, feelings of love, acceptance and effectiveness necessary to establish and maintain family ties as an adult;
- Social and moral development, including concern for others, sharing,
  sense of belonging, ability to cooperate with others, distinction of right
  from wrong, respect for laws and for the property and persons of
  others, resourcefulness, planning, independence, leadership, and other
  capacities needed to live successfully within a social context.[6]

Most of the literature relating work to child development deals only with physical health and safety, and this but superficially. The psychosocial elements of child development are largely ignored. This is far too restrictive a framework for assessing the role of children's work in their overall growth as whole human beings, especially as there is no reason to believe that, for most working children, the relatively neglected cognitive, emotional, and social aspects of child development may be the most important to consider. As a corrective to current practice, this chapter will emphasize the psychosocial aspects of child development, leaving to Chapter Two a summary of research into the relationship between work and physical development.

A review of the child development, education, and anthropological literature has revealed nine broad principles of child well-being and development which apply to children in different social and cultural contexts and which can be crucially affected, adversely or positively, by the work they do. They are:

- The development and best interests of children are likely to be defined differently in different places and contexts;
- Within any given society, children are not all regarded equally and this profoundly affects children's experience of childhood;
- Children are not passive recipients of experience but active contributors to their own development;
- Child development is mediated by an array of personal and environmental factors and hence children's experiences have indirect and complex effects on their well-being;
- The relationships between different aspects of child development are synergistic;
- Children have multiple capacities which need to be fostered and different societies present different demands and opportunities for children's learning, producing different developmental outcomes;
- Different child protection strategies have different child development outcomes and in some societies early exposure to work is encouraged as a strategy of self-protection;
- Children are highly adaptable and develop in the context of constant change and contradiction. This is a source of resilience and strength, as well as of risk and vulnerability;
- Acceptance by the family (however defined) has important developmental outcomes in societies which recognize group rights above those of the individual and, in such societies, child work is one of the most important mechanisms of family integration.

We suggest that these principles, each discussed at some length below, should orientate policies and programmes in regard to children's work.

PRINCIPLE 1

The development and best interests of children are likely to be defined differently in different places and contexts

Popular concepts of child development

For a number of reasons, the idea of a universal process of child development appears quite appealing. Defining development in terms of progressive stages fits the empirical observation that children everywhere grow bigger and stronger with age and master new skills and new insights daily. It also seems to make feasible the measurement of developmental progress in individual children through the application of behavioural and developmental tests. And very importantly, it apparently provides a benchmark of well-being upon which child care services and education programmes at all levels, pre-school through to higher education, can be built. In industrialized societies and among literate people in general, great importance is attached to the markers of development outlined in this model. Innumerable volumes on child development show parents and other lay people how to observe their offspring closely and gauge minute changes in growth, movement, language, sociability, moral reasoning, cognition, and play for their developmental significance. They are also shown how to stimulate and foster development in children whose progress appears to be below average. Children's behaviour and activities are thus seen as important indicators of progress in accordance with the developmental stage appropriate for their age.

Observation of the regularities of development and studies of the pathological consequences of deprivation suggest that there does indeed exist an underlying core of universal biological and psychological processes in child development.[7] The satisfaction of fundamental physical needs for food, health care, and regular periods of rest, together with psychosocial needs such as affection, social interaction and stimulation, and learning through exploration and discovery are taken by developmental psychologists to be a prerequisite for children's health and normal development.[8] Recent research has also highlighted that the quality of care, characterized by the motivation, skill, physical capacity, consistency, and responsiveness of the care-provider is strongly linked to child survival and development outcomes. As developmental psychologist Martin

Woodhead notes: "From these general patterns it is possible (in theory at least) to define broad boundaries beyond which childhood environments (including working environments) are likely to have pathological consequences, by any standards, in terms of stunted growth, emotional disturbance, social isolation, and learning disability."[9]

But childhood embraces a remarkably heterogeneous set of experiences, supported by a broad range of developmental goals. There are many different kinds of childhood in the world today; children in different places face very different challenges, and are raised in very different ways and with very different expectations and outcomes. Different societies have their own ideas about children's capacities and vulnerabilities, the ways in which they learn and develop and what is good for them and what is bad. Even basic concepts such as 'child work' or 'child exploitation' are interpreted in different ways by different people in different parts of the world. Ultimately, children's well-being and development are influenced more than anything by their own competencies and by the opportunities and constraints, social, cultural, and economic, associated with the particular context they live in.

Anthropological accounts of childhood in different social and cultural settings tell us about ethno-theories of child development. These theories define childhood in different contexts and express beliefs about children's nature, what children are capable of doing and how they are integrated in society. They therefore determine to a large extent the kinds of activities children are encouraged to undertake, the social and economic responsibilities they are given and the ways in which they are taught, nurtured, and protected. What emerges from the anthropological literature is that there are some clear similarities between societies with regard to ethno-theories about the human life cycle and the place of children in it and also in terms of the age thresholds of major life transitions. To this degree they substantiate conventional developmental thinking. But the diversity between such theories in terms of the goals of development, and even more so in the strategies for socializing children, is quite striking. Thus, for example, in the industrialized North one of the major goals of development is autonomy and self-sufficiency, while in many other parts of the world integration and interdependence are valued more highly. How children are socialized is closely linked to these goals. Here the pattern of ethno-theories departs significantly from the traditional development paradigm.

All known societies break the ageing process up into phases, distinguished by specific terms, babyhood, childhood, adulthood, old age, and the like, revealing observed regularities in human development, and also theories about their significance for social behaviour.[10] Ethno-theories seldom regard childhood as a single homogeneous block of time but as a period subdivided into phases, each one characterized by different competencies and susceptibilities and prescribed often by specific codes of behaviour and dress, rights, and responsibilities. Such theories echo the ideas of northern developmentalists and in many places children participate in rites of passage which broadly resemble the developmental markers of the northern scientific tradition. These rites express major changes in a child's social status and signal new codes of behaviour and dress.

Nevertheless, it is notable that beyond the industrialized, literate world, the movement of individual children through childhood is not followed with much precision and rites of passage lack the chronological accuracy of northern thinking. Age is frequently treated only as an approximate benchmark; not an exact record. In many places, birth dates and their anniversaries are not acknowledged. Hausa mothers in Nigeria, for example, certainly know the ages of their offspring in the first two months of life because during this period they must observe certain rituals but, as their children grow and with each successive birth, diminishing importance is attached to precise ages.[11]

Despite variations in the way age is conceived, there are some important regularities across cultures concerning the major childhood transitions. It is accepted in most places, for instance, that significant changes or advances in physical strength and agility, cognitive and social competence take place during the second year of life, and again at around 6 or 7 years of age, and at puberty.[12] There is a widespread consensus that the first year is the most vulnerable period in the human life cycle. Infants may not even be accepted as full social beings until one year after birth, when their survival is more or less assured. "In many traditional societies, a child must survive for a certain period of time after birth before it is acknowledged as a 'life'. Naming ceremonies and other rituals marking the arrival of a new life are purposely delayed by those accustomed to high rates of infant mortality."[13]

Another parallel with traditional developmentalist thinking is the idea that very young children lack important psychological and mental attributes. In cultures around the world, infancy and early childhood are characterized as a period of non-reason.[14] The Gonja of northern Ghana, for example, see 'lack of sense' as a major defining characteristic of young children, maintaining that they 'have sense' by about the age of 6 or 7.[15] In Bangladesh, although the stage of non-reason corresponds roughly with early childhood, it is also demarcated by children's lack of economic responsibilities, showing that childhood stages can be altered by context:

33

The word *shishu* does not refer only to the age or physical development of a child. It is a stage determined by the circumstances of life ... a child 'who knows too much', a child who fends for herself or himself is not considered to be *shishu* any more. On the other hand, a child well provided and cared for, and kept away from responsibilities may remain a *shishu* up to the age of 12 or so. In no circumstances is the word *shishu* used for youth beyond puberty.[16]

Hence, the view that early childhood is a period of dependence and weakness is rather consistent across cultures, and in most cultures very young children are greatly indulged by adults. But there is much more diversity in the developmental goals and socialization strategies affecting middle childhood and adolescence. In industrialized and literate societies, for example, economic dependence, characterized by full-time involvement in formal education, is perpetuated throughout middle childhood and adolescence; middle childhood corresponding roughly with the primary cycle. Northern children in middle childhood and adolescence spend almost as much time at school as they do at home and most of their free time is passed with peers in informal play, watching television, and other recreational activities.[17] But coexisting with this economic dependence is an emerging capacity for social and political autonomy, fostered by education systems that stress individual rights and responsibilities.

Elsewhere, children of this age are not autonomous in a political sense and are economically and socially accountable to the wider kin group. And yet, they have important productive responsibilities. At the age of 10, Tonga children of both sexes in Mola, Zimbabwe, participate in the household's agricultural enterprise as farmers, livestock owners and cash earners. They not only work but also own and control arable land and livestock, most often chickens, and sometimes goats.[18] A boy of 10 is expected to build his own house, while a girl should be capable of running the household during the absence or illness of the senior woman and also contribute substantially to the daily household chores, including the gathering of wild plants for relishes, pounding, grinding, and cooking. In industrialized societies, these capacities and responsibilities would probably be acquired much later, in the late teenage years or even in adulthood.

Central to the theme of this book is the fact that work between the ages of 6 and 12 which is disparaged in many industrialized settings is understood in most other societies to play a major part in development. Indeed, entry into work is often the most important marker of the onset of middle childhood and the major strategy for child socialization during this period. Children over the age of 6 or so are believed not only to have the physical and mental capacity for work, but also to benefit from working. In many places, children's work is vital to the transmission of knowledge and skills, the social integration of children, and to their sense of self-worth and self-efficacy. Productive assignments in childhood are normally adapted to age and gender. Normally, early work experience is acquired quite casually by undertaking the lighter domestic chores, running errands, or gathering fodder or firewood, and young children are generally indulged, combining work with liberal amounts of play. Adults generally have few expectations of children's productivity at this point.

In middle childhood, work becomes a serious matter; this being when a recognition of children's increasing physical strength and agility results in their assumption of more complex and demanding tasks. In Peru, children younger than 7 seldom work on asparagus farms, for example, and when they do they undertake simple tasks like collecting and piling up weeds.[19] Between the ages of 7 and 10, however, they become more involved, especially in weeding, the selection of harvest, and spreading the manure. Young children are allowed to make mistakes, but after the age of 7 they are much more likely to be chastised for failing to complete chores properly.

Puberty is recognized as an important time of transition in most societies, although the extension of full-time education beyond puberty in the industrialized North also results in the continuation of childhood dependence. Elsewhere, puberty often marks the transition to social adulthood when young people acquire new economic responsibilities and may marry and bear children of their own. By the time children on Peru's asparagus farms reach 11 to 14, they are generally regarded as having almost adult competence and assume more specialized duties, possibly taking sole charge of the cultivation and management of a field, including the selection of seed and application of manure. As one farmer said:

> I leave my 14-year-old son in charge of the field; he already knows when he has to do each of the tasks, he pays the workers, selects the seed, spreads the manure. He has learnt since a boy by watching me; I never taught him, he always enjoyed it.[20]

For children who combine work and school, the increase in workload in early adolescence may coincide with a decline in school performance and attendance, leading eventually to desertion. Drop-out could be due to the burden of work or to a belief that schooling beyond the primary stage is of little value. The balance between unpaid and paid work may also shift at this point too, there being greater emphasis often on paid work outside the home as opposed to unpaid within.

It is evident that different cultures have very different views about child development, providing very different opportunities and constraints for children. Because different societies may have divergent and equally useful ideas of what constitutes 'developed' behaviour in a child, a single concept of child development no longer seems possible. Thus, within the broad boundaries of what is universally acceptable there is a myriad of sustainable niches for child development.[21]

Emerging views in the science of child development

In recent years, scientific thinking about child development has been evolving under the influence of new research which suggests that 'development' is not a single 'built-in' process through set stages the same for all children. Following the ideas of Soviet psychologist Vygotsky, much recent work has demonstrated the way children's competencies are formed through social relations embedded in cultural context and shaped through cultural practices. The significance of conceiving of child development as an open-ended process is that different ethno-theories of development and different cultural goals and paths of development can be accommodated. It is now increasingly recognized that there is no standard goal or pattern for development: "children's behaviour, thinking, social relationships and adaptation, hence 'needs' and 'developmental appropriateness' are culturally as much as biologically constituted".[22] At the same time, the cultural status of psychologists' conceptions of child development is itself being recognized:[23]

> ... anyone making statements about the 'nature' of child development, or about how work 'harms' 'normal' development needs to recognize the way their experience and understanding of children's work, and their location within a particular cultural niche, shapes how they think about children's 'nature', 'normality', and 'harm' and modifies how they construct it as a 'problem' ... Reflexivity remains an alien principle to most psychologists, who continue to presume they are discovering rather than constructing their subject. But the 'childhood' of which these children are 'deprived' is an idealisation that has grown out of particular historical and social circumstances. It may have little to do with how children themselves, or their parents or the communities of which they are part, understand their young lives.[24]

Charles Super and Sara Harkness[25] have devised the concept of 'developmental niche' as a way of explaining how children's needs and development are mediated and expressed in particular ways in particular cultural and social settings:

> The concept of 'developmental niche' draws attention to three components of children's environment: the physical and social settings they inhabit; the culturally regulated customs and practices of child care, learning and socialization; and the beliefs or 'ethno theories' of parents, or other key individuals in their lives, about the goals and priorities for development.[26]

Social and cultural diversity have important implications in terms of the developmental outcomes for children. Woodhead argues that these niches not only define the environment of child development, but the particularities of development itself, in terms of the emphasis placed on human potential for social integration, autonomy, loyalty, obedience, playfulness, assertiveness, task orientation, physical strength, craft skill, artistic representation, literacy, numeracy, intellectual abstraction, spirituality, and so on.[27]

The emerging view, then, is that children develop in different directions according to the goals and strategies within their environment. Each culture has different ways of initiating children into cultural practices which foster development and, in many contexts, work forms one of the most important strategies of socialization. But this thinking also suggests that children bring inner resources to the process and actively participate in defining their development rather than merely passing through it. That is to say, children have an important role in creating their own development, which is one reason why their initiatives on their own behalf should be treated sensitively.

Whose developmental norms apply?

Because academics have not been proficient in disseminating these ideas, practitioners have continued to be bound to the notion of child development as a unitary process across cultures. But it also emerges that what is defined as universally applicable in traditional child development thinking is in practice culturally and historically bound to the modern urban-industrial complex and the Judeo-Christian belief system which produced it.[28] Its theories, in other words, are not really universal but built on a particular type of childhood, as experienced largely by urban middle-class children in the industrial North. These are the children who have been the subjects of child development research. This is significant because, unlike many other children in the world, they play, go to school, and are thought to be helpless and not able to undertake adult tasks.

Drawing on middle-class urban childhood as the archetype for child development theory makes childhood without economic and social responsibility appear as the norm and hence the corollary that work is harmful for children; working children are to be pitied because they are denied a 'childhood'.[29] It works in effect either to exclude and stigmatize those children whose development and experience of childhood is different or to depict them as victims. This is very serious because it renders working children and other groups vulnerable to exploitation or abuse:

> The presentation of a general model which depicts development as unitary irrespective of culture, class, gender and history means that difference can be recognised only in terms of aberrations, deviations — that is, in terms of relative progress on a linear scale.[30]

Many people working with children in different parts of the world recognize diversity as a feature of childhood and child-rearing across cultures, although they still argue that the norms of international instruments like the Convention on the Rights of the Child serve children's interests best. Accordingly, a high proportion of respondents in the Rädda Barnen postal survey understood the notion of a carefree childhood to be an ideal, recognizing that in many settings children are forced to work in order to stave off greater misery and fulfil family obligations. Quite a few highlighted cultural values as the main cause of children working, noting in particular the perception of children as an economic asset, the corollary being that if they are not productive then they are a burden to the family. For example, a respondent from Indonesia said:

> The economic value of children, as it was expressed in the old saying, 'More children, better fortune'. [sic] This value (inherited from the agricultural consciousness) provides cultural legitimacy for parents to economically benefit from their children.[31]

It could be argued that, measured in terms of survival, physical health, growth, and development, northern values and child-rearing practices do appear to be more effective than those of other cultures and other times. But differences in survival and physical health between North and South are largely attributable to wealth. In any case, as we will show, assessment of the psychological and social aspects of child development sometimes reveals a very different picture, indicating that working children are more capable, resourceful, and resilient than school pupils at the same age. We will also show that the view of children as socially and economically dependent may have drawbacks, even for northern children.

The question of whether some social (that is, northern) ideas of children's best interests are better for children than others, and therefore deserve to be promoted over others that are different, is central to considerations about the effects of children's work on their development and well-being. Much of the recent social science literature does not support the notion that such internationalized norms and values better promote the well-being of children, since the goals and standards of development are bound by context, and what is best for children cannot be defined outside the context in which they grow. In other words, definitions of what is in children's best interests must rest not on ideas about what is developmentally appropriate in the abstract, but on the adaptability of given developmental goals, strategies and practices in each social and cultural context.

Clearly children are raised in different ways and with different expectations in different parts of the world. They thrive, and indeed flourish, in widely contrasting conditions and circumstances and have different capacities and needs, to which a universal child development model – which is based on only one type of childhood – is not sensitive. Although it draws on scientific principles developed by the social sciences, it is not even apparent that the type of childhood upon which the present universal consensus is based suits children's interests more than other types of childhood. Understanding that the culture in which children live shapes both the way they are perceived and treated, and the way they experience childhood, is an important departure from traditional child development thinking based on universalist values which conceive of growing up as a standardized process; the same for all children. As suggested, in many countries work, which is neglected by these same child development models as a thing of the past, is seen as a central feature of child development and socialization in mid-childhood. Cultural support for children's work can have positive implications for children when the work they do is safe, although it can make the elimination of dangerous and exploitative work difficult. After all, hazardous work is continuous with more benign work that children have always done: as such, it does not necessarily solicit disapproval among parents, employers or the general public. Child-centred policies should respond to cultural diversity when implementing national and international standards; rigid imposition of universal norms may not always be the most effective way to promote the best interests of children and risk jeopardizing the very children they intend to assist.

PRINCIPLE 2

Within any given society, children are not all regarded equally and this profoundly affects children's experience of childhood

Within all societies there is great variation in the expectations and experiences of children in different social categories, this being a second feature of diversity in childhood with important implications for children's development. All known societies uphold ideas about how children distinguished by social power, place of residence, order of birth within the family, ethnic or religious status or personal characteristics should be treated and what they should be allowed or expected to do. These ideas also determine to a great extent whether and how much children in different social categories work, what work they do, and also whether and for how many years they go to school. Hence, according to their social power and status, children experience different environmental opportunities and constraints, and occupy different developmental niches, the implication being that they also experience different levels of exposure to workplace adversity.

If we begin by looking at distinctions based on gender, this point comes across very clearly. In many societies, even the age at which childhood ends is prescribed by gender; girls normally passing into adulthood before boys. In Nepal, for example, a girl takes on the work roles of an adult woman at the age of 12, while boys do not reach this threshold until 14.[32] Indian girls reach adulthood at puberty, and boys at 16.[33] Distinctions in the treatment of boys and girls are often justified in ethno-theories by ideas about biological or psychological difference. In Bhutan, girls are perceived as weaker and softer than boys, having before them a life of struggle.[34] Parents prefer their daughters to stay with them because they show greater tenderness and are softer at heart. Girls, it is believed, must help with the care of younger siblings, housework, and looking after the elderly and should not be burdened more by school attendance.

Gender roles during childhood can be highly prescriptive, determining codes of behaviour and dress, education opportunities, work roles, and practically all aspects of life. Gender discrimination often results in girls being cast in a subservient role and subjected to a range of taboos that put severe constraints, not just on their personal autonomy, but also on their income and occupational mobility. Roughly two-thirds of respondents in the Rädda Barnen postal survey felt that girls are more likely than boys to be exploited at work or that, where both sexes are exploited, girls are more vulnerable. Someone from India provided a reminder that the additional risks for girls assaulted sexually at work are pregnancy, early childbearing, the responsibility of caring for a baby, and the social stigma of being a single mother. Some respondents explained the susceptibility of girls as being due to the effect of gender socialization and others, discriminatory attitudes and behaviour in society at large. As an Ecuadorian put it:

> At home there is a tendency to scold girls more than boys, but this will help them to become better employees. In the labour market different jobs are assigned to girls and boys, generally girls are more disadvantaged, but perhaps because of this they perform better at school.[35]

It was pointed out that girls are frequently paid lower wages than boys, even when doing the same work, and they are also more likely to work without pay. Often girls start work before boys. In Jamaica, little girls are with their mothers and older women constantly, imitating and assisting them as they are able. Little boys, although dependent upon the women for almost everything, are not pressed into occupational roles nearly so strongly and are allowed to play more.[36] Elsewhere, girls are required to leave school early or may be excluded altogether while their brothers attend full-time. Sometimes they must work in order to pay school fees for a brother.

But gender identity within childhood is not necessarily fixed, gender segregation often becoming far more pronounced in mid-childhood and especially after puberty. In Bangladesh, the term for child, *shishu*, does not distinguish gender but describes a point in life when infants and very young boys and girls are allowed to associate freely.[37] In a highly gender-segregated society like Bangladesh this phase is curtailed and the words *ballok/ballika* and *kishor/kishori*, which are used to describe subsequent phases, reflect the increasingly gender-specific roles adopted by girls and boys as they pass through childhood. At puberty, many Bangladeshi girls are secluded within the home and away from public gaze.

Ethnicity, caste, wealth, birth order, religion and rural or urban residence also play a major part in distinguishing childhood expectations and experiences, as do the physical or mental attributes of individual children. In Bolivia, birth order and sibling composition profoundly affect gender functions during childhood, often resulting in the reversal of stereotypical male and female roles.[38] In many societies, the oldest child in a family is

41

especially privileged, male primogeniture often being recognized as the norm, allowing the eldest son as the only legitimate heir:

> The arrival of the first-born is celebrated in many communities as the validation of marriage and the inauguration of a new set of family relationships: mother, father, son, daughter. The first child is often given a special title ... perhaps indicative of special family rights and responsibilities.[39]

The exact reverse may also apply, however, in that as the number of children in a family grows, the eldest child (or elder children) is expected to make major sacrifices to help the younger ones. The life cycle of the household has a major impact on the amount of housework done by the eldest daughter for example.

In most countries the rates of work are higher for poorer, rural, and ethnic minority children than for richer children or children from urban or majority communities. Thus, in most cases, rural children begin working at a younger age than urban children. This trend has been documented especially clearly for Latin America.[40] Yet the pattern is different in many northern industrialized countries, where often it is the young people from better-off families and from the majority community who get the jobs. Hence, statistics from the United States analyzed by the General Accounting Office indicate that around 28 per cent of all 15-year-olds and 51 per cent of all 16- to 17-year-olds in the United States were employed for some time during 1988.[41] Children from low-income families (those with annual incomes of US$20,000 or less) were less likely to be employed, however, than children from high-income families (with annual incomes above US$60,000). Minority children were less likely to be employed than white children. However, when employed, children from low-income families were more likely to be employed in agriculture or other 'hazardous' industries and also to be working longer hours. Morrow argues that such a pattern is to be expected where the demand for work among young people is greater than the supply, in that minority or poor children are likely to be the subject of labour market discrimination.[42]

Much earlier child development theory was quite insensitive to the idea that different social groups and categories experience very different childhoods and developmental opportunities, prescribing a merged pattern for all children which paid little attention to gender, class or other factors. Nevertheless, it is apparent that children have very different life experiences according to their social and personal characteristics; even within the same family, siblings may be regarded and treated very differently. The implication is that the experience of childhood is very variable even within a society, suggesting that developmental goals and outcomes alter not just across cultures but also according to children's social status within a culture. This implies that policies to remove children from hazardous or exploitative work should recognize that all children are not equally at risk. On the other hand, they should also avoid facile stereotypes in which all working girls, for example, are automatically massed together as victims. Effective policy needs to carefully identify and prioritize those most vulnerable, requiring thorough disaggregation of data on working children and painstaking analysis of children's actual circumstances, to reveal distinctions between different groups and categories.

PRINCIPLE 3

Children are not passive recipients of experience but active contributors to their own development

We have suggested that the way in which child development is explained has implications for the way children themselves are viewed. Traditional scientific theories from the North, for example, tend to conceive of development as progress along a set course, or through set stages, in accordance with particular expectations of maturity. These expectations have to do with growing adequacy and competence. Implicit is the idea that each stage is a more adequate way of functioning, a more effective adaptation to adult society, than the earlier one.[43] But such theories disguise the unique capacities that children bring to their own development, rendering childhood insignificant in relation to adulthood, the ultimate goal of development.[44] They also justify a theoretical focus on how adults convey their knowledge and skills to children (or, in other words, patterns of socialization) and what children become, rather than on what children themselves are able to do, what they bring to the developmental process and how they perceive the world and their place in it:

> The traditional view of socialization sees adult behaviour, in the context of a society and culture, as an independent variable, based on a fixed set of rules, roles and modes of conduct which children must assimilate before they become significant social actors. The role of child is the role of learner; sociologically, unless he [sic] is a 'delinquent', the child is passive. Thus, child culture is seen as a rehearsal for adult life and socialization consists of the processes through which, by one method or another, children are made to

43

conform — in the cases of 'successful socialization' or become deviants, in cases of 'failed socialization'.[45]

Hence, this approach to child development stresses the acquisition and internalization of adult competencies and adult views; adults acting as 'transmitters'. The categories of child and adult that have been generated by the model underline children's weakness and incapacity, and adults' competence and responsibility: [46]

> A close mother-newborn relationship is the quintessential feature of mammalian adaptation. Mammals are born immature and dependent. Their development and very survival depend on receiving adequate parental nurture and protection. The pattern is even more marked in human beings, who have even bigger brains and longer periods of childhood helplessness and dependency.[47]

By studying and interpreting the development and use of actions and responses in the very young, several theorists began eventually to grapple with and explain the discovery of infant competencies. Drawing on ideas from attachment theory, which builds on evolutionary and animal work, researchers began to emphasize how the human infant is born equipped with a reflexive repertoire of behaviours that function to elicit care, nurture and attention.[48] The behaviour of neonates and infants, then, was thought to be due to an innate predisposition; an adaptive feature of survival which functions as a kind of social signal to care-providers.

Infant behaviour eventually came to be perceived rather differently; it having become apparent that infants are born with a predisposition for social relations. Present thinking holds that infants actively seek engagement with parents and other care-providers as the starting point for constructing an understanding of their social world.[49] In other words, children are more capable than was once thought and arrive at adult ideas gradually, in part at least as a result of their own efforts, although "whether they are capable and how they are capable depends very much on the context and quality of their learning experiences".[50] The process of child development, then, is not one in which children passively receive inputs from adults, but one which involves their active participation in creatively handling the uncertainties of constant change and conflicting pressures. This point is critical because it raises the possibility that how children experience and utilize their work or schooling may be very different from the way adults think they do. It also points to the necessity of viewing children not as victims but as protagonists in their own development:

The way an outsider perceives positive or harmful influences on a child may not coincide at all with the way a child receives those influences. The child is active in defining the effective environment for development, according to what kinds of activity they seek out, what kinds of stimulation they attend to, and what selective interpretation they place on what they see, hear, and feel. At different stages of development certain features of the environment may be more salient than others.[51]

But, more importantly still, there is evidence to suggest that meaningful participation is itself developmental:

Research suggests that resilience is encouraged and developed when children and youths have opportunities to meaningfully participate in and contribute to the environments that embody their microsystems. When families, schools, peer groups, and community all communicate the expectation that children and youths can and will handle their responsibilities successfully and participate in valued ways, the youths respond by developing a sense of autonomy, independence, heightened social competence, and — in a word — resilience.[52]

To the extent it is wished to reinforce child development, then it is incumbent upon social planners and programme staff to listen to and learn from children directly: children contribute to their own development and therefore what they have to say matters. This implies that working children must be provided with opportunities to participate in their own protection if it is to be developmentally productive. Obviously children are not always right; they are not always aware of the hidden perils of work, for example. Nevertheless, the current social science insight that children are social actors in their own right, not passive recipients of policies and programmes designed by adults, is of supreme importance. Children have lots of reasons, both strategic and practical, for choosing work over education and often they are acutely aware of both the costs and benefits of what they do. Experience and research suggest that these reasons cannot be dismissed lightly, for they are intimately linked to the development of the children involved. Moreover, children frequently have sound ideas about how to eliminate exploitation and danger at work. At the very least, children's participation in decisions made in their interests may provide some protection since it implies that they should be given appropriate information and an opportunity to articulate their problems and needs. When social planners ignore the reasons why children make their particular choices, they risk undermining the welfare of both children and their families.

Nevertheless, this raises a very important and challenging issue: how children participate, or the degree to which they participate, needs to be determined in some measure by their age and maturity — it is not appropriate or ethical to expose children to possible manipulation or other harm by having them take part in processes which they do not comprehend or to require a level of responsibility they cannot reasonably give. The problem is that, even today, child development theories have very little to say about the developmental competencies of working children in different cultures in middle childhood and adolescence, having been devised (as noted) with non-working, northern children in the early years of life in mind. The emphasis on school pupils and on infancy and early childhood presents a serious obstacle to identifying how to encourage developmentally appropriate participation in children and young people who work. There is much still to be discovered about the crucial middle childhood and adolescent years and research in which children play a meaningful role is required if programmes with working children are to involve children effectively in planning and decision-making.

PRINCIPLE 4

Child development is mediated by an array of personal and environmental factors and hence children's experiences have indirect and complex effects on their well-being

Conventional scientific thinking about child development emphasizes that children confronted by adversity at home, school or work would deviate from the developmental path or fall behind the developmental stage appropriate for their age. Neglect, loss or abuse during infancy and early childhood are thought to have the greatest developmental impact. At first glance, this notion seems eminently sensible, since we all know that human beings have a number of fundamental prerequisites essential for survival, health, and well-being and we also recognize that the very young are the least able to provide for themselves. Besides, it seems logical to think that children who start out in life by being disadvantaged will be handicapped in the future and will in some way compound their early difficulties with a diminishing ability to cope later on.

But the consequences for children of not fulfilling these prerequisites are unclear. Indeed, the links between cause and effect are still little understood. Is it possible to state that children who experience 'abnormal' conditions or circumstances will be damaged or even deviant? This is a vital question when considering the developmental effects of dangerous or exploitative work. In middle childhood and adolescence the capacity for acquiring information and for using new knowledge in reasoning, thinking, problem-solving, and action increases markedly. This is also when children develop, among other things, new language skills and a longer attention span and when relationships outside the family and with peers become more important. How these skills and competencies are affected by injurious work is not obvious. What happens, for example, when a child works alone for 12 hours a day for a wage well below the national minimum and is scorned and beaten by her employer? Predicting adverse physical effects associated with the deprivation of food, fluid or rest may be comparatively straightforward, but not so the psychological or social effects of exploitation, isolation or maltreatment. Even more challenging, perhaps, is to understand the impacts of work that is not evidently injurious.

It transpires that developmental outcome cannot readily be predicted, even when children are exposed to conditions which appear quite detrimental. While it may be true that children everywhere have certain basic needs in a very general sense, it is important to avoid mechanistic theories of cause and effect, since the developmental consequences of either working — including working very hard and in difficult conditions — or attending school cannot be predetermined. According to the Convention on the Rights of the Child, children have a right to stable and protective personal and family circumstances, to receive a good quality and relevant education, and to be protected from hazardous work. But this is not to say that children who do not enjoy such advantages are necessarily damaged. Some children turn out to be much more vulnerable than others in the same situation. This is true particularly of social and psychological vulnerability, since the psychosocial impact of maltreatment and other infringements is far less direct than the physical effects of malnutrition, disease, exhaustion or injury.

There has been no qualitative research, to our knowledge, which is sufficiently systematic to indicate the factors mediating physical and psychosocial vulnerability and resilience in working children. Most of the research on these issues has been conducted either in the North with children separated from parents, exposed to marital breakdown, violent crime, neglect or abuse or with children in various parts of the world who have been affected by armed conflict. Studies about children who face stressful situations consistently find that some children (in many cases the majority) remain resilient.[53] Studies of children affected by armed conflict are particularly illuminating. War involves innumerable 'stressors' for children, including destitution, separation from family, displacement, bereavement, and exposure to violence. But while most children will experience some kind of stress response in the short term, the majority are protected from debilitating psychosocial reactions in the longer term. A few authors[54] have suggested that children can even gain emotionally or psychologically from exposure to stress: "some children ... are remarkably resilient, managing not only to survive, but even to flourish, in unfavourable conditions".[55] This highlights the urgent need to learn what mechanisms of biological, social, and behavioural adaptability to stress allow some children to grow and develop well in adversity.[56]

What does the literature on risk and resilience in children tell us which helps the assessment of developmental impacts of exposure to injurious work? One lesson is that children's experience of adversity is moderated, or rather mediated, by a range of environmental and personal factors, such that there is no direct link between adversity and developmental outcome. In other words, these mediating mechanisms protect children who experience a stressful event from negative impacts; their absence increasing vulnerability in children and their presence fostering resilience. As far as working children are concerned, beliefs and attitudes about children's work make a significant difference to the effect it has on their lives. Thus, parents, employers and working children themselves have feelings and views about children's work which modify the way in which it affects their lives, in terms of their health, mental state, learning, and adjustment:

> If children's work is valued they are likely to have a positive experience — they are more likely to cope with difficulties. If it is devalued, denigrated in their own or others' eyes, or if they are stigmatised, then working is likely to be much more prejudicial to their mental and physical health and their social adjustment.[57]

There are six main mediating mechanisms that protect children against vulnerability: their personal traits; the continuity of emotional support provided by family members or other important reference persons; the efficacy of wider social support networks; the shared cultural meanings given to stressful situations or events; the nature and characteristics of the situation itself; and the sense of personal control children feel when faced with adversity. It is worth dwelling further on these factors in order that their implications for the well-being of working children can be better understood.

When we talk about the personal traits of individual children, we mean to include factors such as gender, age and maturity, personality, physical health, cognitive capacity, and so on. Richman and Bowen[58] (drawing on Antonovsky) use the concept of 'load balance', to intimate the degree to which an individual's capabilities match the demands of the environment; the point being that children may or may not possess the competencies or resources to cope with the stressors presented. But what kinds of competencies do children need to cope with exploitation or danger at work? Gender seems to make a difference. McCallin and Fozzard,[59] for example, reported boys from conflict zones as more nervous and fearful in the presence of strangers and more often expressing a need than girls to talk about their experience of distressing or unpleasant events. However, they found girls to be more fearful of the dark, more often seeking approval, affection, and reassurance and more likely to feel hopeless about the future. The problem is, however, that much of the research on risk and resilience is woefully neglectful of gender issues.

Age is also very relevant. Indeed, international instruments like the Minimum Age Convention tend to found their analysis of vulnerability in work on the age criterion, taking the younger child to be the more susceptible. This fits with a view of development as progression along a linear path in which children appear to become less vulnerable as they mature. It also fits at least some of the child development evidence:

> ... in general the younger the child the greater the possibility of general behavioural and socio-emotional disorganization accompanying stressful experiences. With increasing age, the child's growing repertoire of coping skills permits greater adaptive functioning in the face of stress. The research literature on the development of emotional self-regulation and coping indicates that young children rely on external supports for coping with stressful circumstances but that with increasing age children acquire a broadening repertoire of emotional self-regulatory strategies that can be applied flexibly to different situations.[60]

Thompson argues that young children's understanding of authority renders them more vulnerable to coercion or manipulation than older children, for whom authority relations are better balanced by an understanding of individual rights. Furthermore, he says, young children's trust of authority makes them more susceptible to deception. Older children legitimate authority by virtue of their training or experience and obey them out of respect rather than unquestioning reverence.

Nevertheless, maturity is not necessarily protective. Leyens and Mahjoub,[61] for instance, note that children between 2 and 5 years of age and adolescents are consistently found in research to be the most susceptible to war trauma; these being the life phases, they suggest, when children are particularly influenced by others. And Thompson points out that in some respects children become more vulnerable as they grow, noting how, in a sense, the same cognitive and experiential limitations that make young children more susceptible to certain harms also buffer them against others to which older children are more vulnerable. He cites as an example threats to self-concept, which become more stressful with increasing age "as children develop a more comprehensive, coherent, and integrated self-image, become more invested in an enduring identity, and acquire a more sophisticated understanding of the components of the self by which the self-concept becomes progressively modified and re-shaped".[62] Thus, older-grade school children are more susceptible to learned helplessness and diminished self-esteem.

Cognitive capacity certainly plays a part also. Children of at least average intelligence can enhance their own coping, solving problems by identifying alternatives and thinking up creative solutions. Critical thinking also helps shield the child from simplistic interpretations of experience that are self-defeating and socially destructive in the long run.[63] Some children are better able to manage stress because of disposition or temperament; this is a matter of personality structure and coping style. For instance, children who are able to remain hopeful about the future, are flexible and adaptable, possess problem-solving skills, and actively try and assume control over their lives are likely to be less vulnerable than those who passively accept their condition.[64] Temperamentally easy children of both sexes have been found to develop consistency, a positive outlook, and flexibility in their responses to the environment.[65] If they live in difficult families, these children manage more often than others to avoid negative interactions. Temperamentally difficult children, in contrast, tend to become the target of overwhelmed or depressed parents and are twice as likely as other children to be the object of parental criticism.[66]

The second factor in resilience and vulnerability has to do with the protection children receive through the consistent care and emotional support of at least one parent, carer or other important reference person. This has been identified in the war literature as one of the most important sources of resilience in children.[67] For instance, unaccompanied children evacuated from war zones to a place of safety tend to suffer greater distress than children who remain with their families amidst the fighting, because the experience of separation has more devastating psychosocial consequences than exposure to violence. Kirby and Fraser note that feeling supported and having the resources that derive from caring social relationships have been found to promote development in children experiencing a range of stressful situations.[68] Positive interpersonal relationships and social support, they argue, can act as a buffer against stress and also protect children by providing models of and reinforcement for skills that improve problem-solving, motivation, and the like. A good relationship with at least one parent or carer has been shown to function protectively against stress by helping children feel secure and promoting consistent supervision and discipline. Parents or other carers may also contribute positively to development by acting as mentors and through their nurturing. A third source of resilience and protection derives from supportive relationships outside the family in that peers, neighbours, teachers, employers, and others can provide friendship, positive role models and practical assistance. The school and the workplace can be important settings for supportive relationships.

Family, friends and role models have another important function in that these are the people who supply the shared cultural meanings given to children's work, valuing and conveying a sense of coherence to what children do. This is the fourth factor in resilience. Thus, it is by internalizing and reflecting on the beliefs, attitudes, and feelings of relatives, neighbours, and friends that children learn about the value of work to themselves and those around them, what is approved or disapproved, what is perceived as detrimental and beneficial, and so on. According to Antonovsky,[69] particularly important for psychosocial well-being are a sense of meaningfulness outside the child's existence; "the ability to comprehend current adversity; experience of managing different situations; and the conviction of having interior and external resources with which to cope with stress situations".[70] Thus, where families can provide the emotional context for the necessary 'processing' to enable the child to make positive moral sense of danger, situations of chronic danger can stimulate the child's moral development.[71] Hence:

> ... a mechanistic model fails to take account of the way social psychological and personal processes mediate the impact of an experience ... beliefs about development are an important part of the developmental niche. Parents, employers and working children themselves are thinking about the work they do and they have feelings and beliefs about it. These aren't just epiphenomena of work — they modify the function that the work plays in their lives — how far and in what way (positive or negative) it affects their health, mental

51

state, learning and adjustment. If children's work is valued they are likely to have a positive experience — they are more likely to cope with difficulties. If it is devalued, denigrated in their own or others' eyes, or if they are stigmatized, then working is likely to be much more prejudicial to their mental and physical health and their social adjustment.[72]

The fifth dimension in resilience and vulnerability has to do with the nature of the situation (in this case injurious work) that children are in. Clearly, this can be of considerable significance in influencing developmental outcome. The war research, for example, has emphasized that unexpected, sudden outbreaks of violence can have a psychosocial effect very different from conflicts that build up gradually. And repeated outbreaks of fighting spreading over a long period are likely to have an impact very different from short-lived conflict. Importantly, the psychosocial impact has been observed to increase when children are exposed to a number of stressors. This is especially significant because many children facing adversity are exposed not to one, but several hazards. Turning to the issue of work, we need to think about the terms and conditions children experience and compare and assess these for the degree of hazard they present and their developmental effect. In Chapter Two we consider the risk factors in children's work in greater detail, but suffice it to say here that the kinds of hazards we need to be concerned with include physically dangerous work, long workdays, low or no pay, and denigration and abuse by employers.

Another finding from the war research is that one of the most important elements in children's subjective experience of stressful situations is the degree of personal control they perceive they have; this being the final protective factor. Being able to exercise some control over events and having a sense of personal mastery or competence in stressful situations are fundamental to resilience.[73] For example, there is quite a bit of evidence that children who participate voluntarily in armed combat are to some extent protected from psychosocial distress while conscripts are likely to be far more vulnerable. This brings us back to the issue of participation, in that children are more likely to have a sense of personal mastery and control when they enter situations with all the appropriate knowledge and skills necessary to make an informed judgement about what they are doing. Of course, society must also give them the appropriate opportunities. Thinking about the implications for working children specifically, this raises many questions about the possible effects of compelling children to work against their will. But it also suggests that children working voluntarily, even in quite difficult circumstances, may be protected from adverse effects.

One of the major implications of the research on resilience and vulnerability in children is that working children should not be lumped together as a homogeneous, 'vulnerable' group, especially when it comes to psychological and social well-being. There are no direct and self-evident consequences of exposure to adversity; the detrimental impacts on children of exploitative or dangerous working conditions being mediated by the cultural, physical, psychological, and social resources to which each child has access. Mediating factors in the case of work might include the social approval children obtain from doing the kind of things adults do, the pride and satisfaction of being able to help their families, and a heightened sense of responsibility.[74]

More importantly, portraying children as helpless victims increases the chance that they or other children will be abused or exploited — by increasing their vulnerability to victimization or stigmatization.[75] Involving children in important decisions contributes to their understanding that they have some control over what happens to them. Recent psychological theory and research clearly tell us that the perception and the experience of personal control contribute to healthy psychological functioning. The positive psychological benefits include greater feelings of competence and effectiveness, increased sense of self-esteem, reduced depression, decreased anxiety, and generally less psychopathology.

Work can be experienced in innumerable ways and have innumerable consequences for children. Relationships between the work children do and its impacts need to be seen as being mediated by a broad range of factors. This shows that a simplistic model of direct relationship between cause and effect can lead to a distorted view of work impacts on children, serious misdiagnosis of problems, and ineffective or counterproductive actions. Children's perceptions and feelings play an important part in determining outcomes; hence the onus on policy-makers to take children's subjective experiences of work, as expressed by them, into account. Asking children about their feelings and experiences in relation to work will enhance understanding of impacts.

PRINCIPLE 5
The relationships between different aspects of child development are synergistic

In the industrialized societies of the North, human distress — physical, social, or mental — is normally viewed as a medical problem caused in one way or another by individual malfunctioning. The medicalization of human suffering has some important implications for the perception of child development and impacts of children's work. The modern medical tradition, heavily influenced by Descartes, the seventeenth century French philosopher, has evolved a very particular view of health and well-being in which the origin of illness and disease is held to be in the physically bounded body, which is understood to function also as the receptacle of the mind. In this biological model of disease, a distinction is made between physical and mental health, and illness is thought to reside either in the body or the mind. Another feature of the model is the pre-eminence given to a person's physical condition, in that psychosocial development and well-being play a secondary and derivative role. This tendency to break health into separate components, physical and mental, has been reinforced by the extreme differentiation of the medical field in which high levels of occupational specialization prevail.[76]

The primacy given to physical matters is reflected in both research and the operational priorities of health interventions. As we will see in Chapter Two, the research on hazardous work and detrimental work impacts emphazises children's safety and physical condition to the neglect of their psychosocial well-being. Similarly, Chapter Four shows that the literature on children's work is highly fragmented; there having been very few interdisciplinary studies. Many studies only examine growth status and the incidence of disease or work-related accidents, for example, while others only look at psychological functioning. This makes it impossible to conceive of child well-being holistically or to understand which forms of work, which work conditions, and which terms are most injurious. It also makes it impossible to explain why some children remain resilient even when exposed to hazardous or exploitative working conditions. Problems with research are also expressed in health interventions with working children, in that there is a clear tendency to attend to nutrition and physical health first; psychosocial programmes being viewed as a luxury to be introduced only when physical health and safety are assured.

As with most belief systems, biomedicine is based on an assumption that it objectively describes a reality that applies universally. Indeed, the biomedical model has gained considerable credibility internationally and predominates in medical institutes and medical centres throughout the world. Yet, most people in the world think about health in a far more holistic way.[77] They not only incorporate all aspects of health into an integrated whole, but also highlight the complementarity between natural and social forces and the condition of individual human beings:

... many ethno-medical systems do not logically distinguish body, mind and self, and therefore illness cannot be situated in body or mind alone. Social relations are also understood as key contributors to individual health and illness. In short, the body is seen as a unitary, integrated aspect of self and social relations. It is dependent on, and vulnerable to, the feelings, wishes, and actions of others, including spirits and dead ancestors. The body is not understood as a vast complex machine, but rather as a microcosm of the universe.[78]

Thus ethno-medical accounts sometimes understand disease to be caused not by individual pathology but by aggrieved ancestors or relatives, malevolent spirits, or the forces of nature. Many also see the separation of nutrition and physical functioning from psychosocial functioning as false.

Child development expert Robert Myers notes the emerging view among social scientists that there is much wisdom in this kind of holistic approach because it is becoming increasingly apparent that children's health and development are both interactive and integrated. In other words, there is an important synergy between physical health, nutrition and psychosocial well-being. To remind us of this fact, he cites the WHO Constitution of 1946 which declares health to be: "a state of complete physical, mental and social well-being and ... not merely the absence of disease or infirmity". Of course, an integrated, holistic approach to child well-being is also one of the most important principles underlying the Convention on the Rights of the Child. So, even if it is convenient at a practical level to make a distinction between the various dimensions of development and well-being, it is important to regard the whole child, taking into account how changes in its various physical, mental, and social capacities affect each other and interact with the environment.[79]

Consistent with the causative preference given in biomedicine to physical matters, the relationship between children's physical condition and their psychosocial well-being is ordinarily seen as one-way.[80] Hence, while the debilitating effects of poor physical health on social and emotional development are widely recognized, the reverse is given much less attention. One of the better-documented synergistic relationships is that between malnutrition and infection.[81] In well-nourished children, both susceptibility to infection and severity of illness are significantly less than in malnourished children. The impact of infection on growth is also less and of shorter duration. Another well-established area of synergy is the relationship between malnutrition and cognitive development; malnutrition being thought to affect the growth and development of the brain and energy levels. Even though the physical influences of psychosocial functioning are little known, a review of the literature suggests that distress can create reactions that impair the ability of the body's immune system to function properly, which indicates a need for much more research on the topic:

> ... the bulk of empirical evidence indicates that people who have been exposed to a high degree of recent life stress have greater degeneration of overall health, more diseases of the upper respiratory tract, more allergies, a greater risk of hypertension, and greater risk of sudden cardiac death and coronary disease than do people who have been exposed to a low degree of life stress. Other research indicates that life style factors and poor mental health, quite apart from life stress, are related to physical health status.[82]

Zeitlin, Ghassemi and Mansour,[83] for example, show that psychological stress has a negative effect on the use of nutrients, whereas psychological well-being stimulates the secretion of growth-promoting hormones.

Rigid distinctions between different aspects of health convey the impression that child development is fragmented and that the impacts of children's work on one particular development can be isolated from others as if there were no synergy. A more holistic view is needed to understand the developmental consequences of working more fully and an effort also needs to be made to identify the specific physiological mechanisms that underlie the relationship between stress and disease. Actions to promote the well-being of working children should take all aspects of child development into account and pay due attention to the synergy of effects.

PRINCIPLE 6

Children have multiple capacities which need to be fostered and different societies present different demands and opportunities for children's learning, producing different developmental outcomes

In order to flourish, all human beings need to be in an environment that provides stimulation, emotional support, and meaningful social interaction. Children in particular also need opportunities to consolidate their cognitive, technical, and social competencies. Children have multiple capacities, which can be fostered in many different ways, but assumptions about child nature, the goals of child development, and how best to stimulate development in children vary greatly between societies; opinions are widely divergent on what is appropriate learning experience in childhood and what is not, and the extent, if at all, to which work in middle childhood and early adolescence is educational.

We have suggested that developmental outcome, or in other words the specific psychological, social, and physical capabilities acquired by children, varies significantly not just with individual capacity but also with experience, and with beliefs and expectations to do with childhood in particular social and cultural contexts. This implies, as Woodhead notes, that questions about whether work is detrimental to development cannot be answered in any absolute sense and should not be separated from questions about the value of schooling: "They need to be contextualized in terms of prior questions about the cultural value placed on particular forms of competence, the adaptiveness of learning experiences provided by work, the relevance and ability of school to support other cognitive values and so on."[84]

Hence, whether children work or attend school and what kind of work or education they experience will most likely make a significant difference to their development; different educational goals and different ideas about child development supporting the development of different attributes in children. Where society does not offer the appropriate opportunities, some individuals may never develop certain skills, simply for lack of experience relevant to their development.[85] This is consistent, for example, with Greenfield's[86] discovery that while some unschooled rural Wolof children in Senegal do not develop the concept of quantity conservation, all schooled rural children do and also with Kohlberg's[87] finding that certain forms of moral thought were absent in preliterate or semi-literate village cultures. Of course, the key concern about the developmental goals of any system of education, whether it is based on work or school, is what kind of life, what kinds of skills and values, will serve children best in the context in which they live. This is an issue we will return to in the discussion of Principle 8.

The global consensus among children's rights advocates and policymakers seems to favour school over work as a medium of learning. Many argue that, regardless of either the conditions of work or the family circumstances, work is an anathema to child development. The Convention on the Rights of the Child expresses a similar preference, providing for school education as a right, while at the same time taking a far more cautious view of child work. Many respondents in the Rädda Barnen postal survey argued not only that schooling is of crucial value in itself, but also that it is one of the most important ways of offsetting the values and attitudes that favour child work. Schooling is also regarded highly by a significant proportion (probably the vast majority) of the world's parents and children. With its reputation for securing access to good incomes, school has become the essential avenue to a desirable lifestyle in the modern sector. Children are sent to school so as to qualify for a wage-earning job; preferably one that does not mean getting their hands dirty.[88]

The global achievements of formal schooling have certainly been considerable: improving children's survival, giving them access to new life and work opportunities, and increasing their wealth. Nevertheless, school-learning should not be viewed uncritically, since "it is eventually limited by the technology of the classroom, formal instruction, uniform stages of progression, prescribed knowledge, a curriculum of self-contained bits"[89] and by the restricted amount of time children actually spend at school. There are two major issues that need to be taken into account when considering work and school as routes for education and development. Firstly, it is not evident that either school or work alone can satisfy children's many developmental capacities and needs given the multiplicity of values and goals of development in the modern world. Secondly, as we show in Chapter Seven, it is questionable whether the kind of schooling on offer in many parts of the world today is of much benefit to children anyway. It may even be that in some cases work has a more positive developmental effect.

Taking the first issue, despite the spread of literacy and establishment of formal school-learning throughout the world, it needs to be remembered that this particular form of education derives from a specific cultural context and gives rise to specific cognitive goals which are quite narrow in scope: "the emphasis on language as a medium of instruction, the emphasis on de-contextualized learning, the emphasis on literacy and symbolic numeracy, need to be understood as a modern adaptation to a particular set of socioeconomic and cultural priorities".[90]

Historically, the pressures of industrial production "required people to develop no more than a range of functional skills (such as reading, writing, and calculation) that enabled them to fit into industrial society – for most people this meant the dull routines of manufacturing industry".[91] Some suggest that what children learn at school "does not liberate their minds for a universally relevant abstract thinking, so much as provide training in particular forms of schooled cognition":[92]

> The developmental endpoint that has traditionally anchored cognitive developmental theories — skill in academic activities such as formal operational reasoning and scientific, mathematical, and literate prac-

58

tices — is one valuable goal of development, but one that is tied to its contexts and culture, as is any other goal or endpoint of development valued by a community ... Each community's valued skills constitute the local goals of development. Societal practices that support children's development are tied to the values and skills considered important. In the final analysis, it is not possible to determine whether the practices of one society are more adaptive than those of another, as judgements of adaptation cannot be separated from values.[93]

There is an emerging view among educators that the current model of school education is quite outmoded and needs to be seriously reappraised. Some advocate the use of non-formal education approaches which have shown to be more effective at attracting and retaining children, especially working children, than the formal. These give priority to basic education and the learning of vocational or life skills and are flexible and adaptable in terms of age range in relation to level of course, schedule, and other factors. Critics, however, are concerned that non-formal education is inferior to formal and can even undermine it. The issue is perhaps to find ways of reforming and adapting the formal education system to incorporate those features of non-formal approaches which are particularly effective for ensuring access to quality education. This is a point that will be addressed further in Chapter Seven.

One key question is whether work has a place in modern education models. Some of the educational principles advocated by reformers fit closely with the learning principles traditionally associated with work. As a context for learning, work provides for children a vital link between experience and knowledge, for example, which many see as lacking and sorely needed in the institutional school setting.[94] Hence, in San Juan, a village in Colombia, it was observed that, while children mastered a range of important practical skills through their work and were competent at solving a range of household problems, they had learning difficulties in government schools.[95] In order to establish why this should be, Catherine Laserna compared a milking lesson on the farm with a mathematics lesson at school, the former faring favourably in both content and method. Children in San Juan accompany their mothers to work and from a young age regularly watch them milking. Laserna concluded that pre-knowledge of the actions and operations the learner is to master significantly aids learning, as does the repetitive and concrete nature of the act of milking. It is an activity that fits in with other household routines and therefore has both utility and social value. Knowing why a procedure should be carried out and how to carry it out, also facilitates learning. Learning in a constructive and unthreatening environment, as with milking, is important, as is the sharing of responsibility for the outcome by teacher and pupil. Milking is an overt and organized activity and so can be examined both visually and mentally; an attribute in stark contrast to the oral discourse of much school-based learning.

But which educational goals have traditionally been associated with work? Firstly, there is the learning of endurance and resilience or the capacity to solve problems and manage an unpredictable, sometimes dangerous, environment (discussed in Principle 7). Secondly, there is the learning of technical skills and spiritual knowledge. These are passed from one generation to the next and are normally prescribed by gender and context, with a further differentiation between everyday skills and the specialist crafts of healers, religious leaders, and the like. A third developmental goal is to instil positive values in relation to work. A fourth is to reinforce sociability, interdependency and filial loyalty — occupational experience not only helping to structure a child's view of the occupational world but also of the social world generally.[96] A fifth goal is to achieve a sense of self-efficacy, gained by undertaking socially valued roles.

Work is normally conceived in ethno-theories as one mechanism in a wider complex of learning, in which play or 'playwork' also has a role, especially in early childhood. Rites of passage may form part of this complex, treated as an opportunity to instruct children in such matters as tribal history and sexual knowledge. Often, work also operates in conjunction with a powerful oral tradition in which specialist narrators or community elders convey to children information about the genealogies of important families, myths of origin, records of land inheritance and descriptions of major events such as battles, invasions, and famines.

In many cases, parents and other care-providers (adults or elder siblings) establish the model for adult work roles, reinforcing the interdependency of the domestic group:

> Seven-year-old boys and girls develop skills appropriate for street sellers through observation and imitation of their mothers and other street sellers, testing out acquired knowledge on the spot. Some *ambulante* mothers work with two or three children at the same time: they find a strategic site in a plaza, a downtown street, or a supermarket entrance in a residential area and direct the children's economic activity. The children learn to hawk their goods, to collect money and make change, and to handle themselves with speed and efficiency in this world of the small entrepreneur.[97]

Children may also be apprenticed to religious leaders or others in order to learn specialist skills. In parts of Africa, for example, learning about medicine is a complex process involving different agencies and many rituals and age-groups, craft guilds, religious centres, and secret societies all play a role.

In most parts of the world today, children's work coexists alongside school education, the duties of adults being acquired through work and the complementary academic skills learned at school.[98] Quite a few observers are concerned about the difficulties children face when they try to combine school and work, while others are coming to see this as potentially very beneficial for children, on the grounds that "good schools alone will never be good enough".[99] They suggest that children's multiple capacities require multiple learning opportunities and these need to be provided in more than one learning environment. One respondent in the Rädda Barnen postal survey emphasized that: "Challenging work in pleasant surroundings with people the child likes can be very helpful to children physically, mentally, spiritually, provided it is proportioned to the child's capacity and allows time for the child's other needs".[100] And quite a few argued in favour of a combination of work and school. More importantly, this is the solution children themselves seek, as we will show in Chapter Seven.

Policies of education and work should be built on considerations of firstly what children need and want to learn in the particular context in which they live and secondly how children learn most effectively, acknowledging that schooling is not always educationally more beneficial for children than are some other activities, including at least some kinds of work. Different environments provide different opportunities and means for children to learn and children in different environments acquire distinct competencies. It is becoming increasingly clear that, to meet children's multiple capacities and address the multiple developmental goals in different social and cultural settings, a variety of learning opportunities need to be provided in a range of learning contexts. The quality, relevance and impact of one medium of learning as compared to others depend on the developmental objectives and content of the education imparted, the methods of learning employed, and the types of intelligence to be developed in each social and cultural context. In this sense, poor quality or inappropriate schooling may be a serious disservice to children. On the other hand, quality education combined with safe and appropriate work may facilitate developmental outcomes that serve children's interests well.

Thus, policy should not enforce formal schooling as the only medium of learning but should look to developing education systems that are sensitive to children's learning needs in specific contexts. These systems may need some innovation, building on some of the more effective principles employed in non-formal education for working children. Part-time work that is safe and appropriate to a child's age and maturity may also be incorporated into such systems.

PRINCIPLE 7

Different child protection strategies have different child development outcomes and in some societies early exposure to work is encouraged as a strategy of self-protection

It is agreed universally that children and adults have distinct competencies and vulnerabilities, although these vary according to cultural and social context. Most societies maintain that children are weaker and less self-assured than adults, and in many ways less capable. How to encourage children to become more capable and self-confident and how to teach them to deal with hazardous or difficult situations, however, can be done in different ways. Perceptions of risk and approaches to dealing with it are relative to culture. While some societies believe that children are best protected by excluding them from all work activities and situations that are potentially dangerous, others are more inclined to let children be exposed to moderate risks, putting emphasis on self-protection by teaching their children how to recognize and handle difficult situations. Learning to protect oneself is often regarded as more conducive to child development than is buffering the child against adversity. All societies use both strategies to some extent, but may differ greatly in how they apply them to specific hazards.

We have learned that in the non-industrial world participation in, rather than isolation from, work is perceived to be in children's best interests, even when it entails some hardship. Reflecting a very distinct approach to child protection and safety, children are encouraged to engage in activities that develop physical strength, endurance, confidence, dexterity, and self-discipline. Children in the fishing village of Angang, in Taiwan, for example, are actively encouraged to take part in activities 'which build up the body person'. A similar strategy is used to enable Inuit children to cope with a hazardous and often unpredictable Arctic environment.[101] Survival strategies learnt by Inuit children include experimenting with uncertainty and danger, the idea being that they should

62

utilize instability and solve problems quickly and spontaneously as they arise. Many of these skills are learnt through play, even before children commence work.

In some societies, resilience tests are formalized in rites of passage. For a boy, initiation into adulthood may involve circumcision or a trial of strength.[102] Among the Sambia, Gisu and Mende, for example, boys become men by passing exacting tests of performance in war, economic pursuits, and procreativity. Mende boys are inducted into the Poro Society through a ritual in which the Poro spirit 'swallows' the boy so that he can be reborn a man. To ensure this metamorphosis, the boy must be thrown to the ground on his stomach and 'sacrificed' on the back, marks being scored in the skin using a blunt razor or hook. Having undergone this rite, boys are then sent into the bush without any help or modern equipment to learn survival.

Discipline, which is sometimes quite harsh, is often used to further reinforce endurance, the intention being to strengthen and protect rather than punish the child. Among the Navajo Indians in the United States:

> ... enforcement of discipline came in areas that were essential for safety and well-being, such as following religious taboos and learning self-discipline and endurance in physical tasks. The expectation that children should learn to endure hardship ... should not be confused with physical punishment used for disciplinary reasons.[103]

Several researchers have found that child-rearing which stresses self-assurance and independence and gives children experience of responsibility, such as sibling care-taking and income-producing activities at an early age, not only promotes mental health but actually accelerates psychosocial development.[104] Some might argue, of course, that this rather permissive approach to children's safety is only feasible in a traditional rural setting where technologies are comparatively simple and familiar to most members of society and can easily be mastered even by those quite young, where children work mainly alongside adults and where child work itself is socially adaptable. Urban children who often work in a differentiated labour market which separates them from other family members and use more complex technological processes are probably more prone to accidents, injury, and other hazards, making a relaxed approach to child protection more risky. The age thresholds for being able to manage potentially dangerous situations could well be higher in environments where advanced technologies and work apart from family are commonplace.

Certainly the protective child-rearing strategies of the modern industrialized countries have had a dramatic effect on children's survival and physical well-being. Children in the North are in many ways faring better than ever before in history; the age group 6 to 12 years generally being the healthiest segment of the population:[105]

> The quarter-century between 1950 and 1975 ... witnessed a spectacular decline in the relatively high levels of child poverty, infant mortality and illiteracy which prevailed in the early 1950s. The nutritional status of children improved rapidly in parallel with fast and steady growth in household incomes, control of major infectious diseases and the spectacular effects from the use of antibiotics. Practically all industrialized countries achieved one of the fastest reductions in the rate of infant (and overall) mortality (particularly in post-neonatal mortality) and morbidity ever recorded ...[106]

Nevertheless, the extent to which improvements in children's physical condition are due to wealth or to cultural attitudes and practices is not evident. Undoubtedly, these developments are linked to the expansion of state provision into various areas of child welfare, specifically health, education, social services and social insurance, the rapid and widespread growth in household incomes, and an overall decline in fertility.[107] But changes in child-rearing attitudes and practices have also played a significant role. For example, parents are now far more aware of the importance for children's survival and health of observing a range of hygiene and nutrition practices.

Another development that has made it possible to buffer children from the harsher realities of life in the wealthier communities of the world is the expansion of formal institutions, public and private, that have a protective function. This, Qvortrup suggests, is an expression of the 'domestication' of childhood in the North and among the wealthy in the South. Children today are subject to a plethora of institutional arrangements and organized activities in both their pre-school years and after school hours: "... never before in history have so many children from such a young age been enrolled in organized systems and structures".[108] For example, it is common for American youngsters between the ages of 6 and 16 to participate in a whole variety of organized out-of-school sports activities.[109] Very large numbers also take part in clubs, religious programmes and groups, take private lessons, and attend camps.

New research, as we will show in Chapter Seven, suggests that the domestication of childhood carries some major disadvantages for children in terms of their autonomy and ability, including to negotiate the world of work. The organization of young people's time into leisure and school activities does little to help them enter the labour market. Many teenagers in the North leave school at the age of 18 or even later without ever having worked. Indeed, finding a positive social role for young people is a major concern of social planners in some countries where many young people resent being forced to remain at school until their mid-teens and youth unemployment is also a major issue. These two phenomena are often cited as causal in youth vandalism and crime. The debate concerning the wisdom of maintaining children in an extended state of dependence and innocence for their own protection has now reached the public domain in the United States. In a recent article in the New York Times, Jeff Stryker questioned whether a degree of exposure would not serve children's adaptation to the adult world more effectively than suspending them in a state of isolation, which may leave them in fear of the world outside:

> ... in trying to warn children about kidnapping, drugs, child abuse and the like, parents may be preparing them for a world that is not necessarily as dangerous as warnings might imply. The real danger is that children grow up afraid of the world.[110]

Whatever the real or perceived advantages or disadvantages of child protection strategies based on exposure, children in industrialized countries and better-off children in developing countries are shielded from the kind of work that adults do, largely on the grounds that it is a threat to their education, safety, and moral and social development. Children in middle childhood attend school and adolescents who work are confined to 'juvenile occupations' like newspaper delivery, babysitting, running errands or working in family enterprises such as farms. Children's work in the industrial context is now carefully prescribed by law and cultural values:

> A job or an allowance are instructional devices that teach children the proper values and attitudes towards work and spending. The usefulness of children's chores is secondary; child work is supposed to train the child, not help the parent. The allowance does not depend on the efficiency or the quantity of child work but on parent's beliefs of what is a proper amount.[111]

Their work is no longer defined in instrumental but educational terms. Children's token participation in household work, for example, is justified as moral training, seldom as a real productive contribution.[112] Such paternalism, which does not permit children the pride and self-satisfaction of having made a worthwhile contribution, may be psychologically more demeaning thàn is some work which on the surface might appear to be less appropriate for children.

This is not to suggest that children's work in industrialized countries, whatever the motive, does not entail risks. For example, a significant proportion of secondary school students surveyed in 1989 by a teacher at Shenendehowa High School in Clifton Park, New York revealed that by the age of 15 nearly 75 per cent of all students had held at least one job. Nearly 50 per cent of those working during the week finished work between 10 p.m. and midnight. Some 44 per cent of those students who held after-school jobs fell asleep in class; the more hours a student worked, the lower his or her grade-point average.[113] Children in America continue to be hurt or killed at work; the greatest proportion of victims being those working on family farms. Likewise, cuts have reduced social support in the UK to the extent that a significant number of children have become the sole carers of chronically sick or disabled parents, often to the point that they fall behind or drop out of school due to frequent absences, stress or exhaustion.[114] So, while industrialized countries maintain that they have resolved the 'child labour problem', their children continue to work as they do in other countries and, whereas the work they do in agriculture and for the family is popularly thought to be safe, much of it is in reality quite hazardous and undermines their schooling. The tension between school and work has yet to be resolved:

> Compulsory school represents a vacuum between childhood and adulthood for some adolescents. Mature physically but immature socially, they may exert their independence in different ways. Some children drop out of school, but are often unable to find a job, precisely because they have not completed their studies. This situation may give rise to frustrations and psychological problems.[115]

With the globalization of modern child-rearing attitudes and practices and rapid urbanization in many parts of the world, shielding children from danger and from the adult world of work is likely to gradually become the prevalent child-rearing strategy in most places. Nevertheless, it is doubtful that children raised in a highly protective setting will have the opportunity to develop some of the competencies essential for effective adaptation to the labour market, such as maintenance of working relationships, endurance of monotony or management of risk. In some contexts, self-protection through participation might mitigate against danger. There is also the vital issue, already raised, that participation in self-protection has developmental value, whereas imposition of protective strategies by others may render children more vulnerable. This also raises the question of whether children share the view that it is in their best interests to be controlled and constrained. The challenge perhaps is to identify work which generates self-discipline, life skills, endurance, and confidence in young people without posing a risk to their school education, health or well-being.

PRINCIPLE 8
Children are highly adaptable and develop in the context of constant change and contradiction. This is a source of resilience and strength as well as of risk and vulnerability.

Traditional child development theory implies that for children to develop 'normally' they must live in a safe, predictable, and unchanging world. When children's development strays from a socially prescribed path, adversity and insecurity at home or in the community tend to be cited as the cause of such deviance. The globalization of modern lifestyles, associated with the international spread of mass media, is also increasingly cited because it presents children with contrasting and competing values and options. Marked environmental change and contradictions in the messages children receive from society are popularly considered to undermine their well-being and development by confusing them or, worse, leading them astray from the 'true' values. As children pass through the age-linked phases of development, according to the conventional wisdom, they should be protected from such confusion and 'bad influences' lest they somehow become irretrievably warped into adulthood. As a proverb puts this idea: 'As the twig is bent, so grows the tree.'

Anthropology has in the past advanced a similarly static view in which culture has been conceived as a fixed set of agreed constructs and change has been perceived as an extrinsic threat to social order and cohesion. Internal inconsistencies within cultural systems were considered to be abnormalities, and were usually explained in terms of outside influences of one type or another. It tended to be assumed that they were disruptive and prone to provoke identity crises and other forms of confusion in growing children.

These traditional ideas emphasizing the value of stability in the development of children have in recent years given way to a far more dynamic view which suggests that change, contradiction, and even crisis are normally a healthy part of childhood and should not be considered inherently abnormal or undesirable.[116] Recent social science research, including in regard to children undergoing the serious stress of armed conflict, has spawned both new views of how cultural values are assembled and sustained by societies and new insights into how children perceive and process discontinuities, inconsistencies and, indeed, outright conflicts in their social milieu. In general, they find that children have considerable inner resources for coping with such events and that popular fears of permanent psychosocial stunting by change, confusion, and adversity may be somewhat overblown. Children may in fact be especially able to accommodate dissonance and change, and they are capable of great personal resilience, changing themselves as they need to. Disagreeing with the old proverb cited above, current insights into how children develop might suggest: 'Though the twig be bent, the tree may grow straight.' As one expert observes:

> The very fact that children's patterns of behaviour are not yet completely determined usually increases the possibility of change. This possibility is made greater since growth often continues despite the barriers of stresses and impediments. In fact, at times, the child's growth may be hastened or strengthened by stress, if it is not too overwhelming and if opportunities exist for surmounting impediments.[117]

Modern views from anthropology complement those emerging from developmental psychology in that they accept the normality of mixed signals, conflicting values, and unresolved conflicts within almost any culture. Perhaps this new appreciation of cultural 'messiness' reflects the state of modern life almost anywhere. At any rate, it is now understood that the cultural systems that inform and contribute to the ways in which people live and experience their lives on a day-to-day basis reflect not only internal coherence, but also a great deal of contradiction and dissent. Culture seems to be almost everywhere in the midst of rapid and uneven change in which some parts always are incompatible with others. People live with this with surprising ease and naturalness, at least until the contradictions become overwhelming or assume overtly threatening forms such as ostracizaton or violence. Hence, it is normal for children to experience different and competing socializing norms and values, and it may be an essential part of growing into a competent and discerning adult able to assume heavy long-term responsibilities in an unpredictable world. It is no bad thing that they should perceive that parents, teachers, neighbours, and other children may strongly disagree in their expectations of what children should be and their ideas about what is beneficial or harmful for children to experience. That is in fact the world, and children need to learn about and deal with it.

Sometimes the social incompatibilities can be very deep and structural. An obvious normative conflict for many of today's children is that which sets the global values associated with an urban industrialized society against those deriving from an earlier cultural heritage with rural and pre-industrial roots. This often is experienced as inter-generational conflict. Shona children in Zimbabwe,[118] for instance, struggle with the clash between the group/family orientation espoused by older generations and the individualist orientation that characterizes modern trends in many parts of the world. Competing ideas in relation to children's development also produce contested views about the value and education of work. In Africa, conflicting norms are played out within the formal education system where there is often a major discrepancy between traditional views of what needs to be taught at school, official government curricula, and what teachers do in the classroom.[119]

All of this is to be fully expected in a modern world that is defined by rapid and often wrenching social and economic change. Children do in fact inhabit a reality that is at any moment subject to vast external forces over which they, their families, and their communities have very little control. Economic globalization is only one of many factors that assure that. Large numbers of children face massive social and economic restructuring, extremely rapid urbanization, increasing social and economic diversity, ubiquity of modern communications and their products, growing centrality of the wage economy, demand for new levels and types of literacy and other skills, and new modern political agenda — such as gender equality — which are in open conflict with older cultural values and systems. Virtually all societies are subject to these or similarly disruptive conditions since society is always in a state of flux, continuously being constructed.

What does all this mean for those who plan policies and programmes to protect children from workplace exploitation and abuse and who wish to promote the holistic development of children? First of all, they should not assume that work affects children principally in one way, or the same way, all the time. The same job may affect the same child in many different ways, and change with time. That is because the way that children relate to their work, and to others in regard to their work, is changeable. For most children, what is important is the way that they transact with their environment. "To understand the impact of work requires tracing the transactional relationships that shape children's involvement in work, their experience of it, the impact it has upon them, and that they increasingly place upon themselves."[120] In sum, it is crucial that they understand not only the nature of the work children do, but also the diverse ways in which children experience that work. In many cases it may be as important to address the experience of work as the work itself; a distinction too often overlooked even though some programmes have employed it to considerable effect. Working children's organizations like MANTHOC in Peru and NATRAS in Nicaragua, for example, often place a great deal of importance on helping working children experience their work with an actively open mind attuned to learning, a sense of satisfaction in their own competence and accomplishments, pride in their ability to contribute to their family and society, and feelings of friendship and solidarity with their peers. Current child development thinking would predict that helping children experience their work in this way should build personal resilience and ability to address and grow through rapid change and other stressful conditions.

Secondly, policy-makers and programme-planners should realize that children do not evolve towards a fixed point according to a stable set of norms, and should not try to force children to do so. There is some practical subtlety to this: essentially the difference between trying to socialize children and helping them find their way. It would suggest the developmental usefulness of giving children richness of experience, opportunity to experiment, and room to change their minds. As will be discussed in subsequent chapters, many children are repelled by the sterility and inflexibility of formal schooling available to them. It is significant that, all over the world, they are requesting more creative work-study facilities that will let them combine work and school, and which provide them with a gamut of opportunities and options for constructing their own futures.

Thirdly, it is important to prepare children not to adapt but to respond. If the goal of policy is to prepare children for life in society which is not very dissimilar from today's, with all its poverty and injustice in most countries, what change can be expected in the lives of the majority of children who are so prepared? Moreover, where will society obtain a new generation of leaders required to embrace and provoke change towards more prosperous and equitable societies in the future? As early as the 1970s, certain Brazilian NGO programmes for street children were encouraging them to reflect on the meaning of their situation, to identify changes that should be made, and to begin working towards those changes individually and collectively. They thought largely in terms of the famous Brazilian educator, Paulo Freire, who envisaged education as a process of becoming both conscious and conscientious; a path of awakening that leads from a life of dispossessed exclusion from society to full participation in it as a citizen with equal rights. This entails actively seeking change — he called it 'transformation' — both in one's self and in society. Many of these children took an active role, including later as adults, in grass roots movements leading their country not only to new ideas and laws for the treatment of children like themselves, but also to renewed emphasis on democratic progress toward inclusion and full citizenship for all. In this process, working children not only espoused change but caused it.

PRINCIPLE 9

Acceptance by the family (however defined) has important developmental outcomes in societies which recognize group rights above those of the individual and, in such societies, child work is one of the most important mechanisms of family integration

We have suggested that the continuity of emotional support provided by family members or other important reference persons is important to the development of resilience in children. Children obtain a sense of security, effectiveness, and self-confidence through their integration with the family or other primary unit of care, particularly in a collaborative family atmosphere. Filial loyalty and achieving a sense of solidarity with the family are therefore important for children's emotional and social development. Filial ties and solidarity are expressed in different ways in different cultures; for example, depending on whether group (family) or individual rights prevail and whether it is considered appropriate for children to contribute to family well-being through work. Especially in prescriptive, hierarchical societies where the continuity and strength of the family group is valued more than the rights of individual members, children may have significant productive responsibilities which are integral to their domestic obligations and to the development of positive moral codes.

Take the Shona of Zimbabwe, for example. The Shona maintain that it is in the best interests of children to blend in with the family, to obey, and to fulfil their filial duties.[121] Shona culture is authoritarian and hierarchical and obedience is important not just when children are young but also when they grow up. These hierarchical family relationships are reciprocal and binding: "A child, according to Shona culture, does not stand as an individual, but as a member of a family. Thus, the family serves the child and the child serves the family."[122] Many decisions are made on behalf of the children, and these are generally articulated with reference to the needs of the family group or of another family member. Children are expected to do many things to serve family interests, but it is crucial that family interests are not perceived to be in conflict with the interests of the child; for example, the concept of 'caring for' a child often includes providing that child with work.

In prescriptive societies, relative age is one of the major determinants of power and authority both within childhood and between the generations and hence of family unity and integration also.[123] Children are precisely ranked in relation to each other — by birth order, according to whether they are either junior or senior — or by generational criteria, through grouping in age sets. Thus, in non-literate communities in Bangladesh: "... children have a sharp awareness and an early knowledge of who is senior and who is junior to them".[124] Kin terms tend to be specific to each relationship, such that: "Kin terms differ for older and younger brothers, older and younger sisters, husband's older brother and husband's younger brother, father's older brother and father's younger brother."[125] Relative age is so significant for the Hausa of Nigeria, that birth order is acknowledged even for twins.[126]

These values of social integration and social responsibility contrast sharply with those of the urban industrial world, in which personal autonomy is one of the most important goals of child development and notions of individual freedom, individual integrity, and individual rights are highly cherished. Accordingly, as we have argued in Principle 7, in urban industrial societies, children's work is no longer prescribed culturally as useful to the family but only to the child, as a form of life-training, and children no longer have the kind of filial obligations that are expressed in economic obligations to help maintain the family.

Some have even suggested that in societies which favour individualism and personal autonomy over group solidarity, children's work affects family unity adversely. In a review of research from the United States, Manning[127] observes that, as more teenagers enter employment, the workplace becomes increasingly important for their socialization, to the point that family control and influence over teenagers could diminish. She cites research by Ianni[128] which suggests that adolescents' experience and involvement in work may disrupt family relations, diminishing family interaction and undermining adolescent-parent relationships. She refers also to the work of Greenberger and Steinberg,[129] who found that family supervision of teenagers lessened when they worked, giving the young greater autonomy. Also significant is that parents can lose control over how teenagers use their money when they are employed. Bachman,[130] for instance, discovered that teenagers' earnings are not used to help families so much as to achieve a higher standard of living for themselves.

Planners need to recognize the developmental value of family integration to children's social and emotional functioning and acknowledge that in many societies it is through work that children contribute socially and economically. As far as possible, policy and programme interventions should support, not undermine, family solidarity. This implies that interventions to remove children from work, even from hazardous work, should take account of the possible impact on children's status within the family and family well-being generally, mitigating adverse effects by providing viable and sustainable alternative sources of work and income for children or other family members.

Conclusion

It will be apparent to the reader that the foregoing chapter, although lengthy, has barely scratched the surface of important issues to be addressed when approaching the subject of children's work from a primary concern for ensuring their well-being and development. It is equally apparent that there is an enormous gap between traditional ideas of child development, which are still largely rooted in theories of Piaget, Erikson, and others in the first half of this century, and the findings of social science regarding human development over 50 years later. The implications of this gap for how we think about working children and children's work are enormous. Newer insights, which call attention to the diversity, cultural relativity, and self-organizing nature of child development, suggest that protective approaches which involve and empower children are more likely to have the desired developmental effects than are approaches which are imposed upon them as passive victims or beneficiaries. There is a hint that perhaps the idea of prohibiting children from work or rescuing them from it should be a last-resource policy reserved for conditions and occupations in which the risk to children is palpable and serious, leaving children the opportunity to enter safe jobs. There is in this material considerable support for the potential value of safe work as an important vehicle of children's development and social integration, which suggests that policy might devote more attention to how to incorporate it into education and other human resource development activities.

The operational question is how to preserve the benefits of work for children while protecting against its risks, which implies that agencies combating the evils of exploitative or dangerous child work need to guard against throwing out the baby with the bath water. It is especially interesting to note the degree to which modern thinking stresses the mediating role that children play in their own protection and development, and the fact that the way society leads them to think about themselves is often more important in determining their health and development than is the stressful situation they live with. Most importantly, there is a clear signal that policy-makers and programme-planners need to devote much more attention to how children experience not only work, but also school, play and recreation, family life, and governmental interventions intended to protect them against workplace exploitation and hazards. In doing this, they need to take a holistic and contexualized perspective. This implies careful assessment of children's actual circumstances and condition, bearing in mind the important distinctions in values and experiences associated with differences in personal and social attributes.

CHAPTER TWO

The Impact of Work
on Children

We have argued in Chapter One that the central concern for planners and practitioners involved in the implementation of measures against exploitative and dangerous child work should be the impact of work on children's well-being and development. But to find out about impacts is a difficult task. Many take into account only the negative aspects of work. Just over a quarter of all respondents (54) in the Rädda Barnen postal survey, for example, stated that the benefits from children's work are either minimal or non-existent, while several others commented that the few benefits are outweighed by the serious disadvantages. Certainly a significant number of children experience highly detrimental terms and conditions at work, many suffering major health and developmental consequences. The susceptibility of children to exploitation, danger, and abuse makes the identification and elimination of the most harmful forms of child work an urgent priority for planners. Nevertheless, the children involved in truly harmful work appear in most places to be but a minority, the greater proportion being in work which is much less detrimental, or even beneficial.

While they were concerned about abuses of children's work, quite a few of the respondents in the Rädda Barnen survey felt that there also were advantages for children in working, citing first and foremost the economic benefits. Some also mentioned that through work children are socialized in practical survival skills and knowledge, and initiated into adult roles and responsibilities, this making them more mature and self-reliant. Several noted that work participation enables children to learn about the work ethic, to gain an understanding of the importance of punctuality and discipline, and how to manage money. Other benefits were thought to include: enhancement of cognitive development (especially problem-solving skills and creativity); learning about self-protection; and gaining a sense of independence, pride, and satisfaction, this latter contributing to children's self-esteem and self-confidence. Some social advantages were also noted, including the reinforcement of children's social and cultural identity, companionship and cooperation, and keeping children from becoming idle and getting into trouble with the law.

Of course, it is likely that the people who describe work as an anathema to child well-being and those who see it as having certain significant benefits are talking about very different kinds of work and working conditions. For instance, there was a tendency in the Rädda Barnen survey for respondents from Asia to oppose all child work and for those from Latin America to favour letting children engage in non-detrimental work. This could well reflect major qualitative differences in the kind of work children tend to be engaged in across the two continents — Asia having a higher prevalence of full-time child work and bondage, for example, and Latin America a larger proportion of part-time and semi-autonomous street workers. But major differences in views also reflect conceptual differences in definitions of detrimental child work. Given the broad range of occupations and tasks children are involved in, the challenge is to develop a conceptual framework which encompasses all forms of children's work and also makes it possible to identify each one, as far as possible, according to the degree of risk or benefit it entails.

Most of the ideas about the effects of children's work held by policymakers and practitioners are heavily influenced by beliefs originating in Europe and the United States in the nineteenth century. Historically, concerns about detrimental child work were confined mainly to young children and to wage employment in industry and related sectors, focusing on the larger and more organized enterprises.[1] Work over the age of 14, agricultural work, and unremunerated family work generally have been believed to be safe and appropriate, as were typically 'juvenile occupations' such as newspaper delivery and babysitting.

But that thinking is beginning to change. Testimony provided by working children and evidence from recent research challenge old assumptions. They suggest that whether children are under a given age, whether they work for strangers or receive a wage are not the determining factors in workplace risk. In many contexts, for example, younger children may be better protected than older ones simply because society chooses to make fewer work demands of them. And children who work for family members sometimes say that they would prefer to be in paid employment because this is less exploitative, has more future prospects, and allows them greater autonomy. As we suggested in Chapter One, more important than mere age in determining risk and resilience are the terms and conditions of children's work, the way work impinges on other aspects of children's lives, especially school, how it is regarded by children themselves and by their families and communities, and how children with different social and personal characteristics in different contexts and at different levels of maturity respond to work. If old ideas are not correct, a new conceptual framework is needed to direct consideration of children's work into more useful channels.

Conceptual framework for assessing work impact on children

In recent years the terms 'child work' and 'child labour' have (in English) been used by some to distinguish activities that are harmless, or possibly beneficial, to children from activities that are injurious. However, forcing a highly complex reality into a simplistic dichotomy of this nature has not proved very helpful, provoking debate on the meaning of the two terms, without advancing insight into the actual impacts of work. Ben White recommends that children's work should be viewed instead as on a continuum of effects, from 'worst' to 'best':

> Such a continuum would begin at one end with 'intolerable' forms of child work – those which cannot be tolerated in any circumstances, which are not susceptible to efforts at 'humanization' and improvement ... Next comes forms of child work which in their *present* form are hazardous and detrimental, but which can *potentially* be made safer and less harmful ... and can potentially be combined with school or continuing education. Then come 'neutral' kinds of work which in themselves are neither particularly harmful, nor particularly beneficial to children; and finally a category for 'positive' or 'beneficial' forms of children's work.[2]

In the last couple of years this idea of a continuum of effects has gained many adherents and now receives support from UNICEF and many NGOs, among others; it usefully points out that work may be either good or bad for children, depending on the circumstances.

The Convention on the Rights of the Child provides another viable conceptual framework by encouraging a holistic view of children's well-being and development. It requires that work should be assessed for its physical, psychological, emotional, social, and spiritual consequences, as well as for the educational opportunities forgone due to work. This opens the way for applying the broad developmental principles presented in Chapter One. However, the information at present available on work impact is highly fragmented, having been gathered to suit narrow concerns or professional expertise of researchers and implementing agencies, rather than embracing the holistic reality of child development. An overwhelming priority has been given to physical health and safety issues. The impact of work on children's education has also received some attention, although not nearly as much as is needed. Studies of the psychosocial effects of work are in extremely short supply.

The International Labour Organization has recently been calling particular attention to what it terms "the intolerable forms of child labour", which it feels deserve urgent action. Separating out work that is so detrimental to children as to merit being considered intolerable is a major challenge, for there has been little serious research on the developmental impacts of child work, and existing child development theories largely ignore work as a major experience of childhood. Moreover, there are but few ethnographic descriptions which place child work in its proper social, cultural, and economic context.[3] Most of the studies of the effects of children's work are undertaken to provide evidence of prejudicial terms and conditions for use in advocacy and programming. Consequently very little is known about the ways in which children can gain from work.

So far, the term 'intolerable' has usually been linked to very visible occupations and activities like commercial sex work or soldiering that seem obviously hazardous and are shocking to adults. But some words of caution are needed. Firstly, many of the most damaging things children are involved in do not attract public attention, because they are concealed from view. This applies, for example, to exploitative work in domestic service or in hotels and catering. In fact, the hidden nature of much children's work is one of the main sources of vulnerability; sometimes being visible is a form of protection in itself. Secondly, activities that appear intrinsically safe, like herding cattle, delivering newspapers and tending a market stall, may in practice be caught up in a web of maltreatment and exploitation. Thirdly, even in some highly inappropriate occupations, the detrimental effects are not always self-evident – the point having been made in Chapter One that negative experiences may be tempered by positive ones, protecting children against harm. Fourthly, there is need to guard against purely emotive responses which are understandably invoked by children's involvement in occupations like sex work, because such responses tend to go hand in hand with simplistic and stereotypical views of children as either victims or having pathological behaviour. Such views disregard the active contribution children make

Activities that appear safe, like herding cattle, may in practice be caught up in a web of maltreatment and exploitation.

to their own lives, as well as their perceptions and feelings about their work. They put children at greater risk by casting them as helpless and vulnerable, ignoring the inner resources children can bring to their own defence and which can be reinforced by appropriate action.

Present thinking about the impact of work on children is mostly speculative. Many myths and assumptions surround the subject. There also are some major conceptual difficulties, and some ideas have little grounding in evidence. The most serious and common problem, we suggest, is a tendency in research and reports on children's work to confuse *hazards* or *risks* with *actual impacts*. Most information about children's work tends to cite risks and not effects. While children have a right to be protected from detrimental work and should not be encouraged to endure exploitation and hazard merely because they are resilient, in Chapter One we argued that the presence of risk does not tell us very much about the precise outcome of work for children, because exposure to a hazard does not necessarily have damaging consequences. Much depends on the social and normative context of work, the nature and severity of a hazard, and how children respond individually.

The discussion of child development in Chapter One implies that working children are not mere victims, but are often quite resilient, and the experience of adversity need have no obvious and direct effect on well-being and development. Moreover, children's experience of work is

79

mediated by a range of mechanisms, personal, social, and cultural, which can either mitigate against harmful effects (possibly even making children more resilient) or increase their vulnerability. In other words, modern research suggests that, given the same set of working conditions, a physically vulnerable child is more likely to succumb to illness or accidents than is a child who is physically robust, and a child whose work is socially approved is better protected against loss of self-esteem than is a child whose job is stigmatized. This implies that citing hazards alone can be misleading, giving a distorted view of work outcomes.

A more effective way of looking at children's work is to identify the risks and the mediating mechanisms and assess outcomes in the light of both. One needs to understand not only the potential dangers of work, but also the resources that children bring to the situation. For this reason, before entering the discussion of impacts, we begin the chapter by looking at hazards or risks. Then we describe what is known about the impacts of children's work, what is not known, and what needs to be done to provide a more sound understanding of this important topic. We explore some of the findings on impacts and discuss some of the difficulties researchers and social-planners encounter in being really precise about them. Some of the more critical mediating mechanisms are then outlined in the third section, drawing largely on children's own words and perceptions. Bearing in mind the point made in Chapter One about how children in different categories show different levels of susceptibility to work, the chapter ends with a discussion about which children are most likely to be affected adversely by detrimental work.

Identifying the hazards of children's work

Types of hazards

Physically hazardous work implies any work process or working environment that is either intrinsically dangerous or inappropriate for children's physical and mental capacity, size or energy levels. Almost every work setting involves at least a low level of one or more health and safety risks; chemical, physical, biological, and stress hazards existing in combination, their effects often being not only cumulative but actually intensified due to a synergy between them.[4] These are problems for all workers, but can be more so for children because of their physical immaturity and particular growth needs. The physical hazards reported most frequently as affecting working children include:

- polluted or dangerous working environments;
- exposure to extreme environmental conditions;
- involvement in physically dangerous or strenuous tasks;
- use of tools, machinery or equipment that are unsafe.

But often children are at greater psychological or social risk than physical. This is because they lack authority and physical power, because their work is not always valued as productive activity, and because they usually have the lowest status of all workers. Seldom are children able to assert their interests or needs in the workplace. Because they cannot refuse adult commands, they are often assigned the most menial and repetitive tasks or the most hazardous ones. They may be subject to rigid discipline, intimidation and physical or sexual abuse against which they cannot defend themselves, and they have little or no recourse to law in the event of injury or injustice. The social dangers cited most frequently as affecting working children include:

- absence or inadequacy of remuneration in money or kind;
- lack of representation, legal protection or compensatory mechanisms;
- work that is not voluntary or occurs under slave-like arrangements;
- work that is socially unacceptable or socially isolating;
- work that is mundane, repetitive, and dull;
- long hours and few or no periods of rest or holidays;
- sexual or physical abuse by employers, customers or work colleagues;
- emotional abuse or neglect by employers, customers or work colleagues.

In many people's minds, the greatest social hazard of all is bondage and other forms of slavery, because this places children at the complete mercy of the employer and can have both psychosocial and physical consequences. Bondage has been associated with abduction and family separation, deprivation of schooling and sustenance, extremely long hours of arduous work, and physical and emotional abuse, leading to grave consequences, both physical and psychosocial, including severe anxiety and depression, malnutrition, vitamin deficiency, anaemia, tuberculosis, and skin and parasitic diseases.[5] It is a problem in fishing in Indonesia, Sri Lanka, the Philippines, India and Pakistan, and industrial manufacturing (in the glass industry of Ferozabad and the carpet belt of Uttar Pradesh, India, for example, and the carpet production and brick kilns of Pakistan).[6] In several parts of South Asia, debt bondage is widespread in agriculture, debts stretching in many cases across several generations in the family.[7]

In Chapter One we noted that the links between physical hazard and physical effect are generally more direct than between social risks and psychosocial consequences, making health and safety impacts easier to identify than emotional or psychological ones. In industry, certain occupations are linked with very specific physical hazards, producing a fairly predictable pattern of physical morbidity. In agriculture, particular crops present specific risks. Children involved in harvesting tea, for example, often develop calluses on their plucking fingers, known as 'tea ulcers'.[8] Steam, smoke, heat, and dust — which can lead to asthma — have been linked to tobacco production, caused by the boilers in the tobacco-grading sheds. In Tanzania, young sisal workers were found to be inhaling large amounts of sisal fibres and air-borne dust during the brushing stage, one of the more serious consequences being byssinosis, a lung disease.[9] Exposure to the sisal liquid when they carry the wet fibres irritates the skin and causes severe itching, and the sharp needle-point of the sisal plant results in injuries during weeding.

Physical hazards can also have psychosocial consequences. Working in a dangerous environment, for example, can result not only in bruising, haemorrhaging, fractures or other physical traumas, but also in anxiety, sleeping or eating disorders, and other forms of psychosocial distress. Not having the right or opportunity to go to the toilet while at work can be a major source of distress. Fear caused by exposure to danger at work is revealed in the Rädda Barnen study on children's perceptions of their work and schooling.[10] The children talked quite a lot about the adverse physical conditions and safety hazards they face, and some expressed anxiety about being exposed to danger. For example, a girl working as a brick chipper in Bangladesh said: "When the hammer hits my hand tears come to my eyes ... I feel scared when I break bricks in the evening because evil spirits might take me away." Others feared the unpleasant things, like traffic accidents and deaths, that occur at work.

Working children usually have quite strong ideas about the risks — physical and social — they run and some may also be able to tie specific hazards to precise outcomes. The Rädda Barnen sample consisted of rural and urban children, boys and girls, engaged in a broad variety of occupations, including domestic work, sex work, brick chipping, street vending, embroidery, weaving, agricultural production, fishing, lead mining, and fireworks production. A high proportion of the children combined work with school, some in addition doing household chores for their family. Martin Woodhead, co-ordinator of the study, notes that, when asked to think about occupations according to a range of criteria, the children demonstrated their ability to weigh multiple considerations about income, independence, autonomy, security, safety, health, abuse, gender appropriateness of occupations, and other factors.[11] Negative comments about work, totalling 121, slightly outweighed positive ones, which numbered 101. These results should give pause for thought to those who claim children are too impressionable or inexperienced to objectively assess the negative aspects of their work.

In the Rädda Barnen focus group discussions about the bad aspects of work, concerns about health and safety and the arduous and boring nature of work predominated. Filipino boys involved in fishing, for example, cited several specific hazards: "Our ears bleed … we are hurt by the spines of crabs, shells, fish, bamboo … we would always drink Alaxan pain relievers … we will become hunchback … there are sharks."[12] A farm boy from Bangladesh recalled an accident at work: "Once, nails from my four fingers were plucked by the sickle as I was cutting sugar cane. I was out of work for four months."[13] And a Bangladeshi girl described the hazards of brick chipping: "It is very painful when a splinter from the brick gets into the eyes. One can turn blind … I don't like sitting under the sun without a shade and brick chipping. My head spins. I often get fever at night. Many people die working under the sun."[14]

The social risks provide a second major theme in discussions of the bad things about work by the children in the Rädda Barnen study. They identified physical and sexual abuse and humiliation by employers, customers, other adults, and peers as a major problem. An Ethiopian boy talked about beatings by older boys. Another said he felt ashamed when people insulted or shouted at him: "I sometimes hide myself when I see my classmates while I clean shoes."[15] Referring to abusive treatment by her employer, although showing some ambivalence by justifying maltreatment in some contexts and decrying it in others, one Bangladeshi girl said: "In the garments factory there are times when we are scolded. But that is to help us learn the skill. Whereas in domestic helping, after working so hard they beat us and verbally abuse us not for our own good."[16] Many of the references to maltreatment and exploitation by employers were made by children talking about other occupations, not their own, reinforcing their preference for their own work.

Several of the concerns voiced by the children reflected the difficulty of managing work relationships, especially relationships involving adults and peers older and more powerful than themselves. These relationships are imbued with threats to self-efficacy and self-respect, associated with feelings of shame attached to some occupations, worries about personal safety, difficulties in meeting employers' and parents' expectations, a distrust of others, and anxieties about not being trusted oneself.[17] Ethiopian sex workers, for instance, described being raped by policemen and robbed by customers. A Filipino fishing boy feared that, if ever he was caught stealing fish, his employer would have a security guard shoot him. Several of the Bangladeshi children expressed sadness and resentment about not being trusted by their employers or other adults: "Whenever *bibi shaheb* is going out she locks me in from outside, as if I am going to steal everything in their house."[18] The working children perceived domestics as especially vulnerable to employers, from whom there is no escape, while porters and street workers were seen to enjoy more freedom.

Shame was an important issue for girls in Bangladesh, firmly linked to ideas about appropriate gender roles.[19] They expressed some discomfort about working in public places, valuing the autonomy but worrying about the possible dishonour. Brick chipping, for example, was regarded as a low-status occupation: "everyone sees you sitting and working on the road and they know the kind of work you do" and even though the brick chippers preferred their jobs to domestic work, they recognized the advantage of the privacy the latter affords.[20] Flower selling was seen as less shameful than working as a porter: "because you carry flowers in your hand ... so people appreciate you instead of putting you to shame". These ideas about the shame and dishonour of working in public could reflect the tendency among Muslim women in some parts of rural Bangladesh and in some socio-economic groups to enter *purdah* after puberty.

As Chapter One pointed out, such feelings of shame may pose a greater threat to children's development than do the actual work situations to which they are connected.

Problems in understanding work hazards for children

Most of the information on work hazards has been gathered by sector, industry or occupation. Research by the ILO, for example, tends to isolate impacts by sector, separating out mining, construction, agriculture, a variety of manufacturing industries, hotel, catering and tourism, sex work, domestic and street work. This kind of approach assists the identification of broad health and developmental risks, accident patterns, diseases, and ergonomic hazards specific to each sector and industry. A strong link between occupation and poor health was found for child scavengers on Manila's Smoky Mountain rubbish dump, for example, the degree of risk being a surprise even to local health authorities. The assumption had been that the illnesses of scavenging children would be similar to those of others in their age and economic group, consisting largely of intestinal and respiratory infections. Many, however, were found to have been subject to mercury poisoning and other life-threatening conditions, such as tetanus, gunshot wounds and battering. Indeed, the risks of tetanus and exposure to toxic, combustible waste were hazards specific to scavenging, as was impaired pulmonary functioning due to the extreme carbon monoxide pollution of the work site (25 times the national limit). There was also a range of debilitating problems such as stunting and malnutrition and skeletal deformities associated with carrying heavy loads, as well as infected wounds, burns and cuts, and skin disorders that are not necessarily occupation specific.[21]

Approaching the assessment of hazards by sector or industry gives an impression that particular industries present particular hazards. At first glance, this impression appears amply justified. Mining and construction, for example, are usually rated as highly dangerous physically, while children working in services are thought more exposed to risks of a social nature, such as sexual and emotional abuse. Thus, jobs in hotels, catering and tourism have been associated with both casual and organized sex work, carrying the possibility of customer violence, sexually transmitted diseases and substance abuse.[22] Domestics risk sexual abuse by members of the employing household. A 1987 study of 100 employing families in Lima, for instance, found that 60 per cent of adolescent males in the household had their first sexual encounter with the domestic — this being how young males obtain sexual experience.[23] Physical abuse is also common among domestics. In Benin, child domestics were found to bear injuries to the back and neck, caused by beatings. In a Haiti study, three-quarters of the children in one sample had been beaten, mostly as a matter of routine.[24] Violent treatment included thrashings with a leather strap and cutting the child with a broken bottle.

Another hazard associated particularly with domestic work is extremely long hours of work. Domestics under the age of 15 in Colombia work an average of 50 hours per week, a working week longer than any other occupational group of children in the country[25]. Female domestics made up the majority of all child workers labouring over 60 hours a week. Such hours are damaging to health, lead to exhaustion, and deprive children of social contact and educational and recreational opportunities. Anecdotal descriptions from all over the world refer to young domestics as timid, listless, and withdrawn.[26] Malnutrition, psychological and emotional stress, fatigue, sleep problems, depression, eating disorders, chronic fear, and anxiety are also common among domestics.

But, in practice, the extent to which work hazards are occupation-specific might be overstated. Due to a shortage of well-grounded analysis, much of what we 'know' about specific occupations and industries largely reflects the professional or ideological inclinations of researchers. It is important to consider whose judgement of risk prevails, what indicators of risk are being used, how these are identified and by whom. Seldom are the views of the protagonists, in this case working children, taken into account, although often their perspective on risk is very different. Take, for example, the literature on child street workers which is replete with statements about impaired moral and social learning, explained as being due to young street workers' association with pimps, criminal gangs, drunks, drug dealers, and sexual adventurers, and high levels of malnutrition, stress and anxiety, and associated substance abuse. In many cases this is little more than conjecture, however, based on stereotyping, as recent research reveals. Jill Swart,[27] for example, shows that street children in South Africa have well-developed moral and social codes with a clear view of right and wrong.

Similarly, when 100 juvenile street vendors in Nigeria were asked about the likelihood of their learning 'delinquent' behaviour like lying, cheating, stealing, and promiscuity, 56 per cent felt that vending was not a cause of bad habits and that children could just as easily learn such behaviour at home.[28] Research in Nepal suggests that street children may experience less stress and better nutrition than several other groups of children of equivalent social and economic status.[29] The importance of avoiding stereotypes in assessments of work is amply reinforced by a surprising finding from North Carolina, in the United States, where farm work is the most important occupation for children of both sexes, that the leading cause of fatal occupational injury for females is homicide.[30]

There are other problems with the way hazards are defined by sector and industry. It needs to be borne in mind, for example, that some children working in industries defined as hazardous may in fact be doing quite safe jobs. By the same token, children working in generally safe industries can be doing a dangerous job. Also, the tendency to list all the hazards associated with a particular industry overlooks the question of their relative severity of impact; whereas some hazards are really quite minor, others are life-threatening. Besides, some of the most serious hazards are not occupationally specific but prevalent across all economic sectors, arising from a general deficit of safety measures and unsafe working environments. Conditions that threaten children in all occupations and activities include lack of clean water and sanitation, poor light and ventilation, absence of first aid facilities, proximity to dangerous machinery, exposure to loud noise, high levels of humidity, and extreme temperatures.[31]

In the absence of literature on the impacts of work hazards on children, it is tempting to turn to the literature on adults. There now exists a significant body of information on the effects of working, unemployment, and job loss on adults, much of which is explored in a useful review by Robert Lane.[32] He shows how task experience and job content affect things like personal and social orientation, intellectual functioning, personality, and so on. He cites research by Kohn and Schooler,[33] for example, which indicates the features of work that contribute adversely or positively to psychological functioning in adult male workers. These authors discovered that whether the work is with things, people or ideas (data) makes a difference, as does the degree to which it is varied or routine, closely or loosely supervised, complex and intellectually challenging or simple and mundane, or to which it is 'dirty' or 'clean'. The degree of bureaucracy and levels of hierarchy in the workplace were also found to be significant, as were the presence or absence of physical risks and job pressures of various kinds. While such studies raise some important questions about the ways in which work might affect children as well as adults, their relevance for children still has to be established.

Identifying work impacts

How do children and adults differ?

It certainly cannot be presumed that the effects of work on children are the same as on adults, there being major physiological, psychological, and social differences between the two groups which significantly influence susceptibility to hazard. Most importantly, because of their immaturity and because they are in a state of growth and development, children may be seriously jeopardized by work which presents little or no risk to adults. Moreover, some damage done to growth and development during middle and late childhood can have lasting effects, stretching into adulthood.

When speaking of children, therefore, it is necessary to go beyond the relatively limited concept of 'work hazard' as applied to adults, expanding it to include the developmental aspects of childhood. Because they are still growing, children have special characteristics and needs that must be taken into consideration when defining workplace risks to them. This means that, in the case of children's work, the concept of 'work hazard' needs to be child-centred, focusing not only on factors of immediate jeopardy, but also those that menace child development over the longer term.[34]

Children differ biologically from adults due to the rapid growth and development of the organs and tissues and the body as a whole. They also differ in terms of body composition, which in children entails a larger surface area in relation to weight. They have a higher metabolic rate and oxygen consumption and therefore a greater intake of air and greater energy and fluid requirements per unit of body weight.[35] But in addition there are major differences between children and adults in terms of psychosocial functioning, although whether this renders them significantly more vulnerable than adults to psychosocial distress is not clear.[36] As indicated in Chapter One, children's patterns of behaviour are in the process of formation and are therefore more adaptable to new demands than adults. Many of the symptoms associated with psychosocial problems in adults are not present in children. On the other hand, some of the symptoms in children with behavioural or other psychological disorders are not usually found in adults. And, as suggested in Chapter One, the expression of psychosocial distress in children varies also with age and developmental capacity. What can be expected of children at different points in childhood may not be connected in any way with what is considered usual or appropriate for adults.

Physical impacts

Although conclusive evidence on this subject is lacking, there are indications that children are more susceptible to environmental hazards than are adults. For one thing, a higher metabolic rate and oxygen consumption increases the intake of air per unit of body weight. Thus, for example, children between 8 and 10 years of age doing exercise have a ventilation rate three times higher than adults doing light work. It therefore seems reasonable to deduce that working children may absorb larger amounts of airborne toxins than adults.[37] The larger body surface area in relation to weight means that children may risk exposure which is far greater per unit of body weight than adults. The toxic effects of exposure to chemicals can be more serious in children because of their small body size, although considerations other than simple weight or body size may be involved, including mechanisms for detoxification which may not be fully developed in children and chronic under-nutrition due to poor diet and parasitic infections. Also, exposure to chemicals during development may disturb the maturation of organ systems and alter their response to other environmental conditions.

All these factors together suggest that, in occupations like mining, children are likely to suffer more respiratory diseases than adults due to the inhalation of stone and coal dust. After prologued exposure, they may develop silicosis, pulmonary fibrosis and emphysema. Similarly, farm children and others exposed to chemicals may be at high risk of immediate and long-term poisoning. The toxic effects of pesticides at low doses are particularly serious for children. In a survey of health facilities in large-scale farming areas in Zimbabwe, for example, hospitals reported that almost a third of their pesticide poisoning cases were children.[38] Children involved in weeding and planting tobacco were found to be susceptible to poisoning from ethylene dibromide and children in sugar, tea, cotton, and coffee production and in horticulture were exposed to agrochemicals after spraying, having entered the fields to pick crops before the pesticide residue disappeared. Local union officials and labour relations officers reported that these children suffered eye, skin, and breathing problems. Long-term exposure to organophosphates on farms was noted as causing chronic neurological damage, although this is difficult to detect in its early stages in the absence of adequate medical surveillance.

Children have a relatively higher level of energy expenditure than adults and energy lost through work can therefore jeopardize healthy growth and development. Physically, children are not suited to undertaking long hours of strenuous or monotonous work.[39] Carrying heavy loads or being forced to adopt unnatural positions at work, for example, can lead to deformation of the spinal column and sometimes of the pelvis. Child carpet weavers experience swelling of lower limbs, skeletal deformities and pain in their joints due to the cramped postures they maintain for extended periods.[40] This is a problem in mining also, since children may be required to adopt unnatural and uncomfortable positions for long hours in a restricted space underground, and may also have to wield heavy tools and loads without adequate protective equipment or clothing. Physical strain, fatigue, and musculo-skeletal disorders are common among children in mines.

Children are more susceptible to accidents and injury than adults. According to the World Health Organization, this is the main cause of death in children and adolescents globally; one child in every five sustains an accident each year, the most common being burns and scalds, falls, and poisoning.[41] Although the data are lacking, it is logical to deduce that occupational accidents are frequent among working children, especially those who work in dangerous environments, with sharp tools or moving machinery. A survey in North Carolina in the United States, for example, revealed that more than 50 per cent of work-related injuries to young people aged 11 to 19 involve a motorized vehicle.[42]

Children have little experience or awareness of danger and do not always anticipate or perceive it correctly.[43] They may have a vague impression of jeopardy, but cannot always discern the relationship between the idea of danger and a particular hazard and therefore may come to the wrong conclusions. Often, children have not developed the muscle coordination and speed necessary to avoid hazards effectively or the expertise to work in a safe and efficient manner.[44] In construction, quarries, underground mines, and docks, accidents involving falling objects and debris, explosions or drilling are a serious risk, as are falls from scaffolding and other structures, fatigue, and musculo-skeletal disorders due to lifting and carrying heavy loads. Crush injuries, lacerations, cuts, and amputations of fingers and toes are frequent in children working in agriculture, as are head injuries, abdominal trauma, fractures to bones, induced hearing loss, and eye injuries.[45] A study in Zimbabwe by the plantation workers' union found children were often injured by farm animals, manual handling of heavy loads, hand tools, knives, and hoes, as well as by falling from moving trailers.[46]

Children's physical proportions, strength and work capacity are not normally taken into consideration in the design of work methods, machinery, tools, and equipment. Hence, children using hand tools designed for adults have a higher risk of fatigue and injury. In Ferozabad, India, children working in the bangle and glassblowing industry carry molten glass and iron rods seven feet long and burns are common.[47] Children and adolescents working in fishing in Thailand use sharp knives and shelling tools and suffer frequent scrapes and cuts.[48] Accidents involving machetes and other heavy, hard-to-handle tools are reported as commonplace among Latin American children working on sugar cane, onion, hemp, and tobacco plantations.[49]

Psychosocial impacts

Because psychologists have largely ignored work during childhood, very little is known about the psychosocial consequences of work for children, and it is clearly not possible at this stage to draw firm conclusions about whether they are more susceptible than adults to psychosocial distress. The lack of information on psychosocial impacts is also partly due to the difficulty of developing appropriate research methods and indicators of psychosocial functioning, especially in a cross-cultural context. As indicated in Chapter One, symptoms of psychosocial distress are generally far more culture-specific than are physical symptoms, and the cultural context may determine whether or not symptoms constitute a recognizable 'disease'. Measuring depression due to mistreatment by an employer or emotional distress due to work that separates children from their family, for example, is extremely difficult.

Assessments of children's psychosocial condition tend to cover intellectual and affective functioning, emotional state, and moral and social learning. In order to gauge the psychosocial effects of work, it is necessary to identify the main developmental features associated with middle childhood and adolescence in different social and cultural contexts and establish the ways in which work affects functioning in each area of development. In Chapter One we found that between the ages of roughly 6 and 14 children develop a growing awareness of self and others, adapt to a rapidly widening social world, learn about autonomy and how to take control of and manage their own lives, and expand their competence in reasoning, thinking, and problem-solving. At work children may be relegated to the activities and jobs requiring the least skill and offering the least social and economic opportunities. Clearly, work that assigns children to the most repetitive and dull tasks and to the most lowly social position is hardly propitious for the development of healthy self-esteem, confidence, and feelings of personal efficacy that are the necessary foundation for other aspects of normal psychological well-being.[50]

A study of the consequences of adolescent work in North America found that many of the jobs open to children and adolescents provide very little scope for skills acquisition and forming collaborative relationships, the conclusions being that work experience is only beneficial if the tasks undertaken have social value, permit social interaction, and embody some educational or other training element:

> Jobs that provide only limited opportunity for decision-making or cooperation are not likely to foster healthy independence or social responsibility. Jobs that are clearly recognizable as adolescent' jobs, and that have little connection with the occupations youngsters will enter as adults, are unlikely to serve as effective bridges into enduring adult employment. And jobs that involve youngsters in repetitive, unstimulating tasks are not likely to facilitate the growth of higher-order intellectual skills, prepare youngsters for adult employment, inspire feelings of self-esteem, mastery, and competence, or foster a clearer sense of identity.[51]

However, there is an emerging view that even dull work can bring some important psychosocial benefits for children. This is reflected, for example, in the findings of psychiatrists George and Caroline Vaillant in the early 1980s which are reported by Lane[52] in his review. The Vaillants decided to explore the question of what characteristics are the best predictors of mental health, including recovery from serious mental health conditions, by re-examining a group of 392 middle-aged adults who had been intensively studied by Erikson more than 30 years earlier when they were about age 14. Erikson had assessed this sample according to a variety of measures indicating the free exercise of dexterity and intelligence in the completion of tasks, which was seen by Erikson as the core competence of development for that age group. The Vaillants tested their sample for a variety of adaptation and recuperative indicators of mental well-being.

The results showed that intelligence quotients and various socioeconomic, family, and other environmental factors measured when the subjects were adolescents proved irrelevant to later success as adults. The factors most predictive of later life success were "work experience (holding a part-time job or performing regular chores at home) or significant engagement in extracurricular, purposeful activities, or performance in school work (which is *work*) beyond what was predicted for a person's measured abilities".[53] Most significantly, in an interview the Vaillants are reported as saying: "The willingness and capacity to work in childhood is the most important forerunner — more important than native intelligence, social class, or family situation — of mental health."[54]

Lane comments that, even though the low level of challenge and self-direction in entry jobs available to young people may not be highly propitious for the development of the kinds of cognitive skills that Khon and Schooler found to be associated with self-directed work, early work experience apparently teaches "preservation and a belief in one's own powers to master some of life's challenges".[55] Research by Lewis Aptekar, Jill Swart and Catherine Panter-Brick, Rachel Baker and Alison Todd[56] suggests that, even under conditions that appear quite adverse, children's psychosocial functioning may not be impaired. As noted earlier, for example, Swart found that street children in Hillbrow, Johannesburg held very mainstream moral values. Similarly, although a sizeable proportion of the street children in Colombia studied by Aptekar were not coping adequately with their lives, many demonstrated "a remarkable ability to make life happy and meaningful in the worst of circumstances".[57] Overall, the children in his sample were found to be relatively healthy, intelligent and emotionally intact, many developing "in an orderly fashion". Significantly, his research supported the notion advanced by Whiting and Whiting[58] in the 1970s that child rearing which emphasizes early responsibility hastens psychosocial development.

As a means of gauging anxiety in homeless street children, rural working children, squatter children, and urban school children in Nepal,

Panter-Brick and her colleagues measured the cortisol levels present in their saliva. Raised levels of cortisol indicate stress. Early results recorded remarkably low cortisol levels in all populations by comparison with children from the United States. Significantly, levels were higher for the school and homeless populations than for village and squatter children, although age was an intervening variable. Although these findings suggest that street and working children are quite resilient, the authors note the need for further analysis for a full interpretation of the results because the meaning of low cortisol is not entirely clear. It could, for instance, show a blunted response to stressful events rather than a total absence of stressful events in the children's lives. This study is discussed in greater detail in Chapter Four.

A study of street traders in Nigerian cities by Beatrice Oloko shows how the psychosocial impact of children's work cannot be isolated from the social and cultural context and is also linked with the personal characteristics of the individual child. She found that gender significantly affected work impact, for example, as did community of origin. There is a long tradition of children engaging in street trading in Nigeria. Economic skills acquired through trading include the ability to calculate quantities, costs, and profits. Social skills include a facility for attracting customers and maintaining their loyalty while minimizing conflict with other young traders whose support is needed in the face of threatening adults. Beyond this, in the context of a hierarchical culture built on strong group ties and obligations, trading also provided children with the opportunity to explore their physical and social environment and enjoy some autonomy away from adult surveillance and control. These freedoms were not available to other children. But Oloko argues that recent social and economic changes have challenged the adaptability of street trading in the Nigerian context. For example, traditional support and protection against exploitation has been undermined by the tendency to work for distant relatives. Urban conditions and a more competitive environment put children under greater pressure to work long hours, and this they do in a more dangerous setting in terms of street crime and corruption. She concedes that, in the past, street trading was a sustainable lifestyle and even now offers socializing benefits, but concludes that: "... illiteracy undoubtedly would create obstacles to occupational success and mobility, as well as personal development and meaningful political participation in an increasingly modern society".[9]

Taken as a whole, available information on the susceptibility of children to adverse impacts in the context of work might imply that working children are likely to fare less well than children who do not work, even when the two populations are of comparable economic and social status. However, it is important to stress that at this point in time this statement is mere conjecture, since there are so many factors influencing how children are affected by their work and so many possible outcomes from working. Very little has been done to compare working with non-working child populations, and in-school with out-of-school children from both groups. Researchers have been especially neglectful of the positive effects of work and the adverse effects of schooling, thereby giving a distorted view of the impacts of both. We urge that well-structured studies of this type be undertaken by competent social scientists.

The difficulties associated with impact assessment

There are a number of important reasons why there remains so much to learn about the consequences of children's work, and why researchers, planners and practitioners have preferred to focus on risks rather than effects of working. In order to understand how best to approach an assessment of work impact it is worth considering first some of the difficulties with available information on the subject, some of the information needs, and some of the factors that influence the effect work has on children. Part of this discussion highlights methodological problems in the research, an issue that is taken up again in greater detail in Chapter Four.

Firstly, there is the fact that cultural and social views on the risks and benefits of work vary enormously. What in one context may be seen as abusive treatment by an employer, for example, could in another be viewed as necessary discipline. What may be perceived by some as working too young might be regarded by others as a good training and preparation for adulthood. Take the practice of informal adoption which is employed in many parts of the world by which rural children are sent to live with relatives in the city to work in their home in return for their keep and possibly some schooling. Child advocates and practitioners often see this as exploitative, a form of child slavery. Parents, on the other hand, may see it as an opportunity for their children to learn the ways of the modern world and in some cases as a strategy essential for survival. Children's views are not often sought.

Secondly, there is the 'invisibility' of many work effects. The most obvious signs of harm caused by work are death, sickness, injury, failure to grow or thrive, or backsliding in developmental growth.[60] But even accidents and death due to work can be difficult to record because they are often kept secret by employers and family members or because of lack of access to medical facilities where diagnosis and registration can be made. And research done at the work site will most likely fail to capture the children who have left work because of sickness or injury or who have died. Besides, many of the effects of work, whether negative or positive, are not very evident. This applies especially to psychosocial impacts.

Thirdly, there is the problem that psychosocial distress, disease, and death generally result from multiple factors and causes, making it difficult to isolate the impact of work specifically.[61] The majority of children who work have poor living conditions and these may be more significant in impairing health than is work. This is the finding of one study, in Tegucigalpa, Honduras,[62] in which market children living with their families were compared with abandoned children living on the streets (referred to as street children in the study). The market children were engaged in general tasks, running errands and selling trinkets, gum, sweets, and the like, while the street children were involved mainly in begging, carrying things for customers, and petty theft. The market children were found to be faring better in terms of physical and mental health and nutrition than the street children, although occupational differences were seen as less significant than were several living conditions. In general, the health and associated social problems of the market children were found to stem primarily from the extreme poverty of their families, whereas the problems of the street children were thought to result from being without family in the first place. Nutritional status and personal hygiene were poor for both groups, causing susceptibility to infectious and communicable disease, the crowded and unsanitary living conditions also contributing to high transmission rates. Air and noise pollution were excessive on the streets, as was the risk of injury and exposure disorders. Trouble with the police, substance abuse, and sexual activity were additional risk factors for street children.

Most existing data do not separate the effects of working from the effects of poverty and other variables already known to have an important influence on children's well-being. The only way to isolate the effect of working is to compare the well-being and development of working children with children from similar economic and family backgrounds who have never worked. Few studies of this type have been done. Exceptions include an investigation by Das, Shukla and Öry,[63] which compared a sample of adults and children engaged in carpet weaving in Mirzapur, India, with a control of non-weavers of similar age and socioeconomic status. Coughs, backache, and eye problems presented more frequently in weavers than the control group, although the authors noted the difficulty of establishing whether these diseases were occupationally linked.

In another study, Mattoo, Rauf and Zutshi[64] assessed the health of 500 carpet-weaving children aged between 6 and 16 and a control of 450 school pupils in rural Kashmir. The overall height of the weavers was found to be less than the control group and a retarding tendency in the rate of growth was noted in boys especially. Although there was no strong tendency in weight, clinical assessments showed that symptoms of nutritional deficiency were more frequent among weavers than in the control group. Conjunctival pallor was the most common sign of nutritional deficiency in both groups, and this was present in a higher proportion of weavers. There were also significant differences in presenting complaints like headache, blurring vision, backache, abdominal and respiratory tract infection.

A fourth difficulty with impact assessments is that many health symptoms are general to a range of conditions, making it hard to arrive at an accurate diagnosis of health outcomes in the absence of trained medical personnel. Data from Bangladesh illustrate this point well.[65] A summary of the medical symptoms that had presented over the previous two years in a sample of working children revealed the type and frequency of morbidity by occupation. However, it is not possible to draw firm conclusions from this because many of the symptoms, such as coughing, fever, eczema, and vomiting, were non-specific and could indicate a range of conditions. Accidents and injuries, on the other hand, obviously present specific symptoms and can be tied to specific episodes; injury to the hands and legs or feet being by far the most common and electrocution, burns, and eye injuries slightly less frequent in the Bangladesh sample.

A fifth problem is that many work effects are difficult to detect simply because they are quite subtle, sub-clinical conditions that present no obvious symptoms. Moreover, many effects are cumulative, or manifest only in the long term, sometimes not until adulthood:

> Damaged vision or hearing, crippled limbs, distorted and weakened bodies, stunted growth, and increased vulnerability to disease are common results of children participating in occupations and working conditions inappropriate to their stage in life. Since some of these symptoms may take years to appear, they are often not recognized by an uninformed public as having been caused by childhood work.[66]

The delayed and changing effects of work cannot be captured in assessments made in the short term; a more accurate view requires longitudinal research. Such investigations are extremely rare, however. One of the few studies of this nature, by Satyanarayana, Prasanna Krishna and Narasinga Rao[67] was published in 1986. They tracked around 700 child paid and family workers and students in rural Hyderabad from infancy into early adulthood, the research stretching over 17 years. The working children and students were matched for nutritional status at the age of 5. The main finding of this study was that the child workers suffered significant growth deficits in the long term as compared to the students, even though there were no height and weight differences between the two groups at the outset.

Learning about work outcomes for children requires that children's strengths and vulnerabilities and the synergistic effects of child development be taken into account. Care must be taken to find out about the 'hidden' effects and especially about the ones with psychosocial connotations. A balance must also be struck between long-term and short-term outcomes. For instance, the immediate benefits of working, such as sufficient food, may be outweighed by the long-term disadvantages of reduced employment prospects and therefore the perpetuation of poverty. Adverse effects also need to be weighed against the advantages, for these mitigate against harm and increase resilience.

Mediating resilience and vulnerability at work

In Chapter One we learned that there is no direct link between adversity and developmental outcome in children because child development is not a mechanistic process of cause and effect. We established that whether work is beneficial or detrimental to children is influenced by a broad array of mediating mechanisms. But there is as yet very little systematic evidence on the influence of these mechanisms on children in the context of work, largely because social scientists have often assumed that exposure to adversity during childhood leads automatically to negative effects, and also because psychologists in particular have done very little research on working children. Added to this is the fact that it is only in very recent years that researchers, child advocates, and practitioners have begun to listen to children and their families, and therefore to see child work in its social and cultural context, which often throws on it a less negative light.

Certainly, work can entail major hazards, rendering children susceptible to harmful effects, but it can also offer some important opportunities and benefits (enhanced self-esteem or heightened sense of responsibility for example) which moderate negative outcomes (such as poor working conditions, or excessive responsibility).[68] Sometimes even what presents a risk in one context or with one group of children increases resilience in another context or with different children. Hence the suggestion made by

White that work be viewed not as a dichotomy between good and bad, but on a continuum from best to worst.

The interplay of positive and negative aspects of work is quite complex. Children who participated in a study in Russia, for example, were mostly satisfied with their work and yet had quite a few reservations.[69] Of those who expressed doubts, 20 per cent criticized the amount of money — especially those in agriculture — while only 4 per cent mentioned the danger of work as a problem. They were aware that the search for work and the work itself are time-consuming and interfere with their studies. Having to travel a long way to work was a discomfort, as was having to get up early, the danger of being caught by the police, the difficulty of the work, exposure to cold, and the risk to their lives. For example, those who washed cars or sold snacks from McDonald's to passing motorists were afraid of being hit by a vehicle. Technical problems such as not being able to get the materials they needed, lack of knowledge, experience, foreign language facility, and so on were also mentioned. Racketeering and extortion were significant problems for some.

From the literature on child work and from the responses to the Rädda Barnen survey of NGO practitioners, policy-makers, and planners it is possible to identify a number of mechanisms which mitigate against harmful impacts of work. These are as follows:

Sources of resilience

We have suggested that whether work is harmful or beneficial for children is determined not simply by the conditions and terms of work but also by the subjective value given to work by the children themselves. This, in turn, is influenced by cultural definitions of the social legitimacy of child work. The degree of legitimacy, in turn, depends in part on the occupation (some occupations bringing higher status to the worker than others). Other factors that can be significant include whether the work is paid or unpaid, and ideas about the roles appropriate for boys and girls of different ages, rural children, urban children, and so on.

Despite an acute awareness of the risks of their work, the children in the Rädda Barnen study generally rated their own occupation more highly than did children from other occupations. This, Woodhead comments, indicates the security of the familiar, even in the face of difficulties, and the importance of maintaining a sense of self-esteem and group, occupational or family solidarity.[70] Feeling pride or shame, he suggests, mediates the impact of more tangible hardships. When flower selling, brick chipping, domestic work and portering were compared by girls in

Bangladesh, domestic work was viewed most negatively overall, largely because of the risk of abuse. Nevertheless, even though they recognized the hazards of their occupation, the domestics themselves were able to identify some important benefits: "We get to eat well and work within the house instead of burning under the sun like in brick chipping. We can rest for a while and don't get electric shocks like in the garment factories".[71] The one occupation that proved the exception to the rule was sex work, since Ethiopian sex workers could find few redeeming features in their occupation and ranked it amongst the worst. As one girl commented: "It is better being called a thief than being called a prostitute."[72]

The negative perceptions of their work held by the Ethiopian sex workers reinforce the idea that one of the most important mechanisms mediating resilience and vulnerability is the degree of social legitimacy attached to a given occupation. Work which is socially valued can enhance self-concept and self-esteem, implying that work which is not approved may render children vulnerable to psychosocial distress. Work that has social legitimacy can be an important transition rite through which children and adolescents become social adults and also confirm their gender roles. Among African bushmen foragers, for example, boys must prove their manhood by hunting prowess. They must undergo tests of hardiness and skill from which girls are excluded. In other words, their manhood is subject to proof and conceptually to diminishment or loss.[73]

Even in more complex urban societies, where formal transition rites are absent, children are drawn to work because of its association with the personal autonomy, rights, and responsibilities of adulthood. Being appreciated by customers or employers for doing a job well was important to the children in the Rädda Barnen sample. They also expressed pride and satisfaction at participating in work which is a preparation for adulthood. Two boys from the Philippines, for example, said: "I learn how to work young so that when I get married I can already feed my family" and "We will learn how to work ... be trained with the skills of a farmer ... follow the good traits of our parents" while a Filipino girl remarked: "I learn to be industrious and helpful ... I am being trained for the future when others will get and employ me."[74]

For many children, the benefits of work are closely linked to helping family, which adds moral value to children's work. Children can also make a significant contribution to family or household income, either through direct earnings or because their work releases adults from domestic or childcare chores, allowing them to take up paid employment. As a Peruvian child notes:

I'm twelve years old and I started working in this market two years ago. My *papá* works as a plumber and as a bricklayer but the money he gets isn't enough to feed us all. I have six other younger brothers and sisters. My *mamá* has to stay home with the little ones and can't go out to work.[75]

A clear distinction is made by Chinese children in London between family labour and employer—employee relations, the former being described as 'helping out' and the latter 'work'[76]: "'helping out' involved work which was meaningful in itself, and which was normatively prescribed, while 'work' was seen in terms of delimited work roles in an impersonal context".[77] Helping out is underpinned by a certain amount of moral and material pressure since it contributes directly to the survival and success of the family business, and is also a 'duty', affirming family membership.[78] Helping out implies good will and a willingness to contribute one's labour. This is seen to derive from the fact that family relationships are 'special': "... working together as a family was inextricable from most young people's understandings and experiences of 'family' ".[79]

Parents exert varying degrees of influence over occupational decisions made by children and this may have an important bearing on the extent to which children view their work positively. Child work can be an important factor in family solidarity and contributing to family maintenance mitigates adversity in many contexts. Parental approval can enhance positive moral identity, as Sui, a girl who works in a Chinese takeaway in London, comments: "In that sense [working hard], I had quite a lot of respect, because I was able to help out and they can't say, 'Oh, my daughter's no good'. Because I did help out and everything, in the ways they wanted."[80]

Work also affects children's adaptation to a wider social network. Children and young people in middle childhood and adolescence begin to identify themselves increasingly as members of broader social groups, including racial, ethnic, and socioeconomic groups. Participation in work can enhance their identification as members of such groups. Chinese takeaway restaurant children, for example, recognize the work they do for their families as a positive emblem of Chinese cultural identity in Britain because, although conscious of the mythologizing of traditional Chinese families, they are proud of the Chinese tradition of collective rather than individual interests.

But it needs to be borne in mind that in the modern world opinions about children's work vary widely between different social groups, and who is approving or disapproving it makes a significant difference in terms of children's psychosocial well-being. Children's views on work are often at variance with those of parents and other adults, as in Russia. The greatest concern of Russian parents is that children's work will interfere with their studies; in their view a child must first be well educated. They worry that the value of education will diminish for children as they begin to see work as making it possible to earn money without lengthy training. Adults and children held different occupational preferences:

> Older adults rated work in production cooperatives highly since these have been and continue to be promoted in the media as the most honourable occupation. In general, teachers and adults tended to value dirty or menial activities such as shoe cleaning, dog walking, and house cleaning as less appropriate for children since they still associate these with the work of servants. One indication of changing attitudes is that adults under 30 are now willing to consider former menial activities as acceptable if the conditions and remuneration are to standard. Adults view street trade as least desirable as this is identified in the public mind with profiteering, which under the previous system had been illegal; the term 'profiteer' is still considered a swear word. Youngest adults tend to be more tolerant of child labour. Children's preference of occupation is almost completely at variance with that their elders would have for them. Children rate occupations largely by their profitability, their cleanliness and to a lesser extent, their safety, whereas adults tend to use moral or social criteria. Thus for children street trading emerges as most desirable since it is more profitable, whereas it is last in the adults' listing. Children are also willing to consider a number of activities that adults do not consider as possible occupations, among them black-market dealing, money changing, boxing or fighting for money, and playing musical instruments in pedestrian subways.[81]

By adolescence, peers often are a more important reference group than are parents and other kin, and sometimes young people do not seek parental approval so much as autonomy in occupational choice. The value of independence was a recurring theme in the Rädda Barnen sample, especially for children working on the streets. So long as they have the approval of their peers, work which is opposed by parents can retain social legitimacy. In one study, children working on the streets in Brazil and the Philippines more often than others viewed work (frequently combined with schooling) positively, as did their parents.[82] Children involved mostly in rag picking and domestic work in India and child workers in

Kenya were less positive, however, many feeling they had been compelled to work by their parents and preferring to be at school. The authors suggest that the children in Brazil and the Philippines may have had more freedom in their work decisions, making them more favourable towards their occupations.

There can be a lot of tension around children earning, and it can bring them both advantages and disadvantages. Certainly economic gain was rated most highly among the various benefits of work by the children in the Rädda Barnen study. The Russian study indicates that the possibility of acquiring valued consumer items imported from overseas may motivate children so strongly to work that they do not feel constrained by adult opinions. This is very much in keeping with the suggestion made recently by White,[83] that the globalization of mass media and lifestyles is so compelling that children all over the world are encouraged to enter work, regardless of whether they have their parents' consent, so that they can buy brand name goods and other luxuries.

Children often value paid employment outside the home more than unpaid work within, because this can bring greater respect within the home and among peers. Surveys have shown that child breadwinners have fewer conflicts with their parents and are less frequently punished than their non-working siblings.[84] In India, paid work was found to give children a purpose away from the drudgery of daily life in the slums: "a boredom which may be relative idleness for boys and hard and repetitive domestic work for girls".[85] White[86] emphasizes that paid work outside the home is often preferred by girls in societies which in varying degrees and in various ways confine girls much more than boys to a secluded life at home. These kinds of factors have led children in some countries to favour factory work which is seen by some policy-makers and practitioners as highly exploitative and degrading.

The subjective value given to work by children, their families and communities, the sense of pride children obtain from what they do, the contribution their earnings make to family income – these are all mechanisms mediating vulnerability and making children more hardy. There are many other such mechanisms; for example, the health status, stamina, and cognitive capacity of individual children play a role. Gender is also very significant, as is personality. As we found in Chapter One, the mediation of impact is one of the central tenets of recent theories about risk and resilience in children exposed to adversity, helping explain why some children succumb to work hazards while others similarly exposed thrive.

Work itself is a mediating force affecting other areas of children's lives. Precisely because they work, working children often seem to have less access to health care, education or other services and resources than non-working children. All child work should be weighed against the comparative advantages or disadvantages for children of other uses of their time and energy, and should be examined in light of the opportunities foregone and opportunities gained due to work. The most important alternatives to work for children in the middle and late childhood years are education, rest, and play.

Most working children have attended school at some time or other and many combine school and work on a regular basis. Sustaining work and school can be difficult for children, as several of the children in the Rädda Barnen sample noted. The tendency to drop out of school, repeat school years, perform poorly, be removed from school early or fall behind are problems faced by many working children. Based on household surveys in ten countries in the Latin American region, a study done by CEPAL asserts that 13- to 17-year-old males who work complete one to two fewer years of education than those who do not work; for girls in the same age group the difference is between 0.5 and 1.5 years of schooling.[87] However, such findings do not indicate whether children are behind in school because they work, or work because they are not interested in doing well at school. These children generally accumulate an education deficit of more than two years compared with those who enter the workforce between the ages of 18 and 24 years, which is reflected in a reduced income throughout their adult life. But it is more than an economic issue, since children made to work when they see school as providing better opportunities for their future may harbour deep resentment.

Levison regards the amount of time in a week given to labour force participation as being one of the most significant variables impinging on children's welfare, especially in so far as it affects their education:

> Part-time work may be a learning experience complementary to formal education and a life experience with positive effects on maturity and self-confidence. On the other hand, long hours of work on tasks requiring little or no skill and providing little stimulation may handicap children for life by impeding their formal education.[88]

She suggests that hours worked is more significant in terms of effect on school performance than whether or not children work. To support this argument, she cites a study conducted in the United States by Steinberg and Dornbusch,[89] in which 20 hours of work per week was found to be the critical threshold for adverse impact on school performance:

> Long work hours during the school year are associated with lower investment and performance in school, greater psychological and somatic distress, drug and alcohol use, delinquency, and autonomy from parents. Workers do not have any advantage over nonworkers in self-reliance, work orientation, or self-esteem. The negative correlates of school-year employment are closely linked to the number of hours worked each week and generally cut across ethnic, socio-economic, and age groups ...[90]

Nevertheless, the relationship between education and work is far from predictable. Thus, for example, while seasonal full-time work in Latin America is associated with high repetition rates, permanent part-time work appears less damaging, at least for children in secondary education.[91] Work can also support schooling. A significant proportion of children throughout the world work in order to be able to pay for school uniforms and utensils, school fees, or the cost of travelling to school; if it were not for their work, many of these children would not be able to attend. Moreover, children who learn responsibility and self-discipline at work may be better motivated to study than children who do not work. As we indicate in Chapters Three and Seven, in many cases school is the problem and not work, in that a large proportion of children enter the workforce not out of economic necessity but because of poor quality schooling.

The children most likely to be harmed by work

In Chapter One we emphasized that children in different categories are regarded and treated very differently and that this affects both the experience and impacts of work. Clearly, for the purpose of planning interventions to assist children involved in hazardous or exploitative work it is important to know which categories or groups of children are most susceptible and in what ways.

Unfortunately, information about the risks and effects of work is often disaggregated insufficiently to reveal distinctions between different social groups and categories. However, gender disparities are sometimes made evident. For example, an analysis of farm fatalities among children in Colorado and Kentucky, in the United States, reveals both gender similarities and distinctions in work impact.[92] In Colorado, almost all farm machinery deaths occurred among boys. Animals (horses and cattle) and drowning (mostly in irrigation ditches, but also in rivers, ponds, and manure pits) were other major causes of fatalities in boys. Girls, on the other hand, were more likely to be the victims of animals, drowning, suffocation caused by house fires, and falls into grain bins or grain-filled wagons. In Kentucky, both girls and boys died predominantly by drowning or from farm machinery.

It is clear that gender plays a critical role in work outcomes in many countries, gender differences possibly being due in part to differences in the way boys and girls respond to adversity:

> Sex disparities start early in life. During infancy and early childhood, girls cope better than boys in difficult conditions. Boys are more physically vulnerable at birth, rendering them more prone to malnutrition, infection and mortality. They also seem to be more vulnerable than girls to the negative effects of family discord, and have difficulties in handling aggressive impulses in an appropriate way ...
>
> During pre-adolescence (10 to 12 years), however, there appears to be a reversal in this vulnerability tendency. Boys perform better scholastically, while girls are more likely to experience major problems relating to dependency ... Resilient girls may benefit from experiences that encourage greater autonomy and independence; resilient boys may fare better in homes that are fairly well-structured, uncrowded and lacking family discord.[93]

A study of work-related stress in young people in the United States[94] revealed significant findings in this regard. Females with part-time jobs showed a higher incidence of physical and psychological symptoms when compared to a non-working group of females, but this pattern did not emerge for males, who showed fewer symptoms with an increase in work-related stress. Despite this finding, there was firm evidence that the more time spent in work, the greater the use of alcohol, cigarettes and marijuana; a possible indirect indication of stress, although it could equally be that 'alienated' children are both more likely to drop out of school and use substances and that therefore the link between work and substance abuse is incidental.

Gender differences in the hazards and impact of work have a lot to do with different societal expectations. In highly gender-segregated societies, girls generally experience much greater work hardship than boys and are also far less likely to attend school. Studies from Nepal, Java,

In most parts of the world, girls have fewer chances than boys to escape oppressive work situations.

and Zimbabwe reveal that girls consistently work longer hours in a wider range of tasks than boys.[95] They are also more likely to have to combine domestic chores within the home with paid work outside. In Bangalore, India, for example, 92 per cent of girls were found to be doing household work in addition to their work outside the home, compared to only 18 per cent of boys.[96] Ideas about gendered roles played an important part in shaping the feelings about work among the children in the Rädda Barnen study. In Bangladesh, girls' occupations were viewed less favourably by both sexes, domestic work and brick chipping being regarded quite unfavourably. There was much concern about the vulnerability of domestic workers in particular to exploitation and abuse by employers. In South Asia, girls are subject to considerable moral pressure in connection with their work: "Girls particularly are imbued with ideas of honour, and are made to internalize how they should safeguard them, by cultivating a spirit of self-denial and performing their domestic duties without muttering."[97] In most parts of the world girls enjoy far fewer opportunities to change occupations than boys, with the result that they have fewer chances to escape oppressive work situations.

In some cases, however, boys are at greater risk than girls. This may be because boys are expected to do the most dangerous or onerous tasks. In many countries in Latin America there is greater pressure on boys to work than on girls. In a sample of 379,000 children between 7 and 14 years of age in public and private primary schools in Bogotá, 87 per cent worked, including those engaged in domestic activities.[98] Especially high rates of work were recorded for boys, for children in the older age groups and for children enrolled in public schools. Of the total, a full 41 per cent were doing paid work outside the home in addition to domestic work within. A more complex picture emerges from Brazil, however, where survey data reveal that below the age of 10 boys are more likely not to be at school than girls, while by the age of 12 this pattern is reversed.[99] The decline in attendance among girls may be linked to growing childcare and domestic responsibilities.

Because they are often confined to reproductive activities in or near the home which are of lower status than productive, girls are less likely than boys to be given the opportunity to acquire skills valued highly by society. In Peru,

> ... the outstanding characteristic or pattern that emerged — as opposed to the working female children — is that boys learn how to buy products and raw materials wholesale for their mother's businesses. Boys are entrusted with capital to invest and establish

the same commercial networks as their mothers. While still in school they make use of their student's bus pass to go back and forth from home to the wholesale market and return to their mother's workplace with the products she needs.[100]

The limitations of learning opportunities provided for girls at work is an important consideration in decisions about the relative value of work and school for their well-being and development.

Age is another important criterion for distinguishing the degree and nature of work impacts in children. When it comes to children in different age groups, it is usually assumed that younger children are more likely than older ones to be affected unfavourably by work, both because of their physical and mental immaturity and also because they are less autonomous and assertive. This is certainly the logic behind legal instruments setting a minimum age for entry to work. But, as noted in Chapter One, young children often are more indulged and seldom required to do strenuous work, the levels of responsibility and hardship increasing with age. Further, even though the risk of physical damage due to work decreases with age, some health problems appear later, especially during adolescence when the body is developing in size, strength and reproductive capacity.[101] The impact of poor health during infancy and early childhood due to impoverished working and living conditions may be felt first during adolescence, for example, because the effects of toxic exposure or infections may be delayed. Likewise, minimal brain damage, visual and auditory or speech defects due to occupational exposure may cumulatively affect the adolescent's ability to learn and consequently his or her self-esteem. Inadequate diet, excessive physical stress or pregnancy may also undermine normal physical development during adolescence.[102] More information about the effects of work at different ages and developmental phases is urgently needed.

Variations in work risk are observable in relation to other criteria, especially ethnicity, religion, caste and class, and rural or urban residence. In most cases, rural children begin working at an earlier age than urban children. This trend has been documented especially clearly as regards Latin America.[103] Nevertheless, rural work is often idealized and it is generally held that rural working children face fewer hazards than their urban counterparts because they are involved in less complex technological processes and work within the context of the family. It is important to guard against assumption or stereotype, however. Firstly, the ambivalence about working for family expressed by many working children suggests that this is an ideal cherished more by adults than by children. But there is also the fact that family work is not exclusive to rural areas, since a significant proportion of urban children also work with family members. In Korea, mothers and children work together in textile production, marketing and cottage industries, and in Bogotá children work with family members in brick making and quarrying. At the same time, conditions for working children in rural areas are often far from ideal. A large number of rural children in South Asia, for example, are bonded and children involved in plantation agriculture and even in peasant farming frequently work with chemicals or dangerous machinery, quite apart from being exposed to environmental hazards due to extremes of temperature and weather.

When employed, children from low-income families and minority children are more likely to be in low-paying and hazardous industries and also to work longer hours. Many minority and depressed-area children are forced to migrate in order to find a job, rendering them even more vulnerable. In Thailand a high percentage of girls in prostitution are migrants from poorer neighbouring countries like Laos, Cambodia, Vietnam, and Burma. In many cases, these children come from impoverished ethnic minority hill-tribe communities. The tendency to employ migrants from overseas in the Thai brothels has become more marked since the risk of contracting the HIV virus has become widely known in Thailand and local families have become more reluctant to expose their girls. A similar disparity prevails in the United States, where migrant children are particularly prone to agricultural hazards, in part because of dangerous work conditions and in part because migrant labour camps are substandard and overcrowded, with makeshift or no housing, unsafe electricity and drinking water, and other environmental hazards. The camps are often located near the fields and exposed to pesticide sprays.[104] As a result of poor sanitation in fields and living quarters, migrant farm worker adults and children have shown rates of parasitic infection ranging from 20 to 75 per cent, compared to a 3 per cent level among the general US population.

Minority children are also at greater risk than other groups of being involved in forced work of one form or another. Thailand's fishing industry employs refugees and migrants with no legal status, including ethnic Karen from Burma who receive no wages, only food and housing.[105] In Nepal also, most bonded families are from economically marginalized and landless indigenous ethnic groups such as the Tharu. Bonded children in agriculture in India are generally from scheduled castes and tribes, including adivasis and other low-caste groups. Bonded children in the carpet industry in Uttar Pradesh are often recruited from low caste families from Bihar and Madhya Pradesh or Nepal. The worst conditions occur in production units that rely on migrant child labourers who have been recruited or lured from their villages.[106] Many of these children work extremely long hours, sleeping, eating and working in the same room and are not allowed to visit home. Those who try to escape or make mistakes are often beaten, deprived of food or tortured.

Conclusion

For a long time, discussion and information about the outcomes of work for children has been confined mainly to the risks rather than to actual impacts. Emphasis usually has been placed on physical and safety issues and on the adverse effects on schooling, while psychosocial effects have been largely ignored. The overall picture that has emerged suggests that in various ways – and especially physically – children probably are more susceptible to adversity than are adults, although conclusive evidence has yet to be provided. Without a doubt, some work is highly detrimental for children and identification of intolerable forms of work should be a major priority for planners and practitioners. But research and children's own testimony suggest that work also can offer some important psychological and emotional advantages which mitigate against detrimental outcomes, contribute to children's resilience, and facilitate psychosocial development. Work can present many dangers, physical and psychosocial, for children. But it can also bring important rewards, teaching them endurance, giving them a sense of pride and self-esteem, and making it possible to buy nutritious food or attend school. It is generally supposed that the majority of working children are involved in work that is quite benign. But until proper research into the effects of work on children is further advanced, it is impossible to conclude whether this is the case.

Policy-makers, practitioners and child advocates most need to understand that work is neither all good nor all bad in its effects on children, but is a powerful childhood experience for many children that can be turned in either direction. Children should be protected from workplace harm, but permitted access to its benefits under appropriate conditions. All policies and programmes and all advocacy measures directed at children's work should be concerned about both its positive and negative effects on children's health, safety, well-being and development. Priority must be given to identifying work which presents an immediate threat, work which does damage in the longer term and work which undermines schooling, recreation, and play, as well as to distinguishing the categories and groups of children who are most susceptible in each and every context. At the same time an effort should be made to identify and make good use of work and working conditions that have a beneficial effect on children. Given the many crucial gaps in knowledge, this means doing further research by activity, occupation and industry, as well as by social group, and comparing working children and non-working children over significant periods of time. It means examining children's own views of their work and comparing these with their feelings about education. Emphasis in all research and action should be on children's holistic well-being and development.

CHAPTER THREE

The Causes of Child Work and its Exploitation

Policy-makers and programme-planners need to understand in detail why children work and why some of them are at serious risk in their work. As we have indicated in the Introduction and previous chapters, ample experience suggests that mistaken ideas about the causes of child work and its exploitation can lead not only to interventions that are ineffective and wasteful, but even to misguided 'solutions' that perversely end up hurting the very children they were intended to help. While such cases receiving widespread attention recently have tended to involve children working in export sector industries, it has also been a persistent problem for informal sector working children. The realities that surround child work are complex, nuanced, and may vary enormously between countries and situations. In-depth understanding must include special attention to children's own views, which are a source of essential information. This entails listening to how they define their problems and recognizing the often subtle connections between the reasons children give for working and what they feel they need to advance their physical and psychosocial development.

The literature treats the subject of causes superficially. One reason is a very common impression that the causes of child work and exploitation are already well known. It is common to hear the question: "Why waste time on what everyone already knows when the important thing is to take action?" The problem with this notion is that attributing causes is not as easy as it may appear, nor is it always an objective exercise. The causes one sees depend upon one's perspective; people who feel they know a lot about child work and exploitation do not always readily agree on what it is that they know. Another reason for inadequate understanding is the feeling from some quarters that knowing causes is not always relevant to taking action. It is sometimes claimed that prohibitions against hazardous conditions of work by the very young, for example, should be energetically enforced regardless of why they exist: "You don't need to know why violations exist in order to enforce the law." This argument ignores the fact that different causes imply different measures if action is to be effective.

Neglect of careful thinking about causative factors has led to a curious inconsistency in the existing literature, which mostly talks about 'child labour' (at least in English) rather than children's work. Despite a current international trend toward defining 'child labour' as child work that is detrimental to children, discussion of its causes is still largely confined to the question of why children work, neglecting the equally pertinent issue of why some working children are at serious risk while many others are not. The conventional approach to the issue of causality reflects a labour market perspective dividing the topic into 'supply' and 'demand' factors that 'push' or 'pull' children into the workplace. The discussion usually begins and ends on that issue, without considering the differential effects of work on children engaged in it. This considers causes but for part of the problem.

Entering into the problem only half-way in this manner implies that the fact that children work merits more concern than the fact that they are preyed upon by adults or otherwise put at risk. But why does this risk occur? Is it because children and their families are ignorant of the risks, or do not know how to avoid them? Or is it that parents simply do not care? Is it a lack of other available alternatives? Does class or gender discrimination consign certain children to the more dangerous forms of work? Why do many employers (often the children's own family) maintain dangerous conditions or practices that could be easily and inexpensively remedied? What economic and social factors help maintain the most abusive forms of child work, such as slavery and slavery-like conditions, prostitution and criminal activities, and seriously hazardous activities that threaten life and health? There is an urgent need for further research into questions of this sort, the findings of which could help target scarce resources more effectively on manageable numbers of children requiring special assistance.

The causes of child work and exploitation, as reported by children

It is conventional to begin a consideration of the roots of detrimental children's work by relating the incidence of child workers to prevailing social and economic conditions such as poverty, discrimination, failure of public services, cultural tradition, and so forth. For some purposes, such as understanding the function of labour markets, this approach is valid. But for those seeking to protect the best interests of children, this 'macro' point of departure can wrong-foot the discussion from the outset by diverting attention away from the reality of the children involved and the motives that drive them to act as they do. Obviously, protective interventions that can succeed only with support of working children themselves have to be reasonably compatible with children's own thinking. It is therefore useful to hear what children have to say about why they work and about why they get into trouble in their work. It is even a good place to start. From that departure point, inquiry can expand to include broader social perspectives, relating them to the specific options and dilemmas which children must face and act upon.

In the last several years, the published and unpublished literature based on child surveys and interviews has expanded significantly. New interest in the topic also has brought some welcome methodological sophistication, which will be discussed in the next chapter. However, the methods and quality of existing research are uneven, which makes it difficult to systematize their overall findings. Moreover, few researchers have been specifically interested in children's thinking about causal factors, and this information has to be derived from their studies in bits and pieces. Most importantly, perhaps, hard-to-reach children who work in some of the worst circumstances — such as those working away from their families and in slavery-like conditions — and may be most at risk are under-represented in such studies, since by definition they are difficult to find and interview. It is inevitable that, for the time being, the voices most heard are those of children whose work allows them freedom of movement and contact. The following discussion is therefore an unavoidably impressionistic assessment by the authors, who have over time seen and worked with much of this information. However, a few broad themes clearly seem to stand out from studies and experience almost everywhere in developing countries, and sometimes in rich countries as well.

Child work as a contribution to the family

Most developing country children feel they work in order to help their families, as the Rädda Barnen surveys of both experts and children themselves suggest.[1] Most working children say they begin to work at the encouragement, request or command of their family. The decision may be taken with the child's own willing support or, at the opposite extreme, may be even brutally imposed. In many homes, children work simply because they are told to, and whether they enjoy or detest what they do is almost beside the point. Most children are put to work in order to help the family, either by doing non-economic chores within the household — typical for girls — or by contributing in some way to the family income.

Although they are seldom asked, it is likely that, if given the opportunity, most poor children would say that it is legitimate and reasonable that they be asked to help the family by contributing their work, especially when family survival and solidarity depend upon it. As was indicated in Chapter One, children usually see and value themselves as part of a family unit, and they derive meaning and development from it. At the same time, many children object to being placed in kinds and conditions of work that they consider unfair, oppressive, or worse — and often this objectionable work is in their own homes. While some adults assume that children are better off when they work in their own homes than in outside jobs, presumably because they are better cared for by family members, the testimony of children does not necessarily support that idea. In fact, children often say the opposite. Studies in Morocco and Indonesia, for example, have found that children prefer factory jobs over what they consider more oppressive, unremunerative, and futureless drudgery at home.[2]

Relatively few industrialized-country children and adolescents claim to work in order to contribute to their families,[3] but developing-country children show much more interest in helping maintain family solidarity and economic viability. Typically, they also claim to receive emotional satisfaction from contributing to the family income and unity. For example, Ethiopian working children in the Rädda Barnen survey of children indicated that what they most like about their work is the good feeling they receive from being able to help their families.[4] Sometimes this satisfaction reflects deeper dependency, as illustrated by a study of street children in Brazil:

> While these children may be economically independent, they often remain deeply emotionally dependent and attached to the idea of 'family'. When we asked a street kid of Bom Jesus da Mata if his mother still loved him, he replied without hesitation, "She's my mother, she has to love me!" But Chico knew as well as we did that his mother had forced him out of the house after trying to give him away as a baby several times to distant relatives. When asked why they beg, steal, or why they live in the streets, poor children in Bom Jesus da Mata often replied that they were doing it to help their mother. Most share a percentage of their street earnings with their mothers to whom they return each evening, or at least once a week.[5]

The fact that children are set to work by their parents, rather than at their own initiative, does not seem to diminish their readiness to contribute. However, children who are taken out of school to work, who are sent to live and work away from home, or whose work is especially burdensome or oppressive frequently report regret and a sense of loss even as they defend the need to assist their families. Family recognition and appreciation of the work children do is important to them, but it may vary with age and gender. The work of older children and boys may be considered more important than that of younger children and girls, in which case the latter may be bitter. For example, a study of child work perceptions in rural Bangladesh found that boys, who generally helped with crop cultivation tasks, liked their work and felt that other family members regarded it as important. Girls, on the other hand, assisted mostly with child care and household duties, which they said their families did not recognize as equally valuable work, and they felt slighted and resentful.[6]

While genuine family affection and solidarity may motivate children to contribute to the livelihood of their families, fear of losing family support and having to fend for oneself unprotected can also be an important factor. The literature does not extensively explore this incentive for children to work, and children seldom cite it explicitly. However, our own contact with working children and adults who work directly with them leads us to call attention to what we suspect is an important motive driving children to work, and we strongly recommend that more research be devoted to this question. In our experience, careful listening and common sense interpretation of children's words and actions suggest that an underlying fear of abandonment often exists. This threat is an everyday reality for many of the world's children. In urban slums, for example, it is not unusual for most children to be personally acquainted with other children who have been pushed out of their homes in order to make their own living. When one considers the frightening prospect of having to face a strange and often hostile world bereft of family protection, it is not difficult to imagine why many children will go to enormous effort in order to guarantee themselves close family ties. Many perceive, often accurately, that making an important economic contribution ensures their acceptance and indispensability. This fear-based desire by children to secure family protection through becoming an economic asset may not always be sufficiently appreciated by policy-makers. For example, enforcement of a legal minimum age standard has been interpreted by many children as a threat to their income and family solidarity, and policy-makers promoting it have not always understood why they are demonized by the very children they are trying to protect. Working children commonly take it for granted that they have a right to seek work in order to defend their own survival and meet their basic needs. On occasion they even have claimed that this right is implied by provisions of the Convention on the Rights of the Child.[7]

Children's work as a means of self-actualization

Even if they did not have to work, many children would want to. That helps explain why, in various industrialized countries, huge numbers of middle-class children seek part-time work. Even if poverty were vanquished from the Earth, and nowhere were children forced to work against their will, some children still would demand the chance to engage in productive work. The ILO explains why with elegant brevity: "Work is an integral aspect of life. It is an end and important in itself, and a means of participation in the economy and society at large. The same is also true of the work of children."[8] As Chapters One and Two pointed out, many children feel that non-exploitative work makes them feel included in and important to society, and more mature and efficacious as individuals. They believe it helps them become competent, successful adults.

Policy-makers and programme-planners need to pay more heed to children's insistence on the developmental and self-satisfying aspects of their work. Interviews with children plainly demonstrate that many of them work at least in part because they like what they do, and they feel that their work helps them grow and progress toward their own objectives and aspirations. Certainly this is not true for all children and types of work, and it would appear to apply mostly to remunerative economic activities that children do not find too burdensome or unfair. Children in oppressive working conditions tend to have a far more negative view of work. Yet this is an important policy issue because it raises practical questions regarding whether children should have the right to engage in work not only to defend their survival, but also to promote their own development and self-actualization through work they feel provides them with important self development and advancement opportunities.

Chapter One indicated that children naturally learn valuable life skills through imitating and participating in the activities of adults, including various types of work. Children often are conscious of the developmental value of work and quick to defend it. For example, child delegates in a 1996 international meeting of working children's organizations from Africa, Asia, and Latin America emphasized that they learn essential skills from both school and work, and insisted that children should not be denied access to either of them. In this meeting in Kundapur, India, they said that children should be freely permitted "work with dignity" (defined by them as safe work that leaves adequate time for school and play) as well as be guaranteed access to quality education relevant to their needs.[9] They insisted that many children find considerable satisfaction and self-esteem in work that is not exploitative or too burdensome, and that they like the feeling of helping themselves grow towards competence, responsibility, and independence. Their position is of course consistent with the emerging view of social science, discussed in Chapter One, that the quality of child development is enhanced when children themselves actively pursue their own growth opportunities and experiences.

Children's claims for the developmental and self-actualizing benefits of work are plentiful in the literature based on child surveys. A fairly typical example is a study of 10- to 14-year-old street-traders in Lagos, Nigeria, all of whom also attended school. The girl subjects of this study considered their trading activities to be essential preparation for adulthood. According to local custom, many of them can expect to be sequestered after marriage, but will nevertheless have to supervise the buying and selling by household members able to leave the home. Childhood is the period when girls normally obtain the first-hand experience needed to play this later role.[10] Similarly, a Nicaraguan study of how children interpret their work experience, based on testimonials from about 1,500 working children aged 9 to 16 years, showed that these children see their work as a valuable learning opportunity even when it is also a burden of necessity.[11] In fact, many children say that they learn more from their work than they do from school; one hears this often from school-age drop-outs. It is not clear that this is so much an elegy of work as a condemnation of the schools. As Chapters One and Seven suggest, even working children who regularly attend school may consider their work to be more useful for learning essential life-skills beyond basic literacy.

Many children work in large part to establish a certain independence for themselves, but just what this means varies with the setting. In some cases the 'independence' obtained would seem to be mostly psychological and symbolic, an example being rich-country children who enjoy earning some discretionary pocket money but still depend on their parents to pay for most essentials. In the poorer circumstances of developing countries, however, children wishing to escape from poverty or oppressive social restraints and to seek out opportunities to advance themselves may find it necessary to earn their own income. This can be glimpsed in the case of girls from highly traditional societies who wish to adopt a somewhat more modern adult lifestyle than their families or communities would prefer. For example, small-town girls in a Morocco garment factory saw in their jobs and income a chance to escape their traditional confinement at home and to enter into a newer and more urbanized society allowing them greater freedom and upward mobility.[12] Similarly, girl garment workers in Bangladesh hoped, by virtue of their income, to avoid being forced by their parents into an early arranged marriage (often as young as 13) and to acquire a respectable dowry that would allow them to marry upwards into higher socioeconomic status.[13]

Analysts and policy-makers impressed by macroeconomic figures demonstrating high economic returns to education often wonder that some children consider work to be a better economic option than is secondary schooling. In some places, children claim that continuing their studies will not change their economic prospects, and there is some evidence this attitude may respond to particular facts of their environment, such as a lack of local jobs that can absorb and pay higher wages to educated workers. Long-term economic restrictions and incentives can appear to many children to favour work.[14] When an unlettered Bangladeshi boy can rise through the traditional apprenticeship system from entry-level helper to skilled machinist in but seven or eight years, and is in high demand, while a child with eight years of schooling faces bleak employment prospects, facile claims for the economic superiority of education may ring hollow to poor children and their parents.

While many adults think of child work in grim terms, many children say they enjoy it, and in some cases may even be attracted to it as a form of excitement or entertainment. For instance, the Nigerian study mentioned above reported that child street traders from wealthier families claimed to work not out of material need but because they enjoy the social interaction, the pocket money, and the fun and stimulation. The claim of children to work because they enjoy it sometimes crops up even in the most unexpected circumstances. The study, mentioned in Chapter Two, of child garbage pickers working on an immense mountain of refuse in Manila in the Philippines reported that socializing with friends and the excitement of finding new things were among the most important reasons children gave for remaining in this sort of work. The programme designed to remove children from this dangerous and noxious occupation had to offer highly attractive activities such as sports, games, and excursions in order to compete with this aspect of scavenging.[15] This is not to imply that all, or even most, children enjoy working. In many studies, children express distaste for their work and would quit it if they could. This reflects the fact that a great deal of the work performed by children is but unrewarding drudgery and is often dangerous and oppressive to boot. However, so many children refer to the pleasure of work that it has to be counted among the important reasons they do it. When about 1,500 Brazilian working children (mostly in street occupations) were asked what they liked most about their lives, nearly a third answered that it was their work. Following at a considerable distance — all at about half the frequency — were school, family members, and playing football.[16]

Some question the self-actualizing and development benefits of children's work and tend to reject the notion that such benefits, if they in fact exist, justify the risks to school performance, family life, and socialization.[17] Yet, the growing literature on the sociology and psychology of work cited in Chapter Two suggests that the intrinsic psychological and social value of work is so important that it must be taken into consideration in the framing of social policy. For example, it is well known that many adults and children acquire useful skills and attitudes through their work, that the workplace often has a crucial socializing role, and that separation from work through unemployment or even retirement can negatively affect both mental and physical health. Given these findings from social science research, it should come as no surprise that some working children and their organizations make similar claims out of their own experience.

Child work to increase consumption

Like adults, many children report that they work in order to earn money to spend on themselves. Research from rich countries of Northern Europe and North America suggests that the income earned by children and adolescents goes primarily for the purchase of fashionable clothing and other luxuries. In the USA, for example, only a few per cent of earnings goes into savings or to pay for necessary expenses such as those related to education.[18] To pick a different economic context, research in Russia suggests that, even in times of severe economic duress, many or most working children and adolescents earn money primarily to purchase consumer goods for themselves, often in response to fashions imported from Europe and America.[19] More surprisingly, reports from developing countries indicate that even children from poor families increasingly work in order to buy non-essential consumer items that are in mode among their age group. This is a growing trend that seems to be linked to the globalization of markets, consumerism, and youth culture, and it shows every sign of accelerating.[20] Various researchers have noted that this trend encourages children to equate their personal value with employment by "explicitly linking their status to the possession of expensive goods, thereby inducing poor children to seek self-esteem through paid work. Working children find themselves clashing with the childhood ideology that places a higher value on the performance of economically useless work."[21]

Still, however, huge numbers of children seek paid work in order to provide all or part of their own support. For example, the literature demonstrates that many children work in order to pay their own school expenses. Without these earnings they would not be able to receive an education. In many urban settings it is common for older siblings (especially boys) to assume voluntarily, or be forced to assume, primary responsibility for their own maintenance so as to free up family resources for younger children. Homeless street children represent an extreme case of children left to fend for themselves, sometimes at a very tender age. They feel they must work to survive. Surprisingly many children support themselves.

What children see as the causes of their vulnerability and exploitation

Studies citing children's own opinions tend to distinguish but vaguely between the reasons children work and the reasons some are at work in activities detrimental to them. Although children themselves do not always make this distinction, it is surprising how often they do. What they have to say, although partial, hints at a view of the problem which may differ from that of others, especially governments and many children's advocates. Avoiding repetition of the obvious, this section will focus on a few points in which children's views often come as a surprise to adults, especially those having little contact with young workers.

Children's notions of what constitutes economic exploitation of their work may differ markedly from what parents and child advocates tend to believe, but may approximate to how some social scientists view the issue. It already has been pointed out that many children prefer paid factory work to unremunerated chores in the house or in the family field or shop, and feel exploited when forced to work at home for less than they could earn outside. It was likewise mentioned that some girls also complain that they are unfairly exploited when the domestic maintenance tasks assigned to them are less appreciated than is the economically productive work done by boys. From the standpoint of theoretical constructs utilized in their disciplines, some economists and anthropologists would agree that these children have a valid point, which hinges on the low status often accorded to the work of children, especially of girls. Researchers also attuned to issues of women's equality draw links between the denigration of work done by children and the short shrift often given to the economic value of women's work. However crucial under-priced family labour may in fact be for the maintenance of low-income households, the fact remains that, from an economic perspective, such work can be considered exploitative, and alert children sense this. Some researchers have called attention to the ironic fact that work at home, which many child advocates assume to be good for children, often tends to be economically more exploitative than is factory work, which is dismissed and inappropriate for children. As one anthropologist puts it:

> Hierarchies based on gender, age and kinship combine to define children's mandatory tasks as salutary work. By legitimizing children's obligation to contribute to survival and denying them their right to seek personal gain, these hierarchies effectively constrain them to a position of inferiority within the family. It is not so much their factory employment as their engagement in low productivity and domestic tasks that defines the ubiquitous way poor children are exploited in today's developing world.[22]

We hasten to add that there are various approaches to defining economic exploitation, and often work in the home may entail learning and other factors that reduce inequity. Nevertheless, researchers justly warn against stereotyping employment outside the home as exploitative and home chores as not. Chapter Two, it will be remembered, also stressed that working conditions in the home can be, and often are, just as detrimental to children's well-being and development as are those likely to be encountered in an outside job. The feelings of some children that they are more endangered or exploited in their household than they are in the job market may deserve more credit and sympathy than they often receive.

Children have a close-up look at exploitation of their vulnerability. Some adults worry that working children may be so innocent that they do not recognize exploitation. For the most part, information taken from children does not support this worry. They tend to know when they are being abused.[23] Statements from children around the world suggest that many of those who work on the streets, in homes far from their own, in brothels, in brickyards, and in many other situations dangerous and oppressive for children understand very well indeed that abuses they face in the workplace are an expression of adult greed, cruelty, and perversity that seeks only advantage without sparing the weak or young. They are no strangers to evil intent masquerading as virtue. Frequently they express feeling caught in situations that they recognize as oppressive and damaging, having no other viable alternatives. When they can move out of them, many do. This could be seen, for example, in a survey of child garment workers in Bangladesh that revealed a very high rate of child migration between firms. One important cause of this volatility was the fact that many children were being cheated out of wages or otherwise abused and would readily leave an unscrupulous employer to take a job in another company.[24] But children frequently say that they feel caught in circumstances of exploitation for lack of better alternatives. Young girls abducted or sold into prostitution in Bangladesh were shown in one study to be aware of their manipulation and risk, but also to feel trapped in it as they could no longer return to their homes and villages. The brothels at least offered a sense of community otherwise lost to them.[25]

It is very common for working children to think about the impact of their work on their education, and those whose work keeps them from school tend to be aware of their loss and regret it. Many report putting in extremely long days in order to accommodate work and still remain in school at least through the primary level. That is why working children consistently ask that instruction be scheduled and tailored to accommodate their need to work. Children who do not go to school because it conflicts with their work-schedule usually reject as impractical the idea that they should stop working in order to attend school during the days and hours normal for non-working students. Some children see no good reason why schools cannot accommodate their needs. They frequently tend to blame not their work, which they consider a basic fact of life that needs to be honoured, but the inflexibility of school systems for the loss of their education. Also, large numbers of children report such discouragement, humiliation, or outright abuse in their school experience that they can no longer bear to attend. The schools that many out-of-school children describe are not the happy, protected places that outsiders from gentler backgrounds might assume. It is not always clear when to blame work for keeping children out of school or when to blame schools for not making it possible for working children to study. Chapter Seven will address these issues in detail.

A similar view sometimes emerges in regard to health care systems too inflexible to reach young workers. Working children are concerned about their health, and some complain that they are ineligible to receive subsidized health services available to adult workers through national social security systems or to school children through school health programmes. Because of their young age, they typically are prohibited even from making social security system payments that would let them join the system and become eligible, like adult workers, for medical services. The exclusion of working children from basic services that by rights should be available to all children raises serious questions about their relationship to a supposedly protective state which fails them. Children often have a lot to say about that.

Older and more worldly-wise working children from poor countries and communities increasingly indicate that they feel discriminated against by poverty conditions that are neither the natural order of things nor borne equally by all. This complaint is hardly surprising in a world of mass communications that nightly bring images of middle- and upper-class life into hovels via the miracle of television. In many places, mass politics also arrive by broadcast. Moreover, poor working children, such as domestics in better-off homes, often live and work in close proximity to more fortunate children who do not have to work full-time, who have access to a full education, and who have ample time to play. Indeed, it is common for a child domestic to escort the children of her employer to and from school every day, while she herself must work full-time and is denied the right to study. Through their work, many children also come to understand that the authority of society protects the rich and powerful at the expense of the poor and powerless, to whom it is occasionally beneficent only by entreaty rather than by necessity. Any child can see that the poor get the worst schools, and far fewer of them, and that the miserably equipped health posts serving shanty towns and rural villages are vastly inferior to the gleaming clinics and hospitals frequented by elites. Parents and siblings of poor children die of common ailments which those of more prosperous families either survive or do not contract at all, and in fact the death or disability of parents is one of the most important factors driving children to work. These contradictions are impossible to ignore, and many children above a certain age and in daily communication with adults tend to lay the ultimate blame for them at the door of uncaring authorities. Geographical factors may be important, with urban children being more sophisticated than the rural. Community mobilization is also a factor; highly politicized slum communities in Peru, for example, produce youth as well as adult activists. It should be noted, however, that 'government' to children is more likely to be the local and familiar authorities they encounter and hear about than far-removed national administration.

The tendency of many working children to blame government for at least part of the risks they incur when working does not stop at edu- cation and health services. National economic, social, and development policies also come in for harsh criticism, especially if children become educated to think for themselves. In some places, especially in Latin America, many working children participate in grass roots programmes and organizations that seek to educate and mobilize the poor to become fully participating citizens. Such groups characteristically stimulate the poor to think critically about the reasons for their poverty and social exclusion, and working children from such mobilized communities often are acutely aware, politicized, and articulate. By their early teens some may demonstrate a reasonably sophisticated grasp of national and international affairs that have an impact on their lives. For example, teenage delegates to the Kundapur, India international meeting of working children's organizations, pointed out that a lack of economic development activity in rural areas produces a large migration of rural children, alone or with their families, to urban areas in search of a living. This occurs in Africa, Asia, and Latin America. They indicated that this rural-to-urban movement accounts for a larger portion of urban child worker exploitation than commonly is realized. Newly arrived children raised in rural areas do not understand the urban environment and are much more likely to end up in degrading and dangerous circumstances, including prostitution and crime. The delegates recommended that national rural development programmes should stimulate appropriate work and education for rural children in their own villages in order to end the need of children to migrate. They dryly observed that governments are in most places quite aware of what could be done to alleviate the poverty and inequality that drive child migration and exploitation, but do not take action.[26] The point is not that children have a better view than adults on such 'macro' matters, although they may be especially knowledgeable about certain particulars, but that they may observe and think about these issues to a greater extent than many adults realize.

To some working children, social responsibility for their vulnerability and exploitation goes beyond mere neglect. In certain occupations, government in the person of police or other officials may be regarded as a bothersome adversary, or even a dangerous enemy to be avoided. This is not hard to understand if one stops to imagine how the world appears through the eyes of poor working children. Children without access to decent education or health care, and who live in relatively lawless slums receiving little police protection, have not personally seen the beneficial face of government and may experience public authority primarily in the form of petty officials from whom they need to protect their precarious income. For example, children in textile trades relate how they hide from labour inspectors, in fear either of being dismissed from employment or of having to come up with the money to buy them off. In developing countries, children in street trades such as shining shoes or hawking small items report that bribing or fleeing from police, on pain of being beaten or having one's goods confiscated, is a normal part of doing business. Children in bonded labour or prostitution sometimes report that local authorities help hunt down and castigate those trying to escape their masters.

At the international Amsterdam Child Labour Conference, in February of 1997, young delegates of working children's organizations from Africa, Asia, and Latin America conveyed this general view that the high-risk forms of 'child labour' stem not only from the fact that children work — which is normal and to be expected — but also from government neglect in performing its proper protective functions. They pointed out that governments often at least try to provide basic protections for adults in their work, but in the case of children not only refuse to protect them, but sometimes actively oppress them as well. To reduce such injustices, some recommended that children be legally permitted to participate in 'work with dignity', be recognized as the workers they are, and be provided with the same legal and service protections offered to adult workers.[27] The children apparently felt that a solution based on equal rights with adults would be more trustworthy than one based on special dispensation leaving government with arbitrary power.

Policy-makers, programme-planners, and children's advocates need to take seriously the crisis of confidence that often separates many working children, particularly those involved in urban street trades, from public authorities. Such mistrust not only exacerbates the problem of reaching and working with these children, but also undermines the role of the state as their official protector as envisaged by the Convention on the Rights of the Child. Where the problem is serious, civil society organizations concerned with working children are likely to be more involved in helping defend children against the authorities than in working with authorities to find and serve needy children. This can make for tense relationships between child advocacy NGOs and local or national government, which is far from uncommon. But such situations are reversible, as is attested to by the many local governments that have recognized the problem and established special programmes and relatively trustful relations with working and street children. Indeed, such programmes have become quite commonplace in some countries, such as the Philippines and Brazil. Experience strongly suggests the necessity of opening channels of communication between government at its various levels and working children; a subject that we shall return to in Chapter Six.

Economic and social research findings

Whereas the preceding section focused on what children themselves say about the reasons underlying their work and its exploitation, the discussion now turns to academic and other research. In the absence of good data on child work and exploitation, it is difficult to conduct definitive studies of their causes. But that does not seem to deter most writers on child work, including us, from addressing the matter, buttressed by such information as can be mustered. The literature from academia, international organizations, research institutes, and elsewhere tends to approach the question of the determinants of 'child labour' from economic, sociological, demographic, and political viewpoints. These perspectives help place the observations made by children themselves in a broader social and institutional context. Three predominant lines of thinking about the origins of 'child labour' merit a brief overview in this chapter. (A fourth, school-system failures, will be deferred to Chapter Seven, on education.) The first approaches child work and exploitation primarily as a product of poverty, the second as a result of family dysfunction, and the third as an expression of culture. They are not mutually exclusive, but are different emphases in a complex subject meriting multiple points of view.

Poverty as the main cause of child work and exploitation

Virtually all studies of 'child labour' in developing countries relate it most fundamentally to poverty. Poor families put their children to work much more than do families that are better off. This is a strategy not only to augment household income, but also to even out the risks of losing one or another income source. For example, if children contribute to the family subsistence, the sudden economic impact of a failed harvest or the loss of adult employment is less disastrous. This added security can be critical for families whose income is so low that any major loss can become life-threatening.[28] Children's contribution can be substantial; the ILO estimates that it commonly may represent at least 20 per cent of the household income. Its importance can be glimpsed in the fact that poor households spend the vast majority of their income only on food – the official poverty line in India is set at just 20 per cent more than the cost of food required to meet the minimum nutritional requirements of a family.[29]

There is some current debate about the degree to which children's own perception of the importance of their economic contribution reflects the reality of their households. Data from the literature can be found to support arguments both for and against the economic indispensability of children. This reflects the large variety of situations studied and the extreme difficulty of arriving at a purely technical answer to the question of how much family subsistence and solidarity depend on children's work. It is not fitting to enter here into a discussion of the thorny methodological problems involved in trying to make such an analysis. Suffice it to say only that the most straightforward approach most commonly attempted – estimating the contribution of children as a percentage of the household cash and in-kind income – is known by economists and sociologists to have serious limitations as an indicator of economic importance that, when not properly recognized, may produce a misleading picture of children's economic significance. For example, the stability of an income source often is as important as its quantity, and a small contribution by children may have a security value out of proportion to its size. Similarly, in many households not all income is equally disposable for meeting basic needs. In much of the world, for instance, income to women is considered more likely to be available for meeting the family's basic needs than is income to men, and children's earnings flowing to mothers may be more important to family subsistence than are earnings appropriated by fathers. Children often take such factors into consideration. In the absence of well-constructed analysis of the economic significance of children's work — which is methodologically very demanding — children's own reports concerning the practical family impact of their economic contribution may be as valid an indicator as any other. This question deserves much more sophisticated social science research than it has so far received.

Even in circumstances of poverty it is not easy to establish the importance of children's economic contributions. As mentioned above, that importance probably cannot be captured in terms of a proportion of household income; children's work may serve vital income goals not reflected by their earnings as a percentage of household income. While attestations of children's earnings as a portion of family income are easy to come by, few if any are econometrically credible, and even the better among them may explain little of the overall economic role and importance of children. Moreover, it is generally felt that perhaps a majority of all working children are unremunerated workers in family enterprises, much like the hypothetical African girl described in the Introduction to this book, and quantifying their economic contribution to family subsistence is very complicated, beginning with the definition of what activities are or are not 'economic'. There is, for example, the extremely common case of children who tend the home and younger siblings virtually full-time so that adults (often their mothers) can hold down a paying job outside the home. By the usual criteria, the work performed by these children would not be considered to represent economic activity, but the impact of their work on the household is profoundly economic. What does seem clear is that the economic dependence of families on the work of their children varies enormously, ranging from virtually none in most industrialized countries to great or near total dependence in households with absent or incapacitated adults – such as are increasingly common in some African countries being ravaged by AIDS. Virtually all indications are that, in poor families, both working children and their parents regard the children's contribution as vitally important to the family well-being. Whether it is indispensable is largely a matter of interpretation, and the poor themselves have not always been quick to agree with analysts and policy-makers about just how poor is tolerably poor, or how dispensable any part of their income is.

The fundamental importance of poverty as a cause of child work is so well demonstrated and is so widely accepted that there is no further need to belabour the issue except to point out that rising worker wage rates are believed by historians to have been a crucial, but far from exclusive, factor in the decline of child work in today's industrialized countries.[30] It should be remembered, however, that there is disagreement about just *how* fundamental poverty is to child work. Some trade union activists, for example, might rank the greed of unscrupulous employers roughly as important as poverty as a cause of detrimental child work.

It is more interesting, perhaps, to examine the limits of poverty as an explanation for child work. If poverty were the sole determinant of child work, one would expect to find the highest rates of child work in the poorest circumstances, but this is not always the case. The relationship between poverty and child work, while real, is vague, varied, and indirect. To begin with, poverty is associated with a high incidence of child work primarily in the developing regions; in rich countries, the relationship is reversed. In the United States, for example, a US Government study found that teenage children from low-income and minority families were only about half as likely to be employed as were well-off children from households having annual incomes of at least US$60,000.[31] Similarly, a large study in Birmingham, England reported that children aged between 10 and 16 from the poorest areas of the city were less likely to work than were their peers from the wealthier neighbourhoods.[32] The best explanation for this seems to be that children in the wealthier environments simply have more work opportunities available. There is some indication that racial, ethnic, and geographic discrimination may play a role in the greater access of non-poor children to earning opportunities in industrialized countries.[33] Also, in both the North and South, certain types of small or medium-sized business generating livelihoods well above the poverty level, such as family-owned farms and shops, commonly depend on the use of family labour, including children, for their economic viability. In fact it appears that most child workers work with their family within the home or family enterprise.[34]

An inverse relationship between poverty and child work may sometimes be found for wealthier versus poorer regions within developing countries. For instance, a Brazilian study of economically active urban children compared the industrialized south and south-east with the much poorer and less industrialized north-east. It was found that children in the richer regions were far more likely to be economically active than were the children from the poor north-east. Even though this particular study could suffer from data quality problems, the best explanation for its findings seems, again, to be that the more prosperous environments provided more employment opportunities for children. As many or more children might have been looking for work in the north-east, but only a limited number of those wanting work could find it,[35] this suggests that increased prosperity and employment in the north-east would not necessarily reduce economic activity by children, at least at first. Even within very local areas, some children from wealthier families may carry heavier work burdens than children from the poorest families. It has been widely noted that children of families owning land or a small business, for example, may work more than their peers from families who own no productive assets and also may depend on employment that is seasonal or otherwise limited. While poverty may stimulate children to seek work, lack of economic opportunity may limit the number who succeed in finding it or the amount of work available to them. Poverty also can limit the ability to establish self-employment in small businesses, or to pay for travel to and from distant jobs.

One implication of these inconsistencies in the association of child work with poverty is that improvement in economic opportunities for the poor could, at least for a time, be expected in some conditions to increase rather than diminish the work burden on children. If these children are also better fed, clothed, housed and educated, and their rights observed, this result might not be negative. However, pulling children out of school to work under exploitative conditions in newly opened employment opportunities would not represent progress. The possibility that development projects can generate unacceptable 'child labour' has lately concerned some international development agencies, and there is discernible movement towards applying some sort of child welfare analysis in the planning of development projects, extending an approach already taken by some agencies in regard to environment or gender. Agencies as different as The World Bank, the Norwegian foreign aid programme — NORAD and Save the Children Fund in the UK, for example, are taking increased interest in the possible child work effects of their development projects. More on this subject appears in Chapter Eight.

The validity of such worries about development programmes as an unintended cause of 'child labour' can be seen in, for instance, a recent case study of child workers in the Moroccan garment industry. This study found that one of the important reasons why young girls were sent to work in the factories was to help pay off the burdensome family debts incurred by participation in a government-subsidized loan programme providing decent housing, potable water, and sanitation to the urban poor. Without the children's economic contribution, many families could not meet these obligations and, when the girls lost their jobs, there was fear that the families would also lose their homes.[36] Similarly, Save the Children-U.K. concluded from a review of projects that "there is some evidence that credit and micro-enterprise projects can increase children's workload … Just as micro-enterprise projects targeting men often result in increased workloads for women, the extra work associated with an income-generating project can easily be shifted onto children who may be least able to refuse … Nevertheless, children may see increases in their workloads positively if for example, they can attend school, eat better or can purchase new clothes or shoes with household income."[37]

Concern about the child work impact of development projects needs to take into account the effects of programme failures as well as successes. The social fallout from failed income-generation programmes can be seen in the case of a government-sponsored credit programme for the adult family members of the previously mentioned child scavengers on the huge Smoky Mountain refuse dump in Manila. An ILO assessment of the programme indicated that virtually all the small businesses which started with the small loans it provided had failed. Many borrowers had not even started a business, using the money for direct consumption instead. In either event, the borrowing families now had the additional burden of repaying their loans. In order to make these payments, even children not previously working were sent out to scavenge.[38]

While it is most common to think of poverty as an explanation for the flow of children into the labour market, it can also play a role in employer demand for child workers. Employers wish to keep their labour costs to a minimum, and poor people come cheap. They are less educated, less cognizant of their rights and have fewer employment options than better-off classes. Children cost the least and are the most docile of all. In the current global competition for investment, some countries with low wage rates have tried in essence to 'sell' their poverty, vying with one another to attract foreign investment not only by advertising their low cost of labour, but in some cases also by keeping that cost low through various forms of wage controls and even outright suppression of worker organization. Such tactics have become a matter of considerable international criticism and dispute, not least by the International Labour Organization and the World Trade Organization. 'Child labour' is one of the central issues of this debate, but it usually focuses on the very small portion of working children, less than 5 per cent, who are involved in the production of goods sold in international trade. Further discussion of this topic is reserved to Chapter Eight.

The contribution of children to economic competitiveness

One of the questions that has arisen in this debate is whether child workers really are necessary to maintain the competitiveness of the highly labour-intensive industries typically found in the poorest countries: those supposedly benefiting from the lowest wage rates. Put simply, is the labour of children so irreplaceable for international competitiveness in some industries that global competition has become an important cause of 'child labour'? It is sometimes claimed that, if the relatively inexpensive work of children is dispensed with, certain major industries providing important income, employment and foreign exchange may be lost to competitors still using children in 'beggar-my-neighbour' competition between poor countries. This assertion, if true, is painful to policy-makers because it seems to imply a conflict between the crucial social objectives of economic growth and child development.

The ILO recently tested this claim through an in-depth economic study of the carpet industry in India.[39] It wanted to know what economic penalty, if any, the industry would incur from a policy of hiring adults only. It also tested the often-heard claim that children are indispensable to the carpet industry because their small hands are uniquely well suited to tying the small and densely packed knots that characterize the best quality carpets. The ILO-sponsored research team undertook multi-faceted studies in selected sites throughout the so-called 'carpet belt' in the vicinity of Mirzapur, India. It interviewed carpet producers and exporters and inspected their facilities. It studied the local economy of the communities involved in order to understand the economic importance of the carpet industry and the availability of schools and other local services. It also interviewed children and their families, as well as actors at different points in the chain of producers and dealers that handle carpets from raw materials to retail sales to customers. This was a 'breakthrough' study in that it for the first time developed a method of economic analysis capable of considering child work from a variety of perspectives. The result was a uniquely contextual view of the industry and the people who work in it. It is an approach worth pursuing in other industries and places.

The study found that the carpet industry does not have to depend on child workers, although they are common enough in it. First of all, there is no truth in the 'nimble fingers' argument. The finest carpets are woven by experienced adults, not children. As the ILO observed: "If child dexterity is not necessary to weave the finest carpets, it is difficult to imagine other trades for which the 'nimble fingers' argument could be valid."[40] The claim of economic irreplaceability did not fare much better. It was found that any savings in the final sale price of the carpet that could be accounted for by use of children instead of adult workers did not surpass 5 to 10 per cent. It was calculated that, at this low level, the commercialization system could easily absorb any added costs of hiring adults only. Competitiveness simply is not an issue.

This finding raised an interesting question: if the economic advantages of using child workers are so modest, even unnecessary, why are tens of thousands of children still used in the industry, especially now that child labour has become a matter generating consumer resistance? The answer had to do with *who* gains, which turned out to be exclusively the small, loom-owning contractors who engage producers (usually working in their own home with materials provided by the contractor) and buy their carpets. These contractors, who often also are weavers, are for the most part poor themselves and work on a very slim profit margin. It was found that they can as much as double their usually meagre profit by using child workers. However, their total income is so modest that a very small increase in carpet prices to the consumer would generate funds needed to subsidize these small loom owners for using exclusively adult labour. The ILO noted that if the value of child work to this extremely labour-intensive industry is so small, it is difficult to imagine that any industry needs to be economically dependent on child workers. At least the burden of proof rests with those who would make such a claim.[41]

It has long been recognized that, in developing countries, many or most of the employers of economically active children are, like the small carpet contractors described above, themselves poor. Much exploitation of the poor is by the poor. Employers of children tend to be involved in agricultural or informal sector activities that are highly labour-intensive and require little capital. In many countries, these employers are primarily the children's own parents or other relatives.

Macro-economic effects

Although the purposes of this book preclude an extended discussion of another much cited aspect of the poverty explanation of child work and exploitation — inequality and injustice in the international distribution of wealth and opportunity — international economic trends have become an important issue in the child labour debate. Economic globalization and national economic adjustment plans are sometimes cited as important underlying contributors to child work.[42] International competition is claimed to hold down developing country employment and development. Negative effects of structural adjustment programmes on investment education have been blamed for declining school attendance and corresponding rises in the number of children at work.[43] At the same time, the World Bank and others point out that economic globalization has driven down world poverty even while causing painful transition problems, and new guidelines for structural adjustment programmes seek to protect education and health services for the poor. While a social services disinvestment trend can in fact be observed in a number of countries, the causes are not always easy to isolate. Economic globalization has so far affected services used mostly by the rich, not the poor. Structural adjustment policy certainly does put national budgets under pressure, but countries also have considerable freedom of action in deciding their relative priorities. It has been noted that, in approximately one-third of the world's countries, military spending exceeds that of spending on education.[44] There is no question that these macroeconomic trends have an effect on all who work in economies influenced by them, but there are so many intervening variables that it is difficult to relate them directly to abusive child work.

While there is no doubt that many inequities are built into the international economic system, and that in many countries they may indeed contribute to 'child labour' problems, it is not immediately obvious what corrective measures would be most beneficial in the long run. For instance, international debt relief is much mentioned as a means of stimulating social investment in countries struggling under a particularly difficult financial burden, but it is not always clear that such savings necessarily lead to education and other social investment for the poor, as opposed to being captured by other and perhaps less worthy interests. As

Chapter Eight will discuss in more detail, the globalization of markets and freeing-up of international trade has made 'child labour' a highly visible and controversial issue but, at the time of writing, the world has not even been able to arrive at a decision regarding the proper international forum for dealing with it. Much of the official discussion is still about where to have the discussion, and there is a great deal of resistance from developing countries to conditioning trade by labour rights criteria.[45] While possible macroeconomic determinants of child work and exploitation need to be kept in mind, they probably can be addressed only in the proper international fora, which inevitably entails long and complex processes. They also can be discerned only through more systematic attention to the issue, especially by economists. At this point in time, the debate regarding the effect of macroeconomic policy on child work is considerably more ideological than empirical, and not much light will be thrown on the subject until that is reversed.

What does all this mean to developing country policy-makers concerned with poverty and child work issues? It implies, first of all, that they should not naively believe either that child exploitation will be eradicated without improving the economic situation of the very poor or that improving the economic conditions of the poor will naturally dry up child exploitation. Poverty alleviation measures are both necessary and, by themselves, insufficient. Secondly, development programmes, especially those intending to raise incomes of the poor, should be analyzed for their expected effects on the social division of work and for what any expected changes in family work patterns may mean to the well-being and development of children. They should then be modified as needed to discourage any systematic incentive towards inappropriate work by children. The mere fact that increasing prosperity may be accompanied by a rise in children's economic participation in some areas or sectors is not necessarily objectionable if it is determined that the added work is likely to be safe and not so burdensome as to detract from education or otherwise hinder children's development. In such cases, however, development projects and programmes may find it useful to include protective measures aimed at preventing harmless or beneficial children's work from degenerating into detrimental exploitation. Marcroeconomic policies should, at a minimum, seek a socially fair distribution of income and ensure adequate investment in basic services utilized by the poor, especially health and education. This is only good development policy. It is today recognized that any good economic growth strategy must include the conservation and development of human capacity, especially that of children and youth.

Family dynamics in child work and exploitation

Another popular explanation holds that children work and are exploited as the result of defective family decision-making or relationships. Child work is seen to represent errors either in families' perception of reality or in their strategic thinking about how best to deal with that reality. A common example is the notion that most parents who keep children out of school to work are ignorant of the true value of education; if they had a more correct appreciation of the return on education they would make any sacrifices necessary to keep their children in school as long as possible. A family dynamics explanation sometimes incorporates moral judgments, for example attributing the exploitation of child work to a breakdown in values in which the family betrays its protective function, perversely placing its children in harm's way in order to obtain some less-than-essential advantage. Often-cited examples of this line of thinking include stories of parents 'selling' their children into bondage or prostitution to help pay for consumer items, a wedding or some other material benefit deemed non-essential. For instance, reference is often made to a custom of sending girls from the north-east of Thailand to enter sex work in Bangkok in order to help their parents purchase consumer items such as refrigerators, supposedly as a sign of family gratitude and loyalty. It is claimed that this practice is generations old and that "girls who refuse to do so are considered selfish, disobedient and ungrateful".[46] Those who believe that child exploitation is largely the result of ignorant or irresponsible family behaviour tend to conclude that children can be protected from exploitation by improving the quality of family decision-making, typically through provision of new information, reinforcement of values or coercion by legislation and its enforcement.

A family dynamics explanation for child work and its abuse often is closely related to the poverty explanation, since much research focuses on the ways in which households organize people and resources to maintain the family's solidarity and livelihood. For example, as this text is being written, a large study jointly conducted by the London School of Hygiene and Tropical Medicine and PROSHIKA, a large NGO in Bangladesh is following about 800 urban poor households over the full year's cycle of activities, investigating the relationships between the ways they allocate tasks and resources to earn their livelihood and the well-being of family members, especially in terms of health and nutrition. The work of children is being documented as but one variable within this broader perspective on the home economy, which is necessary to more precisely understand the nature, importance, and changing dynamics of child work within the family context. This is an important issue for 'child labour' policy because very little is known about what is likely to happen in poor families if the work contribution of their children is curtailed. The issue is critical to a proper understanding of the causes of child work.

Since the 1970s, some research has emphasized the relationship between household size and the incidence of child work among poor populations in developing countries. This issue has not been much interjected into international debates regarding 'child labour', but it is now being raised more assertively by the World Bank, among others.[47] A common finding is that children from large households are more likely to work than are children from smaller households. This fits into a broader pattern in which larger household size is associated with many hindrances to child welfare and development, such as child morbidity and mortality, malnutrition, early school abandonment, and so forth. Sometimes child work is viewed as an indirect effect, the product of some other decision. For example, it has been pointed out that "larger household size reduces children's educational participation and progress in school and reduces parents' investment in schooling. ... This makes it likely that larger household size increases the probability that a child will work."[48] At least one social historian has noted that a decline in family size was one of the most important influences driving the reduction of child work in England.[49]

It is recognized that the effects of household size on child work vary greatly with place, living conditions, occupation, and gender. Not all children in the same family are disadvantaged equally. For example, in some societies it is very common for girls to be kept out of school to help in family work so that the boys can be free to study, and there is some evidence that siblings early in the birth order are more likely to work than those who come later. The education and labour market participation of the parents also has much to do with the likelihood that children work. When mothers work, girl children are more likely to remain at home performing tasks that otherwise would have been done by the adult female, but the more education parents (particularly mothers) have, the less likely they are to keep their children out of school.

There is a long-term debate about whether low-income couples follow a large-family strategy, in part to provide more sources of support for their old age, but also to provide more currently available labour in the form of children. This view emerged some years ago from certain population studies which suggested that there are strong economic incentives for families living from labour-intensive occupations to have many children. Where children begin to make an economic contribution from a very early age, such as in peasant agriculture, it was argued, the value of their labour exceeds the costs of raising them, thereby encouraging parents to produce more of this economic benefit. Many anthropologists have from the beginning been suspicious of so narrowly an economic explanation of family size, and in later years this always academic discussion has become bogged down in debates over methodological issues such as how to value different types of child work or how to properly discount perceived child work benefits to take into consideration the fact that they begin to flow only some years after costs have been incurred. The current feeling is that factors determining family size are more complex than this strictly economic argument proposed, and that field evidence does not substantiate it as a general rule even though it might apply in some particular situations. While an overall relationship between child work and family size does seem to hold up in a vaguely general sort of way, even the very question of whether families have more children in order to put them to work, or put them to work because they are there, seems too simplistic to suit increasingly interdisciplinary thinking about family structure and dynamics.

It should be noted that part of the question of relationships between family size and child work has to do with perceived trade-offs between the 'quantity' and 'quality' (meaning level of education) of children, and that a general trend toward smaller families with greater average education investment per child seems to have been observed. Some economists have asked whether national policies that make it less expensive for families to raise the 'quality' of their children will lead to reduced numbers of children. The World Bank calls attention to a recent study in Malaysia, which gives scholarships to Malays as part of its policy to reduce the economic disadvantage of Malays relative to the Chinese and Indian populations. Chinese and Indian families receive no such subsidy. It was found that household size had no effect on the likelihood that Malay children will attend school but, among Chinese and Indian children, those from large families received less schooling.[50]

One family variable that seems to be very widely associated with higher levels of child work is the single head of household, which is almost always a woman. These families are nearly everywhere among the poorest, and both mothers and their children are particularly vulnerable. Especially in urban areas, the mother may need to work outside the home and, in the absence of accessible day-care facilities, she may leave her youngest children in the care of slightly older ones, typically a girl's task. Other children — especially boys — may undertake income-generating activities. In many places, a disproportionate number of working children appear to be from homes headed by a single woman.

Among the very poor, the security of a family's livelihood can be fatally disturbed by harvest failures, death or incapacitation of an adult earner, loss of a job, severe weather, civil unrest, and many other factors. Households headed by single or incapacitated adults are well known to be especially vulnerable. Under such stresses, family roles and responsibilities may change considerably, and children are much more likely to enter the labour market. Field workers in contact with working children often observe informally that episodic family emergencies and stresses are a prevalent cause of economic activity by children, especially younger children. Many children leave or reduce their work when the period of stress has passed. They also note that, where such family emergencies are an important cause of children entering the labour market, attempts to impede or eliminate children's work without replacing their lost earnings or otherwise assisting the family may have a disastrous effect on the family, including the children in question and their younger siblings. When visiting in the field, one often hears horror stories in this genre, but finds no empirical data to test these assertions. This is a very serious matter which tends to be glossed over by both national governments and international organizations when framing child labour norms and policies. It deserves much closer attention. It may be that, in such emergencies, targeted assistance to afflicted families may be the only humane way to relieve some children of very burdensome work responsibilities. However, it appears that little quality research has been focused on the dynamics of the relationship between children's work and family emergencies, or on the overall importance of such emergencies as a determinant of child work and exploitation. We strongly urge that this issue be properly investigated and addressed, especially in the poorest countries and populations, before governments set about enforcing blanket rules against the economic participation of young children.

Policy-makers, programme-planners, and child advocates also should make good use of the existing studies that cast light on how families under usual circumstances make decisions about the work of their children, assessing how important family decisions really are in determining child work and its exploitation. It is essential to understand the real options that families have before them, appreciating both where there is space to take alternative decisions and where they are constrained by a lack of viable alternatives. Although the base of good research analyzing children's work and schooling from the perspective of household composition and economy is expanding, it has been surprisingly under-utilized to inform national and international discussion of children's work issues. There may be various reasons for this. One is the source: generally speaking, those who generate this literature have come primarily from academia and institutions which have not been much engaged in discussion about children's work questions, at least until quite recently. Another barrier is that most potentially useful research reported in academic discussion is so formal and technically intimidating that it does not communicate well to readers not versed in the social science disciplines. A third reason for the limited impact of this sort of research is the enormous variation in findings from one place to another; it is difficult to extract general patterns that can be turned into policy. Inconclusive social science research producing case studies with contradictory results does not seem helpful.

Social and cultural determinants of child work and exploitation

Chapter One considered in some detail the cultural variation in child-raising systems, and how these differences play out in attitudes towards children's work. It pointed out that culture helps determine not only the different kinds of work children do and the context in which they perform it, but also prevailing opinions about the value of that work. Such opinions are tied to normative ideas about the nature of childhood and how children should be raised, and are emotionally charged. Each society tends to think that its way of raising children is the best way, which it may well be for that society's own reality and purposes, and feels a sense of commitment to it. Any issue relating to the nurture of children is raised, considered, and acted upon within a specific cultural context, and child work is a very culture-sensitive issue. It is so sensitive that some construe a cultural explanation of child work or exploitation to constitute an attack on the South or non-western societies.

Sensibilities notwithstanding, culture *is* one of the most important influences determining child work and exploitation, and ideology about childhood and the raising of children is an extremely important aspect of it. The anthropological and historical literature makes it abundantly clear that some cultural systems are much more likely than others to generate children's work. Likewise, some societies tolerate more pressure on children than do others. For example, anthropological research into childhood in Bangladesh suggests that the culture of child raising calls for children to be coddled when very young, but to be treated rather severely from roughly 10 to 20 years of age in order to prepare them for the rigours of adult life. Girls may be treated particularly harshly and unjustly in order to prepare them for later life under the stern supervision of a mother-in-law.[51] Because all culture is in constant change, any given society may radically change its views and behaviour regarding child work from one period to another. Social historians report that changes in concepts of childhood or in ideas about children's place in society have had pronounced effects on the growth and decline of child work.[52]

This has been amply demonstrated, for example, in the case of the United States, which a century ago valued the usefulness (that is the economic contribution) and quick socialization of children. As would be expected, a cultural framework that valued the economic contribution of children and sought to help them grow up relatively quickly tended to see child work positively, and that period did produce literature extolling the benefits of work in building up the character, skills, and social acumen of children. Over time the top-down social penetration of new concepts romanticizing childhood as a time of innocence and preparation to be set apart from adult concerns fuelled an energetic child labour reform movement to remove children from the workplace altogether. This period coincided with a vision of family life that idealized an adult male breadwinner and a wife who stayed at home to care for the children. Work beyond household chores was considered an inordinate burden on children.[53] By early in this century, the culture moved to a sentimentalized concept of childhood and sought to separate children from adult concerns through an extended period. It now seems to be moving again, some claim, toward a merging of child and adult roles through a new emphasis on children's rights, independence and intra-familial cooperation in household responsibilities, notably including work.[54]

As Chapter One suggested, the ideal of buffered and utopian childhood, nurtured by literature of the nineteenth century Romantic movement, is now apparently being abandoned for a different model of childhood. Some child psychologists, social critics, and others now claim that barriers isolating childhood from productive work (broadly defined to include home tasks) benefit neither the children nor society, and are advocating the re-engagement of children in socially acceptable meaningful work. Such a trend should not seem surprising in rich countries in which children and young people are increasingly characterized by greater independence, unprecedented access to information, increased social and economic participation, and broader legal rights more in tune with those enjoyed by adult citizens. Children now demand more independence and social participation, and are rejecting institutions structured to perpetuate the traditional North ideal of childhood as a privileged time of passive learning while buffered from 'real' life. Social engagement to work is seen by some of them as attractive. In Sweden, for example, a 1997 survey of 1,200 school children from grades seven to nine found strong student disillusion with authoritarian schools in which sophisticated children with access to the world through the Internet and travel are allowed to make no decisions about their school except how to spend the class money and where to go on the class trip. As the researcher reported:

> About 40 per cent of the pupils do not consider that one is allowed to make use of one's imagination in school, and an equal amount say that school does not present any challenges to them ... A quarter indicates that school work seldom deals with real life and that the things they are good at do not count is school. Almost half of the pupils say that their interests are difficult to satisfy at school. Half of all the pupils, or even more, want to have the opportunity to work more with their hands.[55]

As indicated in Chapter One, laws prohibiting all work of children, thus enforcing their economic uselessness, have begun to receive criticism even in industrialized countries. They are felt perhaps to be too discriminatory and inconsistent with a child rights orientation and the holistic development of children. These ideas are arising from a modern social context in which both parents commonly work outside the home, a very large portion of children live in households headed by single parents, and children have access to markets and information previously open only to adults. This new environment tends to value relatively independent children who possess initiative, who can assume responsibilities for themselves from an early age, and who interact closely with adults in maintaining the family's home and lifestyle.[56]

What should policy-makers and programme-planners dealing with child work issues make of the fact that culture can be a cause of child work and its exploitation, shaping not only work but social perception and valuation of it? What is particularly useful about this insight? Three answers come to mind. First of all, addressing 'child labour' is like shooting at a moving target, because the cultural elements that define it are in constant change. One always risks preparing today for yesterday's problems. This suggests that wise policy and programmes will avoid transient and ephemeral issues and, as much as possible, focus on forms of work and working conditions whose impact upon children is so clearly negative that changing culture is unlikely to undermine the good reasons for addressing them.

Secondly, culture provides not only causes of child work, but also tools for dealing with it. In Brazil and the Philippines, for example, widely accepted religious values have been infused into a social critique of the exploitation of children. Culture can generate a passion for social justice just as surely as it can generate disregard for human rights. It has been widely pointed out that traditional means of protecting children have, in many societies, been displaced by the state and other modern institutions which do not perform the job very well.[57] While it is not likely that any society can or wishes to return to the past, it may nevertheless be worth asking which child-protecting elements of traditional culture can be useful in a modern context. There is sad irony in the fact that some rich countries where extended family ties to children have been allowed to wither are now busily establishing programmes with names like 'Foster Grandparents', 'Big Brother' or 'Big Sister' to connect at-risk children to unrelated adult volunteers who try to emulate what used to be the mentoring role of real grandparents, uncles and aunts, older siblings, and other family members.

Thirdly, experience shows that culture can be influenced and those aspects of it that contribute to the exploitation of children can be diminished. Policy-makers are not limited to responding to culture; they can help create it. Because of efforts to deal with the cultural bases of child labour, people in many places now regard working children and the abuses against them in ways that they did not understand previously, and are changing their attitudes and behaviour accordingly. This was demonstrated in Brazil, for example, where a constant effort by NGOs to awaken government and public sensitivity to child work issues has over time created a far more friendly political and social climate for the protection of working children. A change in the cultural perception of children's work and child workers preceded new and more creative initiatives by government and made their public acceptance possible.

Conclusion

The above discussion suggests that children, policy-makers, programme-planners, children's advocates, and researchers tend to hold different views and assumptions about the origins of child work and its abuse. Worse, they seldom even talk together about these issues. Indeed, the differences of perspective sometimes engender open conflict between working children and well-meaning government officials, international organizations, and child advocates who intend only to help them but who have difficulty perceiving how children experience and think about their own reality. Until policy-makers and programme-planners achieve a more sensitive understanding of children's motives for working, they most likely will continue to make rules about work that children oppose and easily subvert. How they think their interventions can succeed in the face of resistance from the children they are supposed to affect remains something of a mystery. There is a clear need for adults concerned about children's work issues to get in touch with the complexity of children's motives for working, and this is best done by systematically consulting with them through appropriate research and including them in discussions. For the latter purpose, children's own organizations can be especially useful.

A second implication of the above discussion is the need to address the social and economic context of children's work and not just the work itself. Voices from the South have long been insisting that too exclusive a focus on the work of children, without intervening in the poverty and social injustice that make it necessary for children to work or that exploit them in their work, may succeed only in reducing opportunities for children to develop while not curing the workplace abuses being targeted.

A third conclusion, echoing the findings of Chapter One, is that the self-actualizing reasons why children work need to be taken far more seriously than they have in the past. The assumption that most children's work is grim, distasteful, and stultifying to their development has seriously distorted both national and international activities dealing with it. A child-centred perspective might respond positively to children's healthy wishes to participate in meaningful work without undermining concern about how to avoid their becoming involved in its detrimental forms. It would be as interested in how to enrich the socializing and learning content of children's work, thereby promoting human development, as in ensuring that children are not abused in that work.

CHAPTER FOUR

Finding out about Working Children

The preceding chapters have made clear three essential facts which point to the need for substantial research regarding children's work:

- The role of children's work in their welfare and development is very poorly understood and much conventional thinking about it is unsupported even by the evidence that exists.
- Interventions unjustified by a thorough understanding of working children, their context and their problems risk being ineffectual or even harmful to the children they are intended to help.
- Almost no effort is being made to assess the impact of legal, educational or other interventions on the welfare and development of the children affected, despite case evidence that the results are at least sometimes poor.

The purpose of this chapter is to introduce the reader to some of the most important research types and issues so as to convey the richness of options open to those who wish to understand the reality of working children and child work more deeply. It aims to provide readers with a general survey of the terrain so that they are able to locate the areas and approaches that interest them for further exploration on their own.

Policies and programmes preventing, prohibiting or regulating children's work, providing protective services, or advocating for the protection of children are seldom based on a strong empirical understanding of the children and situations they address. Policy-makers and practitioners usually do not make adequate use of research. They may think that they cannot afford the luxury of doing studies because they are too costly, take too much time or involve academic expertise they do not have.[1] They may feel that they already know enough about the problem to start a programme without getting more information or fear that resources for research might be taken from programmes benefiting children directly.[2] Many policy-makers believe that it is enough for social policies to express values which exist independently of facts that may or may not justify the policies. But research should not be viewed as an optional extra: it has a crucial role in the planning, realization, and evaluation of projects, programmes, and policies. That role is to ensure that the social values behind policies and programmes are incorporated into practice in ways that do them justice and that avoid the adverse impacts of distortions, errors, and misunderstandings. However, to be an effective tool of social action, research must be theoretically rigorous, analytically sound, and substantiated by properly established fact.

Research is an essential first step towards formulation of successful intervention strategies to eliminate injurious child work. Through research it is possible to learn about:

- the nature and extent of child work;
- the causes of child work;
- the values, beliefs and practices associated with children's work;
- the impacts of work on children's development;
- the children most susceptible to adversity and the situations that threaten them;
- the resources available and possible options for assisting working children;
- the consequences, strengths and weaknesses of interventions, including their impact on children.

Three types of research are especially important for grounding policies and programmes. The first is the baseline assessment, which is made before planning begins. Its purpose is to thoroughly understand the nature and context of problems to be addressed and of children to be reached. A census, however rough and ready, can reveal the number and distribution of working children in a given population. Rapid assessment methods can be used to obtain basic demographic information and identify work that is obviously hazardous, who is affected, and in what ways, so that appropriate goals, objectives, and strategies for action can be devised. Contextual studies can be used to establish the pattern of options before children, especially in education, and to indicate any problems or constraints. More detailed studies may be needed, however, to obtain qualitative information on work and educational experience, levels of school attendance, reasons for drop out and other special topics. A baseline assessment can be used to decide on priorities for action and as a backdrop against which findings from subsequent monitoring and impact studies can be appraised.

The second important category of research evaluates policy and programme action. The type that is periodically conducted during a project or programme cycle is referred to as monitoring. It is used to continuously check whether the policies, activities, strategies and resource allocation of an organization are consistent with agreed priorities, problems, goals and targets and with the needs of the children. Continuous monitoring procedures can also be used to track working children and their families, to determine changes in their condition and circumstance. Periodic evaluations may be conducted to establish the effectiveness of a programme or policy in bringing about improvements in the children's lives. Especially on completion of a project, programme or policy cycle it is desirable to conduct an impact evaluation, which will highlight the benefits and drawbacks, foreseen and unforeseen, for the children, their families and communities.

Advocacy research is a third important component of action to address harmful child work. It can be used to generate information needed for public education and awareness-raising, as well as for the sustained social dialogue of social mobilization (see Chapter Six). It can be especially useful to counter beliefs and practices that put children at risk and to create acceptance, support, and collaboration in favour of new ideas and ways of doing things.

An overview of child work literature and information

For a long time, child work was not considered a worthy subject for research. In most countries childhood itself was neglected. This is especially true of official statistics. Throughout the world, social statistics are generated in large quantities by the agencies of government as a by-product of regular administrative or judicial processes, as well as through national censuses, civil registration systems, and national household and labour force surveys. Yet, as a rule, children have figured little in these large-scale official data-sets. Often, the only comprehensive official information on children concerns under-five morbidity and mortality and education enrolment and retention. The invisibility of children in social accounting and statistics is evident even in the comparatively wealthy countries of Europe.[3]

This situation of invisibility has a lot to do with the very low priority awarded to children by the agencies of government. Especially in family research and population studies, in which they are presumed to automatically share the fate and condition of the family or household, children are seldom studied in their own right but rather with respect to children's institutions such as the school or the family. Hence, most public statistics, social accounting and social surveys report about children with reference to their parent's position in the socioeconomic structure.[4]

As was explained in the introduction to this book, the few childhood statistics that do exist are unreliable, giving rise to a distorted picture of children's lives. Among other problems, are major gender discrepancies in the data because of the concentration of females in domestic work within the family. Available data for Latin America, for example, suggest that there are more males than females in the workforce, 84 per cent of workers in the age group 7 to 17 in Guatemala being reported as male, with similar tendencies in Ecuador, Brazil, Colombia and Peru.[5] New guidelines suggested by the ILO for collecting child work data should eventually help with this definitional problem, but very few countries have begun to implement them.

Sometimes, information about children is amassed and recorded but is neither presented nor tabulated as such, or is simply left unanalyzed.[6] Official figures are frequently estimates based on fragmentary statistical material, qualitative observation and informed judgement. A substantial number of development statistics issued and used internationally, for example, are derived by economists, demographers, educators or others on the basis of models involving indirect data and various assumptions.[7] The frequent resort in official statistics to national averages and the consequent failure to disaggregate geographically or by subgroups within the child population hides the serious sub-national disparities in child survival, development, and work that exist in most countries. Work levels tend to be much higher for low-income populations in developing countries, for example. By illustration, a study from Chile reports that 36 per cent of seventh grade children in poor neighbourhoods have part-time paid jobs, against a national average of only 10 per cent. For secondary school children, the working share rose to 50 per cent in poor areas, as opposed to 20 per cent nationally.[8]

Another problem is the organization of childhood research along fragmentary, sectoral lines, there being no overall integrated system for data gathering. Some sectors, such as education, collect information regularly, while others do only sporadic research. Sometimes the various sectoral agencies employ different definitions of a child, leading to a lack of fit between data sets and making it difficult to cross-tabulate findings. Because of definitional disparities, statistics on child employment are often compiled using age cohorts that are out of alignment with those used in education. These cohorts need to coincide for effective conclusions to be drawn on the relationship between education and work.

Information about the middle childhood years is often particularly weak because it is presumed that, once children reach school age, they are represented in education statistics. Indeed, research with children in this age group is sometimes restricted to education concerns only. Adolescence presents an even greater problem for official researchers, often generating interest solely in relation to unemployment or social deviancy such as substance abuse, delinquency, and crime. Researchers working with official data may be forced to use indirect means to obtain information on children's lives. Children's work, for example, often is studied by looking at school attendance and determinants, on the theory that there is a negative correlation between children's economic activity and schooling.[9] Sometimes, large official data sets can be used as a sample frame for child-specific research. Alarcón Glasniovich[10] for instance took a sample of 630 households from the 1987 General Household Study of Lima and Callao for his study of the relationship between child work and education.

All these factors taken together diminish official measures of the extent of children's work. More importantly, the child workers who we most want to know about tend to be those who are left out. And children who are excluded from official figures are generally beyond the reach of social-planning. The large numbers of children throughout the world without birth certificates or identity papers do not exist officially, for instance, and hence are normally excluded from school due to legal restrictions. On the other hand, incorporation of especially disadvantaged groups in official data can result in their being stigmatized. Thus, working children who are in one way or another in conflict with the law (for instance street workers detained under vagrancy laws) are more than likely to be registered officially, but their inclusion in the data as 'problem children' adds to their social marginalization.

Social science research

But official agencies are not the only ones to have been remiss in providing information about children for there are many discrepancies also in the primary research of the social sciences. Although psychological, behavioural, and medical studies of children have been long established in the industrialized North, we noted in Chapter One that researchers have neglected childhood work on the false assumption that it was eliminated some time ago in these countries.[11] Hence the anomaly that even though the child development concepts from the North underlie international legal instruments like the Minimum Age Convention and the Convention on the Rights of the Child, they have contributed little to understanding the impact of work on child development. Social science research into children's work has been stunted by this general disinterest, and we know of few academic centres that have made any sort of institutional commitment to this subject. Nevertheless, some progress has been made by individual researchers, sometimes working in disadvantageous conditions.

Perhaps the most immediately relevant social science research addresses the psychosocial impacts of work. It was not until the late 1980s that American researchers Elen Greenburger and Laurence Steinberg began to look at the effects of work on the psychological and emotional well-being of adolescents in the United States, the research being summarized in the volume *When Teenagers Work: The Psychological and Social Costs of Adolescent Employment*. Their interest was mainly the effects of work, and especially longer hours of work, on school. There have been several other American studies since then, the majority focusing on school impact.[12] Tackling rather different issues, a few American psychologists (for example Kirk Felsman and Lewis Aptekar) also began at about this time to apply psychological methods to assess the psychosocial functioning of juvenile street workers overseas.

For their part, anthropologists have seldom focused on children, even though the first major anthropological work especially addressed to childhood, Kidd's *Savage Child*, a study of the lives of Bantu children in South Africa, was published as long ago as 1906. Sometimes children's work activities were included in anthropological accounts of rites of passage or socialization, but the main theoretical concern was not children's contribution to society so much as how particular societies or cultures view childhood and successfully change children into adults. Margaret Mead was the first anthropologist to make the study of childhood and adolescence her central interest. Her research in Samoa, the Manus Islands, Papua New Guinea and later, with Gregory Bateson, in Bali, focused on child development. The key assertion of her important book *Coming of Age in Samoa*, sustained by comparing adolescence in Samoa and America, was the primacy of nurture over nature in shaping childhood. She argued that, while adolescence in America could be described as a time of trouble and turbulence, this certainly does not apply universally.

One of the few significant British anthropological studies of childhood from this period was Meyer Fortes' *Social and Psychological Aspects of Education in Taleland*, published in 1938. Fortes' interest was in informal education in the widest sense, as a social process "by which the cultural heritage is transmitted from generation to generation", seeing its function as the "moulding of individuals to the social norm". Importantly, he understood children's work, or the application of practical productive skills, to be a critical component of this process:

> Between birth and social maturity the individual is transformed from a relatively peripheral into a relatively central link in the social structure; from an economically passive burden into a producer; from a biological unit into a social personality cast in the habits dispositions and notions characteristic of his [*sic*] culture.[13]

Fortes was concerned about the conditions and social framework of education in a non-literate society. He noted the important contribution made by anthropology to a concept of education managed by the family, although "seldom regularized or systematized", which occurs as a "by-product" of the cultural routine. He documented the evolution with age of children's economic duties and activities and their play, indicating both educational content and gender-specific roles and he was also interested in the ways in which adherence to moral and conventional rules develops within the structure of parent—child relationships.

By the late 1970s, several economists and demographers had begun to turn their attention to the economic value of children, the main theoretical concern being whether children's work contributes positively to household income. Some researchers argued that on balance the costs of bearing and rearing children outweigh the benefits, at least until they reach mid-adolescence or adulthood.[14] They suggested that only if children are seen as an insurance against risk and a source of support in old age can they be said to contribute economic value. Others disagreed, maintaining that if activities which do not generate monetary income are included, children must be viewed as making a positive contribution to household survival from quite a young age. Several researchers tied the notion that children have economic value to ideas about how child work acts as an incentive to fertility.[15]

While there were some important developments in childhood research up to the 1970s, it is striking that all these early social science accounts of childhood centred on adult views, children's own reports of their everyday lives and experiences, and children's own perceptions, were completely disregarded. Research on child work by development economists, for example, was more concerned about the implications for population growth than about the meaning of work for children. Equally, child development and socialization research was not interested in children's competencies and contributions during childhood so much as with how society turns children into adults. It was not until 1979, The International Year of the Child, that researchers began to question whether children's childhood experiences were quite what adults had imagined, this being when the exploitation and abuse of children in many parts of the globe were first exposed by extensive media coverage and rights campaigns. From this point onwards, children's well-being became a decisive ingredient in studies of child work, and the appalling circumstances of many working children in the world were highlighted. 1979 was also when national and international agencies, non-governmental and multilateral, began to do research and advocacy on children's work.

The early 1980s saw the publication of several major studies on child work, especially the volumes edited by Gerry Rodgers and Guy Standing and by Ben White.[16] In the early 1990s, some anthropologists produced detailed studies on children's life worlds that included a special focus on their work. For example, Pamela Reynolds[17] and Olga Nieuwenhuys[18] graphically demonstrated the crucial importance of children's work in family and community life and the need to conceive of child work in terms far broader than wage employment. They also wrestled with the special methodological problems of describing children's reality in holistic rather than sectorial terms. This was a time when key concepts were being developed and the nature of children's work explored.[19]

The volume of research on children's work has grown considerably since the early 1980s, much of it sponsored by multilateral bodies such as the ILO and UNICEF. This literature has produced trends of its own. Overall, there has been a notable bias towards urban children and especially children who work on the streets. The emphasis on street workers is partly because they are more visible than other categories of working children and also because they are thought by researchers and practitioners to experience distress more acute than many other groups. Child street workers are also favoured because they make good research respondents: they are frequently self-employed and therefore less likely to be constrained by adults than other working children, and many are assertive and articulate and communicate well; these competencies being important for generating income on the streets.

In the 1990s, new information demands in relation to children are being addressed and new ways of perceiving children are emerging. This has coincided with the development of new research methods.[20] The implementation and monitoring of the Convention on the Rights of the Child, for example, has stimulated official research on childhood issues. The treaty provides for UN specialized agencies and NGOs to submit information on implementation in states supplying reports to the Committee on the Rights of the Child, the official monitoring body, and this has acted as a catalyst for non-governmental investigations in particular. According to the Convention, the government of each ratifying country is to submit a report on its steps towards implementation of the treaty two years after ratification and every five years thereafter. In some countries, local NGOs have played a vital part even in the preparation of the official government reports. In others, NGOs have written alternative reports or communicated independently with the Committee. In both cases, original research is sometimes involved. The Save the Children organizations as well as UNICEF, which has a special mandate to support the monitoring and implementation of the treaty, have been fostering government interest through seminars and training on monitoring and by providing technical assistance to agencies responsible for preparing States Parties reports.

Despite the vigorous activity around children's rights in many quarters, the initial round of country reports has shown some serious methodological weaknesses. They also tend to be singularly uninspired. Reporting governments have drawn largely on existing data sets developed at the national and sub-national levels and supplementary information provided by the press and non-governmental agencies, initiating very little new primary research. As with earlier official accounts of childhood, the emphasis has been demography, health, and education. Most reports contain general statements of intent and descriptions of measures (inputs) in favour of children, the types and coverage of services, budgetary and staff allocations, and so on, ignoring the actual status of children's rights or the effectiveness of provision for children. This means that the initial round of reports makes a poor baseline for monitoring future trends in children's rights and welfare. The rather superficial system for reviewing and accepting reports does not suggest their quality will be dramatically improved in the near future.

Nevertheless, the need to broaden the scope of investigations on children's work is increasingly recognized. One priority has been to find ways of improving quantitative information, to gain an overall picture of the nature and trends of children's work, and to discover in which occupations and activities children are most threatened. This is of high importance since bad data and other information produce a misleading picture of the situation. In one initiative, the ILO Bureau of Statistics is attempting to help countries systematize quantitative information about working children through reform of the manner in which child work statistics are collected, analyzed, and reported. The aim is to monitor the nature of the phenomenon, the extent, and trends. For example, analysis of existing country data from circa 1990 suggested a gradual decline in the numbers of working children internationally. However, these figures are known to represent an underestimate of some magnitude, and there is reason to believe that the apparent decline was a product of bad data. Among other things, data for the former Soviet region and China are lacking and, as noted, the existing definition of the term 'child labour' excludes many of the more informal maintenance tasks children engage in.[21] We cannot draw very satisfying conclusions from such data; it might be that urban formal sector employment of children is in long-term decline, but the many exclusions from existing data systems make it impossible to learn whether there is in fact such a trend in children's work as a whole. It also is important to know which children are at risk, and these figures do not tell us anything about that.

Recognizing the limitations of existing databases, the ILO has been collaborating with national statistical institutions in several developing countries in the conduct of experimental surveys and the elaboration of a statistical collection and analysis procedure that is more adequate for monitoring child work trends. This method began in 1996 to be extended to interested countries.

Other assessment approaches

Another priority has been to learn about ways of gathering quantitative information quickly and cheaply thus permitting programming work to proceed on the basis of adequate interim information that can be collected in the space of a few months, where official statical systems take one or more full years to collect and analyze data. The ILO's IPEC programme, in collaboration with UNICEF, has been developing and piloting rapid assessment procedures which provide an overview of the situation, locations and occupations of working children in a given area to facilitate the setting of programme priorities and planning of action strategies.[22] Investigators search out various locations within a given area where children are working and systematically gather information about the child workers, their distribution by sex and age, the industries, activities, and occupations they are engaged in, their work situations, and living conditions.[23] Descriptions of children's work (causes, conditions, and consequences) are obtained from the children, target sites are identified, and teams are trained for future information-gathering and action. Multiple methods are used to obtain the information, each one being designed to yield information complementary to data obtained from other methods.

There have been several large-scale rapid assessments of children's work either at the city level or in selected urban sites, such as in Dhaka, Bangladesh.[24] This kind of mapping exercise has proved useful for establishing a baseline for policy and programming. For example, in a survey of more than 830 establishments (the bulk in the industrial manufacturing sector, with a few in hotels and catering and construction and some informal street-based occupations) in several urban sites in Bangladesh, a total of 47 children's occupations and types of child-employing establishment were identified as certainly or potentially hazardous.[25] The possible risks and health impacts for each occupation, activity, and establishment type were assessed first through observation and then by recording the actual health and accident histories of more than 1,000 working children through interviews with the children, their employers, and supervisors.

The uses and abuses of research

Early approaches

There are some major difficulties in doing research into children's work, not least being that working children are often hidden from the public domain and difficult to access. Research of this nature frequently implies changing the status quo, and thereby poses a threat to the many people who have a vested interest in the work that children do. Finding out about children can prove controversial for the simple reason that it challenges governments or other organizations unwilling to countenance criticism of their policies or practice, as well as individuals who will not accept their responsibilities towards children.[26] Researchers can be foiled by the hostility or suspicion of local government officials, law enforcement agents, employers, managers, parents, and of the children themselves.

There is a widespread popular opinion that children are the responsibility of their families and that investigations of any sort are an intrusion into family life. At the same time, issues that affect children's well-being may be of little concern to adults more anxious to have their own priorities prevail. Properly designed studies may, therefore, be essential for bringing the realities of children's work life to public attention. Children in most places do not have formal institutions that they have shaped to represent their views, although working children's organizations are growing in some regions. Children's work activities can be very hard to distinguish because they are often perceived not as a productive contribution but as part of their own learning and therefore dismissed by adults as trivial. Similarly, because children's work is a normal, everyday occurrence taken for granted by all, both children and adults may be quite perplexed by any interest taken in the subject. Then there is the fact that childhood is not a fixed state, but "... a continuing metamorphosis: 'the category of childhood is concretely descriptive of a community which though relatively stable in its structure is by definition only fleeting in its particular membership'".[27]

Some of the obstacles to learning about children have to do with poor research preparation and design. All too often, researchers use research methods and research tools that are inappropriate for the age group, the context or research issues. How a research programme is conceived, negotiated, and managed can make a lot of difference in terms of the extent to which children, their families, and communities choose to collaborate and participate and the utility of the findings for policy, programmes, and projects. Partly for this reason, and partly to obtain more valid representation of the views of children and their families, participatory research methods that involve them in the design and conduct of research are increasingly being explored. Researchers may have to tread a difficult path, balancing respect for people's right to privacy with a concern to learn about children's problems and needs.

Historically, the topic of research was normally dictated to a large extent by the professional orientation of the researcher and this also determined the research method(s) used. Sociologists and social workers were highly dependent on traditional sociological methods, especially interviews and questionnaire surveys, to obtain data on children's social and economic situation. Medical researchers would do examinations, anthropometry, and biological tests to learn about health and safety problems and psychologists would apply projective techniques, behaviour or symptom inventories, and developmental or cognitive tests to find out about psychosocial functioning. Confined to the ideas and vision prescribed by a particular discipline, most researchers would adopt a partial rather than holistic view of children and child development. This is despite the recognized synergy of child development, which means that the various aspects of children's lives need to be seen and appreciated in relationship with one another. For example, as indicated in Chapter One, adverse impacts of work on physical health tend also to have psychosocial consequences.

Social investigations

The bulk of information on children's work internationally draws on social research using interviews and questionnaires. Interviews, defined as a conversation with a structure and purpose, constitute one of the most fundamental methods of social research. They can range from a casual conversation to a formal, structured set of questions and answers, depending on the degree to which they are directed by the researcher. It is mainly from interviews that the case studies and case histories of children that abound in the child work literature are derived.[28] Interviews can reveal a lot about the context of children's work and also about children's lifestyles, friendships, family life, hopes and aspirations, as well as their school experiences. Sometimes researchers build up a picture of children's work gradually by conducting several interviews over a period of time. Many use a variety of different types of interview to obtain different kinds of information. Campos, et al.,[29] for example, in their study of social networks and daily activities of boys and girls living and working on the streets in Belo Horizonte, Brazil, mixed focus group discussions (group interviews with a defined theme) with open-ended interviews and life history interviews.

Questionnaires can be based on open-ended questions or fixed response categories or a combination of both, fixed response questions being easier to subject to statistical analysis although yielding data of less depth. Questionnaire surveys are particularly appropriate for obtaining a small amount of information from a large number of people and also for making inferences about many people from data drawn from a relatively small number from that group.[30] They have been used extensively in research on children's work .[31] They help the researcher learn about the distribution of a characteristic, or set of characteristics, or a set of attitudes or beliefs, within a population, the aim being to describe and explain statistically the variability of certain features of that population.

Espinola, Glauser, Ortiz & Ortiz de Carrizos, for example, used interviews and in-depth case studies in a survey of 200 children living and working on the streets of Asunción, Paraguay, complemented by photographs and a survey of relevant written sources.[32] The interviews were held in the streets and open questions were used to obtain personal details and information on the context of work, family life, relationships outside the family, education, and other topics. The children were also given the opportunity to comment further on any subject if they wished. In most cases the children were interviewed alone, although some were accompanied by a companion, who might occasionally intercede. The case studies evolved through follow-up discussions with children who had given particularly interesting initial interviews. In order not to inhibit the children, notes were taken after finishing rather than during interviews. Even though this approach yielded much valuable information, systematization of the data was made difficult by differences in the way different interviewers observed and recorded information and wide disparities between responses due to the use of open questions. These in-depth survey studies can reach quite large numbers of children. For example Singh, Kaura & Khan[33] surveyed 876 working children (590 boys and 286 girls, employees and self-employed children not attending school) between the ages of 6 and 15 from slum areas in Greater Bombay. The sample represented just over 14 per cent of a total of 5,939 children, which included non-working school pupils, working children who were attending school and children defined as neither working nor going to school.

Assessing health and safety

Medical research constitutes another major branch of information on children. However, medical researchers have paid surprisingly little attention to children in middle childhood and adolescence, this being under normal circumstances the most healthy and therefore (to them) the least interesting stage in the human life cycle. Health research with children of this age is largely confined to industrialized countries and to lifestyle issues like substance abuse, bad eating habits, lack of physical exercise, and exposure to media images of violence. In non-industrialized countries it is restricted almost exclusively to applied, or therapeutic, studies with especially disadvantaged groups of children such as refugees or children living on the streets. Little has been done in relation to children's work, although the potential for revealing very valuable information on its long- and short-term physical impacts is great.

Physical examinations, biological tests, anthropometry, and personal testimony (self-reporting) can be used effectively to establish the past and present health, nutrition, and growth status of working children.[34] Anthropometric measurements, for example, are straightforward and quick, providing data on height and weight for age, and mid upper-arm circumference and skinfold thickness can be used as estimates of growth status, muscle, and fat deposits. There are, however, some special technical problems in analyzing the nutritional status of children in the mid-childhood range which researchers need to understand in designing their studies. In the study of carpet weavers in Kashmir by Mattoo, Rauf and Zutshi,[35] data were obtained both through interviews with the children and through medical examinations focusing on weight, height, nutrition, and personal hygiene. In another example, the study of carpet weavers in Mirzapur, India, by Das, Shukla and Öry,[36] information on medical symptoms from the previous 15 days was combined with medical examinations including anthropometric measurement and an assessment of lung function made by using a Standard Wrights Peak Flow Metre. These methods were complemented by studies exploring working conditions, work and education histories, and other topics.

Health histories generally are obtained through self-reporting. In one ILO study,[37] for example, a rough measure of the physical impact of work was obtained by asking working and non-working school children to report symptoms. Muscular, chest, and abdominal pain, headaches, and dizziness were stated as common complaints among working children and respiratory symptoms, such as coughs, breathing difficulties, and influenza were reported more frequently among workers than among school children. Nevertheless, the limits of self-reporting on physical health need to be understood. Obviously the main drawbacks are that children cannot give diagnoses but only describe symptoms and are unable to detect sub-clinical conditions or conditions that are manifested only in the long term. At times there may be reason to doubt the accuracy or veracity of self-reporting even of symptoms. Self-reporting is most effective when combined with other methods, such as anthropometry, medical examination, or behavioural observation. Such combinations are essential for gaining a complete health picture including factors, such as drug use, that are important problems for certain groups of working children but are often not picked up by research too narrowly concerned in traditional lines such as occupational health and safety studies.

Psychological research

Psychological research has generated a vast number of psychological and cognitive tests and projective techniques, used to assess children's personality, development, and psychosocial adjustment. However, psychological studies have been confined mainly to studies of pre-school and school populations in industrialized countries. As noted previously, there are very few psychosocial studies of children's work.[38] Because psychologists have not taken much interest in children's work, comparatively little is known about the psychosocial correlates of work in children, and standard psychological methods have been little adapted to the issue of work and to use in cross-cultural settings. The greatest use of psychological research with children outside the industrialized world has been in studies of the psychosocial impact of armed conflict. Even here, research instruments have, in most cases, been standard ones developed in the North and merely translated, sometimes without adaptation, into indigenous languages. In the war research, children's emotional and psychological functioning is mostly assessed in behaviour and symptom checklists or inventories cataloguing the range of stressful or violent events they have experienced, witnessed or heard about. These instruments are completed through self-reporting by the children or reporting by others, generally parents or care givers.

The few psychological studies that have been done in the field of child work have tended to concentrate on street children. In an approach he refers to as psycho-ethnography, Aptekar[39] studied the psychological functioning of street children in Colombia by combining participant observation with three psychological tests. The choice of methods was dictated by validity in terms of characteristics of the sample, the cultural context, and the subject area. Aptekar assessed the intelligence of a non-random sample of children aged 7 to 16 years using the Kohs Block Design Test. He found that, although there were few cases of very high IQ, the mean score of all the children fell within the normal range and there were no more cases of mental retardation than one would expect to find in the normative population. He also applied the Bender—Gestalt Test and the Goodenough—Harris Drawing Test, these giving measures of the children's emotional and neurological functioning. About a quarter of the children scored within the pathological range, although nearly half were entirely without pathology. This suggested that most of the children were functioning adequately neurologically and emotionally, showing an effective adaptation to difficult circumstances on the streets.

Structured observation (where action is recorded at regular intervals during a set period of time), is the method used by psychologists in clinical settings in the North that has been adapted most effectively to field studies of children's work in other cultures.[40] Through systematic observation, it is possible to record what children do during their leisure time, their work activities, and also the context, social relations, schedules, and intensity of their work. In her study of Tonga children in Mola, Zimbabwe, Reynolds[41] found that the method yielded important data on children's conversations, interaction, and mood, the relationships between those who gave orders or requests for tasks to be performed and those who received orders and carried the work out, rules for avoiding work and generosity in assuming another's task, and the manner in which children cared for the elderly and the young.

Structured observation can also be employed effectively in the classroom to learn about children's experience of school. For example, in her study of how children in Tarija, rural southern Bolivia, negotiate their independence as they grow up, Samantha Punch[42] used classroom observation to record pupil—teacher relations and conversations, activities carried out in the classroom, how the teachers coped with multiple grades in the same class, deviant behaviour, and clothes worn by the children. She also studied games played during the breaks, recreation lessons, line-ups, school civil acts, gender differences at school, and children's interactions with peers. However, it is worth noting that it took quite a bit of time to develop a relationship of trust with teachers and pupils and for them to accept her presence in the classroom to the extent that she was ignored and did not disturb the lessons.

Methodological problems

The fact that international research into the lives of working children began in 1979 with denunciation of children's' suffering has greatly influenced the nature of the subsequent discourse, setting it within a framework of advocacy for children's welfare and rights.[43] This has had the effect of diminishing the ethnographic, psychological, and sociological rigour of the literature. Many of the studies of children's work have been done by journalists and children's rights activists as a basis for public campaigns and lobbying, frequently with diminished regard for precise substantiation and reporting of the findings. The tendency has been to define work generally and vaguely as a 'problem' for children and to base inquiries on individual case studies, many focused on a situation of serious peril. While the suffering of children in highly exploitative work should not be minimized, exclusion of attention to the most severe cases can become problematic when it is used to justify blanket policy and programme measures that are ill-suited to the probable majority of children whose work is not particularly hazardous or exploitative and is combined quite successfully with school.

A lack of theoretical and methodological rigour results in poor conceptualization of working children as victims, and their classification, often falsely, into discrete categories defined very loosely by their circumstances or situation. Vague terms such as 'abused and neglected children' and 'street children' are in common usage throughout the world. The imagery of children thus described is static and in some cases has come to depict widely accepted stereotypes which are a serious distortion of reality. For example, classifying children into exclusive categories of those who work and do not go to school and those who go to school and do not work ignores the fact that in many places the majority of school-age children who work also attend school, at least through the primary level, making working children a significant proportion of the school population.

Much research is conducted as a one-off event, providing what is often a fairly static picture of children's working lives and school participation. However, neglecting children's work histories and careers can be misleading because the intensity of their work, their work schedules, and their activities and occupations are often quite variable even over short periods of time.[44] Some children, for example, only work temporarily to cover a specific expense such as medical treatment or a new school uniform; others become economically active only in periods of family emergency. Many are involved in more than one type of activity or job on a regular basis and many integrate work and school in different proportions according to the week or season. Besides, many of the impacts of work are manifested only in the longer term and cannot be captured in a single-stage investigation. Longitudinal research, then, is much more likely to provide an accurate picture of the range, schedules. and intensity of work in different seasons or different phases of childhood, as well as giving an idea of work impacts manifested in the longer term.

Poor quality research presents a serious problem for policy because it influences detrimentally the action strategies and goals that are developed. We have already suggested that information gaps in official data lead to the isolation of large numbers of children from basic services and to a very fragmentary view of children's lives, implying that many of the issues that concern children most are simply ignored by planners. Compensating for these gaps by building projective computer models may make the situation worse. McGranahan et al.[45] warn, for example, that there is a serious danger that those who analyze data generated by models may think that they have discovered important empirical truths when in fact they have merely discovered assumptions of the models.

In practice, research into issues like child exploitation is often anecdotal and of no statistical validity, and so cannot be used in policy or programme development without causing serious distortions. Many of the obstacles have to do with researchers' own views of children, and these also crucially affect the interpretation of research findings.[46] Take conventional psychological research, for example. In Chapter One we stated that earlier psychological research which posits growing-up as a standard process everywhere, defined by established markers and stages, has been questioned in recent years. One of the main arguments, as we noted, is that children's developmental achievements are defined more by their individual capacities and experiences and by the normative context in which they grow up than by universal biological and psychological processes. In light of this critique, there are important concerns as to the reliability and validity of some of the conventional methods of psychological research when they are used in social and cultural settings very different from those in which they were devised, given that the markers of child development used in these methods define only one particular kind of childhood. Similarly, conceptualizing working children primarily as victims makes it difficult to uphold their right to the social benefits enjoyed by other workers. It also clouds researchers' understanding of the choices children confront, the decisions they make, and the pride they can obtain from their growing independence and contributions to the family economy. It thereby renders them more vulnerable.[47]

The emphasis on 'street children' in the research on working children has produced some problems of its own. Firstly, it has diverted policy and programmes away from other economic sectors where children are working in far greater numbers and often in far more damaging circumstances. Secondly, street research has not always been well conducted, producing some misleading findings. For example, for some years policy-makers and programmers throughout the world — and especially in Latin America — have been relying on 'guesstimates' of the numbers of children living and working on the streets. These would consistently exaggerate the size of the former group in particular, with the result that disproportionate effort was invested in housing children, some of whom were not actually homeless, while other important needs were more or less ignored. In the worst cases, a result of flawed understanding was that children working on the streets and living with their families were separated from their homes and placed in government institutions such as remand centres or orphanages under the assumption they were abandoned. For example, as late as the 1980s, Brazilian children working in public spaces were popularly considered to be 'abandoned children' and were as a matter of policy rounded up by local authorities and placed in institutional care without reference to family ties.

In summary, researchers have in recent years developed a better understanding of the special demands of doing primary research with children and the inadequacy of most conventional approaches. Researchers in the 1990s are working with a range of new issues and piloting a range of new methods in the hope of providing more effective information for planning and advocacy.

Methods

Three broad trends can be detected in the development and application of methods of social inquiry at the present time: a move from single-method, single-discipline research to multi-method, multi-disciplinary studies; an increasing tendency to innovate by developing new methods; and an inclination to make research more child-centred and partici-patory. These trends have greatly improved the potential for obtaining qualitative information about children's work.

The emergence of multiple-method, inter-disciplinary research

Short of resources and anxious to progress quickly from research to implementation, researchers at one time would often confine themselves to a single method of enquiry. But extensive use is increasingly being made of multiple methods, frequently cutting across disciplines to generate a more comprehensive picture of children's lives, and some combining psychological and anthropological methods.[48] All research methods entail bias or weaknesses and all leave information discrepancies, especially when applied with only one source of information. In impact assessments, for instance, it is important to canvass the views of children, parents and others, but as we have suggested, self-reporting through interviews entails serious limitations, in that health perceptions may be highly subjective and are not precise diagnoses. Self-reporting needs to be complemented by other procedures. For greater accuracy and to deepen insight, then, more than one method and more than one information source is recommended. Information obtained through one method and/or one type of source can be checked against information acquired in a different way and/or from a different source. This means organizing the research into a sequence, in which one method follows another, consolidating and verifying information provided by the previous one.

The choice of methods and sequence can significantly affect research outcomes. While this choice will be influenced by the kind of information needed, nature of the research population, scale of the investigation, time available, resources and so on, some methods are more effective when used in the earlier stages and others in the later stages of the sequence. One of the first tasks in all good research is to survey existing literature of relevance to the topic. Secondary information of this sort may include published and unpublished material. Possible sources of information on children's work include press reports and television programmes, studies from local and international academic institutions, population censuses, household surveys, administrative and judicial records, school registers, and labour surveys. Material from secondary sources needs to be synthesized and analyzed, taking care to question the validity and reliability of the findings and to check researchers' assumptions.

Primary data collection in the field should always begin with qualitative information arrived at inductively through immersion in the children's world, using observation, the method that underpins all good social science investigations. Observation entails the detailed reporting of events, behaviours, moods, atmosphere, and artefacts in the social setting chosen for study and is important throughout the research process. There are three main forms of observation: systematic observation of the kind used in psychological studies; participant observation, in which the researcher becomes part of the social world of research subjects; and unstructured observation: the continuous and random scrutiny of the research site and subjects. Observation is an extremely versatile method and can be used to select study locations and topics, map where children work and congregate, distinguish which children are working, identify obvious work hazards, and generate initial research questions, as well as to cross-check information obtained through other means at later stages of the research.

Other methods used in the early stages of research should also be situationally driven, employing lightly structured research instruments with open questions or no questions, and allowing respondents to frame their own concerns and concepts and in this way reveal the essential character of the problem.[49] Administered like this, methods such as drawing, focus group discussion, role-play, writing, and photography can yield a great deal of qualitative information about children's feelings, ideas, mood, relationships, and so on. But usually researchers also want to be able to amass their results to some degree to indicate the rate, frequency or quantity of a particular finding. Quite a bit of numerical information can be obtained by coding and aggregating qualitative data, looking for repeated categories and elements. Thus, for example, it is possible to list the negative and positive work impacts children report and thereby indicate whether the majority favour or oppose working. Quantitative information can also be obtained through deductive means, by doing a census or survey based largely or solely on pre-coded, closed questions which favour numerical analysis, although this is most effective if the words and categories emerge from prior qualitative data rather than the research laboratory.

Many researchers[50] start with more informal, unstructured interviews with open-ended questions and move to more structured ones at a later stage. This makes it possible to learn children's words, concepts, and understandings at the outset so that these can be used in subsequent instruments when more quantifiable data may be sought. The need to quantify findings sometimes leads researchers to develop quite structured instruments that lend themselves to statistical analysis, hence the use of questionnaire surveys which at one time were a favoured method of social research with working children.

Recent years have seen much interest in forms of baseline research that are less expensive and both quicker and easier to mount than are more conventional research models. This interest responds to the needs of policy-makers and programme-planners to work within realistic budget and time constraints. One popular approach is what has come to be known as 'Rapid Assessment'. The IPEC—UNICEF rapid assessment procedure, mentioned previously, is an example of sequenced research, one set of information providing input for the next round of information gathering. The process starts with systematic observation and fairly brief interviews in an effort to obtain almost total coverage of the research universe in a given area. Observation provides information on children's work activities and working conditions, and enables counting of children in order to learn the numbers working. Individual interviews conducted with children are both unstructured and structured, and are used to learn their views of work and school, the nature of their activities, the terminology they use for these activities, as well as details of their working conditions and terms of employment. Techniques such as personal histories, recall of the preceding 24-hour or 1-year period, stories, card-sorting tests, and drawings can be included in such interviews. A search of existing information, published and unpublished, and structured interviews with informants selected because of their knowledge about children's economic activities helps build a more detailed picture. Maps and drawings can be used to show the areas under study, and depict the age, sex, and occupation of child workers as observed in each location within the area. Group interviews may be held with selected children or adults to fill in gaps or arrive at decisions about what should be done, as well as to develop inventories of children's economic activities and general perceptions of work. Focused questionnaires administered with children involved in established networks or large organizations like schools can help cross-check information obtained in interviews and also determine the range and frequency of certain key facts.

Innovating new methods

For some time it was assumed that researching children was much like researching adults, and in fact much of the research about children was done by asking adults. It is noteworthy that most of the methods employed in the traditional social science research about children involved minimal interaction with children themselves. Researchers preferred to use methods that could be standardized and were not much influenced by research subjects because these seemed to capture reality more objectively and accurately. This was one of the justifications for devising and applying them in controlled clinical settings rather than the real, often chaotic, world of children. This was especially true of psychological and medical research, which depended on highly structured research instruments like symptom checklists or tests.

But a new generation of researchers has begun to emerge with very different perspectives on children and how best to work with and learn from them. It is now understood, for one thing, that merely applying methods originally designed for use with adults is likely to prove quite ineffective, not least because children are often more spontaneous than adults, respond to research in different ways, value different methods of communication, and have a different attention span. In many cases, considerable adaptation and innovation has been found necessary and considerable flexibility introduced into the research process.

Penna Firme, Tijiboy and Stone[51] chose a novel approach in their evaluation of the impact of programmes for street children in Brazil. The researchers were confronted with developing methods and indicators that catered for an unknown number of children involved in some 400 programmes of enormous diversity in terms of programme goals, size (some with less than 20 children and others more than 3,000) and duration, and the ages and situation of children they assist. They chose to focus on behaviour that would indicate possible changes provoked by the programme, looking at the children's ability to formulate life plans and enter the workforce, developmental and social changes, integration with family and community, and capacity to be self-sustaining or self-sufficient. A bank of indicators was developed to measure these criteria, mainly through observation. Techniques that could have felt threatening to the children, such as photographs or questionnaires were avoided.

The data were gathered through a wide variety of methods, some devised on the spur of the moment. On one occasion, for example, when an evaluator was talking with a group of children, one of them started to communicate through mime. The evaluator took advantage of this opportunity to ask the child to dramatize the status of the children 'before', 'during', and 'after' their participation in the programme, revealing the child's perception of changes. Participant observation was used quite frequently by the team and helped build trust and confidence. Sometimes this was mixed with more systematic observation, which proved especially useful for perceiving relationships, behaviour towards others, the use of critical thinking, and other qualitative information. Plastic arts were used during the children's leisure time as a basis for analyzing personality characteristics. Life histories were obtained in open, informal interviews and individual and collective conversations focused on a broad range of themes and issues, from family life, the police, or school to the programme.

A review of programme documents and formal interviews with ex-participants, staff and community members yielded information about the programme. Five questions were directed at children and staff: What programme are you in? In what way did the programme change you? What was it in the programme that made you change in this way? What do you intend to do from now on/when you grow up? and What message would you like to give children who are not in a programme like yours?

Using a variety of biological and sociological methods, some traditional and some quite new, Baker, Panter-Brick and Todd[2] compared the lives and health of homeless boys aged between 7 and 13 years living on the streets of Kathmandu, Nepal, with squatter children, urban school children, and children from a rural village. Participant observation was the most important underlying method used, providing a consistent grounding in everyday life and prompting the adaptation or introduction of different methods during the research process. Other methods ranged from self-assessments, interviews, and biological tests in groups and with individuals.

An anthropometric survey was conducted by organizing health camps. Height, weight, arm circumference, and skinfolds for the four populations were compared with international referents. The method proved easy to administer and fun. The children were encouraged to familiarize themselves with the equipment first, by attending demonstrations and measuring each other. The homeless street children subsequently took part in self-assessments of their health in group appraisals using a variety of participatory methods. The children demonstrated their ability to participate in a systematic report of health experiences and perceptions. The survey yielded the surprising finding that while, as expected, urban middle-class school children achieved greater height for age, the homeless boys were significantly taller than both the squatter and the village boys. There was no evidence of acute malnutrition in any of the children, only of chronically poor conditions (under-nutrition or infection). Nor was there any evidence that nutritional status deteriorates with length of time spent on the streets for the homeless sample.

The team was also keen to pilot new biological methods. By monitoring heart rate they were able to compare levels of physical activity in the different daily routines of village, school, and homeless children and suggest how these may relate to physical fitness and overall health (as indicated by growth status). The heart rate was monitored by fixing a plastic band containing the transmitter across the chest and a large watch around the wrist. The children enjoyed the novelty of wearing the equipment, although faced some difficulties in resisting theft. The effects of particularly strenuous activities, such as carrying heavy loads and climbing hills by village children, were revealed by different heart-rate profiles. The percentage of time spent at rest and in moderate or vigorous activity (as defined by a heart rate above resting thresholds) indicated that school boys were the least active, followed by the homeless and village boys. Of the three groups, the village boys spent more time doing moderate physical activity. Low-flex heart-rate values (defined as the mean of maximum rest and minimum exercise heart rate recorded during a standard test) indicate that they also achieved higher physical fitness than school and homeless boys.

Salivary cortisol measurements were also used by the team in Nepal as a means of gauging stress and anxiety levels in homeless children and their peers. This method was selected precisely because of its advantages over psychological testing, especially in relation to the research situation and subject population. Panter-Brick found it quick and easy to administer on a large scale, noting that it requires little specialist training for collection in the field and is relatively free from cross-cultural difficulties in designing culturally appropriate questions, as well as being more enjoyable for the children. A sample of children from all four populations was asked to wash their mouths with water, chew medical gum to induce salivation and spit into a small plastic test-tube that was instantly sealed. Stress and anxiety are reflected by raised levels of the hormone cortisol in body fluids. Because cortisol levels are subject to diurnal variation and are influenced by a variety of stressors in the form of physical exercise, food intake, mood, disease or injury, respondents were also asked questions relevant to these variables. Initial findings suggested that all four groups of children experienced surprisingly low anxiety levels. It should be noted, however, that there is still some doubt regarding just what influences cortisol readings and how they should be interpreted.

Participatory research with children

We have noted that, in the past, many studies of children used adults as their informants rather than the children themselves. Many economists and sociologists, for example, found that parents, community workers, teachers, and other adults with an interest in children could provide useful insights into children's work. People who are familiar with the conditions and situations about which researchers need information are known as key informants. Researchers sometimes rely heavily on the knowledge and insights of key informants, especially during the early stages of research when the principal issues and possibly even the research population have still to be identified. But much traditional research never got beyond the key informant stage, or beyond interviews or questionnaire surveys administered with parents or employers. The justification was that adults know more about children's problems and needs than children themselves; "adults routinely set themselves up as the understanders, interpreters and translators of children's behaviour".[3] Children were presumed to have no valid opinions of their own, or to be too inarticulate or damaged by their work to be able to participate effectively in research. Sometimes the possibility that children could not distinguish between truth and fiction, that they might make things up to please the researcher, or merely repeat what they had been told to say by adults, deterred researchers from using children as respondents.[4]

But the premiss that children make unreliable respondents turns out to be false. In any case, by no means are adult respondents always credible. Research about child work that excludes children themselves risks bias, inaccuracy and a lack of depth and may also undermine children's capacity for self-protection and self-actualization. For one thing, as we suggested in Chapter One, how children feel about their work has an important bearing on its impact and so learning about children's perceptions and views can be one of the most valid ways of assessing psychosocial effects in particular. For another, also as indicated in Chapter One, participation in research and other processes affecting children is in itself developmental. Moreover, only by hearing from children themselves is it possible to learn about their particular childhood experiences. Besides,

Only by hearing from children themselves is it possible to learn about their particular experiences.

researchers need to be warned that adults may hold perceptions of working children that are seriously misrepresentative. Teachers, for instance, may be prejudiced against children who work because they are tired and inattentive in class or because they are dishevelled or arrive late. Absenteeism due to work may be interpreted as wilful truancy and symptoms of distress caused by abuse at work as a behavioural disorder.

A growing number of researchers agree that children are competent and do have important things to say. Children's views make a serious source of evidence about their work, although the manner in which they express themselves, their understandings, words, and concepts, may be different from those of adults.[5] Several studies have demonstrated the value, in terms of accuracy, quality of information, and respect for children, of child-centred research. But to involve children more directly in the research process is not as straightforward as it may seem. The implications are twofold: firstly, they must be able to participate meaningfully, in full knowledge of what this entails and in accordance with their capacity; and secondly, methods and means must be devised to help make children feel comfortable about taking part and to encourage them to define their own problems and concerns, using their own concepts and understandings. This may indicate involving children not just as respondents but also in research-planning, data collection, classification and interpretation, finding generating variables and planning the outcome.[56]

It is especially appropriate for children to participate in the evaluation of programmes assisting them, but special effort may be required to make it happen. Children generally have a great deal of insight about the impact of interventions on their lives, although their views are sometimes deeply challenging and difficult for policy-makers and programme-workers. Fear of criticism by the children, devotion to programme implementation, methodological difficulties in developing effective criteria and indicators for evaluation and logistic problems in tracking young people who have graduated from the programme are some of the reasons for the glaring absence of participatory programme and policy evaluation. Many organizations have extremely laudable and ambitious aims and goals, such as to reduce children's exposure to exploitation, increase their self-esteem or improve their image in society. But, as David Tolfree suggests in his appraisal of programmes for working children, some of these goals are quite intangible and are defined in terms which do not readily lend themselves to measuring impact and effectiveness: "... a tendency to use the language of 'process' ... enables them to opt out of a discussion of effectiveness — despite the fact that 'processes' usually do have anticipated outcomes ..."[57] Psychosocial impacts especially are felt very individually and are therefore extremely difficult to gauge, as illustrated by the comments of a former member of the Movement of the Republic of Emmaus, in Brazil:

> The Republic helped me to feel like a person to be valued. I used to be aggressive with everyone. I would have to be the strongest to be sure of getting an advantage ... Perhaps if it hadn't been for the animators, I would have gone into prostitution like so many other girls. By helping me to become more conscious, the movement has helped me see that I could make progress without being aggressive ... It was through the nuclei that I gained a different awareness of what rights are and what duty is and I began to feel that I was a citizen.[8]

Interestingly, Tolfree's appraisal discovered that in one of the case study programmes an impact could be seen clearly in the children, although such an impact had not been framed by the organization as an objective of its work. The point was also made that, since some initiatives are programmes *of* rather than *for* working children, the members have constant input into activities and decisions: "hence there is an ongoing process of self-evaluation, though whether this can be considered as a systematic evaluation of effectiveness is open to question".[9]

Given the broad range of programme and policy options — from prevention to rehabilitation, from abolition to worker's organization and from workers' rights and service provision to self-protection — it is very troubling that so little has been done to assess the relative merits and disadvantages of different approaches and objectives. Tolfree was particularly surprised to find that even organizations that take child participation extremely seriously are not attempting to involve children in participative impact evaluation. "Without this", he argues, "it is difficult to see how approaches and methods of work can develop optimally and for the benefit of future generations of working children".[10] It is even possible that well-intentioned interventions, including those conceived in full consultation with working children, may be having a deleterious effect on children's development and well-being or on family livelihood. It follows that introducing mechanisms for participatory monitoring and evaluation should be an essential component of future action with working children.

Methods that are not heavily reliant on the spoken word and are lightly structured may be the most appropriate for children. Young children in particular inhabit a universe that is phenomenologically very distinct, and they may need encouragement to express themselves through other means, such as drawing. Interviews and questionnaires in particular represent a quite formal, adult mode of communication and need to be used with caution in research with children. Questionnaires really only have a role at the end of the research cycle, after a relationship of trust has been established between researcher and children, and a solid body of qualitative information generated through other methods.[a] Children and young people often find it easier to interview each other than to be interviewed by an adult, especially when discussing sensitive issues. Toby Hecht[a2] found children interviewing children a powerful means of gathering information in his research with street children in Brazil. Using what he termed 'radio workshops', he gave a tape recorder and microphone to the children and asked them to interview each other. Importantly, they tended to view the tape recorder as a means of making themselves heard and would often use role-play, pretending to be on the radio, to conduct interviews. They were not afraid to challenge each other if they thought someone was telling lies and asked questions in words and ways that their peers could understand. Because of their familiarity with the circumstances of their respondents, the questions asked by the children were often more appropriate than those adults might pose in the same situation.

We have suggested that many children are more comfortable with methods that use drama, drawing, games, film, photography, videotape, or writing rather than verbal interviews. For example, by diverting attention away from the child subjects and towards an imaginary character, drama and role-play, improvised or scripted, can be especially effective, making it possible for children to describe difficult or sensitive issues without experiencing personal distress.[63] Essays and other writings have been used in several studies of working children.[64] Children do not have to be expert writers, but can be asked to prepare lists or worksheets, fill in recall forms or write essays on a set topic. In a study of child work in Jamaica, Judith Ennew[65] chose essay-writing in research with more than 2,000 school children in grades 4 to 11 from 17 schools in a range of communities in preference to a questionnaire because it allowed the children to use their own words and concepts and facilitated the collection of a large amount of data in a short period of time. The children were asked to describe in writing what they did outside school. Fourteen variables were chosen from the essays for statistical analysis using SPSS, providing an overview of the sample and a comparison between different schools. She also collected absentee and drop-out rates for each school and conducted informal interviews with several teachers. Children who could not write were asked to draw their out-of-school activities, providing almost 200 drawings from which activities drawn could be counted and tabulated.

Whether such methods are suitable, however, depends on the research topic, the children's age, the cultural fit of the method as a medium of expression, the resources available, and the children's educational background. Ultimately, all research needs careful piloting to assess the suitability of a given method with a given group in a given situation. Thus, in Nepal, children were shy of using role-play because they were unused to drama, whereas they found improvised singing very enjoyable and songs made up by the children made effective data.[66]

Nowadays some of the multiple-method research is being conducted with children in groups rather than individually, using practices based upon a participatory methodology known as Participatory Rural Appraisal (PRA). To reflect the conditions and perspectives of whole communities, researchers start by working with the community (however defined) as a whole and progress to its constituent subgroups (children: adults, boys: girls, and so on), thereby revealing similarities and differences in their perceptions, knowledge and experiences. In this way, children are not isolated from their social environment as they are with many other research approaches. PRA research is conducted by teams, usually made up of a mix of people of both sexes with different social characteristics. In PRA, the researcher acts primarily as a facilitator and the research results are based on a consensus among participants and are used as a basis for social action and policy.

In one PRA study, a range of participatory approaches, including interviews, songs, time allocation and observation techniques, were used to learn about children's roles in the household in Sindhuli District in Nepal. The study explored differences in gender, age, wealth and ethnic status, focusing on how girls and boys share their work burdens with adults and how these burdens shift with environmental degradation and socioeconomic change.[67] In another PRA study,[68] the research team examined the contribution children make to the welfare of their community, Kyakatebe, a village in Uganda. The research process started with some general mapping exercises indicating human and natural resources in and around the village. Songs and other techniques helped make the children feel relaxed. Daily routine diagrams showed the time children devote to work, leisure, rest, sleep, religious observance, washing, and eating. Well-being ranking established the children's views about which households in the community had the most money and status and which were most marginalized. This exercise made it possible to identify the children and families most vulnerable economically and socially. A flow diagram showed the impact of the school environment on school performance and another indicated the impact of income-generating activities on non-school-going children. A seasonal calendar showed how school attendance was influenced by diseases and activities associated with different seasons.

All Kyakatebe children contribute to the food production of the family and are involved in various domestic activities, fetching water and digging occupying most of their time. In addition to the digging they do for the family at home, some also get paid employment picking coffee and growing tomatoes. Several reported doing voluntary work for others, like erecting sun-dryers for families unable to do so. Some important differences were found between children in different categories. When only one sex is present in a family, there is no role differentiation, but when there are children of both sexes, roles are gendered. Among girls, only those who go to school have leisure time. Daily routines and workloads also differ for Christian and Muslim children and for children from wealthier and poorer families.

Use of a team of researchers makes it possible to observe and record several things at the same time. While one person is facilitating, another can observe interaction between children, revealing information about friendships, personal animosity, and social distinctions. In Kyakatebe, for example, it was observed that school going and non-school going, dropout, and never-enrolled children did not mix freely, mainly due to age differences and the different economic backgrounds of their families. Muslim and Christian children, who were attending different schools, also remained quite separate and children from the most vulnerable households did not participate in the research exercises. There was also a certain amount of dominance and bullying by older children.

Increasingly, PRA and similar participatory research approaches are being used with children involved in projects and programmes to conduct baseline assessments for programme-planning and implementation. In West Africa, the NGO Enda Jeunesse Action maintains that, for real and deep change, projects concerning young people should be conceived and realized by themselves or at least with their total and active participation, right from the initial assessment stage.[69] This requires that adults in the project should be facilitators or promoters, the programme activities being conceived, carried out, and evaluated by the children and young people themselves with adult support. The organization works with homeless children, young people living and/or working on the streets and domestics, the majority girls. Animators help the young workers to find out about their problems and needs and identify possible solutions. The needs assessment falls in line with 12 sets of rights identified by the young participants as fundamental to their well-being.[70] These consist of the right to: an education to learn a job; stay in the village and not move away; carry out their activities safely; fair justice in case of problems; sick leave; be respected; be listened to; a light and limited type of work, adapted to age and abilities; health care; learn to read and write; have fun and play; express and organize themselves. When a group of young workers identifies its priorities, the animator is there to help define the activities and approaches best suited to meeting these.

Working children participating in Manthoc's programme in Peru also engage in research. Currently one group of young people is working on a survey of the population in the programme, a study of health and an assessment of working conditions: "right now we have sent a health survey for the group delegates, so they can tell us what health problems they have at their jobs, if anybody is sick, how are they doing at school, their problems, so we can help them".[71]

Some agencies are highly reflective, making it their business to constantly learn from the children's experiences and modify their approach in the light of changing circumstances and thinking. Organizations like FUNPRONOP in El Salvador have undergone major changes in terms of objectives and approach in response to this kind of self-conscious reflection. This can be seen as an informal monitoring process, although risks ignoring longer-term impacts, and unless fully documented is unlikely to aid institutional learning. Developing criteria and indicators for assessing programme and policy performance in relation to stated goals and objectives and building into the programme cycle systematic opportunities for children to conduct monitoring and evaluation is essential.

While it is encouraging to see participatory research methods being used in the identification of problems and design of programmes, far rarer are participatory evaluative studies of programme performance and outcome. The Penna Firme, Tijiboy and Stone study remains one of the very few programme evaluations with children. This lack is extremely disappointing given the very important debate about how best to prevent child exploitation and assist children in detrimental work and the evident need to assess the impact of different policy and programme approaches.

Special considerations in primary research with children

Encouraging children to be active participants in research is predicated on the belief that self-knowledge and self-representation are essential steps in empowering children, carrying the potential to enhance their sense of themselves as active and responsible managers of their own lives.[72] In other words, what is special about the various participatory approaches to research is that full account is taken of the different abilities of different groups of children in distinct contexts, recognizing children's competencies as 'distinct', not lesser.[73]

Nevertheless, there are some important considerations to be taken into account when involving working children in research. Most importantly, research can have unforeseen adverse consequences for the children, exposing them to unwanted publicity, psychological distress, abuse or dismissal. The background, prior experiences, and other characteristics of children sometimes introduce special vulnerabilities to the role of research participant. On the other hand, these characteristics may equip them with greater resiliency and enhance their capacity to make meaningful decisions concerning research participation and to defend their interests in research settings.[74]

For their protection, children need to have the opportunity to consider the potential drawbacks before agreeing to take part in research. Children have a right to know about any intervention affecting their lives, including any research activities. It is therefore very important to inform the children, their families, and others (as appropriate), about the purpose, aims, and nature of the research, and to obtain their informed consent to participate. Obtaining informed consent puts the onus on researchers to explain the purpose and approach of their investigations in ways that children of different ages and levels of maturity can understand. Research into sensitive issues, like the treatment of children by employers or the psychosocial effects of illicit work, can be especially risky and should only be conducted by people who know the children well and have a long-term relationship with them.

People (children, researchers, and others) need to be able to develop skills in order to be able to engage meaningfully in research.[75] Patience and humility, the ability to observe and listen without interrupting are important skills for researchers, as is the facility to respond to and manage distress in children.[76] Putting children at the centre of the research process means using methods that take into account their relative lack of power in families and communities, their different use and understanding of words, and their relative lack of experience.[77]

Research can for several reasons be burdensome to working children. It can be time-consuming and interfere with their work or school schedules, making them fall behind in their studies or cutting their earnings. Especially if children are not told about the purpose of the study, they may not perceive it as having any advantage for them or for others. Research that is not properly designed for children and research topics that are very personal or sensitive culturally may make children feel very uncomfortable. Most people would probably agree that research of this nature which intrudes into children's lives without bringing any benefit is not ethical. In order to make research more worthwhile for children, care should be taken to plan research activities to fit in with their other responsibilities. Emphasis should be given to enjoyment of research by both researcher and respondents, allowing ample time for rest, eating, and play.

Conclusion

Research is an important tool of planning, monitoring, evaluation, and advocacy and so long as a research project is well conceived, time devoted to research is well spent. Until quite recently, research about children was conducted using adult informants or research methods that were impervious to children's special competencies and needs. Much of the information was gathered through anecdotal case studies which were unrepresentative of the wider population of working children or through large-scale surveys which failed to capture important qualitative dimensions of work. In other words, much of our knowledge about children's work is quite misleading and makes an unreliable basis for programme and policy development.

But research with children has developed considerably in recent years and now shows great potential as a tool of programme and policy design. Innovatory approaches, such as rapid-assessment procedures, are beginning to yield important information on the distribution of hazardous and exploitative work. New child-centred, participatory methods are providing insights into children's own perceptions and views in relation to their work and school. And increasingly, children who participate in research are also taking part in the programme and policy decisions that are based on these research findings. These are encouraging developments indeed for, as we stated in Chapter One, when given the opportunity to participate meaningfully in social, economic, and political processes children become more resilient, more independent, and more competent socially.

Nevertheless, the urgent need to use child-centred, participatory research to assess programme and policy performance and impact has yet to be met. Still, most interventions into the lives of working children are an act of faith, based on intuitive feelings about their outcome for children rather than thorough analysis. For example, as Chapter Seven shows, many of the schools which adults believe to support children's welfare and development are in practice quite hostile places for children.

Some organizations keep basic quantitative information on inputs and outputs, such as the number of children enrolled, attendance, drop-out or rates of employment, and others commission the occasional external evaluation. But this information says nothing about the actual effects on children, short- or long-term.

The information on work impacts on children is subject to the same deficiencies, as we indicated in Chapter Two. Data on the physical and, to a lesser extent, social hazards of work abound, but the consequences for children are unknown. Equally seriously, children's views on work impacts are disregarded altogether. Investigators must pay far more attention to the precise effects of both work and programme interventions if children are to be properly protected from harm.

CHAPTER FIVE

Children's Work in National Law and International Standards

Addressing children's work from a child-centred perspective implies, among other things, making, interpreting, and applying national laws and international standards governing child work in ways that are sensitive to the realities, needs, and rights of children. The most recent international conventions dealing with the work of children are specifically intended to increase world-wide respect for children's rights, well-being, and development, and this high-minded purpose is intended to also underlie national laws that use them as models. But good intentions are not sufficient to make legal norms and their enforcement adequately child-centred.

As previous chapters have suggested, social attitudes and rules about children's work often are based on ideological and cultural values rather than on knowledge of the realities in which children live and develop. These values are a given point of departure according to which society is judged to see how well it measures up. A trend of recent years has been to posit universal values, often expressed in terms of human rights. Some seem to be genuinely universal in that few if any societies would argue against them; the rejection of child slavery being an example, since even societies that still harbour it would not defend it as desirable.

However, as Chapter One indicated, anthropologists and other social scientists have in recent years pointed out that many values in regard to the raising of children might not be so inter-culturally uniform as the almost universal ratification of the Convention on the Rights of the Child would suggest. In fact, some of what is ostensibly 'universal' may sometimes be little more than the superimposition of ideas from the North on other societies to which they are culturally alien.[1] While outside influences are not necessarily negative, and often can be helpful under the right circumstances, it is dangerous for children when even the purest of intentions are divorced from the facts of life that determine how they grow up. Children can be crushed between abstract values given the force of law and the intractable realities of their everyday lives. Values unmediated by the facts of life can result in laws or their application that perversely harm the very children they are meant to help, and the previous chapters have suggested that, in the case of laws regarding child work, such unanticipated effects on children have in fact been a big problem.

Damage of this type is sometimes shrugged off as nothing but an unfortunate incidental cost of defending children's rights.[2] To most child advocates such a position is not acceptable, and UNICEF, the Save the Children Alliance, and many other child defence organizations have been calling for a more child-centred approach to framing and applying both national laws and international standards.[3] Such an approach would not negate the existing values, but would add to them a profound respect for the rights, needs, and situation of individual children. It is argued that the well-being and development of children, not an abstract principle of law, should be the departure point for all protective action, including that against abuse in the workplace. An approach that begins with the reality of children does not necessarily conflict with ideologically driven perspectives, but filters and orientates them so that their impact on children will be constructive.

Key elements of a child-centred approach

What more child-centred thinking would introduce into child labour laws and standards is not a superior moral posture, but a new conceptual point of departure based on two factors that should orientate social norms governing the work of children. The first of these is empirical understanding of children's developmental dynamics, situation, aspirations, and socio-economic context. Child advocacy organizations insist that policy and practice must be informed by precise information and data about children who are the subject of national laws and international standards intended to protect them in regard to the world of work.[4] In practical terms, this means that national and international norms governing the work of children should be consistent with the findings of careful documentation, evaluation, and social science research.

The second element that must be present in a child-centred approach is children's own representations of themselves through word and action. This implies that children must be taken seriously and their participation guaranteed in the formulation of official norms governing their work.

This is because "the needs, rights, responsibilities, views and interests of children and adults are not necessarily synonymous".[5] While the right of children to participate in decisions concerning them is today widely touted and officially recognized by almost all countries, as will be discussed below, action to put that right into practice in the formulation of laws and standards is still incipient at best.

A more child-centred approach to national and international policies would change much that is now in them because they do not at the present time incorporate either solid understanding of children's circumstances and development or a serious appreciation of children's aspirations and ideas. In the absence of these two key elements of a child-centred approach, the protective effect of both national laws and international standards is, as earlier chapters have suggested, seriously undermined by a combination of ignorance and insensitivity. This chapter explores just a few of the implications of more conscientiously basing national and international legal norms governing the work of children on empirical research about children and on children's own self-representation.

State responsibility for protecting children from workplace abuse

The framing and implementation of national and international law is the exclusive right of states, working independently or together. They resolve some of society's problems and maintain their integrity through the rule of law. However, states often address social issues by legal means, not because the questions involved are best resolved that way, but because making laws is what they can do. Even in puzzling or complicated situations which governments have neither the wisdom nor the power to resolve, they often find it convenient to legislate national or international laws in order to at least signal their concern and good faith, or sometimes just to express hope for an eventual solution. In this case, the law is not intended so much to be literally enforced as it is to express a social aspiration; it becomes a symbol for what is desirable. Laws dealing with poverty and related social problems, including 'child labour', often have this symbolic function, among others. The fact that laws may play a symbolic role does not imply that they are unimportant, for symbols that articulate social aspirations can be powerful influences in shaping social ideas, values, and priorities. This is, it is suggested, an appropriate role for laws governing the work of children.[6]

States not only help manage mundane realities; they also help societies focus and articulate their dreams, and a society's dreams for its children are among the most important to which a government must give form and content. But there are two important problems inherent in a state's articulating a social vision. Firstly, there is the question of just whose ideas regarding the raising of children, among the many that compete for recognition, ultimately are incorporated into the national aspiration. If only dominant elites may define national policies for protecting and nurturing children, and if those policies are imposed by force on groups who did not participate in defining them, the children of those excluded may be brought to gross injustice and harm. Secondly, there is the matter of distinguishing between the dream and everyday reality. The best policies for moving society towards fulfilment of social goals may not be those that would be appropriate once these goals have been nearly reached.

Far from being merely theoretical, these are burning issues when considering the role of national law and international standards in governing the work of children. That is because, for most of the world, national values and policies regarding child work tend to be articulated by educated elites, often with special affinities for ideas from the North, without the participation of those who are most affected — children and their families.[7] And, in some cases, child labour laws which might be appropriate symbols of social aspiration for the future have been interpreted too literally and forced upon the poor insensitively, to the probable detriment of children and their families. The first issue for a government wishing to ensure that its laws benefit working children is to know how to use them artfully, providing them with the credibility of social inclusiveness and sensitivity to the rights and needs of children.[8]

If one were starting out today to devise social protections against the abuse of children's work, without being already influenced or constrained by an existing system, it is not at all obvious that one would opt for a government role as dominant or as punitively orientated as is that which is the currently prevailing model. The fact that we have such a model now in place is a matter of historical legacy. The notion that the work of children should be actively regulated by the State, the concept of a minimum age for employment linked to an age for education, and the idea of workplace monitoring by means of a public sector inspectorate were originally applied in England in the early 1800s to address child work in textile mills. Historians agree that this particular set of legal interventions had at least a short-term effect in reducing the number of child workers in the textile industry, although modern scholars tend to stress the greater long-term importance of other social and economic factors.[9] This earliest successful model of social intervention against the industrial exploitation of children was soon after adopted by virtually every industrialized country. It is important to note what sort of political context this model was designed to fit. It was developed first of all for use in the industrial sectors of relatively wealthy and quickly industrializing countries in western Europe. It was to be applied through the governments of unitary states and homogeneous societies in which citizens have vested central government with ample social and political legitimacy.

Over the period of more than a century from the invention of this model, the evolution of democracy towards increased political participation of working classes in western Europe and North America strengthened the social penetration of government. In the sort of national society that emerged, government possesses considerable influence to intervene in national culture, processes and institutions as the representative of a broader public interest. Public institutions of inspection and justice, even with all their imperfections, are also understood to represent a social interest beyond the mere personal interests of the particular officials involved. By the middle of this century, the societies for which this model was developed had achieved high average household income levels and had adopted state social and fiscal policies seeking to reduce broad disparities of income distribution and to abolish poverty. They closely resembled each other in many ways, but an enormous social, economic, and political gap existed between these rich countries and most of the rest of the world. Nevertheless, the legislative and enforcement approach to child work developed in Europe was transferred to many developing countries, at first through the colonial system and later with bilateral and multilateral assistance.

Almost all countries now have child labour laws that define the conditions under which children may work. They typically set a uniform minimum age below which no children are to be employed or to participate in certain kinds of economic activity, and they also indicate dangerous occupations or industries in which young persons are not to be engaged until they have reached a higher age, often that of adulthood. In many countries, the age at which children may legally begin to work is coordinated with the age up to which school attendance is compulsory. They may also stipulate the processes for granting eligible children permission to work, such as the issuing of licences or medical clearances. Legislation also provides for a public sector corps of labour inspectors whose job it is to visit workplaces in order to ensure their compliance with the various laws governing health and safety, wage payments, labour relations and other matters, one of which is child work. Most countries also provide for adjudication of labour law cases in special or regular courts, and for penalties such as fines, de-certification or even imprisonment.

In many developing countries the concepts and mechanisms transferred from European and North American experience have encountered a social, economic and political context radically different from that for which they were originally developed. First of all, most developing countries have relatively small industrial sectors; working children are overwhelmingly found in rural areas. Many countries have ethnically and lingually diverse populations, in the face of which central government may not have much influence over culturally diverse social customs regarding the raising of children, which is considered a local matter. In the more extreme conditions, political and social legitimacy of the State may not be accepted equally by all citizens; government may be seen by many not as the representative of all national society but as a symbol of ethnic, tribal, racial or other division and discord. In such instances there may be stiff resistance to government attempts to set national norms for family economic behaviour. Or, owing to corruption, labour inspectors and other officials may be regarded less as representatives of the public good than as privileged individuals using public office to accumulate private wealth or power. Moreover, many poor countries find it difficult to finance the implementing structure required to monitor and apply even modest labour legislation in easily served urban areas. Perhaps most importantly of all, relatively few developing countries have been able to devise fiscal policies that effectively expand employment and income or otherwise stabilize the household economy of the poorest deciles of society. Taking all these special problems of the poorer countries into consideration, it is not surprising that legislative and enforcement approaches to children's work originally designed for European culture and conditions may not have produced in developing countries the same results that were achieved in industrialized countries.[10]

But the reasons for apparent differences between industrialized and developing country effects of child labour laws may be even more subtle; the effects of child labour laws even in the North may not be as is generally imagined. Historian Hugh Cunningham demonstrates in his study of changing English attitudes towards children of the poor through the last few centuries that social ideas about what works and does not work for children — notably including expectations about interventions in children's work — are formed more by popular myths about history than by the facts of history.[11] And, indeed, studies of child labour in present day England raise grave doubts about how well the system of child labour legislation and enforcement invented there, and later transformed into a universal model, really works even in the country of its origin.[12]

Whatever the merits of the model, it is today taken for granted that all countries should establish a clear legal and enforcement structure to deal with the work of children. The ILO, UNICEF, and all major child advocacy organizations agree that every state should make a strong legislative commitment to the protection of its children against abuse in the workplace. The question is exactly what should go into that legislation, and on that matter there are some differences of opinion. It is also recognized that this approach is not by itself adequate to effectively protect children. The ILO has long recommended a 'multi-pronged' strategy that involves simultaneous lines of action on several fronts such as education, health, and social mobilization, along with legal interventions.[13] In some places and under some conditions, the social impact of national law and its enforcement is so limited that legal approaches to children's work can scarcely function at all, and more weight has to be placed on the development of other child protection strategies. If children are to be effectively protected, it is essential that laws do not stand in isolation, but that they be conceived and implemented to fit the reality of their social context and to work harmoniously with other lines of action in a national policy.[14]

At this point in time, two important international conventions articulate principles that are intended to guide countries in fashioning national legislation in respect to child work. They are the ILO Minimum Age Convention, 1973 (No. 138) and the 1989 United Nations Convention on the Rights of the Child. Each approaches the issue of child work in its own particular way. Each brings its own particular view of childhood and of child protection. For the purposes of our discussion, it is convenient to utilize these two orientating conventions as the departure point for a brief exploration into the possible implications of taking a more child-centred approach to legal norms governing the work of children.

International standards orientating national legislation on child work

The ILO Minimum Age Convention and related instruments

The initial international convention against 'child labour' was adopted in 1919 as one of the first items of business of the newly established International Labour Organization. Such an international instrument against the industrial employment of children was sought by activists in Europe and North America, where the problem was considered to be one of the most important social issues of the time. Being orientated by the European experience, the convention prohibited children below the age of 14 from working in industrial establishments. In subsequent years it was succeeded by a series of additional conventions which expanded the application of the minimum age principle to other economic sectors. In 1973, the ILO passed a more comprehensive convention to consolidate, succeed, and improve upon all the previous child labour conventions. This was the Minimum Age Convention, 1973 (No. 138), hereafter referred to by either its title or its number. It expanded prior sectoral coverage to now include "all employment or work", thus applying its provisions to all sectors of economic activity, and beyond just wage employment. Only child work in education institutions and on small family farms that produce for local consumption was exempted. Activities technically considered to be non-economic, such as maintenance work in one's own home, were excluded by definition.

States ratifying the Minimum Age Convention are called upon to establish a national policy to eventually abolish children's involvement in "employment or work" by progressively raising the minimum age for admission to work consistent with "the fullest physical and mental development" of young persons. This clause makes three telling assumptions. The first is faith in the efficacy of government when working through formal policy. The second is the supposition that raising the legal minimum age for admission to work is so powerful a weapon that it should be the centrepiece of national action against the economic participation of children. The third assumption is that the physical and mental development of children will be enhanced by excluding them from all work until at least middle adolescence. It seems to us that each of these assumptions is open to question in light of the enormous diversity between and within countries. While some governments are indeed powerful or influential enough to make such a policy effective in their societies, many are not. As will be seen later, the minimum age strategy has proved rather weak and patchy when applied to non-industrial and developing country settings, which is of course where the vast majority of child work and exploitation is concentrated. And, as Chapters One and Two explained in considerable detail, the effects of work on children's development are not necessarily age-dependent and, even when age is a factor, it does not seem to apply uniformly across cultures and conditions. Moreover, child work has positive as well as negative potential for children, and prohibiting engagement in it until almost adulthood may result in costs as well as benefits to children's development.

States ratifying Convention No. 138 are obliged to establish one or more minimum ages for the admission of children to employment or work. There should be at least a general minimum age, fixed according to the principle that the lowest age at which children can be admitted to work should be no less than the age through which children are required by law to be in school. The convention stipulates that this age should not be under 15, but then allows countries with relatively undeveloped economies and educational facilities to temporarily adopt a lower standard of age 14, provided that employers' and workers' organizations are consulted and agree. There are other minimum ages as well. The convention sets a lower limit of 18 for involvement in work that is "likely to jeopardize the health, safety or morals of young persons", but will allow children as young as 16 in such work if they have been adequately protected and instructed. The ILO points out that use of the term 'likely' is important, because it intends to take into account the fact that "activities which are not in themselves hazardous may become so in certain circumstances".[15] It is left to countries to designate work that is to be considered hazardous. The convention sets a lower minimum age for admission to "light work", which is understood as part-time work that is in no way hazardous and that does not impede schooling. This age is generally to be set at no younger than 13, but may be lowered to 12 for those countries with poorly developed economies and education facilities. It should again be noted that the convention explicitly exempts from its minimum age provisions, work carried out in the programmes of education institutions subject to consultation with workers' and employers' organizations.

A very important provision of the convention permits countries to decide that some sectors may be excluded from minimum age coverage if they raise serious problems of application. What these might be is left vague, although in the context of discussions leading up to the convention it appears that this clause is meant to accommodate types of employment that are very difficult to inspect, such as small family undertakings or domestic work.[16] The practical importance of this provision is that those sectors and occupations in which children mostly work — small agriculture, the informal sector, and domestic service — tend not to be covered by national laws which apply mostly to industrial undertakings in which only a small percentage of children are employed. There is a limit to this flexibility, however, for the convention does not permit the exclusion of certain important sectors, including mining, manufacturing, construction, and plantation agriculture, among others, which are considered to be especially dangerous.

It is important to recognize that, in line with the usual practice of the

ILO, Convention No. 138 was drafted through a formal process involving representatives of the organization's constituents — governments (usually represented by labour ministry officials or professional diplomats), trade unions, and employer associations — as well as lawyers from the secretariat. It does not pretend to be a product of social scientists and child welfare and development experts, who in fact were little involved. Like many or most conventions, its inspiration is more political than technical. The convention's assumptions, approach, objectives, and provisions reflect the primary orientation of its authors toward economic and labour market issues, a natural outgrowth of the ILO's mission to promote employment and economic justice.

An accompanying set of optional suggestions (Recommendation No. 146) was adopted at the same time as Convention No. 138 in order to help countries establish and implement a national policy to withdraw children from the labour market. It especially advocates the expansion of employment and education and welfare facilities so that the economic participation of children will be neither necessary nor attractive. The convention and accompanying recommendation are quite conscious of the poverty element in child work, and they attempt to deal with it by being flexible. Recommendation No. 146 also calls the attention of governments to the basic social infrastructure they must provide if children are not to keep on flowing into the labour market.

As mentioned above, the dream that Convention No. 138 is designed to help realize is one of social and economic justice, a free and democratic society in which all work-seeking adults can find dignified employment without exploitation and live and raise their families beyond the grip of poverty. This is a vision closely allied to the historical concerns of trade unions, and of modern social concern for peace and fairness in the workplace. Seen through these eyes, the employment of children is perceived to pose a threat to adult employment and wages. It is also thought to perpetuate poverty and social injustice. The convention was designed to, among other things, neutralize these threats. Ultimately, Convention No. 138 is meant to be more about the health and development of society than about the health and development of children.

As of mid-1997, 52 countries had ratified Convention No. 138. While on the surface this appears to be a reasonable number, as far as most ILO conventions go, the subscribing countries tend to be small and not among the most worrisome cases. For example, only about five per cent of the population of developing regions lives in countries that have ratified the convention, and no Asian country is yet a member as of the date of writing. The ILO recognizes a certain developing country resistance to ratification, and attributes it largely to the convention's complexity.[17] Others would mention additional factors. For example, some societies traditionally incorporating children into family economic pursuits as an integral part of their socialization may be uncomfortable with the broad range of activities ("all employment or work") proscribed by the convention. Other countries may feel that, in the face of massive poverty, they cannot for the time being implement the provisions of the convention, and they see no point in attracting the inevitable criticism that would result from making commitments they cannot keep. Moreover, most countries already have ratified other ILO conventions that also can be used against the abuse of children in the workplace. Even the new ILO Homework Convention (No. 177), adopted in 1996, incorporates a minimum age provision, and its accompanying recommendation (No. 184) suggests lines of action to help eliminate children's involvement in homework.[18]

Perhaps the most important of these related instruments is Convention No. 29, a basic human rights convention dating from 1930. It prohibits forced labour, which is defined as "work or service which is exacted from any person under the menace of any penalty and for which the said person has not offered himself voluntarily". For various reasons, many countries have found this convention, and their own laws based upon it, more useful than Convention No. 138 for legally attacking some of the most egregious work violations of children's rights. It is relatively clear and straightforward to define and prosecute cases of forced labour — such as when children are virtual prisoners of their employers — and since most societies readily agree that their children should not work in conditions of slavery, it produces few political problems. Indeed, ILO committees that regularly review the performance of states in regard to this and other conventions have in recent years examined a number of cases of forced or compulsory labour of children under the aegis of this convention. The forced labour convention has, for example, been useful in attacking child prostitution, which is in line with the fact that the United Nations Working Group on Contemporary Forms of Slavery also classifies the sale and sexual exploitation of children as a form of slavery.

Comparing the ratification and application experience of Convention No. 138 with that of Convention No. 29 has suggested to some that an international standard targeting children in the most hazardous forms and conditions of work — in which general world-wide consensus could be expected — might be more successfully ratified and implemented than one that applies far more broadly and controversially to virtually all work.[19] As Chapter Six will describe, views of a wide variety of organizations concerned with child work issues seem to be gradually converging towards a consensus that the top priority for national and international action should be concentrated on the worst forms and conditions of work and the children most at risk. For example, the ILO and UNICEF recently collaborated in a publication making precisely this argument.[20]

Accordingly, the ILO has now proposed the creation of a new convention against the most intolerable forms of child work. In an early formulation of the idea, it is intended to include the following sorts of work:

- Firstly, forms of labour or activity that are contrary to fundamental human rights; for example, work performed by a child in slavery, debt bondage, bonded labour or other slavery-like practices; child prostitution; or the use of children in drug trafficking or the production of pornography;
- Secondly, work which, because of its nature or the conditions in which it is usually performed, exposes children to particularly grave hazards to their safety or health or prevents them from attending school normally, it being understood that such work would be regularly identified by the competent authority in each country following consultations with the representative employers' and workers' organizations in the various branches of activity, as well as representatives of other appropriate groups of civil society.[21]

It is proposed that this new convention provide for rigorous sanctions, possibly including penal sanctions, for those using children in the situations covered. It would be made clear that the provisions of this convention would not apply to forms of child work that do not endanger the development, safety, health, or morality of children. The ILO secretariat suggests that the new convention also include a commitment by member states to formulate and implement a national policy aimed at gradually eliminating these other forms of child work. This proposed provision is roughly similar to Article 1 of Convention No. 138, and is intended to serve the same purpose. Some have noted that it may represent an attempt to slip the broad Convention No. 138 commitment to eliminate all work into a more palatable convention that more countries might ratify. At any rate, a ratifying country would through this provision be expected to eliminate kinds of work that are not even necessarily detrimental to children, let alone "intolerable". There is a question whether such a provision would not import into the new convention an issue that has impeded widespread ratification of Convention No. 138, namely, the obligation to eliminate even child work that is in no way harmful to children if it is below the stipulated minimum age.

One noteworthy principle of the new convention would be compensation and rehabilitation measures to be offered to children and their families when removing children from intolerable forms of work. Such a provision would represent a highly significant step towards direct consideration of children's needs and rights, and in that sense an important advance over Convention No. 138.

Discussion on the new convention is scheduled for the 1998 and 1999 meetings of the International Labour Conference (the ILO's policy-making body, which meets annually). Although the minutely prescribed procedures that the ILO must follow in developing a new convention provide only for direct participation from its formal constituents (governments and workers' and employers' organizations), the ILO has indicated its intention to open indirect participation to NGOs, working children's organizations and others through the establishment of special consultative mechanisms.[22] Until that time, positions on the conventions are fluid. For example, as of the time of writing, it appears that the ILO is backing away from defining as "intolerable" work which interferes with schooling, presumably for fear that such a provision might erode support from certain important countries. Of course, that does not change the ILO's overall position, which remains clearly against work that denies an education.

The United Nations Convention on the Rights of the Child

In 1989 the General Assembly of the United Nations adopted a new convention which commits its ratifying states to the observance of a whole package of children's rights. It grew out of a desire by child advocacy organizations to consolidate widely dispersed and frequently vague guarantees of children's rights into a single document treating children holistically and requiring states to create proper mechanisms for their implementation. As in the case of the ILO conventions, it was heavily influenced by industrialized country concepts and experience. The Convention on the Rights of the Child has now been signed or ratified by virtually every country in the world, making it the most widely accepted human rights treaty in history. One article (Article 32) of this convention is devoted specifically to the work of children. It obliges member states to "recognize the right of the child to be protected from economic exploitation and from performing any work that is likely to be hazardous or to interfere with the child's education, or to be harmful to the child's physical, mental, spiritual, moral or social development." The term 'child labour' is not used in the convention, but can be construed in context to mean any work done by children which presents the dangers specified in this clause. This requires going beyond immediate threats to health and safety to also encompass concerns for a child's education and overall physical, mental, and social development. The social objective to be served by protection is the holistic development of children, which broadens the earlier Convention No. 138 concept that the minimum age should be set at an age level that will promote children's fullest physical and mental development. Article 32 also reflects Convention No. 138 in stipulating that member states shall establish a legal minimum age or minimum ages for admission to employment, although no specific ages are indicated. It also commits member states to regulate the hours and conditions of children's employment, extending protection in the workplace for children who do work, and to provide for effective enforcement of the law through penalties and other sanctions.

The CRC's broad concern with the multi-dimensional development of children is also reflected in the wide variety of rights the treaty includes. There is one underlying principle, however, which orientates the application of all these rights. It is the Article 3 requirement that "in all actions concerning children ... the best interests of the child shall be a primary consideration". In the context of the full convention, this means that all policies and programmes that affect children are bound to take into consideration the full gamut of children's rights and needs. In dealing with the issues of child work, for example, policy-makers and programme-planners should plan their initiatives not only in accordance with Article 32, but also with other pertinent rights stipulated under the CRC, including the right not to be discriminated against (Article 2), the right to life and development (Article 6), the right to birth registration (Article 7), the right to remain with parents (Article 10), the right of children to express their views in all matters affecting them (Article 12), the right of free association and assembly (Article 15), the right of protection from physical and mental violence (Article 19), the right to health and health facilities (Article 24), the right to a standard of living adequate to support the child's development (Article 27), the right to education that develops the child's personality and talents to their greatest potential (Articles 28 and 29), the right to rest and leisure (Article 31), the right to freedom from sexual abuse and trafficking (Articles 34 and 35), and the right of rehabilitation from exploitation and abuse (Article 39).

Because of the nearly universal ratification of the CRC, virtually all countries are now committed to protect children according to its multi-dimensional criteria. Few, if any, however, have yet realized the practical implications or worked out the procedures for applying a holistic perspective to policy and programmes in each sector of concern. In framing a national policy on children's work, for example, what actors and means should be utilized to ensure that all rights guaranteed under each of the above-mentioned articles are properly considered and reflected in the resulting policy? Also, how should a country balance the various rights when they cannot all be met equally, or, more vexingly, when they conflict? What does one do, for example, in cases where immediately applying the right to a standard of living adequate to permit the child's development may conflict with the right to education, or the right to education may conflict with the right to freedom from violence? Are some rights to be preferred over others and, if so, by what criteria? Who should decide that sort of trade-off and how? The answers to such questions are not yet clear, and probably will not become so until they have been lived through and learned from in the crucible of experience.

Applying a child-centred perspective to the minimum age standard

The implementation of minimum age standards lies at the heart of the ILO Minimum Age Convention and constitutes the main action called for under Article 32 of the Convention on the Rights of the Child. It is in fact the linchpin of legal approaches to dealing with children's work. Therefore, it merits closer examination to discuss how it might be affected by a more child-centred approach that recognizes the child development principles presented in Chapter One. In making such an analysis, one notes first of all that, in line with its European history, the minimum age standard expresses an ideal of childhood as a privileged phase of life properly dedicated only to play and schooling, and with an extended period of dependence during which economic activity is discouraged or actually denied. Where it prevails as the custom, this model of childhood seems so natural and right that it is assumed to represent the universal norm for how all children should be raised. Yet, as we pointed out in Chapter One, there is no scientific evidence that this particular sort of childhood produces children who are happier, better adjusted, or more fully developed than do other types of childhood. Quite to the contrary, we said, there is evidence that children thrive in a variety of different child-raising environments, including those in which they are raised to mature quickly and become economically productive at an early age. Responsible parents in many societies may consider a prolonged period of enforced dependency and economic isolation in which children are deliberately kept from learning important things they need to know to succeed in life a very odd way to raise children, and one perhaps even bordering on child neglect. The idea that this exotic child-raising philosophy should be enshrined in international law as the one to be preferred can seem a bit strange to them, which of course may be one reason that non-Northern countries have been so slow to ratify Convention No. 138.

The minimum age standard as conceived in the Minimum Age Convention and Article 32 of the Convention on the Rights of the Child restricts the freedom of all children below a given age to work for any of several reasons. In some cases it may be based upon the belief that all work is bad for young children below a given age. An example of this position at the national level comes from Sri Lanka where, as early as 1939, legislation prohibited all labour of children below the age of 12 as intrinsically harmful to their health and development and an infringement of their right to childhood. All work of children under that age is considered hazardous to their welfare and a violation of their right to be cared for and protected.[23] A country does not have to take so categorical a stand in order to justify the exclusion of young children from all work; legislation may prohibit it on the less extreme rationale that engagement in work places children at more risk of abuse than society should tolerate. According to this line of reasoning, the freedom of all children to work should be restricted in order to prevent harm to some of them.

A related but more operational justification of minimum age prohibitions is based on the practical problems of targeting workplace protection to just the children who require it. The Sri Lanka case, in which children between 12 and 14 are allowed to work under officially regulated conditions, has been cited in some detail as an example of the impracticality of trying to intervene on behalf of individual working children when their whole age group is permitted to work. Goonsekere graphically describes the difficulties of trying to prove in court that a particular type of work is harmful to children.[24] A totally different argument holds that children's work competes against their education, which education is more beneficial for both the children and society. Children should therefore be legally banned from all work in order to ensure their adequate schooling. This position has recently been eloquently defended as the most appropriate for Latin America.[25]

Recent years have seen increasing debate about whether a uniform minimum age standard is a good idea and, if it is, how it should be implemented. Each of the above lines of justification has come under attack. As Chapter One pointed out, the first rationale, the proposition that all kinds of work are detrimental to children, is not compatible with the findings of social science or with modern thinking about the processes of child development. It has been rejected by important NGO groups such as the Save the Children Alliance[26] and the International

Working Group on Child Labour[27] as well as by UNICEF[28] and the ILO.[29] It is widely recognized that the most fatal flaw of the Minimum Age Convention may be its explicit prohibition on all economic activity by young children (except that performed in educational institutions and on family farms producing for local consumption), regardless of the purpose or conditions of their work. As the ILO points out: "One of the major difficulties impeding ratification of this convention apparently lies in its very general scope. It covers all branches of activity and all types of work, both paid and unpaid."[30] Consequently, it suggests that an improved standard would not seek to so broadly prohibit all work, but would focus on priority cases, particularly what it calls the "intolerable forms of child labour":

> The reality of child labour today provides the best justification for standard-setting geared mainly to combating the intolerable forms of [child] labour. A close look at this reality has shown that not all forms of work are necessarily harmful to children and that certain activities, if they are appropriately regulated, may even be beneficial for the children themselves and for society, in particular if they further the transmission of occupational skills from one generation to another. For example, should one reject traditions that require children to provide limited assistance in the family undertaking after school or during holidays? Obviously not ..."[31]

The second rationale, the notion that denying all children the freedom to work will effectively protect the smaller number who otherwise would be at unacceptable risk, has been weakened by information suggesting that blanket prohibitions are turning out to be little more practical to implement than are targeted interventions against hazardous work. There seems to be widespread consensus that, for whatever the reasons, it has proved nearly impossible to monitor and control the work of children in the rural, informal sector and domestic service situations in which the vast majority of them work. While specific enforcement problems will be discussed later in this chapter, suffice it here to say that the inability to enforce laws for the huge majority of children undermines the logic of this argument.

Finally, the assertion that excluding school-age children from work is necessary to ensure their education has been virtually demolished by data indicating that many children successfully combine education and work, and that many work to be able to pay for their education. Moreover, the presumption that school drop-outs who work have abandoned their studies for that purpose has been eroded by an accumulation of information suggesting that huge numbers of children abandon school because of discouragement and disillusion with the school experience, and that they then seek work as a productive use of their time. In some places, more school drop-outs seem to be idle than working, although problems in data collection and interpretation might help feed this view. The issue of work as a detraction from schooling is further explored in Chapter Seven.

The question about the effectiveness and practicality of a minimum age approach to protecting children against workplace abuse, which ought to be primarily a technical issue for open research and discussion, is in fact a highly charged political matter that is difficult to discuss objectively. The problem is that not only does it question the worth of a central intervention at the very heart of national and international action to protect children against abusive work, but it also is surrounded by now venerable intellectual doctrines, institutional traditions, and ideological commitments that parties on all sides of the debate feel strongly about. Moreover, most societies do protect younger children more than older ones, as we indicated in Chapter One. Despite the discomfort it may entail, international discussion needs to address concerns that a blanket minimum age standard may be based on false or outmoded ideas about child development, that it may be incompatible with new concepts of children's rights, that it may be impractical to implement, and that it may be unreliable or even counterproductive in its effects on children. Questioning is not tantamount to pre-judging. All of these issues have at least two sides, and individuals and organizations of unimpeachable expertise and dedication to the protection of children can and do differ on them. But they are important issues in terms of their impact on children, and all policy-makers and child rights advocates seeking to serve the best interests of children should think them through carefully. For this purpose, it is useful to quickly summarize some other important issues that emerge from a consideration of minimum age standards in terms of child development.

The minimum age from a child development perspective

Both the ILO Minimum Age Convention and the Convention on the Rights of the Child refer to the fact that interventions in children's work should have the effect of promoting child development. It is plain in context that the framers and advocates of both conventions would expect the proper application of minimum age standards to result in more child development than would occur if they did not exist. This raises the logical question of whether the expected child development gains can be observed when minimum age standards are applied in real-life situations. The matter cannot at this time be resolved empirically, for there seems to have been no systematic research into the general child welfare and development effects of policies excluding children from work. There is not the slightest indication, based on accepted standards of research, whether or under what circumstances a blanket minimum age policy benefits or hinders the development of children. What one chooses to believe is a matter of faith, and on this issue there are divergent faiths.

This is rather startling when one considers that minimum age policy has been around for well over 150 years, and the ILO Minimum Age Convention for nearly a quarter century. One wonders how the assumptions behind so important an item of social policy could have been left untested for so long. A child-centred approach to policy certainly would place high priority on finding out whether this historical and continuing centrepiece of action against child work does in fact affect child development as expected. It might be noted that the question about child development outcomes is different from the one asking whether minimum age standards have been successful in removing children from the workplace, which issue has in fact been researched. It is generally conceded that minimum wage laws have at least helped to reduce children's involvement in the formal sector.[32] What is not known is how this successful exclusion from the workplace has changed the welfare and development of the children affected. It seems to have been assumed by government, trade unions, child protection groups, and others that the effect would naturally be good. This has to do with the fact that in earlier times the child work targeted for action was observably burdensome, dangerous or otherwise inappropriate for children. As the exclusion was broadened to include all work, regardless of type, however, this assumption would seem to be less justified. As Chapter One demonstrated, there is little reason to think that, as a group, children who do not work develop more successfully than children who do, and in some cases the reverse might be true. Since the question is open and important, it should be researched to understand both the child development benefits and costs of excluding all children below an accepted minimum age from work.

In the absence of direct evidence about such effects, one might inquire into what could be reasonably expected on the basis of modern understanding of child development dynamics. While this in no way resolves the question of what actually happens in practice, it does raise interesting and relevant questions for further exploration. We note, for example, that the minimum age provisions of the two conventions appear to presuppose universalist views of child development that are out of tune with the pluralist drift of present social science thinking reported in Chapters One and Two. In particular, they do not reflect the current understanding that 'childhood' is a culturally relative social construct that is not always age-based. The reliance on age-based legal prohibitions as implementing tools in Article 32 of the CRC and the detailed specification of various minimum ages in Convention No. 138 both attest to this. The crux of the problem is that they view age as the key source of vulnerability in the workplace and, while modern child development thinking would indeed recognize age as one important factor, it would not give it such pride of place at the very centre of national and international laws governing the work of children. As we pointed out in Chapters One and Two, other determinants of risk such as gender, ethnicity, household income, and access to basic education and health services, are at least as important as age and are probably more amenable to protective interventions through policy.

The notion of a single universal minimum age standard would also seem outdated in the light of present-day understanding of the great variety of social roles children may play and the many routes they may take to development. Moreover, the age specified by ILO Convention No. 138 as a universal standard (15 years) for admission to "all employment or work" is especially puzzling when viewed from a modern child development point of view. It is, for example, above the age at which girls in various societies are free to marry, have children and take on major family responsibilities, all of which define them as adults. Especially in rural villages, many children have completed all locally available schooling well before 15 and cannot be taken seriously by their community unless they have assumed proper work and family roles. Also, as Chapter One notes, in many societies conscientious families begin to introduce their children to appropriate part-time work, including participation in earning the family livelihood, at around 6 to 8 years of age, according to the child's ability to learn and accept responsibility. There is little inherent reason why such activities, usually important to a child's mental and social development, should be stigmatized under the blanket prohibition on "all employment or work".

The minimum age standard of 15 years of age becomes more understandable only when recognizing that it is based on a highly industrialized concept of work that imagines 'child labour' primarily in terms of full-time paid employment in mostly urban-based undertakings outside the family. Of course, as we have seen, the biggest block of children is thought to work part-time or seasonally in rural non-wage activities, including in their own families. The problem underlying Convention No. 138, and perhaps reflected in the CRC, may be that its authors viewed children's work in industrially orientated terms, using concepts and suppositions derived mostly from urban and formal sector experience, whereas the vast majority of working children are found in rural areas and the informal sector. A more child-centred approach would have paid more equal attention to all forms of child work and to children's own realities, taking the broader picture into full account even if the convention finally intended to address only, say, children working full-time outside the home.

One also notes in the conventions, and national laws based on them, a lack of awareness of the degree to which children mediate their own development. There is no reflection of modern findings that the development of children is strengthened when they participate in their own protection and advancement, and that treating children as powerless victims tends to be psychologically damaging to them. A child-centred approach would maximize opportunities for children to actively participate in their own protection, as increasing numbers are now doing through creation of their own formal and informal organizations. There is a sad irony in the fact that the ILO, which is the United Nations agency charged with defending and promoting the right of workers to organize in their own cause, has conceived of child workers or potential workers in thoroughly passive terms, having included in neither Convention No. 138 nor Recommendation No. 146 any provision for their self-organization, or even for their organization and protection as workers under the aegis of existing trade unions. The CRC does step gingerly in that direction, in that it includes a general right of children's participation (Article 12), but its provisions on child work (Article 32) prescribe only top-down protection through legislated prohibitions and their enforcement. These rather thin and conventional legal provisions, even if fully implemented, would in most countries still be inadequate for guaranteeing the broad child development called for in this section. We will return in Chapter Six to the subject of children's organization in their own protection.

Beyond evaluation applying modern principles of child development, a more child-centred perspective on the two conventions and their implementation could be had by listening to the experience and ideas of people who are in close contact with working children and child work issues. For the most part, these are people from NGOs that directly assist or advocate for working children. The Rädda Barnen postal survey of expert opinion on child work issues raises some interesting issues in regard to minimum age concepts. First of all, the 199 responses left it clear that even child advocacy and services organizations do not share the dynamic view of child development that is emerging from social science research. It is highly unlikely that they even know about it, for researchers and practitioners move in entirely different circles. Even respondent organizations based in developing countries tend to share the 'North' view of childhood as a series of universally age-based stages through which everyone passes more or less uniformly, and as a privileged time that should be reserved primarily for study and play. A majority feel that children below a designated minimum age should not work. They also believe that young children are generally at greater risk than older ones.

That said, there is some indication that respondents see age as a less important risk factor than is gender. Some also argued that, while the very young do need legal protection, there is no internationally valid standard minimum age, since this must be culturally determined. One respondent pointed out that a young person of 12 years of age is not considered by all societies to be a child. Another suggested that minimum age standards are necessary, but that they should be set according to country, and that all age limits should be reviewed every five years.

It is worth noting that, despite solid majority backing for minimum age laws, 77 per cent of the respondents in the Rädda Barnen survey agreed that social, educational and economic measures are more effective than are child labour laws in protecting children from work risks. However, a large majority of those agreeing with this view went on to comment that they believed both types of intervention to be necessary. This is very much in line with the multi-dimensional approach recommended by the ILO and others.

Chapter One pointed out in some detail that different protection strategies have different developmental effects on children, and that these effects should be explicitly considered when deciding on protective approaches. This raises the question of what might be the developmental impact of the inclination, implicit in both conventions, to isolate children from risk, whereas many societies might prefer to prepare children through supervised experience to recognize and cope with dangers. The strategy of separating children from any work with hazards eliminates the risk that children might be harmed by it, but it also eliminates any chance they might benefit from it. This approach would seem reasonable where potential detriments to child development appear to be serious. The strategy of controlled exposure accepts some risk so that children have the opportunity to benefit from learning how to cope with it, which approach might be preferable only when the perceived risks to development are slight and the expected benefits very significant. The operational question is how to determine which strategy is preferable in a given situation. In the current absence of evidence that the 'protection through separation' approach apparently favoured in the two conventions is in fact generally superior, it might be sensible to allow more room for the 'protection through learning from direct experience' approach to be developed as well. This implies that a child-centred choice between removing children from work and protecting them in it should be determined not only by the nature and extent of the risks involved, except in patently dangerous situations where separation is a must, but also by the positive developmental potential of the remedy selected.

If adults working closely with children are divided on the question of the minimum age standards, what do working children themselves think? By all available evidence, children also are divided about the value of minimum age standards. Whereas the Rädda Barnen postal survey suggests that adults in favour of a minimum age standard might well be a majority, there is no equivalent international survey of working children. Based on an impressionistic overview of local surveys appearing in the published and unpublished literature, recent meetings in which working children have participated, and responses on the Rädda Barnen survey of children, however, it would appear that the trend among children probably is towards scepticism of minimum age provisions but not necessarily their rejection. Some are solid supporters of a minimum age strategy. For example, the National Movement of Street Children (MNMMR) in Brazil backs minimum age standards because, among other reasons, it feels they direct social attention and energy towards creating a future in which children below 14 hopefully will not have to work. Working children's movements from other Latin American countries, on the other hand, tend to oppose the idea that children below a given age should be systematically excluded from work altogether, although they do not indicate objection to limits that protect children from detrimental situations. They point out that making children's work uniformly illegal essentially criminalizes it and provides hostile or corrupt authorities with a convenient pretext for violence and extortion against them. Targeted regulations to guarantee their safety would, on the other hand, tend to place the law on their side.

What does all this mean for policy-makers and others wishing to make child labour legislation more child-centred? First of all, there is a clear warning that the child development benefits of blanket minimum age laws need to be demonstrated rather than merely presumed. By the same token, they should not be assumed not to exist. Our suggestion is that the minimum age standard should be open to question for serious research and policy analysis, and that it should be addressed as a technical question rather than as a political one. We do not take the position that the minimum age standard is inherently useless or counterproductive, although misuse can sometimes make it seem that way. Even if it turns out to be true that the ILO Minimum Age Convention overreached itself in encompassing "all employment or work", as we tend to think is the case, that does not by any means disqualify more carefully targeted use of age criteria in those circumstances where they can be shown to be relevant and constructive. It is up to research and evaluated experience, however, to provide a clearer indication of what the appropriate circumstances for their use may be. They almost surely will not be universal. Most would agree that there is some age at which children are too young to be, for example, in paid employment outside the home, but that age may differ with place, gender, and so forth. The point is that minimum age interventions should be based on empirical understanding of the particulars and children involved, and be planned accordingly.

It could be that determination of specific age limitations would be better made locally than nationally or internationally. Perhaps the precise level and operation of minimum age laws could be made more useful for children if they were orientated by properly diagnosed local conditions, maybe employing research strategies suggested in Chapter Four, than by blanket national or international standards which may or may not be appropriate to a given situation. To the extent that this is true, it suggests that the protective purposes of international conventions and national laws might best be served by decentralizing and devolving minimum age decisions to levels best able to relate them to specific situational needs and characteristics. Also, there is an implication that children should have a role in determining what is in their best interest. Without detracting from a Chapter Six discussion of working children's participation, suffice it to say here that, when working children oppose a legal approach that cannot be effectively enforced upon them, it becomes too weak a tool to be effective. It is difficult to imagine how any human rights instrument could remain credible when the very people it is intended to protect denounce it as injurious rather than helpful to their situation. Clearly, it is necessary either to help working children understand that existing minimum age laws and standards do in fact protect them or, on the contrary, to amend these laws and their application so as to gain the support of the children involved. In either case, substantial dialogue with working children is necessary to arrive at a solution amenable to them.

The question of enforcement

Child labour law enforcement issues, faced from a child-centred point of view, throw into high relief the question of what should be done to enforce the law when it is apparent that the law and the best interests of children do not coincide. Approaching enforcement issues from a child-centred perspective necessitates a radical revision in how 'enforcement' is defined, the purposes it serves, and the lines of action it implements. It raises disturbing but unavoidable questions about the role of the State and the degree to which it should be trusted to use its power to fulfil rather than to distort or subvert its protective responsibilities for working children. In the case of ambivalence about state trustworthiness, it becomes necessary to pose additional questions regarding what other alternatives are available for providing children with needed protection from workplace abuse. This in turn raises thorny questions about the citizenship status of children, including what should be their rights when systems intended for their protection work against them. This is a huge subject lying mostly beyond the limitations of this chapter. We will raise only a few issues to help encourage the thinking of others.

The conventional model of child labour law enforcement

The literature dealing with child labour legislation and enforcement is virtually unanimous in pointing out that the failure of legal approaches to protect children owes more to failures of enforcement than of legislation, even though the latter can be a factor. This failure is generally blamed primarily on problems with the government inspectorate which, under the model inherited from experience in the North, is supposed to regularly visit and inspect all work sites, impartially ensuring that their operations and conditions are in accord with the law. Even though the civil service inspectorate was invented in England specifically for dealing with the use of child workers, its tasks have since been expanded to include inspection on a full gamut of issues regulated by law and ranging from workplace health and safety concerns to employer—employee relationships. In most places, concerns about child workers today comprise a relatively minor part of the inspectorate responsibility. The system is highly formalized, with inspectors working under set procedures prescribed by law. Employers are in most places required by the law to maintain an up-to-date register of all children working for them, providing information on their ages. The basic task of visiting inspectors is to confirm that only children registered are working at the site, that their ages are in accord with minimum age laws, and that their hours and conditions of work meet standards laid down in legislation or administrative rules. The latter typically include prohibitions on the presence of children in certain industries or occupations deemed hazardous and limits on the hours and conditions in which children below certain ages may work. In some countries, children must have a licence from the government, and perhaps a medical and school attendance certificate as well, in order to work legally. Where applicable, it is the job of labour inspectors to confirm that any working children have met these conditions to be eligible for work.

There is no secret about why this system is not working well to protect children. In developing countries, government inspection services usually reach only the urban formal sector, and that neither well nor frequently. Typically, each inspector is responsible for visiting several hundred or more firms, and it is far from unusual to find that their caseload is so great that they cannot manage to visit each workplace even once a year. Even these visits may be rapid and cursory. In many countries the inspector is barred from making surprise visits and must arrange all inspections with the employer in advance. Inspectorates are commonly short of qualified and trained personnel and of transportation and travel funds necessary to reach rural areas and small towns outside core metropolitan areas. Inspectors tend to be relatively low-level public servants who are poorly paid, and this often gives rise to corruption. By all accounts, the labour inspector's job is in many places granted as political patronage in full expectation that the incumbent will make use of it to secure lucrative bribes and favours. In these situations nobody even expects the inspectorate to offer a public service other than a guarantee not to harass those who are properly paid up. It is not only employers who must pay off corrupt inspectors. Child workers in factories and other businesses reachable by inspection routinely report pay-offs to inspectors among their problems and expenses.

Other problems faced even by the most honest and conscientious labour inspectors include opposition from working children and their families. They find it thoroughly discouraging to be feared and hated by those they supposedly are protecting, and prefer to devote their limited time to less stressful matters than enforcing child labour laws. Last but not least, inspectors frequently complain about political interference to protect particular businesses, or all business in general, from rigorous inspection. Sometimes this is a matter of informal policy from governments wishing to create a climate that will attract outside investment and create more business and employment.[33] It is not unusual for government inspectors to collude with employers in the exploitation of children. For example, in an in-depth case study of the experiences of 12 girls laid off from a Morocco clothing factory, described in Chapter Eight, the informants detailed how government labour inspectors refused to do their legal duty to help the children make complaints against employers or claim wages they had been cheated out of.[34]

Conventional enforcement procedures are not working very well even in the industrialized countries for which they are best suited. For example, surveys of work by school children in Great Britain found that the vast majority of their jobs presented one or more legal violations.[35] Inspector caseloads in industrialized countries are not necessarily lighter or easier to handle than those in many developing countries. It should be noted, however, that industrialized country 'child labour' law violations mostly tend to revolve around relatively minor issues such as working hours and rarely include gross abuses, such as bonded labour, highly hazardous work, and violence against young workers that are common in some developing countries.

The usual complaint about enforcement systems is that they do not manage to enforce the law. Assuming that this is the proper measure of their success, the ILO has devoted considerable attention to the issue of what can be done to upgrade inspectorate performance in regard to children's work, including through formal training courses and materials. This is seen mostly in terms of improving the frequency and quality of inspection, the proper identification and reporting of violations, the education of employers about child labour law and their responsibilities under it, and the motivation of business and industry to observe the law and to eliminate 'child labour'. The ILO has a fundamental policy commitment to the concept and institutions of government inspection of workplaces and has, over the years, provided much technical assistance to the establishment and improvement of public sector inspectorates in developing countries. There has always been nagging doubt about whether this peculiarly western institution, which sometimes seems designed to stand in splendid isolation from the rest of society, can be successfully grafted onto non-western societies having very different social dynamics. Perhaps no issue challenges the essential wisdom and viability of an independent government inspectorate more visibly than does child work. The ILO recognizes this and is attempting to rise to this challenge.

To begin with, the ILO has reviewed the enforcement problem in some detail, and out of that review it has produced a manual for the training of inspectorates in 'child labour' inspection procedures. The methodology promoted in this manual places high priority on a gentle, educative approach to both employers and working children. For example, it suggests workplace interviews not only with employers but also with working children themselves in order to obtain first-hand information about their work and background socioeconomic and family status. The idea is to help both employers and children resolve the problems that result in the workplace abuse of children, finding ways to make illegal work unnecessary.[36] Not everyone agrees with this 'soft' approach; some feel that the inspectorate should take a 'harder' line, rigorously enforcing the letter of the law and moving underage children out of workplaces as soon as possible.

The IPEC programme has made considerable investment in training courses and other action projects to improve inspectorate performance. While the ILO reports some encouraging successes, they have not been predictable or across the board, and it does not at this time appear that the provision of training alone can be counted upon to bring lagging inspection services to a level of adequacy necessary to meet the need.[37] The trouble is that training is an effective solution only where lack of inspector know-how and motivation are the main impediments to adequate performance. More often, it appears, the problems run far deeper and are therefore not resolvable by training alone. In that case, far more structural interventions are necessary to make major improvements. The ILO is attempting this strategy in Bangladesh, where it has been handed the opportunity to design and install a complete inspection system for the purpose of monitoring children's work in the export garment industry. This is a specialized semi-public system, established parallel to the government inspectorate but with its collaboration, which tests the degree to which it is possible to suppress and monitor children's involvement in an industry when all the required expertise, resources and procedures can be mobilized, even at considerable expense. It remains to be seen whether deep problems such as corruption, outside political pressure, employer suspicion, and others are amenable to solution. It is worth noting that various multinational firms and industry associations now trying to eliminate child workers from the manufacture of products they export from developing countries are creating private-sector monitoring systems rather than depending on the public sector inspectorates.

At the time of writing, it is still too early to draw conclusions regarding whether the ILO—IPEC initiatives will prove it feasible to achieve lasting improvement in government inspection systems that are adequate to the task and cost-effective. If these rather substantial efforts fail, the idea of enforcing child labour legislation through a government inspectorate may need to be reconsidered and the emphasis placed on other mechanisms for protecting children against workplace abuse.

Alternative means of monitoring and enforcement

Alternatives to government inspectorates have in fact been suggested, and it has been elegantly argued that at least one of them could be more effective and socially productive than is investment in law enforcement. The assertion is that the resources and effort necessary to improve and expand labour law enforcement would achieve a far better result if invested in education. The most elaborate and best-known version of this argument has been made in regard to India, where the high incidence of child work is attributed to the lack of adequate school facilities and to popular apathy toward education. It has been asserted by Myron Weiner in a well-known book[38] that a national policy of compulsory education (which India does not have), combined with investment necessary to make adequate education facilities available to everyone, could be expected to reduce full-time economic participation of children by far greater numbers than could be achieved by investing the same effort in improved and expanded inspection facilities. The argument that education can replace law enforcement in eliminating 'child labour' is controversial among experts. However, as Chapter Seven explores in detail, it is now generally accepted that achievement of universal education probably is a necessary condition for a permanent solution to the massive exploitation of children.[39] It has been noted that when the very poor state of Kerala in India managed to achieve universal basic education, children's full-time work declined to almost nothing despite the fact that no special effort was made during this time to enforce child labour laws.

A second alternative to enforcement through public sector inspectorates might be greater involvement by community groups and local governments in monitoring the work of their children and intervening when necessary by means other than the law. This has been done for a long time on an *ad hoc* basis by communities where the law and its agents do not reach, but the results have proved very uneven. Some have maintained that the way around the weaknesses of both local systems and government inspectorates is to forge operational links between the two. There is historical precedence in some industrialized countries for such cooperation between community activists and labour inspectors,[40] but so far such partnerships have not much advanced in developing countries. It has been suggested that the inspectorate could help support community initiatives, providing training and other forms of back-up, while the community could extend the reach of the inspectorate, and provide it with moral and political support as well.[41] While some exploratory activities do now link communities into the enforcement mechanism, a systematic model that can be taken to scale has yet to be developed and tested. We strongly suggest that such a model should be more intensely pursued and that working children themselves should be included as essential partners.

Even if education or community initiatives could completely replace law enforcement activities, which may not be possible, some believe that it is still worth retaining the latter. This is revealed, for example, in the Rädda Barnen survey of expert opinion on child work issues. In that study, two-thirds of the respondents agreed that working children, and children at risk of having to work, would benefit from strict application of 'child labour' laws. They generally felt that, if nothing else, this would move social and government thinking in the right direction. It would, as one Indian respondent put it: "force governments to take positive action regarding children living below the poverty level on one hand, and strengthen the hand of voluntary groups working toward the abolition of child labour on the other".

However, it must be noted that a vocal minority of the respondents were more concerned about the detrimental effects of a narrow focus on minimum age laws, and they tended as a group to argue for a more comprehensive approach to the problem which takes into account the cultural and socioeconomic situation. They maintained that strict application of the law is not the most effective way to deal with a problem as complex as children's work, which is linked to widespread poverty. As one of them said: "laws cannot provide a way to fill stomachs". It was suggested that blanket prohibitions on work provide neither protection for the moment nor a solution in the longer run and, that where children have no better alternatives, applying minimum age laws only makes the situation worse. Various respondents reported that enforcement of minimum age laws provides government officials such as labour inspectors with a chance to extort money from working children. One referred to them as "a purchasable commodity".

Working children themselves tend to take a more immediate view of the effect of law enforcement. Although some of them do leave their work under pressure from enforcement efforts, there is evidence that more of them are likely to look for ways to circumvent any inconvenient prohibitions on their work. For example, the Rädda Barnen study of working children asked what the children would do if the government tried to prohibit children under 15 from working. To pick but a couple of typical responses as illustration, a focus group of Ethiopian shoe-shine boys generated the following answers: (a) work secretly so the police will not find us; (b) change to an occupation that can be done indoors; and (c) show opposition through demonstrations, by writing to the authorities and by enlisting parents in opposition. A Philippine focus group of fishing children answered the same question as follows: (a) work secretly during the night or dawn; (b) work anyway as long as parents approve; and (c) do not work. Responses such as these suggest that children do not necessarily understand or sympathize with child labour laws or see their enforcement as in the interests of children, and therefore undermine them.

Enforcement issues raised by a child-centred perspective

The above-mentioned debate between 'soft' and 'hard' lines on law enforcement points directly to the most fundamental of issues raised by a child-centred perspective. What should be the ultimate objective of enforcement? Is it to enforce the law, or is it to protect the welfare and development of children? By extension, what is the proper measure of success for evaluating enforcement? Is it the number of inspections, prosecutions and fines? Is it the number of children turned out of workplaces, or the number of workplaces that do not hire children? Is it the number of children working in conditions that meet the specifications of the law? Is it perhaps the number of working children who attend school and work in safe environments?

The issue is crucial because, as is recognized by virtually everyone who has studied it, national 'child labour law' legislation tends to be a blunt instrument that, when insensitively applied to particular cases, can easily harm the children it is supposed to help. For that reason, conscientious inspectors have long been selective in applying the law, declining to push it when they sensed that the children involved and their families would be driven to even greater poverty and vulnerability. To many, this has represented a flaw in the enforcement system, a sort of dereliction of duty. On the other hand, it might also be regarded as a way in which the enforcement system protects the long-term credibility of the law by inserting flexibility where rigid application of the law would lead to counterproductive results and a loss of public trust.[42] One view places the letter of the law above all; the other places ultimate value on the welfare of children, presumably the purpose and spirit of the law. The second view is certainly more child-friendly, and it implies that the success of law enforcement ultimately must be measured by the welfare of the children involved.

From this perspective, an enforcement action that removes children from a workplace in accordance with the law, but which exacerbates their vulnerability in the process, should be counted a failure rather than a success. This idea has yet to be generally accepted; as of the time of writing, the various proposals for a global child labour monitoring mechanism to be situated in the ILO refer only to tracing how many children work, or are removed from work or hazardous forms of work. There is no reference to what happens to the children involved, when the point of the whole protection exercise should be to improve the lives of children. How can the success of child protection be assessed without inquiring into whether the protective activities actually improve the lives of children? This is an important question, given the tendency of insensitive enforcement to impinge on children's rights and well-being. It raises the issue of methods and indicators. How would one measure whether children are left better or worse off by protective policies and programmes in regard to their work? There are no apparent easy solutions, although some of the techniques discussed in Chapter Four are highly pertinent. Clearly, this is an area in which considerable research and evaluation technical capacity will be necessary.

The task is made no easier by the fact that an appropriate approach will surely require taking a holistic view of children's well-being and development, and a comprehensive perspective on their rights, as represented by the various relevant articles of the Convention on the Rights of the Child. A holistic approach to children's needs and rights suggests that the implementation of national and international standards must do two essential things that normally are not formally included inside child labour laws and their enforcement, but which sensitive inspectors have taken into consideration on their own. First of all, it must take into account the problem of poverty, which is to say the stark necessity that drives many children to work. And secondly, it must recognize and act upon the fact that some work is beneficial, including as a developmental learning experience. Taken together, they suggest that laws seeking to remove children from even hazardous forms of work need to be implemented in tandem with economic and learning activities that create viable alternatives to inappropriate work.

As noted elsewhere, children from many parts of the world, both developing and industrialized, have long been requesting work-study programmes that allow them to both earn and learn. Owing to institutional inertia, little attention has been paid to this issue. Moreover, some national and international organizations have discouraged this approach for children under the legal age for employment, fearful that it could furnish a pretext for abuse of children's work. That worry is doubtless merited, but the huge number of children who drop out of school altogether because they do not have practical alternatives for combining work and education should be of even greater concern. Article 6 of ILO Convention No. 138 opens the way to such cooperative solutions between education and work by specifically exempting from minimum age standards such work as is performed under the aegis of legitimate education institutions. This option needs to be much more aggressively explored.

Conclusion

This brief discussion identified and explored just a few of the many challenging issues that arise when a child-centred perspective is brought to the framing and implementation of national laws and international standards governing the work of children. Important questions concern the responsibility of the State, the social significance of child labour laws, the social source of values and objectives to be encoded in law, the inclusion of working children and poor families in the definition of laws, the compatibility of laws with child development dynamics and conditions, the various means and meanings of enforcement, and the monitoring of interventions to learn their effects on the children involved. Each of these issues easily merits a full chapter in its own right. The time is ripe for qualified persons in any of various disciplines to undertake a far more profound reconsideration of what it would mean to approach child work legislation and enforcement from a child-centred point of view, reassessing the value of both national laws and international standards, such as the minimum age mechanism, in light of rigorous empirical information about children and their situation and with the participation of children as crucial actors in representation of their own interests and aspirations.

CHAPTER SIX

Mobilizing Society
in the Best Interests
of Working Children

In order to be successful, any effort to protect children from abuse in the workplace must reach beyond legal measures and the confines of government to also mobilize the interest and creativity of civil society. Writers on the subject of child work policy are virtually unanimous on this point, and both the ILO and UNICEF have found social mobilization to be essential for dealing with detrimental child work. Such mobilization must in particular secure the involvement of those groups who are most intimately involved in the issue — working children and their families, employers, educators, and organizations providing basic services to children or advocating for their rights. This mobilization of broader society is essential for three reasons. Firstly, and most importantly, it is the only practical way to induce change in the ideas and practices of massive numbers of people. An attitudinal and behavioural transformation has to occur in both urban and rural areas, among both men and women, among both children and adults, and in all socioeconomic classes. Without such change, children simply will not be protected from dangerous work and abusive working conditions.

Policy-makers and programme-planners face the question of how to get large numbers of people to adopt the changes required in order to better protect children from work-related harm, and then to make those changes. One way, of course, would be for government to coerce the desired behaviour through the force of the law. As Chapter Five pointed out, however, that has been tried and, despite some limited success in the formal sector, labour inspection and enforcement do not effectively protect most children. They simply do not penetrate society very deeply even under the best of conditions, and they have virtually no potential at all to reach into the private homes, family farms, and small informal sector establishments where the vast majority of working children are to be found. The plain reality is that change in most children's work patterns and conditions depends almost entirely on the voluntary behaviour of people who act out of conviction rather than fear.

A second need for social mobilization is to create an enabling cultural and political environment that encourages public action to protect children and dissuades predatory people from exploiting them. Government is often loathe to intervene in child work issues unless it is sure of ample political support from the public.

A third reason why social mobilization is necessary is that ending the detrimental work of children requires a set of different activities that no single part of society — including government — can carry out alone. A complete strategy for protecting children from harmful work may involve changes in legislation, research and statistical methods, private sector employment and supervision practices, media communication about children, health, recreation and welfare services for children, literacy and other non-formal education programmes, family economic security, community organization for children's protection, and employment and income opportunities for the poor, among others. The specific activities that must be included vary with place and conditions, but they almost always imply a team effort that demands cooperation between government and the various sectors of civil society, including children and their families. Social mobilization is best conceived of as the process that brings all these necessary pieces and actors together.

But simply getting people together to undertake cooperative action is not enough. The joint effort has to be channelled in the right directions. There is the problem, for society can mobilize to do the wrong things as well as the right ones, and this in fact happens as regards the work of children. Previous chapters already have indicated that not all interventions intended to protect working children succeed in doing so, and Chapter Eight will describe how international campaigns mobilizing public opinion against 'child labour' in international trade have in some cases rebounded negatively on the children involved. In such instances, it is not surprising when children vociferously protest that actions supposedly intended to protect them have in fact subverted their best interests and harmed them. It is no exaggeration to say that while social mobilization is absolutely necessary in order to protect children against abuse of their work, it is also a double-edged sword that can exacerbate the vulnerability of children when it is used carelessly. In fact, the irresponsible and arbitrary use of the consolidated power of mobilized society to protect children, when misguided, can be as dangerous to children as are the work-related risks that are being targeted.

Therefore, policy-makers and children's advocates wishing to enlist civil society against the workplace abuse of children must ask: "Which social mobilization approaches reliably protect children, and which approaches risk harming them?" While, as indicated in Chapter Four, a scarcity of empirical evidence makes this a difficult question to answer, combining available information with child development principles presented in Chapters One and Two makes it possible to identify certain key issues and to trace the outlines of a social mobilization approach that safeguards working children's best interests.

Social mobilization as a process of dialogue

How 'social mobilization' is conceived of and implemented can have an impact on how well it protects children. Many believe that democratic approaches involving all major interested parties in sustained dialogue and cooperation have the best chance of protecting children and avoiding counterproductive results. Mobilization can of course occur from the top down, as authoritarian states have demonstrated over the years. Or the strong can simply impose their will on the weak. However, modern societies valuing ideals of democracy and social justice prefer voluntary consensus arrived at through internal communication, discussion, and negotiation. For them, social progress occurs through commitments born of mutual agreement, as admittedly partial and imperfect as such a process must be.

For purposes of this chapter, social mobilization is considered to be the open and dialogical process through which a society consults with itself and collectively (1) identifies a particular problem and deems it important, (2) defines the social reasons and objectives for addressing it, and (3) agrees on lines of action and devotes resources to them. This democratic model is what United Nations agencies, international NGOs, and most governments have in mind when they call for social mobilization against exploitative and dangerous work by children. They generally believe that children's rights are best served by an unfettered, socially inclusive process of "internal discourse and cross-cultural dialogue".[1] Proceeding in this way, social mobilization works by changing culture, social attitudes, and social behaviour. As cultural values and priorities change, the spontaneous independent action of millions of individuals and their organizations also changes to reflect the new social attitudes and objectives.

This open dialogue has little in common with top-down, one-way public information campaigns that sometimes also are referred to by the term

Change growing out of true social dialogue reaches the roots of culture, the way people go about living their everyday lives.

'social mobilization'. In this case, a particular group simply sets out to sell its point of view to the rest of society, often with intensive use of the media. While this 'advertising' approach may be an effective way for one party to convey its views to the rest of society, a single-minded intent to persuade at the expense of also listening and learning undermines the search for common ground that is the hallmark of more democratic social mobilization.

There is a profound difference between processes in which a few powerful groups impose their views on the rest of a reluctant or apathetic society and the reciprocal dynamics through which a large portion of society evolves awareness, values, objectives, and behaviour in regard to a particular issue. While the influence of a top-down campaign may penetrate only as far as the power of the particular groups imposing their perspective, change growing out of true social dialogue reaches the roots of culture, the way people go about living their everyday lives. Change of this type is considered by most agencies involved in social development to be especially profound and self-sustaining, and therefore it is favoured by international NGOs, United Nations agencies, and others as the most powerful for increasing the protection of children. It is especially important in regard to dealing with children's work, in which the social penetration of the law is extremely limited and effective child protection must depend on huge numbers of people acting properly of their own accord and conviction. It needs to be noted, however, that preference for this dialogical model is based primarily on common sense reasoning, democratic values, and faith in participative processes. At least so far as we are aware, no social science studies have compared the relative merits of the 'social dialogue' and 'top-down' approaches to mobilization against detrimental child work, and the empirical case material available has not been systematized in such a way as to ask this question.

Considering the fact that the 'how to' literature on combating abusive children's work always recommends social mobilization among the essential activities, it is surprising to find that there is virtually no analytic literature which assesses what works and does not work. This may reflect a lack of awareness that social mobilization can go wrong for children, and that sometimes it might not work. There seems to be an assumption that anything a society gets together to do against the exploitation of children will be good for the children involved. Yet the Rädda Barnen survey of expert opinion included an open-ended question in which respondents were asked whether they knew of activities in which social mobilization had actually worked against working children rather than for them. A surprising number and variety of instances were cited, although some of them — like the now infamous Bangladesh case, to be discussed in Chapter Eight — were not from the direct experience of the respondents.

What does one do to avoid campaigns or other forms of mobilization that may hurt instead of help the children involved? One answer would be to try managing the process. The literature does suggest that broadly consultative processes of social dialogue and cooperation can be successfully catalyzed and managed. Various large organizations now do this on a national or international scale. For example, the ILO—IPEC programme seeks, as a part of its capacity-building strategy, to motivate "ILO constituents and other concerned partners to engage in a dialogue on child labour problems and create alliances to overcome them".[2] This dialogue may be local, national or international in scope, and it usually involves both organizations and individuals. The process may incorporate both formal and informal procedures, but must in any event be open to a wide variety of actors and ideas, and it must be able to accommodate a fair amount of spontaneous evolution. It usually entails broad and spirited public debate, and absence of debate may mean that proper communication is not occurring. It requires mechanisms by which this debate can come to fruition in actionable decisions that enjoy at least a reasonable degree of support both from those most affected and from the public at large. And, of course, social mobilization finally manifests itself in tangible action that melds diverse human and material resources, from various government and civil society channels, into roughly coherent movement toward agreed-upon objectives. In short, from what one can see in the existing experiences, social mobilization consists of starting and managing some form of social dialogue which leads to or affects concerted action.

It is now generally recognized that effective protection of children requires participation of non-governmental sectors ranging from children and their families through child advocacy and services organizations, to the various religious and educational organizations, service clubs, trade unions, and business associations. Countries lacking a civil society infrastructure are at something of a disadvantage for dealing with child work abuse. There also is a major role for the media. Experience also suggests that civil society, rather than government, usually must provide most of the moral, intellectual, and even much of the political leadership necessary to confront harmful child work effectively. The mobilization of civil society may be necessary even to motivate government to assume its own proper responsibility. As UNICEF puts it: "The best guarantee that a government will take its responsibilities seriously is when all sectors of society become involved in a genuine national movement. As the implications of child rights and the principles of the Convention of the Rights of the Child start to permeate society, attitudes, assumptions and values will correspondingly change."[3]

However, if the diverse parts of society are to cohere and cooperate in the battle against child exploitation, they must all be permitted voice and participation in developing a common vision and sense of purpose that can occur only through open dialogue. The history of the struggle against 'child labour' suggests that this dialogue can be extremely fertile, and that nurturing it is the central task in mobilizing a society to protect its children against abuse in the workplace. This is apparent even in early nineteenth century England, in which a new amalgam of labour organizers, middle-class crusaders, writers, educated elites, and parliamentary reformers managed to have an effect, at first on government policy and eventually on the prevalence of child employment itself. This success established an early mobilization model — "the twin forces of law and philanthropy".[4] As the phrase implies, it was constituted of parallel but cooperative actions by government to constrain demand for child workers and by civil society to raise public awareness and to provide for certain education and welfare facilities. In one form or another, this model has prevailed down to the present, and is today more commonly phrased in terms of a separation of roles between government and non-governmental organizations. In recent decades, social mobilization has been at the very heart of action against the abuse of working children in various developing countries. Reflecting new environments differing in important respects from countries of the North, these newer experiences not only have adapted the 'law and philanthropy' combination in new ways, but also have evolved other mobilizational ideas. Some of this experience has been reported on by the ILO and UNICEF, among others.[5] This base of new experience has been greatly expanded through a constantly growing number of countries, actors, and projects attacking the workplace exploitation of children, often with financial or technical support from the ILO, UNICEF, bilateral donors or international NGOs. Many of these new activities initiate or coordinate mobilizational strategies. The time is now ripe to review this experience, trying to answer the question of what approaches to social mobilization are most consistent with the best interests of working children.

Making social mobilization more responsive to children's best interests

A few case studies apart, the literature does not directly address the question of how social mobilization against detrimental child work affects the children involved. Only very recently are doubts being raised about the long-standing assumption that national and international campaigns against the workplace abuse of children are necessarily beneficial for children. This historical neglect to check on how generalized campaigns to rescue children from the presumed ravages of work have affected the lives of real children can be taken itself as a warning. The few case studies now trickling out confirm this warning; the cure can sometimes be at least as bad as the disease. A recent film from UNICEF in Bangladesh, for instance, explores what has happened to children who were laid off from garment industry jobs after a concerted campaign by American consumer, labour, and governmental forces against the involvement of Bangladeshi children under 15 in this industry. While some of the dismissed children have now entered special subsidized schooling belatedly provided for them, others are shown in work which is clearly even less appropriate and more hazardous for children than were the garment industry jobs from which they were sacked.[6]

In the absence of more developed analysis, modern social science thinking about children's development, presented as nine principles in Chapter One, can provide a convenient departure point for assessing the likely impact of mobilizational activities on children. Viewing the world through the lens of these principles immediately throws into relief a whole series of issues that are almost never mentioned in relation to social mobilization. The following discussion raises only a few of them, which is nevertheless sufficient to suggest how much is to be learned from testing social mobilization outcomes in terms of their welfare and development impact on the children involved.

Making room for diverse childhood

The modern understanding that there are many childhoods, and that different childhood contexts present very different growth and development challenges to children, should warn policy-makers and programme-planners wishing to mobilize society against simplistic assumptions about the problem they are dealing with. Even the most cursory look at historical and present-day mobilization activities aimed at eliminating 'child labour' reveals enormous gaps of misunderstanding not only between countries but between socioeconomic groups in the same country. There is the bizarre fact of frequent strong disagreement between some adults who are ostensibly 'helping' children and the children who are being 'helped'. Often there is a senseless and bewildering lack of communication, trust, and good faith between those whom one would ordinarily expect to be the closest and friendliest of allies — children in need, their families, and benefactors wanting to assure children's needs are met. In our practical experience we have found that, when poor children and their families argue against protective measures advocated by elites for their supposed benefit, their disagreement often is dismissed by the would-be 'benefactors' as ignorance, stupidity or even immorality to be expected of under-educated lower classes. Discrimination can too easily displace sensitivity. Rarely, it seems, does a government policy-maker, a trade union administrator, a salaried child advocate, or a professional expert stop to seriously consider the possibility that popular resistance to social agendas imposed from above may stem from essential factors that he or she has overlooked.

In retrospect, events do indeed sometimes confirm that children or their families have held views that might be interpreted as too immediate or too narrow to serve their own long-term interests. However, it also frequently turns out that working-class families and children may have all along possessed a far broader and more accurate picture of their situation than have reformers who complain of their intransigence. Elites, we must say, do not have a very impressive record in recognizing and responding constructively to the problems of the poor, which is one reason we called attention in Chapter Four to situation research methods, such as PRA, that community adults and children can undertake to define and address their own problems. A particular obstacle is the widely recognized fact that educated elites who make policies and plan programmes tend to have social agendas differing significantly from those of the poor, frequent rhetoric to the contrary notwithstanding. Even actions supposedly for the direct benefit of children may in fact virtually ignore the best interests of the children involved.

An example of the displacement of children's best interests by elite agendas can be found in the campaign to introduce government-funded schools and compulsory education in nineteenth century England, which has sometimes been seen as an important milestone in the struggle against 'child labour'. The provision of government-sponsored schooling is popularly considered an unqualified benefit for the poor, who are thought to have been overwhelmingly illiterate. However, social historians point out, most working-class children did in fact receive instruction through privately operated voluntary schools, often sponsored by churches and charitable institutions, which usually offered practical vocational skills along with basic literacy. These so-called 'free schools' generally had the flexibility to accommodate the various work schedules of children and, since families usually had to pay at least something for tuition, were responsive to what client families and children wanted and needed. Government schools, on the other hand, had less useful (that is, impractically academic) curricula and were renowned for treating children violently with beatings and other cruel punishments. This is hardly surprising since a government priority was to teach 'discipline' and nationalist loyalty to a lower class that the elites feared as potentially rebellious and unfit for submissive military service — apparently a rather greater government concern than was children's inability to read, write, and think critically. Despite prolonged popular resistance to them, government schools finally achieved a monopoly, not so much by winning over converts or providing a superior service as by introducing laws and regulations (ostensibly to ensure 'quality') that fatally hampered operation of the 'free' schools preferred by the poor. It seems that literacy among poor children might have actually declined for a time. Hugh Cunningham, a noted social historian of British childhood, indicates some doubt about whether the establishment of this system of government schools actually served the best interests of children of the poor.[7] Presumably, however, the supply of docile workers and willing cannon-fodder was expanded satisfactorily.

The issue of contradictions between elite and popular views is also raised by the Chapter One observation that children's development is highly sensitive to the regard in which they are held. It was pointed out that, in many cases, the development of children is undermined less by the risks they face in their work than by public denigration of that work and, by extension, of the children's own worth. Children themselves pick up on this dynamic and articulate it clearly, underlining the importance of work for their self-esteem. This comes out very clearly in field research and meetings in which children can express themselves in their own words. It is interesting to note that working children from various parts of the world said in the earlier mentioned 1996 Kundapur meeting that one of the things they most want is respect for their work contribution and for themselves as workers.[8] By the same token, working children almost everywhere reject terms (for example 'street children') which they feel demean their status as persons and as contributing workers.

Building expanded opportunities for children

Great care should be taken with the social and cultural message that is being sent to children regarding their work and persons. Portraying children as helpless victims to be rescued is not conducive to their development. Even more seriously, it has been noted that the language of 'elimination of child labour' is sometimes understood by children as elimination of child labourers. When one takes into account that many working children, especially those in public places, already have to deal with extortion and violence from the authorities, one can appreciate that the threat of 'elimination' has a very frightening resonance. It is worth noting that many experienced NGO programmes with working children build self-esteem by accenting the positive in children's work and building on children's strengths. At the time of writing, for example, Street Kids International (SKI) in Canada is developing a curriculum for use by street educators and others to teach basic business concepts and practices to child street vendors and other autonomous workers. It is presented in terms of a story about a small group of friends who work together and who contribute their particular talents — which correspond to the typical business functions of product development, sales, production, and so forth — in ways that allow them to succeed in their work, education and personal life. This up-beat approach communicates a healthy image of working children as smart, responsible, innovative, and capable of solving their own problems, which is calculated to strengthen these characteristics in the children who use this curriculum.[9]

The idea of helping children use their experience as workers to learn how to run a proper business is an apt example of how programmes can take advantage of learning opportunities in children's everyday lives to help them develop their multiple intelligence and competencies. It also is in line with Article 29 of the Convention on the Rights of the Child, which demands that children be educated to develop their full potential. Social mobilization could do a great deal to enrich working children's environment, greatly expanding appropriate options for both learning and economic survival, if it defined its mission positively as the promotion of child well-being and development rather than negatively as the prohibition of economic participation. For instance, what would be the long-term result for part-time street-trading children of linking them through something like the business-teaching curriculum imagined by SKI to, say, both formal education and groups of adult business people who could act as volunteer mentors to them? Again, there is more to be gained by social mobilization to create options for impoverished children and their families than by mobilization to restrict even further the few routes to survival they now have.

As we suggested in Chapter One, one way to create alternative opportunities for working children is to structure their work so that it provides a vital learning experience as well as income. Even some work that is currently detrimental to children can be changed so that dangers are eliminated and learning content is enhanced. As has been prominently pointed out, one basic strategy for eliminating harmful child work is to correct bad working conditions or other factors that make work harmful while retaining the income opportunity for children in a more acceptable form.[10] While this strategy does not satisfy the objections of those who feel children should be dissuaded from engaging in work, it is a realistic option when the problem being targeted is defined as danger to children rather than as economic participation. Obviously, making work safe for children is above all an employer responsibility and a powerful form of protective intervention for which employers are uniquely qualified. Despite the fact that even as far back as the last century some employers have taken measures to make their workplaces more appropriate for children (for example, by giving children time off to study and sponsoring school facilities in or near factories), relatively little of this sort of activity has been documented or analyzed. At the current time, of course, at least the multinational private sector seems absorbed primarily in removing children from their workplaces — responding to pressure from consumer groups, trade unions and others — and the child development possibilities to be realized by transforming children's work into a safe learning experience are receiving scant attention. That is not difficult to understand, since commercial firms would naturally be expected to place higher priority on protecting markets than children. When public opinion insists that employers totally exclude children from work they create, no matter under what circumstances, it is not realistic to expect employers to adopt strategies to improve children's work rather than to abolish it.

Non-profit-making organizations, who find it easier to be child-centred, have long been active in making work into a vehicle of their education and social advancement. The literature of non-formal education, especially from Africa, is rife with experiences of this type.[11] Programmes based on 'learning by doing', in which the students earn money in a particular trade while in the process of learning it, have a long history, including through traditional apprenticeship systems. In modern times, many attempts have been made to meld the 'hands-on' and income advantages of learning through apprenticeship with the efficiency of school instruction in groups. Some of these experiments, such as the Swareng Hill School in Botswana, were widely publicized and much discussed in both education and development circles as the potential solution for ensuring that education would directly contribute to the modernization and development of rural areas. In a more or less typical programme of this type, children and young people would receive basic educational instruction in reading, writing, and maths within the context of operating a group development project, commonly in agriculture or construction. Under the guidance of one or more teachers, the group would undertake practical money-making activities which would serve both as a learning vehicle for the children and a source of financial support for both the children and the programme. Productive work-study programmes of this type have been especially associated with Africa, where some are known as 'brigades', and have been widely studied and discussed as a possible new model of popular education and local economic development.

Interest in such work-study combinations seems to have peaked during the 1970s, which period saw broad international discussion of this 'education through production' approach and attempts to incorporate it into the regular education systems of at least Botswana and Zimbabwe. However, the daunting problems of fitting a highly non-formal and pragmatic process that is business oriented into the hierarchical structures and rigid procedures of Ministries of Education were never adequately solved. There is some suggestion that activities of this type are far more successfully sponsored by civil society than by government. Also, work and study elements have not always cohabited easily in this hybrid model, which sometimes is criticized for under-perfoming both as business and as education. In fact, in the brigade experience, it did prove difficult to make farms or construction groups economically efficient when they were staffed mostly by youngsters still learning the business, and the education received often was considered by parents and educators to be inferior, especially since it did not lead to coveted certificates that opened the way to government and other white-collar jobs. Interest in making work an educational tool has not been limited to Africa. Certain Brazilian projects of this type have been prominently mentioned in the literature on child work, for example.[12] And, as has been mentioned previously, the idea that children's work should be treated as a key learning experience and a valuable social contribution has been at the centre of the philosophy and activities of some of children's own organizations, such as MANTHOC in Peru. In some recent contexts, this line of thinking has been closely identified with advocacy for children's right to economic and political participation.

This is especially important when considering the significance of social science findings, reported in Chapter One, that children contribute to their own development, and that their development is facilitated by opportunities to pursue their own life projects and aspirations. As Chapter One suggested, development is something children do, it does not just happen to them and they need ample space to do it. Society needs to provide that space for them and creating an environment conducive to the well-being and development of children, including in regard to work, should be a high priority of both policy and practice.

Social mobilization against detrimental child work but for expanded opportunities for children to learn runs up against the popular ideas about childhood that permit the exploitation of children to occur. Obtaining long-term changes in social practice involves changing these ideas, which entails helping a society reflect on them and their consequences. However, this process is complicated by the fact that any complex society contains different concepts of childhood, what childhood ought to be, and what is right for children. As Chapter One described in detail, gender, ethnic group, caste, socioeconomic status, religion, and other factors all influence the particular childhood that children live. Social mobilization reconciles ideas about child rights and development with these different 'childhoods' so that a general consensus on principles can emerge and each kind of 'childhood' can internalize and implement these principles in its own way. Parents, children, employers, teachers, government officials, and many others may have to change the way they think about children and childhood in order to arrive at agreement on how to deal with hazardous and exploitative child work; first of all they must delve into the specifics of each sort of childhood. Unless harmful child work is considered within the framework of a particular social group, many crucial insights into that work and how to intervene in it will be missed. For example, motives that lead children to work, the recognition of dangers, and the psychosocial rewards and risks of working can be very specific to a given culture or life situation, and out of context are easily misinterpreted.[13] Countries need to establish ample opportunities for diverse parts of their societies to come together in dialogue regarding how children should be nurtured and protected. Part of this dialogue should address issues of children's work, reconsidering old assumptions and ideas, and opening the way to new perspectives.

Some organizations, in this case most notably the ILO and UNICEF, recommend that this social rethinking of the rights and roles of children as regards their work be pointed toward the development of a national 'child labour' policy. It is here, they feel, that the many 'childhoods' finally can be brought together in agreement on how society should regard and address the exploitation and dangers children often face at work. They suggest that countries should frame such a policy by bringing government and civil society together to jointly examine the national situation with regard to children's work by means of a dialogue between the various groups having a stake in these issues. The ILO tries to jump-start the policy-development process through formally structured national and regional seminars at which government, trade unions, and employer associations, with participation from non-governmental organizations, jointly review the child work situation (mostly on the basis of official data) and prepare a suggested draft national plan of action. These seminars last several days and receive technical and financial assistance from the ILO. It is intended that they be followed by a longer and more detailed policy-development process. UNICEF tends towards more informal and varied approaches. In Latin America, for example, it has published situation analysis guidelines for use by informal working groups made up of persons from government and civil society interested in the issues of child work. In Bangladesh, on the other hand, it has pioneered the use of innovative 'future search' workshops in which interested parties are invited to project their hopes and knowledge into the future as a basis for setting collective policy goals and parameters. It is interesting to note that none of these processes yet includes the systematic participation of working children, either as individuals or as representatives of their own organizations. One of the first and most important ways to improve the quality of these existing mechanisms would be to include working children in them.

This vision of a tidy process in which an explicit national policy expresses and coordinates social consensus against detrimental child work may be slightly utopian. Not many societies work in so orderly a fashion. As was pointed out in Chapter Five, it is not clear that even the best national policies are particularly effective in reducing workplace abuses against children, except perhaps in certain parts of the formal sector. Neither current experience nor the hindsight of historically conclusive scholarship shows how policies governing children's work can be made to guarantee children's best interests. Some of the most important forces acting on the problem — such as changing cultural notions of childhood, long-term wage rates, lower birth rates, and technological changes in industry — are only marginally amenable to government policy manipulation, at best. And, again recalling Chapter Five, some governments have more popular legitimacy and are taken more seriously by their citizens than are others.

But there is some evidence that a dialogical process leading to definition of public policy can, by providing a participative framework for public debate, become a powerful vehicle of social mobilization. In at least some societies, widespread cultural changes of attitude and behaviour achieved through open public discussion might have a greater impact on the protection of children than can be achieved through any policy. The case of Brazil already has been cited as an especially good example of what can be achieved through a highly socialized process of policy discussion.[14] There, starting in the early 1980s, limited action in favour of children living and working on the streets burgeoned into a massive grass roots movement. That movement ultimately resulted in a constitutional article defining children's rights, and an innovative implementing structure of watchdog councils that decentralized responsibility to the community level. There was nothing tidy about this process, for public discussion outgrew and developed beyond each event and mechanism designed to hold it. It in effect set its own agenda as it went.

Brazil probably represents a fairly realistic picture of what can be achieved through social moblilization. A national movement of working children has now been long established in Brazil, and national congresses of working children are held every few years. The media have covered child work issues assiduously. The government has taken a firm stand on the issue and the Brazilian trade unions and employer associations lead the world in their engagement against the workplace abuse of children. Yet, as the newspaper-reading public well knows, children on the streets are routinely killed and otherwise persecuted with the reported indifference or collusion of some authorities, and reports of children in bondage and other intolerable forms of child work are common.

Brazil today symbolizes both the potential and the difficulties of social mobilization against the abuse of child workers. The problems that remain are enormous, especially in the informal sector, in rural and frontier areas and in marginal activities such as prostitution and drug trafficking. The country's school-completion rates are among the lowest, and its malnutrition rates and inequality of income among the highest of countries near its GDP per capita. Nevertheless, it has managed to forge a large child defence movement strongly rooted in both government and civil society, and this movement is energetically confronting the country's infamous oppression and exploitation of its children. The battle for children's rights in general, and against harmful child work in particular, is far from over. But a new set of ideas and values has been released into society: ideas and values that are defended by dedicated supporters of children's rights representing a full spectrum of society, ranging from working children and their families to private sector, NGO, and government leaders. A chain of solidarity in defence of the best interests of children spans the width of Brazilian society. In a difficult situation such as that of Brazil, a determined, organized, and broadly based establishment for the defence of children may be the first result of social mobilization that can reasonably be expected.

If consideration of the best interests of children is slighted, however, social mobilization can go awry. As mentioned earlier, societies can agree to do the wrong things as well as the right ones, and social mobilization is a powerful force that enhances the costs of failure as well as the benefits of success. It can easily damage the best interests of its intended child beneficiaries by overwhelming them under misguided ideas and 'solutions' that are backed by the full force of a mobilized society. Sometimes the offending mobilization effort does not even have to come from the same country as the children. For example, as already cited, the campaign by US labour, consumer, child advocate, and government interests to end the participation of children under 15 in the Bangladesh garment industry was demonstrated to have had a negative effect on the well-being of the very children its organizers intended to protect.[15] UNICEF and the ILO had to get involved in order to counter those ill-effects, and went on to develop a positive intervention model to help avoid them in the future. This experience, which is further detailed in Chapter Eight, provides one more indication that social mobilization against harmful child work may greatly benefit children when its actions are competent and sensitive to children's realities, but it can be a disaster for children when irresponsibility is magnified by power. It is therefore imperative that the enhanced force it can generate be guided by rigorous consideration of the facts at hand, and the best interests of the children involved.

Stimulating the participation of children and young people

Children should participate in social mobilization on their own behalf. It is not only a matter of common sense, making use of their unique information and perspective, but it also promotes children's development as they take active responsibility in forging their own lives. The participation of children is one of the overarching principles of the Convention on the Rights of the Child, which in Article 12 provides that its member states shall "assure to the child who is capable of forming his or her own views the right to express those views freely in all matters affecting the child...". "For this purpose," it continues in the second paragraph, "the child shall in particular be provided with the opportunity to be heard in any judicial and administrative proceedings affecting the child, either directly, or through a representative or an appropriate body, in a manner consistent with the procedural rules of national law".

Strange as it may seem, however, social mobilization against detrimental child work almost everywhere tends to ignore the participation of working children themselves, except perhaps in a small or symbolic role. They are the persons most involved in the problem, but are usually little involved in its solutions. We argued that the prevailing public view of child workers has regarded them as passive prey to exploitation, and therefore as needing protection by adults. Perhaps more to the point, a child that is perceived to be little more than a helpless victim is considered to be not "capable of forming his or her own views", implying that he or she is unqualified to participate under the terms of the CRC. It is worth noting that staunch opponents of working children's participation in national and international 'child labour' policy discussions have questioned the independent capacity of working children — even adolescents — to represent themselves and one another, claiming they simply have been indoctrinated by adults. Evidence shows, however, that working children tend to be especially independent and capable of making decisions in their own interest, as well as of contributing to the social dialogue regarding children's work. Preliminary findings from an evaluative study of five programmes for working children, characterized by different degrees and types of children's participation, strongly suggest that children can be remarkably capable, that they maintain independence of critical judgement and action even in programmes with strong adult leadership, and that participation does in fact stimulate mental and social development.[16]

It should come as no surprise that working children can be quite independent and capable of defending themselves. By necessity, they depend much of the time on their own personal skills to avoid the worst situations. For example, studies of garment industry children in Bangladesh have found a surprising degree of mobility from one employer to another within the industry. Few children stay in the same place even for a year. Part of that volatility has to do with the structure of the industry labour market — children are often employed during periods of peak labour demand when extra workers are brought in to help meet large orders. However, it also was found that many children leave one employer for another, or leave the industry entirely, when they object to working conditions, feel they are being cheated on their pay or otherwise exploited, or find they cannot be promoted.[17] They refuse to stay where they feel exploited.

An ILO—IPEC project in Indonesia demonstrated that the ability of working children to defend themselves in the factory environment can be substantially increased by equipping them with proper information and skills. Using an alternative education approach, the project helped nearly 200 factory children, many of whom worked in hazardous conditions, to master the organizational and negotiating techniques necessary to present their complaints and ideas to national and local government leaders,

NGO representatives, and the media as part of an awareness-raising campaign on detrimental child work. At the end, 13 factories employing some 1,500 children removed them from hazardous tasks and extended wage, insurance, and leave benefits, previously available only to adults, to the children as well.[18] A number of community and NGO projects have sought to help children develop their individual capacity to protect themselves in informal sector activities as well. For example, Casa de Passagem in Recife, Brazil works with street girls, who often are involved in prostitution, so that they can protect themselves against HIV infection. While the programme tries in the long run to assist these girls to leave the street life, it tries to protect them in the short run from contracting this lethal disease. It also works to raise their self-esteem, which is a critical element in helping them to develop and to adopt more successful strategies for their lives. In this work, it uses street educators to make street contact, provides a drop-in facility where advice is available along with showers, meals, medical attention, and other assistance, and recruits the girls who come to the centre to spread the message about AIDS to other girls on the streets.[19]

Since working children often have to depend so much on themselves, it is not surprising that, in a number of places, they have organized into a variety of informal groups and formal organizations to defend themselves and promote their interests. In some areas of Asia, Latin America and West Africa, such collective activities are now numerous and have established even national and regional organizations. Informal children's organizations are common in the Philippines and are networked with each other. In the port city of Olongapo, for example, child street workers have long been organized into groups according to occupation: sack makers, newspaper vendors, scavengers, vehicle washers, and so forth. They discuss and resolve many of their problems together. Organization of this type is increasingly present in the cities of various countries. Much is now known about how to successfully start and support such organization.

Protections offered by a small group may seem modest but are important for the children helped. A typical example from a West African newsletter for and by working children is illustrative, and shows children defending their right of free assembly granted under the CRC. Akofa is a ten-year-old maid who wanted to join the local association of working children, a self-help group of children and young people that promotes the rights of working children, but her employer was reluctant to let her go to its Sunday meetings. One of the association members then approached the employer to explain the organization and ask that the girl be released to participate in it. When Akofa still did not appear, the contacting child asked her activity leader (the role is unexplained) to accompany her on still another visit to the employer. The activity leader not only insisted that Akofa should be able to attend the meeting but also called attention to her overly heavy workload. At last Akofa was permitted to attend, and is reported to have since brought other children along with her.[20]

At a somewhat higher level of organization, The Working Children's Movement in Peru, a national association of local working children's groups, reports that it has finally achieved a long-sought goal, which is medical coverage for working children under the national social security scheme that already provides for adult workers. The government originally balked at the idea of insuring children, while the children complained that their exclusion had no reasonable basis and was purely a matter of age discrimination since they were willing to pay the same premiums as adults. A tenacious committee of children and young people pursued and negotiated with the national authorities and, over time, won an agreement that has brought young workers into the programme, complete with their social security identity cards.[21]

Ignorance of the critical role that working children can and do play in their own protection has led to a plethora of adult-planned interventions that working children, or for that matter their families, do not find relevant or helpful. As Tolfree puts it:

> It is the experience of organizations who work in a more participatory way that working children are resourceful, capable and competent people; conversely, those organizations who treat working children as dependent, irresponsible and incompetent will quickly find this to be a self-fulfilling prophecy and will then find many reasons for continuing a non-participative way of working. In the process, children will feel little or no sense of ownership of the programme and will probably have little commitment to achieving the goals of the programme if they have had no involvement in establishing them.

> ... At the very least, the need to consult children about their own perception of their needs, problems and resources is an essential precondition for the development of programmes designed to support and assist them. Programmes based entirely on adult perceptions of working children's needs and priorities are almost certainly destined to 'get it wrong' and hence to waste valuable resources. The importance of basing programme planning on participatory research in which working children can freely articulate the prob-

lems, needs and resources within their social world of work, school, family street and so on, cannot be overestimated.[22]

The main resource in any project, Tolfree stresses, is the children themselves. Based on his appraisal of five programmes for working children,[23] he has identified other important benefits of children's participation very much in line with those suggested by the recent child development literature discussed in Chapter One. First of all, he confirms that participation in decisions about their lives and the programmes that serve them contributes to the positive self-image of working children, and this works at the social as well as the personal level. He finds that a high level of participation leads children to regard themselves as significant agents of change in their communities and societies, and encourages their sense of citizenship and social activism. He also finds that participation helps avoid or mollify the dangers of children's dependence on programmes in which they take part; what he calls 'creeping welfarism'. Yet another important benefit is that, through participation, children learn to co-operate with one another, and this helps alleviate harsh and mutually destructive competition between them. This is an important consideration for child street workers, for example, since naked competition for favoured work sites, or access to special resources or customers, is a common cause of violence between children.

Despite its undeniable benefits, Tolfree warns, participation can involve certain risks that need to be guarded against. One is that, in cultures generally not favouring a pro-active role for children, it can lead to feelings of cultural dissonance in the children, or even to their alienation from family and community. He worries that instilling more forwardness in children might expose them to abuse in families or cultures already inclined towards violence. In such environments there is also the question of whether children highly engaged in programmes facilitating their participation are being socialized into false expectations not realizable in the 'real world'. He also shares with others a certain worry about the potential for conscious or unconscious manipulation by adults. It is worth noting, however, that this concern generally is less acute the more fully and transparently children are involved in decision-making processes. In this sense, the way Hart defines participation in his much circulated essay on children's participation is of particular interest: "the process of sharing decisions which affect one's life and the life of the community in which one lives. It is the means by which a democracy is built and it is the standard against which democracies should be measured. Participation is the fundamental right of citizenship."[24]

A rural area in India provides an interesting example of children being brought into the democratic decision-making process. India's system of government includes a system of village councils which operate as the most local unit of government. Concerned for Working Children, an NGO that addresses the issues of poor and working children, helped start a local association of rural working children and young people, the objective of which is to assist in the development of the local area as well as to defend the rights and opportunities of children. This association, Bhima Sanga, has helped establish representation for children within village government and claims that, in less than two years of experience, the majority of requests made by children — many of which had to do with improving schools and access to them — have been attended to.[25]

Article 12 of the CRC is interpreted by some child advocates and working children's organizations as giving working children the right to participate in national and international discussions regarding what should be done about detrimental child work. While there is widening agreement that working children should participate is designing, operating, and evaluating local programmes that serve them directly, there is at this time fierce disagreement regarding whether children should have a voice in forming public sector policy. The CRC makes no such distinction in its provisions. While its intent is clear enough at the national level, it does not address the question of children's participation in international fora and processes. Nevertheless, when the Government of the Netherlands sponsored an international policy child labour conference in Amsterdam in February of 1997, it followed the spirit of the CRC by formally inviting the participation of working children's own organizations. The participation of working children also seemed particularly relevant to the purpose of the meeting, which was to mobilize international support for a new ILO convention on "the most intolerable forms of child labour". This was the first time that the participation mandate of the Convention on the Rights of the Child had been implemented in a major international meeting, and considerable innovation was necessary in order to make that participation meaningful. In the unfamiliar environment of a typically formal international meeting, developing country children from rural villages and urban poor areas presented their views with equanimity, balance, and eloquence. Their contribution was clear indication of the feasibility of children's participation in such international meetings, and was a successful example of the right of expression guaranteed by the CRC. And there is little question that enthusiastic support of working children for a new convention would add to its credibility, expand its interest and attractiveness to the general public, open new opportunities for social mobilization, and improve the chances of its being ratified.

However, the child delegates voiced certain opinions not in agreement with positions being promoted by trade unions and some other groups represented. This led to stiff resistance to the participation of children's organizations, except symbolically, in a follow-up conference in Oslo in October of the same year. The host government refused the request of children's organizations for full representation. The situation was ultimately mollified when the Norwegian government changed, a new minister invited child participation in a compromise form, and a parallel children's forum was mounted by the Save the Children Alliance. Despite complications arising from the newness of children's participation, working children did manage to express their views in both conferences.

The above discussion suggests that there is now some movement towards the further inclusion of children in social mobilization against detrimental child work. However, only the first steps have been taken, and one of the most important social mobilization issues, at both the national and international levels, is how to include children much more completely into both dialogue and action. As has been mentioned above, however, there is considerable discomfort in some quarters with the idea of children's participation in such meetings — especially those intended to lead towards national and international laws such as the proposed new ILO convention. There is particular resistance to seating children as accepted delegates representing children's own organizations. At the time of writing, such resistance appears strongest in the trade union movement, which is something of an irony given the movement's devotion to the ideal of workers being represented by freely elected colleagues, and the fact that it has generally been unwilling itself either to organize children or to extend its protections to them as workers. In our view, this hostility stems from a gross misperception of the nature and position of the working children's organizations, but it nevertheless raises some important issues that need to be addressed.

Governments, international organizations, trade unions, employer organizations, and others need to establish strong connections with working children; one which early on in the planning cycle enables them to take into full consideration the children's motives for working and their views about the main risks they identify with their work. These connections should include both empirical studies *of* children, especially surveys and case studies which carefully document children's observations and opinions, and direct dialogue *with* children, including through their own organizations where such exist. Only by responding to how children regard both the value and the risk of their work will it be possible to devise policies and programmes that children themselves will comprehend and support. Actions conceived with the understanding and support of working children are more likely to be effective in promoting their full development while safeguarding them against workplace abuse. Only policies and activities developed in this child-inclusive way can overcome the suspicion with which many working children regard outside attempts to protect them. And unless that hostility is assuaged, children will continue in many parts of the world to deliberately ignore or subvert child labour laws and other actions which they perceive to be irrelevant to their reality and obstructive to fulfilling the needs and aspirations that motivate them to work.

The leadership for viable participation methods and channels probably rests with child advocacy NGOs, at least for the next few years. It is significant that, even after the controversy regarding lack of children's participation, the Oslo child labour conference statement at the end – a proposed international 'Agenda for Action' – did not specifically include the participation of working children among its recommendations. In the face of strong trade union and some government opposition, neither UNICEF nor the ILO were willing to defend the issue. Given that some 30 countries, representing the main actors in respect to child work, were present in the meeting, the challenge looks formidable. It needs to be remembered, however, that most progress in child rights has first been spearheaded by non-governmental organizations, and most of the progress made towards the protection of working children is a direct result of their initiative. Both national governments and international organizations such as UNICEF have seldom led the way, but have appropriated and disseminated ideas and methods pioneered by civil society. The eventual participation of working children in determining the policies intended to protect them will, it seems, have to be achieved by the same route.

The special role of adults in facilitating children's participation

Perhaps the major issue is the relationship between working children and adults who work with them, especially in highly participative contexts such as working children's organizations. The question is complicated by the fact that even working children's own organizations could not exist or operate without adults in critical roles. First of all, in most places, organizations must be legalized in order to receive direct financial support, and only adults can assume the legal responsibility necessary. Secondly, children are children for but a very limited period of time, so the organization cannot build up an experienced cadre of members in the same way that adult organizations do, so adults must assume considerable responsibility for maintaining the organization and constantly preparing new children to participate in its activities and management. Thirdly, adults have certain skills and life experience that children need to consult and rely upon.

Because working children are dependent on adults to help facilitate their participation in programmes, even their own organizations, the adults working with these children need special skills and sensitivity to play their role without being intrusive. This issue is well recognized and, among programmes serving working children, there typically is a great deal of discussion regarding how adults should relate to children in a democratic framework. In addition, a variety of resource materials and training courses are now widely available for street educators and other adults who work closely with working children in a non-directive mode. Clearly, this is an art still in the early stages of experimentation and evolution. In his appraisal, Tolfree noted the delicate issue of adult roles, and indicated that he observed certain situations in which "it did seem that the main impetus behind some of the children's organized activity came from adults rather than from the children themselves. ...It is not being suggested that any of these ...organizations are, in any sense, manipulating children or encouraging participation in a tokenistic sense." He goes on to note, however, that "this experience does raise the question of what are the principle concerns of child workers and what are the principle concerns of organizations which are supporting them: they may not be the same".[26]

Another issue raised by critics of children's participation in national and international decision-making about child labour laws and standards is that of representation. They question the right of some children to speak for others. The question is apt, for in those cases in which adult- operated programmes simply hand-pick children to participate in an event, no representative credibility can be attached to the child. That is why various organizations insist that children must elect their own representatives, and the democratic election of leaders and spokespersons have in some places been the rule for many years. It is usual for the voting children to thoroughly discuss the main issues of concern and to provide those elected to represent them with a list of particulars that they are to present as the official voice for other children. So far, relatively few organizations serving working children make use of such evolved democratic procedures. They remain at this time largely the province of a very limited number of children's own organizations. Another question of representation involves age differences. Some have criticized the fact that working children's representatives before national or international bodies tend to be adolescents rather than younger children; the implication is that young children can be fairly represented only by children roughly their own age. While there is no easy answer to this question — very young children could be considered by some too dependent to meet the CRC Article 12 criterion for personal capacity — children's own organizations suggest that children as a group should be free to elect whomever they think will best represent their interests, and if that is a highly articulate older child, such is their right. Their line of reasoning is that any democratic system is intended to push the best leadership to the top so that the constituency will be represented as well as possible. One could ask why, in a democratic framework, children should be bound to paternalistic representational expectations that put them at a disadvantage *vis-à-vis* adults.

Even with these problematic issues still unresolved, the right of children to be heard is so clearly established by the CRC, and so fundamental to success, that there is no logical, legal or moral alternative but to facilitate the full participation of working children in framing national and international policies governing children's work. The operational question is about workable mechanisms and how to develop them as quickly and responsibly as possible.

This limited discussion cannot undertake a lengthy description of the various ways through which creative NGOs and others are developing children's participation as regards child work issues. It is possible, however, to suggest some of the patterns found in what appear to be successful efforts. First of all, they are organic, growing out of pragmatic attempts to identify and meet real children's needs. Anthony Swift portrays such an instance in an in-depth historical study of a programme for working and street children in Belem, Brazil.[27] As this case points out, the participation of children was supported by a full ideological, organizational, and methodological context; in this case a religious institution trying to live its message within the context of urban poverty. A second characteristic is an objective of empowering children and promoting their psychosocial development. As Chapter One suggests, participation has positive developmental effects for children, and programmes thinking in terms of child growth and social learning have a relatively easy time mounting appropriate participation efforts. A third element of successful approaches is a firm belief in the right of children to be heard, to participate, and even to defend views and objectives that influential adults do not agree with. This is essential because children have unique perspectives, some of which may upset various adult assumptions and doctrines, as the above discussion indicated. But they have a right to present their ideas, which often are embarrassing because of their unvarnished truth, and adults facilitating the participation need on occasion to actively defend children's right to have inconvenient notions. Lastly, successful programmes of participation are patient, realizing that children – like adults – need time to learn how to discuss productively in groups, articulate collective options, and so forth. They also know that children's dynamics are not like adults', and that the process of discussion and decision-making for children will differ greatly from the forms familiar to adult organizations.

Seeing children holistically and in context in social mobilization

Much of the public debate about child work and exploitation is far too narrowly focused. This can be disastrous for children. Child street traders, for example, have been cruelly mistreated by local authorities who see them only in terms of a possible public-safety issue. Child factory workers have been left even more vulnerable than before by regarding their work as but a matter of labour law violations. Such restricted views of children's reality, amplified in public debate through social mobilization processes, can lead to serious public misconceptions about the problem and eventually to inappropriate action. It is of the utmost importance that social mobilization against the exploitation of children avoids the pitfalls of blinkered vision. A review of the literature and experience of recent years suggests that two specific measures, if incorporated into social mobilization activities from the very beginning, can do much to provide the required holistic and contextual view of children that is necessary to guarantee their well-being and development.

Taking an intersectoral view

The first way to ensure that social mobilization takes an adequately holistic view of both child work and the children involved in it is to institutionalize the social dialogue in one or more groups that include a variety of views on the problem. Experience of this type was first tried and studied in Brazil during the early 1980s, and has long since been documented as a standard fixture of social mobilization in other Latin American countries, the Philippines, and elsewhere. Community councils made up of the various governmental and NGO groups concerned about working children have become something of a norm. A version of the practice has been installed by ILO—IPEC through an intersectoral 'steering committee' in each country having a regular programme to advise its activities. Such committees would typically include delegates from different government ministries, and perhaps NGOs as well, representing different sectoral perspectives, such as education, labour, and health and welfare. UNICEF field-office guidelines for the development of programmes for child workers have recommended beginning with a formal or informal working group comprised of interested persons and organizations having a variety of complementary perspectives on the problems and the children involved.

The idea is that the various viewpoints on children should be present from the very beginning, starting with the planning and conduct of situational analysis research, including surveys of children and case studies of particular places and problems. Someone — usually a health professional — needs to take particular interest in the physical health and development of working children, while other participants concentrate on matters of their educational, emotional, and social development. In some societies, religious institutions take considerable interest in working children and their moral and spiritual development. Starting early on in its national programme for street children, the Philippines established such interagency, intersectoral councils in each major city, the idea of which was to provide such multi-dimensional perspective on programmes and the children reached through them. Brazil began with similar local councils, at first informally constituted, and has since institutionalized them in a far more ambitious national system to protect children's rights through legally mandated councils in every municipality.

Putting an emphasis on families

Chapter One emphasized the importance of understanding and intervening in the work of children within a family framework; treating the work of children in isolation from their family situation and expectations risks loosening the family ties that are the child's first line of protection. It is therefore impossible to pursue the best interests of working children without taking their family connections into careful consideration. Family ties must also be part of the foundation for any holistic approach to the development and protection of working children.

The second way to ensure that social mobilization will treat children holistically and in context is to stress the importance of their connection to family, making ample opportunity for family views to be heard and discussed in the process. When adequate attention is paid to the importance of links between working children and their families, the issues that surface virtually force a holistic perspective on the children, and children's most immediately significant context is usually their family.

It is widely recognized that the family should be the first line of defence against the exploitation of its children. However, not only does that first line often break down, but families are often among the serious exploiters of their children, directly placing them in harm's way. As mentioned in Chapter Two, the common assumption that children who work for or with their families are more likely to be protected against work risks than are those who work outside is not necessarily borne out by experience. It is a proposition that has to be tested according to the case. Sometimes the problem seems to be that families do not sufficiently appreciate the dangers that their working children may face, and in other cases they either do not sufficiently care or they feel constrained by lack of other possibilities. Whatever the reasons, just about all recommendations for social mobilization against harmful child work say something about the need to reach and mobilize families.

Various programmes and projects do this by providing parents with useful information about child work hazards in order to help them better supervise the work participation of their children accordingly. In Brazil, for example, the National Confederation of Workers in Agriculture (CONTAG) has utilized its extensive radio network of 160 stations to reach highly dispersed rural families with information about the hazards attendant to farm work — such as equipment and toxic chemicals — for children who work with them. It also produced and disseminated 10,000 copies of a book on the rights of rural working children and provided training courses to union leaders.[28] In Cebu in the Philippines, municipal social workers began to educate mothers about the dangers of work and the advantages of education as part of their regular visits to village mothers' groups. This was done through informal, low-key group conversations, maintained over a period of time, in a friendly and educative manner. It was observed that most school-age children who had been engaged long hours in splitting rocks or in other types of inappropriate work were gradually removed from such tasks, while school attendance increased.[29] In a like vein, the ILO—IPEC has found that parents often can be educated to find ways of reducing the workload and risk exposure of their children in order to enhance their school attendance and performance, sometimes even when poverty would appear to be an impossible barrier.[30] In many places around the world, governments or civil society organizations provide family subsidies, often termed scholarships, to free children from burdensome work and allow them to attend school. Freeing children for education was one of the important reasons leading to the establishment of welfare assistance programmes in Europe and North America, and many believe that provision of an effective social safety net for families became one of the most important factors keeping children of the poor in school and out of the workplace.

In regard to social mobilization against injurious child work, the main issue about families is that their voices are seldom heard. There are many 'social communications' projects which beam carefully prepared messages about child work to a target audience of parents, but there are very few activities which provide means for parents to convey their concerns and experiences to others. As a result, they are virtually excluded from the dialogical process of social mobilization. It is strangely ironic that the social institution nearly everyone agrees should be the first line of defence against the economic exploitation of children, the family, is vastly underrepresented in social discussion of the issue.

Why has surprisingly little effort been made to hear out parents and other family members systematically and to learn what they feel is needed to help them play their protective role more effectively? The literature does not throw much light on this critical question, but the authors are left with the disturbing impression that national and international agencies sponsoring social mobilization might tend to have unfairly low expectations of families. Sometimes there seems to be an almost automatic assumption that families are unaware or neglectful, that they need instruction more than voice, and that they probably have few useful insights or opinions to offer. Moreover, in fieldwork one sometimes encounters a presupposition that poor families have a vested interest in the work of their children and, for that reason, they will defend child exploitation rather than help abolish it. This is why there is some fear that increasing their influence in the social dialogue could prove an obstacle rather than an avenue to child protection.

However, the literature reporting parental attitudes and aspirations regarding the work, education, and future of their children does not, on the whole, justify such pessimistic expectations of families. While exceptions are not difficult to find, they are just that: exceptions. Negative preconceptions against parents may too often represent hasty judgement by outsiders who do not understand the full limitations under which parents struggle to ensure the survival and meet the basic needs of an entire family.

Even a casual review of available case studies and surveys suggests that most parents want their children to receive an education, do not want them to work in conditions that undermine their health or development, and tend to do what they feel they can to prepare their children for successful adulthood. They often express deep frustration when poverty or other factors inexorably put the health, education or development of their children at risk, and they can be very explicit about what is needed to solve the problem. In many places they join forces in direct action — such as building schools and hiring teachers at the expense of the community when government education systems fail to serve them. Ways need to be found to bring parents much more centrally into social mobilization efforts as partners rather than as targets of action.

It is admittedly difficult to mobilize families in households or small groups and to take the time and effort to understand their situation and ideas completely. However, some programmes manage to do this. An example is the Bonded Labour Liberation Front in Pakistan, which has long had a practice of involving parents through committees attached to its schools as part of its programme to release children from work in brick kilns and elsewhere and assure their education. It is more difficult to find mechanisms for bringing parents' views and voices to national attention, and the authors have not discovered positive examples to cite. It may be that this is an aspect of social mobilization in which innovation, badly needed, has yet to occur. It is fervently hoped that it will occur at an early date.

Conclusion

The most important challenge before social mobilization is to make it sufficiently inclusive. Decisions that are now taken by political, social, and economic elites about the work of children should be the subject of broad social dialogue that fully includes both working children and the poor families and communities that most of them come from. Without at least reasonable social dialogue, consensus, and cooperation, it is unlikely that children can be adequately protected against workplace abuse. The process of social mobilization must be democratic, open and two-way. One-way campaigns by large, powerful or rich organizations to convert the public to their way of thinking may play a valid role in making the positions of important stakeholders known to the public, but they are not social mobilization, even if they sometimes misappropriate the term.

Some social mobilization efforts have not been very child-friendly; societies can agree to do the wrong things for children as much as the right ones. Therefore, it is necessary to ensure that social dialogue and consensus about child work issues take a sufficiently holistic view. Experience shows that organizing society to take a too narrowly focused approach to the problems of child work and exploitation can be counterproductive for the children. One of the most important ways to make social mobilization more child-friendly is to open space for children themselves to participate, especially through their own organizations. Experience shows that children can and do represent themselves very well, including in international fora, and more support should be channelled to helping them make their voices heard. Children's families also need to be brought fully into the social dialogue regarding what should be done to make children's work more appropriate and developmentally beneficial for children. Without their support, little change in social behaviour regarding the work of children can be expected.

As this text goes to publication, word has arrived that the Union of Working Children and Youth in Senegal has been invited to be a member of the board overseeing the national programme to eliminate the exploitation of children at work, which programme is the result of a cooperative agreement between the Government of Senegal and the ILO. This progressive move to include working children's organizational voice in national policy and programme-planning deserves to be widely praised and emulated.

CHAPTER SEVEN

Education and Children's Work

M any who are worried about detrimental child work look to universal primary education as potentially the single most powerful instrument for removing children from the labour market, or at least from types of work inappropriate for children. Education is seen by them as both a replacement activity and a source of changed mentality. This view of education as a tool of social reform has a long history. In the past, work was thought to be good for children everywhere but, by the mid-nineteenth century, social reformers in Europe had begun to amass information on the perils of child employment in factories and mines. They denounced employers of children and parents of working children as exploiters and asserted children's right to remain free of productive responsibilities. Education was proposed by the reformers as the most effective deterrent against idleness, on the one hand, and detrimental work on the other. Gradually, education came to be seen as serving children's interests better than work.

The earliest developments in formal education, characterized by paid teachers performing roles within institutional settings (schools), usually with age-specific groups of children, were associated with the spread of world religions like Islam and Christianity. In addition to their educational responsibilities, schools were expected to fulfil a moral and social function. Although most schools provided a minimum core of secular education, consisting usually of basic literacy and numeracy, initially the prime pedagogical objective was religious instruction. Soon, among the wealthier families of the world at least, school education was to replace work as the most important medium of learning and the school and the family were to become the main institutions for the social integration and socialization of children. School education was also to compensate in cases of inadequate care and authority within the family and prevent delinquency, street crime, and other violations by juveniles.[1] And with the emergence of nationalism, it was to have a central role in building allegiance to the state and its ideologies. Several of these ideas are reflected in present-day schooling which, in many countries, remains at least in part a vehicle for religious and moral instruction.[2]

Another aim of schooling has been to produce a numerate and literate workforce for industry and public administration, the massive global investment in formal education having been stimulated by evidence that it fuels economic growth.[3] This was one of the prime motives for the gradual withdrawal of European children from the labour market at the end of the nineteenth century, for example. In the countries once ruled by European colonial powers, education was aimed initially at local elites and schools were concentrated in towns and cities where the expatriate rulers, white-collar workers, and industrialists lived. This pattern persists even today, the interests of the urban elite prevailing in both curricula and the location of schools. Rural areas and poor urban communities made up of informal or illegal housing are still grossly underserved in terms of both schools and teachers.

In order to secure the transition of European children from work to school, compulsory education laws were passed. Although compulsion was resisted by many families, these laws certainly acted as a deterrent against child employment in quite a few countries, since children made to attend school could not work full-time. In Britain, for example, compulsory education (introduced in 1880) was associated with a decline in the proportion of children aged 10 to 14 in the workforce and also with the progressive raising of the age at which it was legitimate for children to enter the workforce.[4]

Globally, modern mass education — embodied by the state school system — has received its greatest impetus from the rapid urbanization and industrialization that has occurred since the mid-twentieth century. Mass education has gained wide political endorsement in recent years in a series of international events and developments. The Convention on the Rights of the Child establishes the right of all children to receive an education (Article 28), which education shall be directed not just on cognitive growth, but to "the development of the child's personality, talents and mental and physical abilities to their fullest potential" (Article 29). This implies that member countries will endeavour to reach all children with an education whose efficacy can be assessed according to the degree to which it promotes not only a narrow range of basic academic skills, but broader physical and psychosocial development as well. At least primary education, presumably meeting these standards, is to be mandatory and free of charge. Various forms of secondary education, including general and vocational education, are to be available and accessible to all children, whereas higher education is to be accessible to all on the basis of capacity. Measures to encourage school attendance and reduce drop-out are also envisaged.

Another important event was the 1990 'Education For All' conference in Jomtien, Thailand. This brought educators from more than 100 countries together to assess the state of education globally. They agreed to work for a future in which all children, everywhere, will have access to quality basic education. Also in 1990, 71 heads of state and government and 88 other senior officials attended the World Summit for Children at the United Nations, at which the commitment to deliver basic schooling and literacy to the 100 million children and nearly one billion illiterate adults globally without access was reconfirmed. Specific measures were recommended, in particular the expansion of early childhood development activities and universal basic education, vocational training, increased acquisition of knowledge, skills, and values through all education channels and adult literacy.

Recent decades have witnessed some important advances in education coverage at the primary and secondary levels particularly; the assumption having been that access rather than quality was the key priority.[5] Education budgets increased in the 1960s and 1970s in many parts of the world, with a corresponding growth in literacy, schools, teachers, and enrolments. Literacy rates in Latin America, for example, rose from 72 per cent in 1970 to 83 per cent in 1985 and gender inequality in enrolment and retention was practically eliminated. Children in some developing countries — including Chile, Cuba, Bahrain, Panama, and Tunisia — are now reported to receive roughly as many years of schooling as do children in the North.

Education holds the promise of improving survival, well-being and wealth and yet, despite the global spread of education in recent decades, many problems in making it a viable reality for all children remain. In this chapter we explore some of these problems, especially in regard to children who work. We examine some of the key issues surrounding the relationship between school education and work, highlighting how the shortcomings of present-day schooling relate to children's work, the ways in which work can harm schooling, and how children view school as compared to work. We consider the options that exist for children, both realistically and ideally, and discuss what needs to be done to make school more accessible, relevant, and interesting for children, and cater more effectively for their multiple developmental needs. Finally, we look at some of the key elements of good practice in education and the ways in which these have been implemented in several countries, especially for children from poor families in general and working children in particular.

The core issues

Like the social reformers in Europe last century, social-planners, educators, international organizations, and others today are strongly supportive of education as being in children's best interests for a whole variety of reasons. This was apparent from the responses to the Rädda Barnen survey of expert opinion, which endorsed education as the most important social measure benefiting children. It is usually assumed that most working children would be benefited by abandoning work and dedicating themselves exclusively to school. On first appearance, national census and labour data generally suggest that children who work have lower school enrolment, attendance, and completion rates than do non-working children of the same age. Even when in school, their performance tends to lag behind that of non-working peers. Work can seriously disrupt education in a number of ways:

- children may often start school late or leave early because of work;
- work may take children away from residential areas where schools are located or take up so much of their time that school attendance is impossible;
- work may provide an opportunity to gain income and independence, enticing children away from school;
- children who learn to become assertive and confident at work may be spurned by teachers as disruptive;
- working children may be so humiliated by teachers and pupils for being dirty or unkempt, that they are too embarrassed to remain at school;
- work may make children too weary to go to school, concentrate in class or do their homework;
- work can cause health problems which make it impossible for children to attend school;
- children who miss class because of work responsibilities may fall behind their peers and become discouraged, especially when they have to repeat school years;
- children who are abused or exploited at work may not have the confidence to attend school, or may became so distressed that they cannot do their schoolwork.

In the light of such evidence, the conventional wisdom is that work by school-age children impedes their education. It is concluded therefore that school-age children should be prohibited from working in order to ensure high levels of school attendance and achievement. To many, it is an almost uncontested assumption that children will benefit from being separated from work and exclusively devoted to school.

The apparent success of historical compulsory education measures has encouraged some to suggest that this is the most effective means for attracting children away from work and into school in developing countries today.[6] They advise not only that primary education be made compulsory (as the Convention on the Rights of the Child also provides), but that the minimum legal age for admission to work be set no lower than the upper age of compulsory education (as provided for in the ILO Minimum Age Convention, 1973, No. 138). In most countries, education is now compulsory and, in many, the ages for compulsory education and the minimum age for employment are coordinated. However, the relationship between schooling and child work is much more complex than this rather simple formula suggests:

> If the introduction of compulsory schooling is indeed the most effective way of combating child labour, the British evidence adds some important qualifications: opposition to child labour is not necessarily the reason for introducing compulsion; enforcing compulsion is no easy task; and the experience of school may be such that it is not entirely obvious that children are better off at school than at work.[7]

Experience clearly demonstrates that, in today's world, both compulsory education and minimum age standards are extremely difficult to enforce.

Since a large number of children throughout the world appear to combine school and work quite effectively (although many pay a price in terms of school attendance and performance) it would seem that the incompatibility of the two activities has been overstated. British, Italian, and Russian children, for example, have continued to work in the morning before school begins, in the afternoon when it finishes, and also at weekends. In Bangladesh, children recently withdrawn from work on the assumption they would go to school sought other jobs instead, some of which entailed far greater risk than did the work they left. Condemning all child work and compelling children to go to school without first securing viable alternatives can make children more vulnerable, making it impossible for them to pursue and realize their own aspirations and potential.[8] Besides, in richer countries where compulsory education is enforced, there are reports of older pupils becoming bored at school as they wait impatiently, even resentfully, for their official release.[9] Truancy, vandalism, discipline problems, inattention during lessons, and even violence against staff may suggest some questionable results of compulsory school attendance from a child development point of view.

Seeing how many children combine work and study in one way or another, the expectation that school will remove children from work is probably not reasonable. In fact, the short hours of many schools, especially those using shift systems, facilitate work before and after class.[10] Besides, as has been pointed out in previous chapters, school often serves as a cause of work rather than a solution to it. Nevertheless, while education may not deter children from working part-time, it could stop full-time work, in that non-school-going children consistently work longer hours than school-going children.[11] In other words, it appears that children engaged in full-time work are seldom able to keep up their schooling, the corollary being that the expansion of education might at least lead to a reduction of the hours worked by children. If schooling reduces the hours and possibly the intensity of work, it may also lessen children's exposure to some of the most dangerous or coercive work, since the more exploitative work arrangements often impede participation in other activities.

This implies that the real protective power of education may be to keep children out of the worst types of exploitation rather than out of the labour force. In other words, some claim, children who turn up at school most days of the week may be less likely to fall into bonded labour or other intolerable forms of child work which seek to monopolize their time. It should be noted, however, that this is speculation based on but thinly documented evidence. Proper research is badly needed in order to test this assertion. Of course, education has other protective capacities. Teachers can monitor pupils, identifying those who are in trouble at work or those at risk of dropping out of school and drifting into detrimental work. Schooling of the right sort can provide companionship and inspire the development of self-esteem, giving children the confidence to stand up for themselves against adults seeking to take advantage of them at work. Education approaches are also being successfully used to inform children about dangerous work situations and how they can avoid them.

In cases where the conventional idea that work and education are mutually exclusive does not hold true, educators face complicated and subtle issues. When is child work competitive with education and when complementary to it? Under what conditions does it detract from a child's education and under what conditions might it even promote learning? What should the education system do to protect children against harmful and exploitative work? How far, and in what ways, should it bend in order to educate children who work? Finding practical answers to such questions demands an in-depth understanding of the relationship between child work and education. The fact of the matter is that educators and policy-makers do not have a sufficient understanding of this relationship, even when they think they do. Moreover, what they think they understand often conflicts with how children and families regard the relationship between school and work. Besides, as Chapter One indicated, new studies, thinking, and experience have reopened the question whether child work necessarily undermines education and whether an institutionalized educational process isolated from work and other life activities is necessarily the best vehicle for child development. It is increasingly thought that children benefit most from exposure to a diversity of learning environments.

Child work and systemic problems in education

While the conventional view of school participation preventing work fits some children, it glosses over the question as to just why so many children are not in school. Despite the enthusiasm for education in most parts of the world, the goal of basic education for all children is far from being achieved. Many children are still not enrolled in school, and recently there has been a fall in the rate of growth of enrolment globally. Approximately 20 per cent of school-age children in developing regions still do not receive even a primary education and these are almost all children of the poorest classes and living in rural areas. Roughly two-thirds are girls. In some parts of the world, the problem is one of resources and facilities for education. But many education administrators, policy-makers and experts also regard child work as an important competing activity drawing children away from school. Some speculate that most of the out-of-school children work essentially full-time, although there is still little statistical confirmation of this. Some argue that families do not properly value education. They often play down complaints against the education system and blame low school-enrolment, attendance, performance and completion primarily on external factors such as a lack of child motivation and parental ignorance or neglect, family poverty, and children's work. But this belies the evidence that, all over the world, severe education-system problems and failures are also a major deterrent against school attendance. A significant proportion of working children are in the labour force not out of sheer economic necessity, but because they have dropped out of school and wish to make productive use of their time. This factor is so important that it is worth digressing for a moment to consider the overall problems of education systems as background for understanding how they infringe on the work of children.

In the 1980s, education spending declined in many parts of the world, especially in Latin America and sub-Saharan Africa, often because of national indebtedness and structural adjustment. Today, major discrepancies in access to education and educational levels still are found in many countries, often correlating closely with distortions in spending. Budgetary allocations to the various levels of education across national boundaries are now extremely uneven, including in the distribution of funds between the different education levels. Take Brazil, Chile, and the Dominican Republic for example: in all three, the share of education budgets for primary schooling rose in the 1980s, but higher education still received a greater proportion of government funds than primary education. Thus, in Brazil in 1986, more than a quarter of government spending on the sector went to higher education. In Argentina, the share of primary education fell in the 1980s while that of higher education rose. These were not unusual cases. This tendency was especially detrimental to poor children, in that investment in higher education benefits the better off disproportionately. Recent years have seen a concerted international effort to correct such imbalances by shifting more attention to universal primary education and, while some success is being achieved, it is still uneven at best.

There is also evidence of a widening knowledge gap between the richest and poorest countries. This is associated with a growing divergence in total enrolment in education at all levels as a proportion of the population nationally aged 6 to 23, as well as in the average grade levels to which children study (school life expectancy). In some countries, school life expectancy remains below the level — four years — considered the minimum duration of formal education for the acquisition of literacy and other basic knowledge and life skills. In 1993, UNESCO reported that in certain sub-Saharan African countries the average 6-year-old could expect to receive little more than two years of formal education, and girls not much more than a year, compared with nearly 16 years for boys and girls in the United States.[12]

Even in the wealthier Latin American and Caribbean region, where over 90 per cent of children start school, education expansion has been achieved in part by cutting teachers' salaries, shortening school days, introducing school shifts, transferring the costs of schooling to pupils' families, and other quite damaging measures.[13] This has had a serious adverse effect on education quality, as expressed in the problems of over-age students, grade repetition, and functional illiteracy. Some 20 per cent of children start primary school late; 40 per cent repeat the first year and 30 per cent repeat the second, with an overall average of primary school repetition of about 30 per cent per year.[14] As many as half of all children in Latin America graduating from the basic cycle are not functionally literate. The emerging evidence of the problem of repetition triggered evaluations in seven countries in the region. These confirmed very low levels of achievement by comparison with other developing regions. It is now accepted that low educational achievement is a major factor, along with a lack of relevance, in school drop-out in Latin America.[15]

Chapter One emphasized how children's individual and social characteristics often dictate their life experiences and expectations. An education system that is poorly designed can reinforce social inequalities. Serious equity problems associated with income and place of residence were also identified in Latin America. While repetition rates average nearly 30 per cent for the region, they rise to over 50 per cent for students in the lower half of the income distribution, and are probably even higher in the bottom quintile.[16] Over 80 per cent of students in the lower half of the income distribution do not master reading comprehension. In rural and urban slum communities, not only are schools fewer, they are also likely to be older, more dilapidated, far less well-equipped and have poorly trained teachers. Until recently, the rural illiteracy rate for the region was three times higher than the urban for women and four times higher for men. Aggregate achievement scores of students in state primary schools in urban slums and rural areas (particularly in indigenous areas) are usually about half those of better-off students, even though teaching is of similar quality.

In some parts of the world, gender is a major factor in educational difference, females consistently faring less well than males — especially at secondary and higher levels. At primary level, the gap between male and female gross enrolment is widest in the poorest countries. In South Asia, girls' primary school enrolment trailed behind that of boys by 29 per cent in the period 1986 to 1989 and the situation was little better in sub-Saharan Africa or the Middle East.[17] Gender bias in inheritance and marriage practices, and in the labour market is a decisive factor in the low participation of girls in school. Girls' education is less valued and girls start work younger than boys. They also work longer hours and more intensively, undermining school attendance and performance and leading to drop-out.

The problem of out-of-school children is not only one of lack of facilities or interest in education; there is also child or parental refusal to make use of existing facilities, reflecting the poor quality and irrelevance of education available to them. While educators have tended to interpret parental reluctance to school their children as ignorance about the value of education, increasing evidence of abysmal school performance and lack of benefits to children suggests that parental attitudes may be more rational than believed. Thus, apparent indifference to education is more likely to be symptomatic of a dysfunctional education system than a failure to value education.[18] Poor families make considerable sacrifices to get their children into decent schools and basic coverage is expanding but, at the same time, huge numbers of children enrol only to drop out early, disappointed by their experience of school. Many repeat one or more grades, utilizing space and resources which otherwise could be devoted to reducing those children now out of school. This raises doubts about the extent to which inferior schools really contribute to child development and, by implication, about whether decisions by children to prefer work to school should always be regarded as the fault of children instead of the fault of schools.

Working children comprise a very large group of school-age children (as mentioned in the Introduction, the ILO estimates roughly a quarter of a billion) whose right to an education is not being adequately recognized and served. While most school-age children who work at least part-time apparently manage to receive a basic education, a significant portion do not. Many of those who are at school find it hard to attend regularly, to keep up with their peers or to complete their education. This is partly for the same reasons that girls, children of the poor, and children in rural areas tend as a group to have lower school-enrolment, attendance, and completion rates. Since most working children are from low-income families and live in rural areas, and at least half are girls, they are disadvantaged educationally in comparison with other groups even before the effects of working are taken into consideration.

Children's work presents a number of obstacles for schooling. By starting school late, repeating school years, and lagging behind their peers, many working children gradually come to view school in a negative light and work as a far better use of their time. Quite a few of the education problems encountered by working children are not due to their work, however, but to the failure of education to take their special circumstances into account. Often, educational facilities are not realistically available to them. Schools may keep to hours or calendars that effectively exclude working children, such as children of farm families who must assist their parents during particular agricultural seasons. Children in cardamom cultivation in Guatemala, for instance, report that they must stop school a month before the end of the school year and are not released from the fields until six weeks after the new year has begun.[19] In other cases, children must attend school only where they live and are not permitted to take more practical advantage of schools located near their workplace.

The single entry point method employed in most formal education systems disadvantages children who are forced to start school late because of their work since they generally find themselves in a class with much younger children using materials ill-suited to their developmental capacity. This is a cause of embarrassment and frustration, leading to a disinclination to continue at school. Often, working children are met at school with undisguised hostility by teachers, and sometimes by peers, and may be actively discouraged from attending. While such rejection may be linked to broader ethnic, gender or class discrimination, it has been especially noted for particular occupational groups such as street traders or scavengers. Teachers are frequently reported to stereotype working children as dirty, disrespectful, unintelligent, criminally inclined, and a negative influence from which other children should be protected.

While poor countries generally experience the most acute problems in education, worrying trends can be detected in several wealthier nations, where schooling may not be an added incentive for children to work but cannot, by any stretch of the imagination, be described as a feature of a carefree and happy childhood. In some countries, education is less a medium of self-realization and liberation and more an all-consuming way of life, nearly every minute of the day for young people being organized around school and, in particular, examinations.[20] With high levels of compulsion and extremely long and gruelling hours of study reducing drastically the opportunities for recreation and play, this kind of education shares some of the more negative characteristics of detrimental child work.

The education system in Japan, for example, has become so competitive that even infants are affected, the 'infant education industry' selling devices like the 'Athleticot', a crib that promotes infant development by providing monthly age-appropriate challenges.[21] The device was developed by The Organization for Child Development, which is headed by Ibuka Masaru, author of numerous books championing an extremely assertive approach to early childhood development, with titles such as *Why Age Zero? Life is Decided at Age Zero* or *The Foetus is a Genius: Education Begins before Birth*. Research by Arita and Yamaoka[22] points to the incredible pressures experienced by Japanese school children. Fifty per cent of children in the capital region in the fourth to sixth grades, for instance, attend crammer schools for three hours each evening on top of homework, revision and other education obligations. Corporal punishment within schools is commonplace and a confidential report, *naishinsho*, on each child, which goes with the child from school to school, polices behaviour, instilling great anxiety in children and their families. Competition is underpinned by regular examinations and tests:

> ... the routine of constant testing habituates children from an early age to their insinuation in a hierarchical world, where their place is "objectively" determined by their standard deviation score (*hensachi*, a household word), which for upper-level grade school students, junior-high students, and high-school students becomes an identifier more substantive than their names since it denotes the rank of school they can aspire to.[23]

School refusal — technically defined as absence exceeding 50 days per school year — is recognized officially as on the increase in Japan.

The pressure to attend and perform well at school which is felt by children in many rich countries and by many rich children in poor countries is accompanied by other significant changes in the way children's lives are organized. In Chapter One we discussed how, in the wealthier communities of the world, one strategy for compensating children for the loss of their productive role and for protecting them and fostering their development in a safe and appropriate environment has been the expansion of formal childhood organizations and institutions, educational, social, and recreational. This 'domestication' of childhood is symbolized by children's confinement within their homes and in organized activities and settings and also by their isolation from the adult world of responsibility and autonomy. A study of English children aged between 7 and 11 by Hillman, Adams and Whitelegg, conducted first in 1971 and repeated in 1991, indicates serious costs in terms of children's freedom and their ability to negotiate the world around them:

> Whereas nearly three-quarters of the children in 1971 were allowed to cross roads on their own, by 1990 the proportion had fallen to a half. There was an even more marked decline in the proportion allowed to use buses on their own: half were allowed to do so in 1971 in contrast to only one in seven in 1990 ... Perhaps, most disturbingly, very few children are allowed out after dark by their parents — effectively a curfew for them. Younger children are most affected, with the difference, as would be expected, declining with age: few 11 or 12-year-olds now or indeed then would accept such restrictions on their independence.[24]

There were also important distinctions according to gender, girls having far less freedom to go out than boys. By contrast, German children of comparable age and social circumstances were found to have much greater freedom and only when it came to going out after dark was gender a major distinguishing factor. English parents mentioned the fear of assault and the unreliability of their children as the main reasons for confining children within the home, while German parents were more concerned about traffic hazards. This 'domestication' of childhood in tandem with demanding full-time schooling replicates detrimental aspects of full-time work in a confined atmosphere, and should by no means be considered an acceptable model of child development and empowerment.

If education is to help reduce the most intolerable forms of child work and provide protection for children in part-time work, a great deal needs to be done to make it more effective and interesting for working children. However, this does not imply adoption of industrialized-country schooling and child-raising models that disempower children and place them under great stress. In both poor and rich countries, education needs to be more child-friendly. Education reform is most likely to succeed if education-planners take into account the reasons why children fail to attend, repeat school years or drop out. This means listening to children.

Children's assessments of education

That educators and policy-makers view the relationship between child work and education rather differently from parents and children is hardly surprising since they almost never ask the views of children and their families, or discuss with them the meaning and implications of other types of information available on the subject. Most information coming to education policy-makers is from official statistics, from internal reports, and from special studies conducted by academics or other outside experts. They also see education from the standpoint of providers rather than consumers. Ultimately, however, universal education can be achieved only when children and their parents truly want and value school, and this depends a great deal on the quality and relevance of education on offer and the degree to which it is really accessible.

Parents and families have a strong influence on how their children regard education. They are generally well-predisposed towards school, although they often fear that it may undermine the child's ability to survive in an environment of poverty, high unemployment, and malnutrition.[25] They note the lack of secure, well-paid jobs even for school graduates and often decide that there is little point in children staying at school when early work participation enables them to learn important practical skills and establish a foothold on the ladder of employment. On the other hand, it is also true that: "the worse unemployment becomes, and the more a given school certificate is devalued, the stronger becomes the pressure for more education".[26]

In some of the countries where children are at school and out of the workplace well into their teenage years, planners have felt obliged to introduce compensatory mechanisms for delaying entry to work through the vocationalization of education and training. In Britain, there have been discussions about paying young people for staying on at school and various measures have been instituted, ranging from the Technical and Vocational Education Initiative (TVEI) to the Youth Training Scheme (YTS), now Training Youth, to facilitate the smooth transition to work. Nevertheless, vocational and non-formal alternatives are not always greeted by children and parents with enthusiasm because they are perceived to be of inferior quality and status. And Mizen comments that such schemes fail to provide: "... a grasp of the meaning of work for young people and its centrality to their experience of growing up. At its most immediate, young people gain intimate knowledge of work through child working and this is significant for growing up ... this is how young people gain knowledge of the social relations of production."[27]

Most children wish to receive at least a basic education, and studies inquiring into the education experience and aspirations of working children show they fit the mode. In several parts of the world, working children have taken part in campaigns to secure their right to an education. The United Children of Marcacao, a union of child sugarcane and crab factory workers in Brazil, occupied the mayor's office and demanded and won transportation from the factory into town for evening classes.[28] In 1991, the All Nepal Trade Union held a demonstration in Kathmandu in front of the parliamentary house. The Child Labour Union, Bal Majdoor Sangh, was formed and a letter was submitted by the Union to the prime minister demanding, among other things, the provision of school facilities for all working children.[29] When representatives of organized working children met at the International Meeting of Working Children held in Kundapur, India, and set out ten recommendations, the fourth was a demand for an education system "of which the methodology and content are adapted to our reality".[30]

Children in the Rädda Barnen sample had many positive things to say about school. They saw it as a way of escaping poverty and the drudgery of unskilled or semi-skilled work: "I will not be just a house helper for life ... I can be hired in a decent office ... I can go far to other lands ... I will not be poor forever."[31] They also acknowledged the importance of skills like literacy and numeracy learned at school. Some valued the opportunity of wearing a uniform or receiving a school snack, while others said they enjoyed playing games with their friends during break time. Quite a few mentioned that there was a sense of achievement to be had from passing exams and winning games and a sense of pride at being held in high regard by family and community: "If I go to school people around are going to say 'see her daughter knows how to read and write' which is going to please my parents".[32] As was suggested in Chapter One, this kind of social endorsement is fundamental to the development of children's self-esteem and confidence. Some of the children appreciated school because it offers the chance to learn good manners and avoid anti-social habits like substance abuse or stealing. A significant number perceived their teachers as a positive influence and a source of support: "They guide us, love us, support us and take care of us; they teach us new things."[33]

In fact, many children go to surprising lengths to obtain an education even while they work. Having considered the good and bad things about both work and school, over 200 of the children in the Rädda Barnen sample commented individually on whether, in their present family circumstances, they thought only going to work, only going to school or going to work and attending school was best for them. Most of the children valued education, although not to the exclusion of work, and combining school and work was the preference for an overwhelming 72 per cent, with more girls than boys favouring school only. There were some important variations in these findings by country and occupation. Filipino children in particular viewed school and work as interdependent: One girl remarked: "Work provides support to schooling" and a boy said: "We need both of them, so why not do both?" The two activities were seen by these children to offer different benefits: "... we won't become poor financially and mentally ... it is flattering to be called working student". In contrast, few of the Bangladeshi children were able to attend school and none viewed 'school only' as a realistic option.[34] Of the 24 per cent who favoured 'work only', the majority were boys employed in embroidery and sari workshops who felt that their present jobs were incompatible with school attendance. Similarly, sex workers in Ethiopia felt unable to attend due to their hours of work and the social stigma of their occupation, which would lead to insults by teachers and other students.

The majority of children probably feel that they receive an acceptable quality of schooling, but some are ambivalent about school, reflecting legitimate concerns about both its quality and its relevance. Indeed, when given a chance, children and their parents loudly criticize irrelevant curricula that spend more time on, say, colonial history or the biographies of political leaders than on practical information and skills that will help children survive and prosper. Most children find it difficult to memorize information of this kind which has no obvious value to them, making it difficult to consolidate their learning. Distaste for or boredom at school were cited by children in studies from Bangalore, Brazil, and Lima as very significant in non-enrolment and drop-out.[35]

Children are acutely aware that one of the gravest problems is lack of resources for education. From every developing region come widespread reports of schools that lack even the barest essentials such as books and blackboards. Many cram large numbers of children — 70 to 80, or even more — into a single class, frequently combining several school years in the same room. Children may be required to share desks and chairs or to take turns to sit. Many schools have insufficient space for play and exercise and lack basic facilities like potable water, lavatories, and lighting. Often, in highly gender-segregated societies, a failure to provide separate facilities for males and females makes it impossible for girls to attend once they reach puberty. The cost of school is another serious concern and turns out to be an important reason why many children work. In Latin America, for example, state education is supposedly free, but all the same, parents now pay up to one-third of school operating costs and part of their already small income is allocated to various school 'contributions', as well as to transport, uniforms, books, and the like.[36] In government schools, fees are often levied informally by teachers, often to make up very poor salaries. Children regularly report that they must work in order to help earn money that will permit them — or their siblings — to attend school. The income forgone due to school participation is another major consideration for many families. The problem of school expenses can be especially serious for large families. As one girl said:

> "When I can no longer attend school because of failure to pay fees, my father tells me to sit home and help with work in the coffee fields. After some time he tells me to forget about school completely so that I can give my younger brothers and sisters a chance to attend school. The problem is he is still producing more children."[37]

Children in Kyakatabe, a Ugandan village, felt conditions at school to be more decisive in undermining attendance and performance than work. They were critical of the poor state of school buildings, which let in the wind and rain, and feared that they might collapse on them. The dusty floors were said to be a breeding ground for jiggers, causing fevers. School chairs had protruding nails which tore uniforms.

Almost as common are stories of teachers who have not mastered the skills they are supposed to teach, or who use class time primarily to sleep or conduct purely personal business, or who seldom show up in class, simply collecting their pay, or who come to school inebriated, or who accept no questions and punish children who try to ask them.[38] Kyakatebe children had many complaints about their teachers, who they said were unqualified, poorly paid and had insufficient land to keep their families, accounting for their low morale and frequent absenteeism. The children felt that they were blamed by teachers for their problems, and were exploited by them, being required to get food from home and do chores, like fetching water and digging the school garden, to make up for the low pay. Children in the Rädda Barnen sample from the Philippines and Guatemala also mentioned teacher corruption: "Our teachers ask many donations from us." And they complained that teachers are extremely unreliable: "Teachers many times lie to us. They say, we are going to come such and such a day and then they don't come anymore."[39]

There is an even far darker side: many children associate school with violence and threats of violence. Enquiries into the school experience of working children frequently reveal complaints of beatings, cruel humiliation, and other forms of abuse. These include not only fights and intimidation involving other children, but also serious instances of violence, threats, and public ridicule by teachers. In the United States, the fear of pupil violence or exposure to actual violence at school or on the way to school is one of the main reasons for non-attendance and drop-out.[40] In Britain, bullying in schools has led to several suicides and many attempted suicides. Because accounts of physical and mental violence by teachers do not readily surface from education-system reporting or evaluations, the scope of this problem tends to be ignored by educational bureaucracies and the public at large, but children readily point it out, and many flee it by dropping out of school and going to work. In Sudan, punishment by teachers was found to be an important cause of children running away from home.[41] In many parts of the world, children consider even severe corporal punishment to be an integral and normal part of the teaching method, which is not to say they necessarily approve of it. Even in some industrialized countries otherwise concerned for the safety of their children, schools are expected to liberally mete out corporal punishment to school children. The idea of school as a major source of violence against children may surprise some readers, but child reports of this nature are extremely common and widespread. We do not hear much about it in the literature because it is a nasty little secret of education that is hidden away.

The problem is exacerbated by the fact that, in various cultures, adults sanction school violence against children in the name of 'discipline'. A boy at a school in Ethiopia, for example, was punished by a teacher at the request of his mother, because of an argument he had had with his brother.[42] He was hung upside down and forced to inhale smoke from smouldering peppers. This made him violently sick and he remained ill for a week. The mother was eventually obliged to seek medical assistance. Physical punishment of children of the same town at both home and school included pinching, beating, slapping, inhalation of pepper smoke, tying up, being thrown out of class, and being made to kneel for long periods. Some reported fainting and nosebleeds after being forced to contort their bodies in unnatural positions and remain there for long periods. Other disciplinary measures included threat of exposure to wild animals, punishment by the police or community leaders, isolation, dismissal from school, and insults. Behaviour that precipitated punishment included fighting with other children, talking or laughing in class, inability to answer a question, failure to do homework or follow the teacher's instructions, and theft.

Teachers in Addis Ababa, Ethiopia, also reported that they use corporal punishment as a matter of course, maintaining that students are conditioned to beatings and would not respond to lesser measures.[43] Boys in Bangladesh provide similar testimony: "They beat us with a cane or a bamboo stick on our palms or back"; "At times they also push our head under a table and hit us on our buttocks"; "We are also made to stand on a stool holding our ears".[44] Sexual humiliation and abuse was a complaint made by a Bangladeshi girl: "Some teachers have bad intentions. They kiss some girls on the cheeks, pinch their cheeks and even touch their bodies. One of them often said 'I will tear your chest apart and eat it'". And a Filipino boy remarked: "Our teachers undress us, genitals exposed."[45]

Children tend to consider corporal punishment unjust and humiliating and are critical of its use as a disciplinary measure: "I would have gone to school if the teachers taught me properly instead of beating me."[46] Students in Addis Ababa maintained that it was not merely cruel but also ineffective. They argued that frequent castigation dulls the mind and makes the student remember the punishment not the misdemeanour.[47] Some children, they commented, become unforgiving and resentful towards the teacher leading to a dislike of learning, causing them to quit school. Certainly, such treatment is inconsistent with the CRC's insistence that education should promote the broader personal development of children.

Work is a cause of punishment at school, as children in both the Rädda Barnen and Kyakatebe studies testified. They talked about being punished for late arrival at school, which was generally due to work done at home early in the morning, and highlighted the injustice of teachers refusing to listen to their reasons for being late. Work before school causes some Kyakatebe children to go without breakfast, the weariness and hunger leading to poor performance and castigation. These children were fearful of their teachers, indicating a reluctance to ask questions in class because they might be penalized. A nine-year-old boy said: "Refusal to be punished also results in being chased away from school".[48]

For a significant proportion of children, then, school attendance constitutes a traumatic experience which undermines rather than promotes overall psychological, emotional, and cognitive development. Many of them do not consider school to be the safe, child-friendly place that adults assume it to be. The problem is by no means limited to developing countries. There are reports of both new morbidity problems and a rise in the incidence of so-called adult diseases among children in several industrialized countries and school pressure is quoted as the main cause. Thus, in South Korea the stress of preparing for university entrance exams is cited as the cause of over 200 suicides a year among third-year high-school students.[49] In Japan, a nationwide survey of grammar school children conducted in 1990 indicated that 63.2 per cent were suffering from high levels of blood cholesterol, 36.2 per cent from ulcers, 22.1 per cent from high blood pressure, and 21.4 per cent from diabetes.[50] There are also reports concerning a new pervasiveness of eczema and chronic constipation among Japanese school children. And Aderansu, the leading artificial hair transplant manufacturers in Japan, is said to be selling wigs to school children suffering from stress-related baldness attributable to the pressures of attendance at crammer schools and bullying in their regular schools.[51]

Discouragement and low self-esteem are natural products of child-unfriendly education systems that readily consign children to failure without having first made a real effort to help them succeed, and out-of-school child workers are eloquent in describing the pain of school failure. On the other hand, people in contact with working children frequently comment on how clever and curious many of them seem. There is evidence that many bright school children become bored and depressed from lack of stimulation and eventually drift into work as a more interesting and challenging, and sometimes safer, activity. It is obvious that education that is unavailable or discriminates, that stunts or warps personality, that disparages children's own skills and talents, or that discourages mental initiative is inconsistent with child development and with the basic intent of the Convention on the Rights of the Child and the Jomtien and World Summit for Children declarations. It is also obvious that such education cannot reasonably be advanced as an instrument of reform in connection with children's work. The irony is that education is by far the largest investment made by the public sector in supposedly promoting the development and well-being of children. Such widespread experience of school as a source of physical and mental violence adds credibility to the claims of many working children, already cited in Chapter Three, that government — not merely the fact of working — is directly to blame for much of their abuse and exploitation.

What needs to be done?

Some might say that, on balance, it is far better to strengthen the genuinely developmental aspects of school education than to try to bolster up the developmental side of children's work while also trying to protect children from workplace abuses. Clearly there is an urgent need for education reform in many countries. But, as we have indicated, it is not so clear that most children need to give up all work in order to be able to reach their full developmental potential. Indeed, as suggested in Chapter One, work may have far more to offer children than is at present apparent, although work may not always be compatible with successful performance and school completion. And, as we indicated in Chapters Two and Three, when working children are given an opportunity to be heard, many of them insist that their work is in itself an educational experience from which they learn a great deal, and are reluctant to give it up in favour of school only. As the Rädda Barnen study found, many children claim that the best education is to be had from a combination of school and limited work under safe conditions, and they insist that they should have a right to quality schools or other education facilities that are available at affordable cost and according to schedules that permit that combination. This is entirely consistent with modern child development thinking, described in Chapter One, that children have multiple intelligence and learning needs and that they require diverse learning environments and experiences to develop these various capacities.

It appears, however, that opinions about the educational value of work are sensitive to the kind of work and working conditions involved. While possible educational aspects of street trading, for example, might be observable, it is more difficult to imagine how simple, repetitive tasks performed for long hours under duress could have educational value. In this vein, as noted in Chapter Two, some critics of child work point out that children performing obsolete, low-technology tasks are not being prepared to cope with the modern world, and others have suggested that even 'modern' jobs, such as tending the counter in a fast-food restaurant, may be so narrow and repetitive that they provide no worthwhile skills. Children, on the other hand, often insist that they learn generalized work skills and behaviour (such as how to get along with co-workers and supervisors) even in jobs with narrow or routine tasks. But they draw the line at work that is abusive, too burdensome, too long or otherwise beyond what they feel to be reasonable.

Working children frequently resent the lack of appropriate educational facilities and what they consider to be unfair educational discrimination against them. At the same time, they generally resist efforts to coerce them into unacceptable school situations or into abandoning their work if that means that they or their families must suffer undue deprivation. They usually say that they want a curriculum that effectively teaches not only basic literacy and numeracy, but also some vocational and life skills that can help them make their way now and in the future. That is to say, they request some sort of practical connection between education and work or other income generation.

Most government school systems are not prepared to offer that connection, and many actively resist this request for economic relevance as inappropriate 'vocationalization' that will lead to an 'inferior' second-tier system for the poor. There is great irony in this refusal when one considers that children are asking for better rather than worse education, and that many industrialized countries are moving quickly away from purely academic schools and towards a whole variety of work-related activities for all children — and not just a 'vocational track' minority — because they have found that the conventional school does not provide a holistic education and leaves children too unprepared for life. In those countries, career orientation, skills training, and work experience organized through the schools now may begin at ages equal to those of developing-country children asking for similar facilities, and this is considered a hallmark of educational progress. Developing-country education, however, is in many places at an impasse in which working children are malserved or not served at all by the rigid standards of government school systems, and governments refuse to consider what the children and their families insist would help.

As we saw in Chapter One, present-day understanding of child development increasingly emphasizes multiple intelligence, the importance of recognizing the present competence of children, the centrality of diverse relationships with adults in the development of character and life skills, and the educational importance of child participation in a broad spectrum of family and community life. If working children are to benefit from schooling, planners must cater to their need to integrate work, study, recreation, and play — acknowledging that work can have developmental value for children whilst also being sensitive to the risks to recreation opportunities, school performance, and completion which such a combination may entail. Doubt is increasingly being thrown on the developmental and moral validity of the conventional northern model of childhood, which excludes children from social and economic participation by treating childhood as but a preparatory period for adulthood, free of productive and other responsibilities and bereft of civic rights. It also questions the educative value of isolating and institutionalizing children in schools buffered from other aspects of life. The concept of holistic child development envisaged by the Convention on the Rights of the Child as a goal of education cannot be achieved in school alone. In order to become efficacious in their society, children need to experience a broad spectrum of social and economic life as participating citizens.

At the same time, research into how children learn indicates that different children learn in different ways, and all children must have a variety of learning environments if they are to develop their various capacities. When this is taken into account, it becomes clear that implementation of the Convention on the Rights of the Child calls for a more holistic approach to child development that provides for a broad spectrum of learning situations, not all of which can be accommodated in the conventional school classroom.

The first important contribution that education can make is to stop being part of the problem by pushing children away through its failures. The minimum objective is universal basic education, which is "education for all children that successfully equips them with at least the basic knowledge and skills necessary to participate as full citizens in a modern society and to take advantage of other opportunities to realize their individual potential".[52]

Achieving this objective entails attracting out-of-school children into school, retaining all children there until an appropriate age, and reintegrating children who have dropped out.

These aims will be best served by finding ways of structuring schools to fit the needs of working children, their families, and communities.[53]

This means increasing government investment in education to make schools more welcoming, safer, and more accessible to all children regardless of gender or class. It implies creating an educational environment that fully accepts children who work, even if they are unkempt or slightly unruly, and also making education more attractive and useful to working children and others. Since most children want an education and many make considerable sacrifices to get one, this approach would appear to be more promising than one based on compulsory education laws. It is more likely to bring children to school and keep them there and, in any case, is more beneficial for children because it entails improving education quality.

Educators increasingly understand that schools have to be linked more organically to the family and community life of the children they serve, and that they need to help equip children to deal with their present world as well as to prepare them for adulthood. This suggests finding ways to help children meet their family roles and responsibilities — including work responsibilities — and building education around them rather than competing with them. In many places, this may imply that education should assist them to cope with their work duties; in others, it may entail providing educational alternatives to inappropriate work. A growing inclination towards encouragement of broader child participation in family and community life as a developmental strategy, as proposed in Chapter One, raises the question of when children should be protected by isolating them from risk, how to identify children who are at risk (whether from injurious work or school drop-out), and how to help children to recognize risks and deal with them on their own.

More energy needs to be applied to reaching working children and pulling them into both educational and recreational activities. This entails considerable innovation and the use of non-traditional techniques, shifting towards a more reflective, problem-solving approach to education.[54] It involves upgrading teacher training, school materials, and other educational resources, looking to alternative funding sources, and introducing greater flexibility and creativity in education management, teaching and learning methods, curricula, school schedules, and location. It means mobilizing civil society, especially children. As Chapter Six indicated, non-governmental models are often more responsive than government to the circumstances and needs of working children. Several NGO non-formal education programmes have been successful in reaching working children with adequate education, finding innovative ways to make the connections that governments usually will not. Children tend to respond very positively to such programmes, but NGO resources are far too limited to deal with the immense scope of demand. In some instances, innovative approaches developed by NGOs for working children have proved so useful that they have been adopted for more general use. Publicly funded formal school systems have, by leaving more flexibility in their calendars and curriculum-planning procedures, managed to attract and retain out-of-school working children and to raise their education performance to fully satisfactory levels. Much more work of this nature is needed.

Creating a favourable environment for education

For working children to gain confidence and self-esteem through their participation in school, education needs to have broad societal recognition. Even the most innovative and creative of education programmes will fail unless it is credible to children, their families, and communities. Often, non-formal education is disparaged because it is considered second-rate, but this unjustly overlooks its superior ability to target especially needy groups of children and to act as a transitional mechanism bringing them into education systems. Programmes need to seek ways of providing both the skills needed to improve survival chances today and those compatible with lifelong learning that facilitate entry into society's more traditional means of upward mobility. In other words, every opportunity should be sought to provide skills consistent with the formal education system and/or the acquisition of valued credentials. Hence, many non-formal programmes serving working children use the national curriculum as a basis, while some have as a goal preparing children for entry into the state school system. This can be quite challenging because, due to different work demands, working children might be ready to enter school at different ages and bring a wide variety of life experiences and competencies to the classroom. Many children will have attended school for a while and dropped out, others may have attended intermittently and, some may not have been enrolled previously. When working children are involved, learner groups may be extremely heterogeneous in terms of their age, social or ethnic status, competence, work and family responsibilities, and previous educational and work experience.

Strategies for bringing schools closer to children and serving them more effectively are many and varied and must respond as far as possible to the children's actual needs and circumstances. Addressing children's specific circumstances emphasizes the need for a baseline assessment of children who work, highlighting the terms and conditions of their work, their education history, and education requirements. This is best done through the kinds of participatory processes, involving the children, their families, and community discussed in Chapter Four. By first learning about the precise circumstances of working girls, the Self Employed Women's Association in Ahmedabad, India, has been able to accommodate the specific needs of different occupational groups, in this case patch-workers, paper-pickers and cart-pullers. The three occupational groups were different ethnically and also had different educational experiences, necessitating individually tailored curricula. The cart-pullers were totally illiterate and so needed to learn basic literacy, while the paper-pickers had attended school and the patch-workers were still attending and so could be offered language classes. All three occupations are associated with low incomes and so an additional objective was to train the girls in weaving, circuit board assembly and other skills offering the potential for a higher standard of living.

Frequently, one of the most serious obstacles to the provision of education for working children is that making time for schooling is seen by employers as a distraction, a threat to children's productivity. However, experience demonstrates that many employers can be persuaded to allow or provide for children's education. Critical to the successful outcome of education programmes for working children is the identification of individuals and groups with a vested interest in their work and the development of mechanisms for ensuring the collaboration of employers, parents, and others. It is worth remembering that 'factory schools', in which children and unlettered young persons were released from work for a limited period of instruction, were in many places a major means of mass education during the industrialization of Europe and North America. In many countries, industrial associations, firms, service clubs, and other private sector groups are becoming more interested and involved in improving the effectiveness of local schools. They can play a major role in persuading employers of the importance of ensuring adequate educational time and opportunity to any children who work for them, including those who work only part-time.

Managing and administering education

A key concern with programmes targeting working children is whether they can be sustained on a large scale and with a wide variety of occupational groups, each one of which may have different competencies, work experiences, and educational needs. This question is especially relevant for programmes that offer stipends and other financial incentives. One important strategy for sustaining an educational approach that is responsive to the needs of working children in different groups and categories is decentralization of certain decisions to the local level. Decentralization of education planning and management has recently received strong support from the World Bank, which has provided loans to facilitate this process in several countries. The Bangladesh Rural Advancement Committee (BRAC) has successfully developed a national education programme which has achieved high levels of community involvement and allows considerable autonomy among parents and communities in the planning, implementation, and continual evaluation of education, providing basic literacy for almost 1 million out-of-school rural children in 30,000 schools in rural Bangladesh. The programme began as a response to the problems of bringing education to rural villages in which children were needed to participate in certain agricultural and household tasks. Although not intended exclusively for working children, BRAC schools recognize the need to accommodate children's economic roles by adjusting school calendars and teaching style, and applying to the regular primary curriculum some practical relevance. Currently, these schools are achieving completion rates of over 95 per cent for the three-year course, after which most children enter fourth grade in government primary schools.[55]

In several countries, community schools have proved particularly effective at improving gender and geographic equity in education, increasing the enrolment of rural children in areas where there are few schools and of girls in societies where their education access is constrained by social restrictions on leaving the community. Under an agreement with UNICEF and the Ministry of Education, community schools were first piloted in Dar El Salam, a district of Upper Egypt, in 1992 with the explicit aim of removing regional and gender disparities in education. Teams seeking potential sites found that there was a strong interest in education for girls, but only if it could be made available within the community. Schoolrooms were provided by local families close to their homes and management committees were formed to ensure regular attendance. Schooling was offered free of charge and local women were trained as para-professional teachers. Whereas previously in many villages less than 15 per cent of girls were attending school, by the end of 1995 they made up 70 per cent of pupils in 110 community schools. When pupils of the first four schools took the Ministry's standardized third-year exam, they all passed, doing much better than children from government schools. The aim is to provide 200 more such schools by 1999.

Community decision-making does not always guarantee children's best interests, since, as we discussed in Chapter Four, adults close to children are not always aware of their real problems or needs. To provide effectively for working children, education planners and administrators need to furnish opportunities for children's representation in bodies that make decisions about their education and also for their participation in planning and evaluating their own schools or other educational programmes. As already indicated, this is implied in Articles 12 and 13 of the Convention on the Rights of the Child, which provide children capable of forming their own opinions with the right to express their views freely and to participate in decisions made on their behalf. It is also consistent with the finding discussed in Chapter One, that children benefit by meaningful participation in civil and political processes. And it is desired by the representatives of organized working children who met in Kundapur, India, in December 1996, who stated: "We want to be consulted in all decisions concerning us, at local, national or international levels."[56] Chapter Six addressed some of the general issues pertaining to such participation by working children in programme and policy decisions.

Experience with children participating in the planning of their own school activities is gradually spreading. For example, it is a matter of policy for the New Schools (Escuela Nueva) educational reform in Colombia, where children's councils are now common and the formation of children as participating citizens is an educational objective. The Panchayat Toofan experience in India, described in Chapter Six, has included systematic participation by children in local decisions about many aspects of the education programme. In one case, children were during a short experimental period offered different styles of education, and afterwards they suggested elements from each that could be incorporated into a model best suiting them, which was done.[57]

Children can also be given much more scope to participate meaningfully in the education process itself. As Chapter One stated, treating children as active participants in their own learning rather than passive recipients of knowledge is developmental, confirming the integrity of children's background and experience. There are many ways in which learning can be made child-centred. First and foremost, it requires that educators act as facilitators, organizing activities, providing materials, and otherwise stimulating, guiding, and advising, rather than teaching or delivering knowledge.[58] Learning sessions need to be built as much around children's own experience, knowledge, and skills as around what children do not know. Educational materials can be developed with children, drawing on their own ideas and perceptions. The pace of learning can be adjusted to the children's potential rather than matched against formal age and grade requirements. And beyond the core subjects of literacy and numeracy, children can be given greater choice in selecting their own curriculum options according to their specific interests and circumstances. A focus on citizenship and awareness, as in the self-advocacy and liberation education programmes in some parts of Latin America, can be particularly effective in programmes for socially and economically marginalized groups (especially girls) who are denied access to decision-making processes.

Facilitating access to school

Accommodating working children may entail considerable adjustment of school schedules. Many working children simply cannot attend school daily for six to eight hours. They may be able to attend short courses, or shifts, however, or every-other-day or break-time classes, night classes or weekend schooling. Flexible schedules may prove the best option in many situations. Arranging lessons to fit work routines, including seasonal variations in work, and condensing curricula can help give children maximum possible access to education. For example, typical northern school years with long summer vacations reflect an earlier time when the school calendars were adjusted to specifically accommodate the summer work of farm children, assuring the chance to both work and study. In the BRAC programme in Bangladesh, there are wide variations locally in the school calendar, no homework, a shorter day than in government schools, very short vacations, and about 20 per cent more total days in session than government schools. Escuela Nueva in Colombia, which also caters for rural working children, has adopted a different approach, based on the existing calendar but with self-instruction as a means of allowing children to proceed at their own pace and not to fall behind when they miss classes.

However attractive some of these options may appear, they need careful monitoring. Research shows that the intensity of education — or the total number of hours of yearly class attendance — contributes vitally to its effectiveness, indicating that intermittent classes or short shifts may not always be efficacious. Shortening an already inadequate amount of time that disadvantaged children spend in schools can ensure that they continue to experience second-rate educational opportunities unless quality is high enough to compensate. Of course, time needs also to be set aside for recreation and play. Shift systems in particular can overstretch teachers since running two or more classes a day can be extremely tiring. Having younger children in school for longer hours, including 'extra curricular activities', can also be a positive contribution in terms of childcare for hard-pressed families, especially those headed by single mothers. In Latin America, the shift system has been identified as part of the problem, not the solution, in that it undermines education impact. Conceding that at present only 50-70 per cent of the available time is used for active teaching — the balance being taken up by administrative procedures, discipline or idle time — additional learning time has been provided in Argentina, Chile, Costa Rica, Mexico, and Venezuela by lengthening annual or daily schedules for all students or by providing time for remedial work for low achievers.[59] Chile and Uruguay are planning an extension from five to seven contact hours per day. The issue of contact hours needs further sorting out in regard to working children. It is fairly common for non-formal education programmes to achieve literacy with far fewer hours than do government schools. It still is not clear what motivational quality or other factors account for their greater productivity.

Another way of bringing schools closer to working children is to site classes near to or at the workplace. It is often assumed that purpose-built school buildings at the centre of a community are an essential component of a good education system but experience suggests this is not necessarily the case. Children frequently leave their community to work elsewhere, making access to community facilities impossible. In some cultures, school access is a particular problem for girls, who may work within their homes and not be allowed to venture beyond the boundaries of their community to attend a school in another village or town.

Use can be made of improvised venues close to or at the children's workplace, enabling them to study in shifts throughout the working day. In Bangladesh, Pakistan, Kenya, and Mali, governments have accredited mosque schools which make it possible for girls to be educated within their own communities and under the supervision of the respected local leader, the Imam.[60] Some non-formal education programmes run work-site 'pavement schools' for children working on the streets, in markets or railway and bus stations. Others make extensive use of street educators or distance learning, the latter supported by home visits and occasional classes held outside working hours. The Institute of Psychological and Educational Research (IPER) in Calcutta decided against night school because the children work long hours during the day and are too exhausted in the evenings to benefit. Instead they offer working children the formal primary school curriculum in 'holiday schools', classes being held on Saturdays for two hours and Sundays for four, supported by individualized lessons and home-teaching programmes. Additional services include health care, free books and utensils, local outings, and drawing competitions. An evaluation showed that almost 80 per cent of the children came to school for more than 40 per cent of the year and at least 25 per cent achieved 80 per cent attendance.[61]

Street educators in Brazil make initial contact with working children and provide transitional non-formal education to prepare them to enter the formal school system. This entails reaching children through activities and channels that they are familiar with and have both reality and attractiveness for them. The AXE programme in Salvador in Brazil has made use of local music and dance culture, for example, as a way to bring street and working children into educational activities. Involving them in drum corps and *capoeira* (a local combination of dance and ritualized combat) activities is a stepping-stone to literacy and other activities that prepare children to enter or re-enter school as successful students.[62]

Distance learning has been facilitated by the creation of mobile schools and mobile libraries in China, Peru, and Brazil as a means of reaching dispersed rural populations. In China, where some communities are not served by roads, horses were used. In the *'escola volantes'* (rolling schools) of Lages, a municipality in southern Brazil, four vans enabled teachers to reach children within an area of over 5,000 square kilometres. They would meet with children three days a month and leave assignments and materials to be completed before the next three-day session.[63] Providing creches in schools can benefit working girls particularly, making it possible for them to leave younger siblings in the care of others while they attend classes.

Learning and teaching methods

Research comparing schools that serve very similar populations of students often reveals very different levels of achievement by school, indicating that some promote learning far more successfully than others.[64] School size, school values, classroom organization, teacher attitudes and behaviour have all been found to affect achievement. However, changes to the content and methods of education are less agreed upon than adjustments to school location and calendar. Traditional educational approaches based on authoritarian teaching methods, certification, fixed schedules, and a structured environment have been tried, tested, and found wanting in the case of many working children. Nevertheless, it is not possible to get away from the essentials of reading, writing, and counting, because these are the cornerstone for other kinds of learning as well as for successful integration within the modern world. Current thinking, however, emphasizes that an academic education does not have to be esoteric or irrelevant.

As a means of increasing the effectiveness of school education, the priority should be to strengthen the genuinely developmental aspects of education (including school-supervised extracurricular activities) in line with the latest child development thinking, as discussed in Chapter One. Educationalists sometimes advocate the introduction of effective learning principles long employed in traditional systems of informal education based on work, although when considering the popular view of education as an instrument of child labour reform, this is perhaps a little ironic. This entails drawing as far as possible on children's own skills and knowledge. It also means devising learning models that are sensitive to the special needs and achievements of the children who, as indicated, may be very heterogeneous in terms of aptitude, background, age, and experience. To sustain children's interest in learning and also to make education more relevant, comprehension, critical analysis, problem-solving, and adaptation to changing conditions and new learning situations should be given precedence over the acquisition of knowledge or learning by memory. Experiential learning, or applying the knowledge and skills acquired to practical situations, is another crucial educational strategy. These approaches allow children to practise and learn on their own terms, using their own language, concepts, and understandings and in this way to build children's confidence, self-esteem, and self-efficacy. Such methods also allow children to incorporate learning into their own aspirations and life effort, what some educators see as the true meaning of literacy. It will be recalled that Chapter One emhasized the critical importance of a life project in children's development.

Another aim is to create an informal atmosphere that provides ample opportunity for student discussion and interaction. To enable children to learn free from anxiety, an effort needs to be made to help teachers understand better and respond more effectively to the competencies, problems, and needs of working children. Monitoring systems conducted by supervisors, educators, and pupils, as opposed to competitive learning procedures and exams, can be established, and extensive use made of local educators whom the children know and trust. Art, dance, mime, song, drama and role-play, games, and stories relevant to the children's daily lives can be employed in place of formal teaching sessions. Classrooms can be made to look attractive by covering walls with posters and artwork and locally generated materials, including recycled waste collected by the children, can be adapted as learning aids. In various parts of the world, 'joyful learning' movements are successfully rejuvenating classroom instruction and raising school attendance and completion rates. Some feel this to be among the most powerful of all interventions.

We have already argued that, because of the diversity of experience among working children, learner groups comprised of young workers tend to be extremely heterogeneous. The orthodox view is that homogeneous learner groups are better in educational terms, but heterogeneity should be seen as an opportunity and a strength. By introducing flexible promotion mechanisms and multi-grade teaching, the Escuela Nueva programme has managed to keep almost 80 per cent of children in school in the country's vast coffee-growing areas where their help during harvest is essential.[65] Students learn at their own pace and those who are absent for work can continue from where they left off when they return. Personalized and group learning and school relevance are key objectives. The programme has achieved significant reductions in desertion and repetition and improvements in primary school completion rates and education quality. Job satisfaction among teachers has also increased.

With heterogeneous learner groups it is particularly important to allow children to progress at their own pace rather than according to a predetermined schedule based on age and grade. Also important is to find ways of encouraging over-age children to enrol and attend, a task that may require specially developed materials and adult-education styles of teaching and learning. Imaginative strategies may be needed to keep children in school and an effort made not to penalize them for being absent. This means learning about and responding to the children's individual problems and needs as and when they arise. Older children should be given special attention in this regard, since their participation in school will be undermined if education is not relevant or has no practical value. Education promoters and others can assess home circumstances and assist with the referral of children with special needs.

Some multi-grade classes are divided into groups of learners by levels of competence on the basis of written and oral tests. Elsewhere, individual tuition is used to bring pupils into line with each other. To maximize the learning opportunities of such groups, teachers, auxiliaries, and volunteers need to be trained in multi-grade teaching and to allow for diversity by facilitating and providing resources rather than instructing. Project work and task cards undertaken individually can be complemented by collaborative group work and peer teaching, used as an alternative to more traditional class-based teaching. Individualized learning plans and peer teaching are particularly effective for enhancing children's confidence and absorptive capacity.

With heterogeneous learner groups it is very important to assess the materials and curriculum for their utility and acceptability among children of different ages and social backgrounds. Flexibility in entry and exit into classes helps older children who are educationally behind their age group especially. Evaluation of performance is often particularly difficult in the multi-grade system. However, where monitoring and evaluation is possible, special attention should be paid to the problems associated with children's work that prevent their attendance or affect their performance at school.

Curriculum

It has been suggested that, if education is to instil a sense of self-worth and self-confidence in children, it should build on their competencies and strengths. As noted, one way of achieving this is by involving working children in the analysis of educational problems and needs, the development of curricula and education aids, and formulation of application activities. In another approach, the Escuela Nueva programme has adapted the national curriculum to make it applicable to the lives of rural children. Use is made of tested and relevant materials that provide many opportunities for self- and group-learning, observations from local context, group discussions, implementation of projects and experimenting with alternative approaches, simulations, interviews, discussions, comparisons and contests, sharing of learning experiences, use of previous knowledge as well as reporting findings in writing, and on-the-spot evaluation by teachers (rather than mere grading).

Education that helps equip working children to deal with the realities of their life also needs to address their work specifically. Children can not only be taught basic skills useful to them, but also informed about workplace dangers and how to deal with them. Training in vocational subjects like automobile mechanics, electronics, agriculture, crafts, and other skills is offered in many programmes to improve income-generating capacity, provide greater occupational choice, and increase independence and self-confidence. Throughout the world, there are large numbers of NGO technical and vocational education programmes for street children, many run by religious organizations. In some countries, large-scale vocational and technical education programmes are managed by major public institutions. An example is the Servicio Nacional de Aprendizaje (SENA) in Colombia, which operates under an agreement with the Ministry of Education to provide vocational education for children from low-income families. However, working children are often excluded from consideration for such programmes, which may also require academic precedents that are beyond the reach of most poor children in general and working children in particular. Most vocational training for such children comes through non-formal education programmes run by NGOs or from informal and traditional apprenticeships.

There are a number of different ways of approaching vocational training, the most formal and traditional being courses provided in special training centres. This model has been heavily criticized, however. Not only are educational requirements for entry often too high for working children, but trainees are often isolated from the local labour market because the training is based on capital-intensive, modern productive processes very different from the labour-intensive operations typical of most informal economies. Seldom are they planned on the basis of a prior market survey, so that there may be no demand for either the labour or products of programme graduates. Frequently the skills imparted through vocational training are only modest and of little practical value, not providing the problem-solving skills needed to maintain a successful trade or business.[66] For example, trainees in auto mechanics may repeatedly take apart and reassemble the one or more engines in the training centre, learning their function, but have no opportunity to diagnose faults or make improvised replacement parts. Publicly funded vocational educational systems have been notoriously resistant to reforms seeking to overcome their many problems, and education experts seldom regard them as a viable large-scale option for children of poor families.

Because of the problems associated with formal vocational training, education-planners are showing greater interest in supervised apprenticeship as an alternative, the advantages including the automatic relevance of the training to the materials, techniques, products or services and business methods of the local economy.[67] Also, a well-run apprenticeship programme can ensure a better dispersal of trainees by trade and geographic area than is possible in the more rigid institution-based programmes. But the risk is that, if not properly supervised, apprentices may be exploited by unscrupulous employers. The cost of apprenticeship schemes varies considerably, depending on the equipment involved and the degree of supervision. Most indigenous and traditional apprenticeships are self-financing, since the apprentice serves the master either gratis or for negligible recompense in at least an initial period of no or low productivity. That is one reason their potential is attracting some interest.

To reduce the cost of training and to increase outreach, some programmes use a third approach, integrating teaching with the rest of children's lives by structuring work so that it is educational. Non-formal, self-help skills training is conducted within and by the family or community. This approach is particularly common in Africa. The brigade model in Botswana, for example, provides for out-of-school young people to work together with a teacher, earning and learning at the same time. This enables young people to acquire traditional skills appropriate to the local market within their homes or communities. Of course, the success of this approach depends largely on the availability of people in the community with the skills, patience and interest to train children. It also depends on sympathetic education policy from government. It is worth noting that attempts to incorporate 'education with production' models into formal education systems have met with great difficulties. They make great technical demands, they tend to be threatening to some education bureaucracies, and they may be looked down upon by parents and children who want only academic studies leading to white-collar jobs.

Funding

We have suggested that a shortage or poor distribution of funds is one of the main obstacles to the delivery of effective education to working children. More funds are urgently needed at the primary level especially. Most educationalists accept that primary, and preferably also secondary, education should be free, although cost recovery in one form or another is increasingly viewed as essential in higher education. At the very least, books and uniforms and other direct education costs should be free or subsidized at the primary and secondary levels for the poorest families. Large numbers of NGO and government programmes now subsidize these costs, but much more is needed.

Economic incentives for school enrolment and attendance

As mentioned in Chapter Three, the ILO estimates that children may often contribute as much as a quarter of the income in poor households. These combinations may be critical for ensuring family survival and hence it is often very difficult to reduce children's workload for them to attend school if some offsetting source is not available. Programmes sometimes provide this. Although policies and programmes that provide income replacement and economic incentives to stimulate school attendance have been utilized for over 20 years, many new programmes have been designed in recent years in order to address the need for children to earn. It is not very well known, however, how effective these approaches are and until recently almost no data on the subject have been available. Recently, however, literature on the subject has begun to appear. We will summarize a few approaches here and a more complete discussion of economic incentives will appear in Chapter Eight.

There are five main types of economic incentives. The first consists of cash payments to low-income families to make up for the loss of children's earnings. For example, in the Borsa-Familia programme in Brazil, a subsidy equivalent to a minimum salary is paid to families with school-age children when those families are in the lowest quintile of the income distribution. The money is deposited in a savings account. Half of it can be withdrawn after four years and the balance after eight years. In 1996, 14,000 students benefited from the scheme. Preliminary assessments of this programme have found it to dramatically increase student retention in school.[68]

A second approach is the school voucher system. One example is the Programma de Ampliación de la Cobertura (PACES) in Colombia, which provides school vouchers for low-income students who have completed their primary education in a state school but failed to obtain a place in state secondary school. The voucher is equivalent to half the cost per secondary student in the state system. In 1996, the scheme accounted for 10 per cent of the total increase in secondary school students nationally, subsidizing a total of 100,000 children, and even encouraged the establishment of several new private schools. A similar programme in Chile is more comprehensive, covering all types of education, from pre-school through to the end of secondary schooling. Subsidies are paid to schools in accordance with actual attendance, as reported by schools.[69] This approach raises questions about equity and the ethics of transferring resources from public to private education, especially if education quality does not improve.

Thirdly, school-based food programmes have been used widely in many countries. These have the advantage not only of being an incentive for poor children to attend, but also of improving education performance by reducing hunger. Food may either be provided to schools in low-income areas or to low-income children in any school. The Brazilian Programa Nacional de Merenda Escolar covers 32 million students in some 5,000 municipalities with an annual cost of US$650 million. An evaluation found that the programme had reduced drop-out and repetition. The funds are allocated at municipal level and each municipality selects the best mix of food to meet needs and cost, although attempts to prioritize the poorest children are comparatively recent. In Colombia, the funds are made available to schools and parent associations according to an index of basic need, 30 per cent of costs being covered by the programme and the balance (including premises and personnel) being provided by the community. Low-income students pay US$0.50 for a lunch.[70]

A fourth approach has been adopted in Guatemala, where transportation costs are provided to families in accordance with school attendance. Transportation subsidies can make a significant difference in the many cases where pupils live a long way from school. Of course, working children may have even greater distances to cover than others because they may need to travel between home, school, and work.

The final approach consists of the previously discussed education-with-income programmes, in which work and school are combined by apprenticeship schemes involving a modest salary paid to trainees. There seems to have been a steady growth of such programmes in several countries,[71] and street children have been among those targeted.

Conclusion

Education is often advanced as the most effective deterrent to child work or to work that is detrimental to children, for it is believed to change their outlook on life and keep them so busy that they have no time for work. But many school pupils work part-time and, for many, a combination of work and school is the preferred option. Besides, school is not always a very positive experience. Sometimes publicly funded education is less responsive to the development needs of children than to other social purposes, such as national integration, continuity of the social or political status quo, economic competitiveness, ideological indoctrination, or even removal of children and youth from the workforce. Education practices evolved to serve these objectives are not always consistent with child development and the best interests of the children involved, especially for children of the poor. The education available is frequently so irrelevant, incompetent, and repressive that its very character may constitute a violation of education rights guaranteed to children under the Convention on the Rights of the Child. Programmes devised specifically to promote the holistic development of children in general, and of working children in particular, look very different from the schools that now serve most children of the poor. Everywhere the worst schools are concentrated in the poorest communities, which of course are home to most working children. Schools are in many places so bad that they drive children away from school and into the workplace, themselves becoming an important cause of child work.

Reaching the goal of universal primary education necessarily involves not only the creation of new school places for an expanding population and the now out-of-school 20 per cent (most of whom are likely to be working children) but also dramatically increasing school-system efficiency, the levelling up of years of schooling, and improving quality. Radical reform is required in many areas to increase educational choice, upgrade curricula, devise methods that build on children's experience and competencies and focus on the learner rather than the teacher, and improve delivery systems. Emphasis needs to be given to the provision of schools for children rather than of children for schools and to the aim of education for living, rather than a preparation for moving up to the next level.

Most working children want to go to school. But often they have very specific needs which affect their ability to attend and benefit from school. They cannot always attend during the regular school hours, for example, and may be forced to begin school late or drop out early. Their experience, expectations, and competence are likely to be very different from those of full-time pupils. But instead of being valued for their resilience and capacity, often they are shamed and ridiculed at school, precisely because they work. As indicated in Chapter One, denigration of this nature can undermine self-esteem and social development.

School education needs to become far more creative and flexible if it is to fulfil its protective potential in relation to children's work. It needs to offer support and encouragement to children who carry economic and social responsibilities rather than penalize them for their intermittent attendance or unkempt appearance. There is much to be done if school is to become a serious alternative to detrimental child work.

CHAPTER EIGHT

Economic Approaches to Children's Work

D uring the last several years, certain economic issues, as they relate to child work and exploitation, have been brought forcefully to world attention. A large part of this new interest in how children relate to the economy is driven by a worldwide debate on whether and to what extent world trade should be made subject to international standards governing various labour rights matters, including detrimental child work. Discussion is also fed by resurgent concern that the poor are falling even further behind, both inside countries and between them. That raises serious questions about the role of children in poverty-stricken households and how to ensure that the human resources of children will be properly developed through education and other means. Still another source of interest is an expanding notion of children's rights, including a new insistence on their right to participate as full citizens in all aspects of their societies, including in economic life.

Some of these issues merit special attention, largely because they are so publicly visible and politically controversial that policy-makers and programme-planners will find it virtually impossible to ignore them. Important questions most likely to come before them include:

- To what extent are child development goals compatible with social and economic development goals when dealing with children's issues?
- Should children be excluded from involvement in the production of internationally traded goods and commodities? What would be the effect of this on poor children and their families?
- How effective are mechanisms to monitor children's involvement in export products and to ameliorate the economic impact of removing them from it?
- What economic incentives are effective for poverty alleviation and

encouraging school enrolment and attendance and discouraging the involvement of school-age children in detrimental economic activities?

The following discussion will examine these questions.

The compatibility of child work with economic and social development

Chapters One and Two established that children's work often is conducive to their development. Chapter Three pointed out that, over and beyond reasons of economic necessity, many children work because they like it or because they feel they receive psychological rewards such as feelings of self-esteem, independence, and personal efficacy. Others work to achieve personal aspirations, whether for learning and advancement, for purchase of fashionable consumer items, for changing lifestyle, or for other reasons. Traditional thinking about 'child labour' policy has not been blind to the desire of children to work, nor has it denied that work can be beneficial for children. However, it has taken a position against the work of young children, and for the regulation of work by older children, in part to protect society from the presumed pernicious effects of letting all children of whatever age who want to work do so, even if good for individual children and their families.

We have indicated that this position harks back to England in the late eighteenth and early nineteenth centuries, when almost everyone took it for granted that the children of the poor would eventually comprise most of the workforce in textile mills.[1] Adult workers were alarmed, and early trade union movements sought to forestall their displacement, unemployment, and impoverishment by restricting the work of children. Since that time, the popular wisdom has claimed that child workers exacerbate adult unemployment and perpetuate poverty by reducing adult wages and lowering their own lifetime earnings by cutting short their education. The assertion that child work perpetuates poverty and adult unemployment is so commonly heard that it has become virtual doctrine not only among trade unions, but also elsewhere. At the same time, surprisingly few economists have been interested in researching child work issues, at least in comparison to experts from other disciplines, such as anthropologists, sociologists, and lawyers. Consequently, there are few empirical answers to fundamental questions regarding the economic consequences of child work for society.

For example, it is reasonable to assume that child work perpetuates poverty in those instances in which children's work robs them of an education or ruins their health.[2] It has been amply demonstrated that low educational attainment generally reduces lifetime earnings, and bodies weakened or disabled young by occupational disease or injury may also impede making a livelihood later in life. In these cases, child work clearly degrades society's stock of human capital. On the other hand, as explained in Chapter Seven, many children have to work in order to pay their school expenses, in which case work helps support education. It would also seem logical that work by school-attending children outside school hours and during holidays may in fact forestall or alleviate poverty, rather than promote it. And useful skills acquired through work increase, rather than decrease, human capital. In the absence of serious economic research on this issue, there is no way to know whether the balance of children's work in a country represents a net contribution or a net loss to human capital.

The same ambiguity exists in regard to the argument that child workers displace adult employment. As the ILO puts it:

It is also frequently contended that the participation of children in economic activity aggravates poverty by increasing the unemployment or underemployment of adults. Again, evidence is insufficient to substantiate this assertion as a general rule; such displacement effects vary with the types of work that children perform. In wage labour, such as in factory work, the substitution of children for adults may indeed have the expected effect of depressing adult employment, wages and other working conditions. At the opposite extreme, however, child labour often facilitates adult employment. For example, many adults, especially women, are able to enter the job market because their children assume essential home tasks. Similarly, it is known that many farmers and small entrepreneurs maintain the adult employment viability of their enterprises by relying on unpaid work from their children. Children working on their own account in the informal sector may have little effect on adult employment, filling niches that are not attractive to adult workers — carrying bundles for market shoppers, selling petty goods such as matches, shining shoes, etc. Finally, many child maids work for families who could or would not pay an adult salary, and hence would no longer hire maids if this meant hiring adults.[3]

The unsupported general notion that child work necessarily promotes poverty and unemployment ignores other complicating factors. It should be noted that this argument refers to children whose work keeps them out of school or keeps them from learning when there. But how does it apply to the complicated case of child workers who must work in order to meet the expenses of attending school, but whose performance in class is impaired by having to do the work that makes school possible? How does it deal with the many children living in rural areas where schools provide no more than the first few years of primary education, and who begin work at a young age after having finished the schooling available to them? In this instance, not work, but the lack of availability of schools and the inadequacy of the teaching and curricula for poor children, depreciate their education, and hence its contribution to human capital development. Another complicating factor is that in some places, such as Kerala, India, unemployment is so rife among educated and skilled people that it has become difficult for even secondary school graduates to obtain suitable employment without political or family contacts that the poor seldom have.[4] In many places, children of particular castes or minorities, regardless of education, face employment barriers that tend to restrict their occupational options. Does education that cannot be absorbed in the job market contribute to human capital? These problems complicate the facile assumption that the economic return on education should be a positive incentive for all children. A much harder analysis of economic expectations in such situations is badly needed.

Research is also needed to determine the extent to which children learn and acquire marketable knowledge, skills, and attitudes at work, such as through informal apprenticeships, in comparison with school. As indicated in Chapters Two, Three, and Seven, children often claim to learn more that is practical for making a livelihood through their work than in school. But school can have a conserving effect on human resources aside from the knowledge it imparts. For example, one positive effect of school attendance on working children can be a lighter work-load in terms of daily and weekly hours of work, as observed by Aragão-Lagergren,[5] thus decreasing the risk of damage from overburdening. As Chapter Seven suggests, positive economic effects might also reflect the social impact of school attendance.

In the Bangladesh case, discussed below, there are indications that when the girl children had to leave their employment, some of their mothers had to leave as well, because the daughters could not be left unattended at home. It is supposed that certain industries relying heavily on child workers, such as the beedi industry in some places, could become unviable if they cannot employ children, as paying adult wages would mean having to raise the prices so much that they might lose the market.[6] If this is correct, the adults also would lose their jobs when children were moved out, although the scenario assumes that technological changes or other means of increasing efficiency are not available. There is very little analysis of these sorts of case, and it is far from clear how common or intractable they are.

Research also is needed into the question of the degree to which children, if removed from employment, would be replaced by adults. Not all children in the garment factories in Bangladesh were replaced when they left.[7] It seems clear that, for many reasons, there is not usually a one-to-one substitution relationship between children and adult workers, and that oft-heard claims that X million working children are to blame for a roughly equal number of unemployed adults are economically untenable. The simple truth is that the net social effect of child work on adult unemployment is utterly unknown, and will remain so until properly constructed empirical studies tackle the issue. Until then, the idea that child work exacerbates unemployment is probably better expressed as a concern than as a fact. It may be somewhat more likely that child workers in at least certain situations depress adult wages, but here again evidence is so lacking that a general assertion to this effect is unwarranted.

The exclusion of children from production of internationally traded goods

Even though less than 5 per cent of working children are estimated to be involved in the production of goods entering into international trade,[8] they are the object of the most intense debate about child work today. In rich countries, this focus of interest is so overpowering that it obscures virtually all other children's work issues from the public at large. In some developing countries, the issue is highly visible because it involves industries important to the nation's economy, foreign exchange earnings, and international reputation. In countries of the North, and in countries of the South involved in the export of labour-intensive products, the question of children's involvement in the export sector is inescapable for child advocates, policy-makers, programme-planners, and others interested in children's work and working children. Despite their reasonable doubts regarding the wisdom of dedicating so much time and effort to so small a portion of working children — and probably an even smaller portion of those in serious danger from their work — major governmental and non-governmental organizations probably cannot avoid the question of what to do about the involvement of child workers in the export sector.

Those export industries that most commonly employ children include the garment, carpet, shoe, small-scale mining, gem polishing, food processing, leather tanning, and furniture industries. A list of goods where children might have been involved in the production includes, among others: textiles; garments; embroidery; carpets; footwear; leather goods; matches; fireworks; toys; sports equipment and games; flowers; coal; tin products; chrome products; gems (emeralds, diamonds, sapphires, rubies, lapis lazuli, turquoise, corals, garnets, amethysts, topaz); gold; brassware and base-metal articles; locks; glass and glassware; ceramics; silk; wood and rattan furniture; handicrafts and folk artisan items; surgical instruments; granite stones; hemp; jute; sisal products (twine, cord, rope, cable); cotton; fish and seafood (shrimps, crabs, mussels, sardines, squid); cardamom; vanilla; nuts (cashew, macadamia, groundnuts); cheese; chilli peppers; cinchona; cocoa; coconuts; coffee; tea; copra; fruits (bananas, oranges, grapes, melon, pineapple, strawberries and fruit juices); vegetables (mangetouts, corn, broccoli, tomatoes); palm oil; resin; rice; rubber; sugar cane and tobacco.[9] These products come from about 60 major producing countries.

Most public pressure, and private sector response to that pressure, is focused on removing all children's work from the production of export goods and commodities. Most of those clamouring to exclude child workers from this sector believe they are defending the well-being and rights of the children involved. They are for the most part among the many who believe children should not work at all before the age of 14 or 15, and that childhood should be reserved for school and play exclusively. They take a position closely allied to that of the ILO Minimum Age Convention (No. 138), as described in Chapter Five. They seem to assume that children, if released from factories or farms, will replace a life of work with a life of study and leisure. It does not occur to everyone that children may simply move from work in the export sector to other kinds of work elsewhere, perhaps in activities even less appropriate for children.

Taken as a group, children working in the export sector cannot, in general, be considered to have worse working conditions than other working children, and they might in fact fare somewhat better.[10] For example, in Bangladesh, work in garment production, which is not completely hazard-free, nevertheless tends to be less hazardous, more financially lucrative, and with more prospects for future advancement than almost all other forms of employment open to children in either the formal or informal sectors.[11] There are, however, some flagrant exceptions; the carpet industry and some agricultural production (such as tobacco and sugar cane), for example, can be considered to have general working conditions seriously detrimental to children.

Many NGOs and others most directly involved with working children are less inclined to believe children should be excluded from all work in general, or from the export sector in particular. Those taking to heart the long-term development of children, as the Convention on the Rights of the Child demands, are more likely to question the position that all work by children is inappropriate, and that excluding them from the export sector altogether necessarily would help protect their well-being and development. Some of them point out that the export sector may in fact include some opportunities that children value, and which might be open to them in ways that assure the safety, health, education, and development of the children involved. As earlier chapters indicated, new understanding of child development processes suggests that provision of the right sort of work opportunities, especially if they are linked to education, could in the right cases be more conducive to child protection and development than is outright prohibition of all children's work in a sector that is generally regarded as providing scarce modern jobs with a future for young people to grow into.

So what are policy-makers, programme-planners, firms, employer groups, and child advocacy organizations to do when they find themselves caught between those campaigning to abolish all children's involvement in export industries and those seeking to promote child rights and child development opportunities even within the export sector? Are there creative ways to reconcile abolitionist pressure from trade unions, consumer groups, and others with the insistence of child-centred NGOs, advocacy groups, and others that the economic role of children should be respected, that children should have at least some rights in their work, and that it is often better to improve working conditions for children rather than to eliminate their work altogether? The following sections address these questions, beginning with a consideration of specific lines of action that have been taken or suggested in regard to children's work in the export sector.

Consumer boycotts

Among the means proposed to address the use of child workers in export industries are measures to reduce the market for countries and firms that involve children in the production of goods. The first of these is refusal by rich country consumers to buy certain products perceived to be produced with the involvement of children. Mass media reports of children working in the manufacture of clothing, sports equipment, and so forth have awakened the concern of western consumers, who feel that one of the few ways they have to protest against the economic exploitation of children it to refuse to buy the goods the children produce. NGOs, trade unions, and consumer groups have launched campaigns encouraging consumers to 'boycott child labour', mentioning some products from some countries like carpets from Pakistan, garments from Bangladesh or toys from China. So far, there have been more threats than campaigns, and even these are not very focused. They also generally do not deal with a potential 'spillover' problem, in which sales of a country's products that are 'child-free' can be negatively affected by these campaigns. The problems of targeting only the guilty and not damaging the innocent, including child workers, have been obstacles to organizing successful boycotts.

Boycotts raise special moral and practical problems which make them more complicated than they first appear. As Ben White points out:

> ... consumers should have the right to know about the conditions under which goods are produced (whether in their own country, or at the other end of the world) and to make informed choices based on that knowledge. But any boycott or international sanctions must first, select the right target; and second, ensure that the objective is one with which the 'target group' (in this case, exploited working children) can agree.[12]

Boycotts also run into the problem of not being able to distinguish between good and bad working situations for the children involved. As was suggested in Chapter Two, a child-centred perspective would inquire not so much into which products children help produce as into the circumstances of their work, identifying those that endanger children. Much coffee, for example, is grown by very small producers who depend mostly on their own family labour and who export through their farm cooperatives. It is also cultivated on large plantations depending on migrant workers for the harvest. The case of farm-family children who work at home may be very different from that of migrant children, who tend to travel long distances with their families and live in squalid conditions and without essential health and education services. It is worth noting that Colombia's innovative 'New School' (Escuela Nueva) programme began in coffee-producing areas dominated by small farms in order to fit education to the schedule and content needs of farm-family children. Virtually all such farm children in areas served under this programme now receive at least a basic education. In Guatemala, on the other hand, where large numbers of migrants work on commercial plantations, there have been reports of adult males being substituted by women and children at lower rates of pay, as well as of very young children working long hours in health-endangering conditions and without access to school.[13] Both examples are in the export sector, but one wonders if it would be good child-protection policy to treat the two situations equivalently.

When consumers are urged not to buy goods made by children, little is said about what happens to working children if boycott actions are successful. Rich country consumers probably presume that if children are not working they will be in school but, as earlier chapters have indicated, this is not likely to be the case unless it is specifically planned for. If provision is not made to furnish alternative means of surviving, children may simply be left more exposed than before. For that reason, many NGOs working directly with child workers tend to ask rich countries to take an interest in the children's welfare through more constructive means than the boycott of products made by poor people. Working children themselves tend to take the same position. Children at the international meeting of working children in Kundapur, mentioned earlier, included in their final recommendations a statement of opposition to boycotts and import bans, which they feel hurt mainly the very children and families they are supposed to help.[14] While some consumer and other organizations have put a lot of effort into raising awareness of rich countries about the situation of child workers in developing country export industries, an equal effort has not yet been made to consider the full context of children's work and the issue of viable alternatives. While the interest of industrialized country consumers in the well-being of developing-country children is in general to be commended, a simplistic view born of ignorance about children and child work in other countries can and does lead to socially irresponsible action that hurts rather than helps children. Certainly there is a need to better educate the public in industrialized countries about the realities of children in other countries so that they can use their economic power — including that of financial support to worthy causes — more discerningly.

This is an objective that has recently been receiving increasing attention by some child advocacy organizations, and especially the Save the Children organizations. Rädda Barnen, for example, raises these issues through participation in radio and television broadcasts, through school assemblies and through seminars for the business community, trade unions, and media journalists. It also raises awareness among its members, consumers, importers, and retailers about the broad issue of child work. Rädda Barnen has worked for several years with private companies to advise on the elaboration of child workers and find good solutions for them. A working group was established in the early 1990s on the initiative of Rädda Barnen, in which carpet importers, trade unions, and other NGOs try to raise awareness in Sweden and in South Asia about the situation of child workers. The group has visited South Asia to review the situation of children in carpet manufacturing areas. IKEA, a large multinational furniture and housewares retailer, which is part of this group, has recently begun extensive in-house training on child work for its staff.

Import bans

Import bans differ from consumer boycotts in that they are imposed by governments. Whereas in the case of boycotts each consumer decides whether he or she will purchase a particular product from a specified country, an official import ban prohibits the banned product even from entering the country marketplace. It cannot be placed on sale. It is a far more severe measure than is a consumer boycott, and can be a serious economic blow to a country against which it is levelled. Even the mere threat of an import ban by a rich country with major markets is a very sobering matter to a poor developing country whose economy depends on being able to export to this country. So far, no import ban has been placed on any product or country because of child work. However, since 1993, the threat of such a ban from the United States has been hanging over developing countries that produce for the large and rich US market.

In that year, the United States Congress introduced a draft law calling for a prohibition of the import to the US of any goods that were manufactured, wholly or in part, by children under the age of 15. This 'Child Labour Deterrence Act', generally called the Harkin Bill, has since undergone several modifications but has not yet become law, and it is not clear that it ever will. Nevertheless, it has caused much anxiety in several developing countries, and particularly in Bangladesh, where, at the time of the presentation of the bill, roughly 15 per cent of the garment industry workforce was said to be under 15 years of age; the large majority of whom were girls.[15] Bangladesh is one of the world's major garment exporters, and the garment industry is its most important source of export income. In 1993, more than half of the country's total export earnings came from trade with the United States alone, and some 1,500 garment factories employed 750,000 people or more.[16] It is worth examining this case in some detail in order to understand the ramifications of an import ban for working children who are caught up in it.

It was trade union concern that first brought the garment industry of Bangladesh to international attention. In 1991, the women's network of the United Food and Commercial Workers Union in the United States launched a nationwide campaign, charging the country's largest discount retailer with purchasing Bangladeshi garments made with the use of 'child labour', and selling them under false labels as made in the US. The Harkin Bill grew out of this campaign as organized labour, now allied with consumer organizations, pushed for official action. Driven by fear that the bill might pass and Bangladesh lose its largest market and attractiveness for outside investors in its largest industry, the Bangladesh government and the Bangladesh Garment Manufacturers and Exporters Association (BGMEA) encouraged garment firms to divest themselves of workers below the age of 15. As BGMEA is responsible for arranging export licences and there was talk of a large fine being imposed for every child found working, the result was that up to 55,000 children were abruptly dismissed from the industry at the beginning of 1993.[17] These children, most of whom were from very poor families, were suddenly on the street with no job, no explanation or severance pay, and no prospects. It was reported that some women also had to leave the factories, since they could not leave their children at home unattended, and alternative day care facilities were not available. Non-governmental organizations were shocked at the sight of so many thousands of desperately poor children suddenly cut adrift without either income or school, and asked for assistance in trying to control the damage to the children.[18]

UNICEF and the ILO were among the organizations who got involved in order to keep the situation of children from deteriorating still further and to see what could be done to support those who had been dismissed. One of the first steps was to conduct a quick study of the children's situation, which was undertaken by the ILO.[19] This research provided some significant unexpected results. First of all, not one child in the sample of 115 children with garment industry experience had returned to school. Few had ever attended in the first place, and on dismissal at roughly 12 to 15 years of age they were too old to enter the formal system. Besides, given family poverty, most had no choice but to work. Half of the dismissed children soon had found a different job and half were still seeking work at the time of the investigation. Those working had gone into jobs that were less remunerative and more dangerous for children than was work in the garment factories. The ILO study also suggested that child factory workers ate considerably better than did children who either stayed at home or had taken up other types of work. There was no evidence from any source that dismissed children were better off, and there was considerable reason to believe that they were worse off than before. Clearly, this counterproductive result for children was not what US activists had hoped for when insisting that the Bangladesh industry rid itself of child workers. But no study of the probable impact on children was done in advance either of drafting the Harkin Bill or of applying pressure on Bangladesh. This was a totally irresponsible omission, in our opinion, since some of the worst effects were entirely predictable had US pressure groups or members of Congress cared enough to look.

As the story gradually unfolded through subsequent studies and experience, it became clear that the best interests of children had not even been considered in the rush to clear the garment industry of 'child labour'. It was a case in which the supposed protection of children was sadly (some say cynically) distorted by economic protectionism, and some 55,000 children paid a harsh price.

It became apparent that children's work in the garment industry had complex antecedents which, when understood, suggested points of intervention far more effective and humane for children than the brutal firings that occurred. Girls, mostly above 11 years of age, were in the factories partly because they were safe there in the company of other women; strict local mores would not let them be at home alone. But their earnings were also important; they made major contributions to the family budget, and in about 20 per cent of the households, children were the sole breadwinners. For reasons of age, most would not now be allowed back in school, and no alternative education facilities were available to them. Garment work is one of a very few reasonably well-paid occupations open to poor women (80 per cent of garment workers are female), and girls tried very hard to get into the industry since they saw it as security for their future. It was regarded as a place to learn and to gain experience that would help them to enter and assimilate into a modern world. It was more than just a job; it was a way for women to open space in their lives beyond the very tight formal religious and cultural structures under which they lived. By working in the garment industry, for example, girls felt that they could put off early marriage (girls of the poor are commonly given by their parents in marriage as young as 13 or even less), accumulating a dowry that would let them make a good marriage at a healthier age. Although respondent children did have complaints about their work, on balance they considered it beneficial and identified no major negative impacts.

It was obvious that there would be no solution for children in the garment industry, unless these factors were taken into account. It was equally clear that seeing child work in the garment industry narrowly, as a child labour violation, led to great violence against the children, which is perhaps the single most important lesson to learn from this experience. The US Department of Labour notes that Bangladesh is one example where "international media attention and threats of boycotts and cancelled work orders led to the dismissal of thousands of child workers from the garment sector — unfortunately with no safety net in place for them. Thus, it is possible that in the absence of government programs to assist the children, the precipitous dismissal of child workers can endanger, rather than protect them."[20] One conclusion of the ILO study was that it is possibly the social disadvantage engendered by dismissal that has had the most serious and long-term negative consequences.

As mentioned above, a common argument against child work is that the children take jobs away from adults. The ILO study found that not all children were replaced by adults as labour-saving technologies make children's unskilled contribution increasingly redundant. The children might never have been very important in the production process since they were a minor fraction of the workforce and engaged mostly in auxiliary tasks, such as removing strong threads from finished garments. This raises the question of why it was assumed from the start that they should be dismissed. Bissell and Sobhan report that:

> ... local NGOs began questioning the rationale behind dismissing children especially those aged 12 and above, arguing that in most cases, the children were performing tasks that could be characterized as light work under the terms of ILO C. 138. They argued that the real problem was conditions of employment, hours worked and the fact that with few exceptions, the children were not attending school and pressed for reforms along those lines. Of course, this had no bearing on the industry that was more concerned with complying with the Harkin Bill, which does not make any distinction between work and labour.[21]

After reviewing the details of the Bangladesh case, it is difficult to find much that is praiseworthy, from the standpoint of a child-centred approach to child work, in a unilateral import ban. The arbitrary exercise of raw economic power by a single nation that parades its own particular agenda under the banner of child protection, but does not bother even to first hear from or learn about the children it supposedly would protect, seems awkwardly out of place in an era of multilateral instruments such as the Convention on the Rights of the Child. The problem is structural, not merely one of actors, for an approach of this type is accountable to nobody, least of all the children whose cause it ostensibly champions, and it is freed to pursue its own narrowest self-interest. It can turn children's vulnerability against them. It is worth noting that the ILO opposes unilateral import bans, feeling that only multilateral actions can avoid arbitrary injustices imposed by the interests of a single country. The Bangladesh garment industry case suggests that there is wisdom in the ILO position.

Social clauses

One strategy for getting around the problems of unilateral labour standards actions is to agree on multilateral measures. A current suggestion is for a social clause including prohibitions against child work to be introduced in world trade agreements and administered under the World Trade Organization. There is some question about what a social clause is and what it would entail. As a general concept:

> A social clause in an international trade agreement is intended to improve labour conditions in exporting countries by allowing sanctions to be taken against exporters who fail to observe minimum standards. A typical social clause of this kind makes it possible to restrict or halt the importation or preferential importation of products originating in countries, industries, or firms where labour conditions do not meet certain minimum standards. Producers who do not comply with the minimum requirements must choose between a change in working conditions or the risk of being confronted with increased trade barriers in their export markets.[22]

The debate on 'social clauses' is complicated, technical, and controversial. Child work is only one of the ingredients in this debate. Whether a social clause is an effective tool to support human rights and prevent labour exploitation in a general sense is a question outside the scope of this book. As 'child labour' is usually mentioned as one of the human rights issues a social clause would deal with, it is essential to see, however, what effects an eventual social clause would have on the protection of working children. The literature on social clauses does not, in general, dwell on the issue of child work. As observed by the British organization Anti-Slavery International, it is not clear what would and would not be included in the social clause and how it would be implemented.[23] For this reason, it is difficult to evaluate the possible implications of a social clause for working children in the world.

The International Confederation of Free Trade Unions, ICFTU, which is energetically campaigning for a social clause, proposes that its adoption would put an end to one country undermining another through abuse of basic labour standards. One of the practices they target is worldwide trade in goods made with the involvement of children. According to them, the social clause would also, in a more general sense, promote government action against child work in non-export sectors. The ICFTU considers that exploitation by others is the main reason why children work. Their recommendations are that child workers should be replaced by unemployed adults and the former working children should be supported by funding to allow them to go to school.[24]

The British NGO Oxfam contributes to the discussion about social clauses in relation to child work in an interesting way by suggesting that a social clause should include the Conventions Nos. 29 and 105 on The Abolition of Forced Labour, but leave out the Convention on Minimum Age for Employment (No. 138). The reason for including the former is that they are conventions on basic human rights which should and can exist in any country irrespective of its current state of development, and bonded labour and child slavery are unacceptable and should be abolished immediately. The reason given for Convention No. 138 not to be included in a social clause is that this "in the absence of adequate investment in poverty alleviation and education, could be counterproductive".[25] Oxfam also holds the door open for including the new ILO convention on 'the most intolerable forms of child labour', if it will cover the most hazardous forms of work, child servitude, bonded work, the sex industry, and work of the very young.

It is not evident how the social clause would promote government action against children's work in non-export sectors. There is no clear evidence that a social clause on child work would lead to fewer children working or to less harmful child work. However, there is reason to suspect that the results of the introduction of child labour standards in relation to trade would include a migration of children from the export sector to sectors not covered by the clause as the Bangladesh case implies.

Actions by individual firms

In the overheated atmosphere of international sensitivity about the use of child workers in the production of internationally traded goods, multinational firms in clothing, sports equipment, and other industries have become aware of their vulnerability to attack by the media and others if children are found working on items they sell. When actually attacked, their response often has been self-serving, putting on the face and language of child protection, but treating the children involved in making their products with indifference, dishonesty, and even brutality. A case of this type in the Morocco garment industry has been recently documented and publicized. It revolves around the alleged dismissal of about 100 child workers from a garment factory in the small city of Méknès. Because it shows how many factors interact in the situation of children, the case study prepared under the auspices of the International Working Group on Child Labour merits exposition in some detail.[26]

According to this report, events started in January 1996, when a British television company presented a programme on child work. It had secretly filmed a garment factory in Méknès, and discovered that, according to them, underage girls were involved in the production of pyjamas and other garments for the British multinational retailer Marks & Spencer. The announcement of this 'discovery' seems to have led to the summary dismissal of all workers aged under 15 from the factory without any prior notice.

This happened in a country where half of the children aged under 15 are estimated to live in deprivation. In the Méknès region, migration from the surrounding rural areas owing to a hard drought has increased the number of unemployed. In a society where education has traditionally been limited to a minority (Morocco has one of the world's highest illiteracy rates), and where handicraft production represents an important part of manufacture, young people generally learn their trade by working as apprentices in small shops or homes. Traditionally, these children were not paid, because they were sent to the master to learn a skill or trade. Although this one-to-one relationship between master and trainee has changed with industrialization, the perception of parents who send their children to work in these areas has not.

In rural areas, far fewer girls than boys attend primary school and there is a general distrust of education as a key to jobs in the future. The rate of unemployment is increasing among educated young people and many parents, themselves illiterate, are not willing to make the necessary sacrifice to send or maintain their youngsters in school. When a family, because of limited financial resources, has to decide who is going to school and who has to work, it is usually the boy who is sent to school. Girls are asked to work outside the home, or to take over the domestic chores, to allow the mother to work outside the home.

The textile industry is important. It accounts for 40 per cent of Morocco's exports and employs 200,000 people, predominantly female young workers. These so-called 'apprentices' are estimated to number around 10 per cent of the adult contractual workers and are allowed by law to be paid less. There are about 1,800 manufacturing units in the country, out of which 28 are situated in Méknès. The Sicome factory, where the children in this case study used to work, is the largest factory in the area, employing around 1,200 workers.

In Morocco, as in most other places, working conditions and respect for labour laws regarding apprenticeship and minimum wages are, in general, better in those enterprises that export than in those producing for the local market. The formal export sector tends to employ children from the age of 12 (the legal minimum age in Morocco) as apprentices. The multinational partners check that their principles and guidelines are respected. Export-orientated factories also tend to be more mechanized and less work-intensive. In this respect, the Sicome factory in Méknès is reported to be different in that it is work-intensive, relying on young apprentices to do finishing jobs rather than investing in modern machines.

At the time of the case, Sicome was subcontracted by a British retailer, Desmond & Sons, to supply about 30 per cent of their output to Marks & Spencer. The television programme was made following an investigation into allegations that pyjamas manufactured at Sicome were falsely being labelled as having been made in the UK. During the course of its investigations into these allegations, the television production team, posing as British buyers, discovered that, according to them, underage girls were involved in the production of these pyjamas and other garments in the Marks & Spencer line of production. Marks & Spencer reacted by launching a major public relations campaign in Britain, claiming its abhorrence of child work and sued those responsible for the television programme for libel. The company dispatched its lawyer to check Sicome's factory records for any employees under 15 years of age. Marks & Spencer later claimed that it used as a standard the regular minimum age set in ILO Convention No. 138. When interviewed in the television programme, and in subsequent media reports, Desmond's executives admitted the wrong labelling. On the other hand, Marks & Spencer categorically and repeatedly denied any knowledge of child workers "below 15 years of age" at Sicome. When Sicome decided to dismiss all workers aged under 15, the girls were just asked not to come back the next day. Some received token severance pay; others were not compensated.

This case came to the attention of the International Working Group on Child Labour, IWGCL, a project jointly sponsored and supported by a variety of international NGOs and development cooperation programmes. In February of 1996 it decided to try interviewing girls who had been dismissed from the factory to find out why they chose to do factory work, their working conditions, and what impact the dismissal had on their personal life and the well-being of their families. While the exact number of girls dismissed as a result of the Marks & Spencer intervention is not known, the study located 12 girls and the IWGCL researcher found the girls' stories strikingly similar in their account of events in the Sicome factory. They confirmed that around 100 young girls were employed, in the majority of cases as apprentices, for periods ranging from a few months to a couple of years. They were all aged between 12 and 15 years when they first entered the factory. The girls were hired in accordance with the national legislation, which states that children can be employed as apprentices at the age of 12 for a limited period under the provision of learning a trade or skill.

The interviews with the girls reveal that the girls and their parents were little aware of their legal rights as workers. This ignorance was used against the girls when they were dismissed. For example, one of the girls told the researcher, that after having worked in the factory for one year, she was asked to sign a paper. Thereafter, she was informed that what she had signed was her resignation papers. "I told her that I didn't know what I had signed, but she told me that I was the one who wanted to quit." Another girl's mother recounted a similar experience: "Close to the end of the first year they asked her to bring back the contract and gave her another one which I had to certify, but that one was only for one year. Unfortunately, I had not kept any copies of these documents; I did not know. Soon after that, they just turned her back at the gate and told her that she was too young."

The IWGCL report points out that provisions of the apprenticeship contract, signed by Sicome and approved by the work inspector were violated, the light workload was not respected, none of the girls interviewed received the scaled-down minimum wage nor the reduced number of working hours specified by the applicable labour legislation. The girls had to stand up all day, from 7.30 in the morning to 5.30 and often later in the evening. They had a one-hour lunch break when they were also standing up outside the factory gates. There was no training to speak of, and the workers often received no overtime pay for the considerable and apparently routine extra hours they worked. In reality, the young girls were less protected than the adults. Imane, 15 years of age, recalls: "The union had obtained from management that the adult permanent workers leave on time at 5:30 but the apprentices could be kept behind to catch up with any unfinished work that may have been caused by a power cut during the day or any other cause."

For these girls, all with a low socioeconomic background, the textile industry represented one of the best employment options. When the girls entered their apprenticeship at Sicome, they thought they had some guarantee of secure employment and of learning a real skill. They also aspired to become regular employees when old enough and 'trained'. Some time should actually have been set aside for learning the skills needed to advance in the job, but in practice there had been no training or career path envisaged for the girls interviewed. When the management needed someone to work on the machines they hired a person with the appropriate experience. Only a minority of the apprentices ever got promoted to work on the machines.

These girls, at the time of entering Sicome, had made a clear decision to seek employment. In part, their reasons were tied to economic difficulties, though inability to cope and succeed at school was also a major determining factor. For many of these girls, work is seen as fulfilling part of their responsibilities towards their families. "I want to help my family at least by buying my own clothes, paying for my bath. I want to be financially independent and not have to ask for every penny I need. It's enough for my parents to pay for my younger sisters." Work was also perceived as a liberating factor, offering an opportunity to take paid employment outside the home rather than unpaid work within, which they all confirmed they did not enjoy. Work was also seen as means of securing some form of financial independence which allowed them to meet their own personal needs to a certain extent. Finally, work was a factor of improving what they perceived as a yet undetermined, unspecified, and unarticulated prospect of a better life in the future.

Although these young girls found the working conditions at the Sicome factory hard and exhausting, Sicome appeared to them to offer the best of limited opportunities available in Méknès. Free and secure transportation to and from work in the company bus was also considered a major plus by both the parents and the girls. Despite the exploitation, they all felt bad about losing their jobs as a result of foreign pressure and kept returning to Sicome hoping to be rehired.

The immediate impact of the intervention was strongly felt by the girls and their families. These incomes were an important part of household revenues. All the girls interviewed expressed both a need and a desire to find another job. And subsequent visits by the researcher revealed that some of the girls went into domestic service, while others were married off. It is believed that at least one girl went into prostitution. None of the girls gave the slightest hint that they considered a return to formal schooling a possible avenue open to them. Their low level of education and their absence for a long period from the formal system meant that they could not go back to school under the current educational system. Their only hope and the only viable and real alternative open to them today is to find a paid job outside the home.

When the girls in the study were asked about their wishes and hopes for the future, none was able to express a desire. The researcher was struck by their inability to imagine or dream of a future, which they rather considered predetermined and remote. This submissive attitude was in contrast to that of their brothers. Even younger brothers could respond to the question about their future without hesitation. The boys envisioned learning a skill, a profession, a trade. They had a dream about their future.

The IWGCL study concluded that the overriding concern by both Sicome and Marks & Spencer was to protect their own interest; they showed little concern for the girls. There does not seem to have been any violation of national minimum age legislation. The 12 girls interviewed had been legally employed at Sicome, one at the age of 12, all the others at the age of 13. On the other hand, other provisions in the labour law related to working conditions, appear to have been routinely violated. Thus, the solution to dismiss the children was a simplistic one, when the most logical solution would have been to ameliorate their working conditions in accordance with the existing law. The IWGCL fears that, without more viable provisions for children, raising the minimum age, as recently proposed by the government, would only lead to more children working illegally, putting them out of reach of the legal protection they would otherwise be entitled to. What was needed, concludes the IWGCL, was a collaboration between contracting multinationals, subcontracted companies, NGOs, and national and local authorities to establish programmes capable of helping these girls develop a skill while working, along with literacy programmes. As of mid-1997, Sicome, Desmonds, and Marks & Spencer seemed to have ignored all calls for support to the children.

The result of these events was that children who were considered to be badly off in the factories, were made worse off by the intervention of 'the Europeans'. So far, the children seem to be the only losers. They were never consulted before the intervention, they did not know they were being filmed and that this would eventually cost them their jobs, and they were consulted afterwards only because an NGO was interested in finding out about them.

This case raises questions about what should be corporate moral responsibility, in this instance by a foreign retail firm and a domestic producing factory. Questions are also raised about the moral responsibility of the mass media, in this case a television company that taped the girls secretly and profited from their words and images while essentially destroying their livelihoods. The IWGCL pointed out that in this case nobody accepted any responsibility for the fate of the children, who were exploited in their supposed defence as they were exploited in their work and dismissal.

What, realistically, could have been done differently that would have benefited the children? The IWGCL suggests that Marks & Spencer could have demanded improvements in existing conditions in apprenticeship contracts for workers who were legally employed as apprentices. It could have worked with the local employer to put in place a scheme of good child-worker practices that would ensure vocational training and relevant quality education in accordance with the convention signed between the government professional training centre and the Moroccan Association of Garment and Textile Manufacturers. The television company could have had a positive impact if it had taken the trouble to examine the context that led these girls to work in the first place, thereby raising the awareness of British consumers about the complexities behind children working. It could have discussed ways of improving working conditions at Sicome instead of looking only at the girls' age. Constructive corporate actions were available that were not taken. Chapter Six pointed out the need for greater corporate sensitivity to children's needs and rights, and this case illustrates the point.

That said, it needs to be remembered that corporations do not live in a vacuum, and they generally respond to what society demands of them. In this case, corporate irresponsibility towards the girls also reflects the failure of other organizations. The Government of Morocco could have better fulfilled its responsibilities for labour inspection and education. The labour inspectorate should have made sure that the children were working under the conditions stipulated in the apprenticeship contract. The Government could have reformed the education system to better accommodate girl children of the poor, and improved its development strategies. Finally, the trade unions could have intervened to defend the girls' rights and they could have demanded compensation for them. They could have demanded the implementation of labour conditions applicable to apprentices and young workers. Had government and trade unions been more sensitive to the child workers and taken a more enlightened attitude towards them, corporate neglect would not have been so likely.

Codes of conduct

The Morocco case raises the question of what can be done to help firms deal with the question of child workers in a more responsible way. More and more corporations involved in international trade have adopted internal standards, so-called 'codes of conduct' or 'best practice' for the employment of child workers. Such codes commonly have the following characteristics:

- They concern the export sector only.
- They are used by companies to advertise their products and win points against competitors.
- They often lack any implementation mechanism.
- Workers concerned may know nothing about them or be too intimidated to insist that rights recognized by the codes be respected.
- They are not binding. The first reaction of importing companies that face criticism is likely to be 'cut and run', resulting in workers losing their jobs.
- There are yet no clear standards and methods for independent monitoring.[27]

Although the reasons for adopting codes of conduct vary, the most common is probably to avoid criticism and bad publicity. Multinational corporations generally realize that they have little, if anything, to gain by keeping underage workers in their production units, as the difference in cost of hiring a child compared to an adult tends to be negligible in relation to overall production costs. They have much more to gain, for example, from protecting their good name and reputation from public criticism. Increasingly, responsible companies are coming to realize that they need to establish and implement standards that protect against exploitative child work and address the rights and needs of the children they employ. Those who have tried to tackle the issue have found, however, that there is very little experience to build on — even western NGOs, trade unions, media, consumer groups, and child rights advocates who criticize the powerful companies for using child workers have problems suggesting solutions that are in the best interests of the child. In the countries of production, usually there are no trade unions who are willing or capable of helping the companies find solutions. Companies and trade associations are increasingly sharing information on codes of conduct, but solid data about their practicality and impact on children are lacking.

There is no guarantee that codes of conduct that successfully protect a company from public criticism also protect children. A code of conduct that is good for a company may be bad for children. Even when companies have the best of intentions, their codes may function in a way that reduces opportunities and enhances risks for the children they are meant to protect. The result of adopting and implementing codes of conduct may be the same as from trade restrictions and import bans against child work: the children might lose their jobs, without being offered alternatives to the work which could make their and their families' life better.

The US Department of Labor has gathered information on the extent and implementation of US garment importers' codes of conduct containing child labour provisions through a voluntary survey of the largest US retailers and apparel manufacturers.[28] 36 out of 42 companies indicated that they have adopted a policy specifically prohibiting the use of children in the manufacture of goods they import from abroad. However, the standards used to define 'child labour' varied significantly from company to company. In some cases, policies prohibiting 'child labour' in the production did not contain any definition of the term.

The US report underlines the importance of transparency of the codes: "or the extent to which foreign contractors and subcontractors, workers, the public, NGOs and governments are aware of their existence and meaning. Transparency reinforces the message of codes and leads to more credible implementation."[29] They found, however, that the respondents in general had not communicated the existence of the codes to a wider audience or engaged in educational efforts. They did not know whether workers were aware of the existence of the codes. Although most of the codes did not contain detailed provisions for monitoring and implementation, and many of these companies did not have a reliable monitoring system in place, only a few respondents solicited input from international organizations, trade unions, NGOs, or government agencies in developing or implementing their codes.

The vast majority of respondents stated that they had never found any violations of the child labour provisions of their codes. If this happened, however, they would first investigate to confirm the use of child work. The enforcement measures they would impose ranged from immediate termination of the business relationship to corrective actions, such as dismissal of underage workers, cancellation of specific orders, and placement of the violating supplier on probation. The conclusion of the Department of Labor is that codes of conduct can be a positive factor in solving the global problem of child work, although they are not a panacea. The Department's recommendations all deal with the adoption, implementation, and monitoring of the codes of conduct. There is no recommendation that deals with, or even mentions, the working children and their welfare. A more child-centred view certainly would suggest that codes of conduct include specific provision for monitoring and responding to the best interests of the children involved. This should apply to all subcontractors in the firm's supply chain.

One example of a well-elaborated best practice guide is the one of the World Federation of the Sporting Goods Industry, WFSGI,[30] in which their members commit themselves among other things to take specific actions to achieve:

- no new hiring of employees aged below 15 (or 14 for countries with insufficiently developed economies and educational facilities) and, for those already working, a reduction of hours to permit education/training,
- return of working children under the age of 13 (or 12) to some form of full-time education,
- where the workforce is predominantly female, consideration of the provision of childcare facilities,
- special measures (defined in the practice) in outworking situations.

The WFSGI also recommends its members to take certain steps to ensure the protection of older children. To start with, they should establish age records of employees and record the number of hours that those under 18 years of age work, in order to avoid overtime work. Members of the WFSGI should also examine their operations for potential hazards to young workers and cover child workers for social security and insurance. There should be no punishment, and employees should have equal pay for equal work — paid directly to the worker. Working children should have a right to at least 12 hours' rest at night, two days' rest weekly and an annual holiday with pay for at least four weeks. Finally, children should be encouraged to continue their education.

Serious and well-thought out codes of conduct must carefully consider what is in the best interests of working children. This presupposes assessment studies of the situation of the children, so that the company can offer alternatives to children who are too young for the work they do, protect older children from harmful work, and enable those concerned to understand the codes (the first step being to translate them into the working children's mother tongue). Companies that are willing to make an effort to involve the working children themselves and their families in the elaboration of codes of conduct would certainly have greater possibilities to base the codes on the children's realities and best interests. An independent monitoring system is needed to make sure that the codes are respected.

Whatever the motives of the companies are for introducing codes of conduct, they should be welcomed as a means to protect working children. However, it is important for NGOs and individuals with special experience in protecting working children to help and guide companies so that the texts adopted are well thought out, meaningful, and in the best interests of the children. Companies establishing codes of conduct may need assistance in ensuring that their codes will be progressive rather than regressive for children.

Monitoring mechanisms

NGOs, governments, firms and industries, and international organizations have in the last several years been attempting to create new mechanisms that can realistically accommodate political and economic pressures to remove child workers from export industries but at the same time protect children from the negative impact of lost jobs. This is done by providing them replacement income and expanded opportunities for schooling. The principle involved is that children should be left better off, not worse off, by measures that transfer them from export sector work to other activities, especially education, deemed more suitable for them. But what are these fledgling mechanisms, and how well do they work? Most importantly, do they really succeed in their objective of protecting and promoting the well-being and development of the children involved? To answer these questions, it is useful to consider two experiences in some detail: labelling initiatives in the carpet industry, such as the Rugmark, and the planned transition programmes, as implemented in the Bangladesh garment industry.

Labelling

One new strategy that has received much attention in recent years is that of providing consumers with the choice of purchasing products they can believe to be made without the involvement of child workers. In some cases, the aim is not to guarantee that the item is 'child-labour-free', but the customer is supposed to contribute to the welfare of working children by purchasing the product. When the aim is to offer 'child-labour-free' products, this is often done by establishing a voluntary system of inspection which certifies that the products of member companies are subject to regular inspection verifying that they do not employ children. A small premium is often added to the export or sale price, which money is to be utilized in providing education or other services to former working children who are no longer employed in the industry. This is a complex undertaking which combines and coordinates the tasks of compliance monitoring, funds management, and rehabilitation. So far, the labelling approach has been applied primarily to the hand-knotted carpet industry in South Asia.

The last five years have seen a flood of mass media and NGO reports describing the disastrous conditions for children in the carpet industry. Subsequently, a number of initiatives have emerged in order to stop child work in the industry, focusing mainly on India but also on Pakistan and Nepal. Little has been done, however, to find out about child involvement in the carpet industry in other countries such as Iran, Afghanistan, the People's Republic of China, Morocco, Egypt, Turkey or countries in the former Soviet Union. This overwhelming interest in the carpet industry might be explained by the fact that carpets are made in poor countries almost solely for export to rich countries. And the contrast between the hand-knotted carpet's air of luxury and abundance and the children's slave-like conditions yields the possibility of good illustrations for campaigning against detrimental child work.

The carpet industry employs relatively fewer children than is generally believed. For example, while estimates of the number of children working in India's hand-knotted carpet industry range from about 50,000 to 1,050,000, a study by ILO[31] found that the total number of children in the industry is in fact closer to 130,000. This is still a large number but a small proportion in relation to the many tens of millions of children who are toiling in other sectors and occupations in India, doing work that is equally harmful to children.

The best-known attempt to get 'child-labour-free carpets' is the Rugmark label — an initiative which started in the beginning of the 1990s and was formally established in 1994 as the Rugmark Foundation, RMF. The Rugmark label became a legally binding international trademark in December 1995 and April 1996 respectively in the two major carpet-importing countries Germany and the United States.[32] Starting in India, Rugmark has recently been introduced in Nepal and there are attempts to introduce it in Pakistan as well. There are licensed carpet importers primarily in Germany, but Rugmark-labelled carpets are also exported to other European countries, the USA, and Canada.

Carpet exporters with a Rugmark licence bind themselves legally not to employ children under 14 years of age and to pay adult weavers' salaries that conform to legal minimum wage requirements. The exporters must furnish information to RMF about the looms working for them and the looms are inspected by professional inspectors but could also be inspected by NGOs. The licensed exporters have the right to affix the Rugmark label onto the carpets. Every carpet can then be traced all the way back to the loom through a computerized code number, indicating the details about the exporter, manufacturer, loom owner, the weavers, and so on. The Rugmark label is said to provide the importers and consumers with a visual guarantee that the carpets are manufactured without involving children.[33] According to Rugmark's own figures,[34] there are 180 carpet exporters in India with Rugmark licences (out of 2,700 exporters in total) and 40 in Nepal. Almost one million Rugmark carpets have been exported from India and Nepal, primarily to Germany, the world's largest importer of hand-knotted carpets. German importers pay a contribution of at least 1 per cent of the export price of carpets to the RMF to finance social and rehabilitation programmes for children. The exporters also pay a fee of 0.25 per cent of the value of their carpets which goes towards financing inspections.

To gain credibility for the Rugmark label, huge efforts have been made in order to lay down norms and rules for the issue of licences and labels and to make the inspection and control system function. The RMF has made some efforts recently to find a good answer to "the most often repeated question"[35] of what will become of the children who are freed from the looms through the Rugmark initiative. For instance, they have opened three schools and a rehabilitation centre in India.

Another initiative is STEP (Foundation for fair conditions in carpet production and carpet trade). Starting as an informal collaboration between Swiss NGOs and socially committed carpet traders, STEP was formally established in 1995 as a joint venture by five Swiss development organizations[36] and a national organization representing the carpet trade.[37] Through signing a licence agreement with STEP, the Swiss carpet firms and individuals commit themselves to respect socially just, economically fair, and ecologically sound standards in their business. This means paying producers a fair price which would allow fair wages to weavers and a production without child workers.

STEP differs from Rugmark in several ways. While Rugmark is a label on individual carpets showing that they are 'child-labour-free', STEP has a more 'pragmatic' approach. It is a company label, expressing the company's dedication to improve the situation in carpet production and trade. Companies with a STEP label do not aim at guaranteeing every single carpet to be 'free of child labour'. The initiative takes into consideration the desire by the companies to sell off old stocks and the difficulties to reach full control over each stage in the manufacturing and trade. Swiss firms that have signed, pay a licence fee per square metre of sold carpet to finance the organization's operational costs as well as development projects in the 'carpet areas'. These fees are supposed to lead to slightly higher prices for the consumer.

The control system is thought to work through double checking. On the one hand, the Swiss importers and retailers should make sure that minimum conditions are respected by their suppliers and manufacturers. On the other hand, a STEP monitoring-system of independent specialists is supposed to countercheck information provided by the carpet trade. The carpet trade involved in the programme has a responsibility to set up minimum standards to producers and to control that the agreed conditions are applied. The foundation reports that a 20–25 per cent representation of the overall Swiss market actively participate in the initiative. STEP supports projects and programmes in India and Nepal, carried out by Swiss and international NGOs.

Care & Fair, an initiative of German carpet importers and dealers, started in 1994 with the aim to improve the life of children in the carpet industry in India and Nepal.[38] Each member of C&F pays an annual fee and a fee on the value of the imports from these countries. The money collected goes to C&F schooling and rehabilitation projects controlled by a special C&F committee. C&F also differs from the Rugmark in the sense that it does not try to certify  that carpets are '100 per cent child-labour-free'; it does not directly engage in any monitoring or inspections of work sites, but focuses on finding alternatives for the children working in the carpet industry.

Finally, the Kaleen labelling programme was set up in 1995 by the Indian Government through its Carpet Export Promotion Council, CEPC. Kaleen describes itself as a commitment of the Indian carpet industry to totally eradicate the use of hired child workers and to introduce suitable welfare measures for the education and rehabilitation of children in the carpet industry in India.[39] The initiative includes a labelling system for all handmade carpets, druggets and dhurries certifying that the user of the label is following the code of conduct adopted by the CEPC, which is responsible

for enforcing the labelling system. A weavers' welfare fund has been established for education, health care, and vocational training. Exporters must be members of the CEPC, pay a fee in relation to the value of their exports to the welfare fund, provide an affidavit certifying that they do not use child workers, and provide information about the looms where their carpets are produced, in order to get the right to affix the Kaleen label to their products. A registration system and enforcement mechanism has been set up based on a total registration of looms used by exporters. According to the CEPC, regular random inspections are made by an independent agency and loom owners and exporters/manufacturers found in default will face deregistration and blacklisting procedures under the CEPC's voluntary code of conduct.

There are numerous other labelling initiatives addressing child work, for example, in the footwear, soccer ball and tea industries.[40] As most of these programmes started very recently, there is little information on their operation.

There is no doubt that those benefiting from the serious labelling initiatives are a group of working children in urgent need. Another positive effect of the efforts made in this area is the attention they have attracted to the issue of harmful child work. One of the weaknesses of the labelling initiatives, however, is that they are expensive and time-consuming in relation to the very limited number of working children benefiting from them. Another problem is that they have, in general, so far focused more on the elimination of child work in the industry in question than on the rehabilitation of the working children. If this latter problem could be solved, there is a certain value in "liberating" these children as they perform work that can be very damaging.

However, the labelling model presents special questions which have yet to be answered from experience. Firstly, can labels implying 'child-labour-free' manufacture be made truly credible through watertight inspection or other means? Secondly, do consumers care enough to search out and prefer the labelled product? Thirdly, is it feasible to fund support or prevention activities from small fees attached to use of the label? Fourthly, are compensatory and support services to children losing jobs sufficient to offset what the children and their families have lost? Fifthly, is there systematic monitoring of the welfare of children involved in order to know how they are being affected? Until those questions can be answered positively, it is not possible to conclude that the labelling model is economically and socially viable. In addition, there are today all kinds of faked labels, but which in reality have no monitoring system and are only meant to dupe the consumer.

The ILO, UNICEF, the Save the Children Alliance, and many other NGOs recommend that removal of children from their jobs should always be accomplished through planned transition programmes that assure them education and/or income alternatives that are more attractive and appropriate than the work they leave. The mechanisms of such an approach are left to each case, but are never simple. The main experiment of this model is now occurring in Bangladesh, having been established by the ILO and UNICEF in conjunction with the garment industry employers' association, BGMEA, and in cooperation with government and various NGOs.

Soon after the dismissals of the children from Bangladesh's garment industry (see above), trade unions, NGOs, and UNICEF started discussions with BGMEA and the Ministry of Labour. It was agreed that, although the removal of children from the work force was desirable in the long term, abrupt dismissal was more likely to force children into other jobs, in order to avoid destitution. The alternatives to garment jobs are in general less safe and less well paid, such as domestic service, brick chipping, rickshaw pulling, and selling flowers on the streets.[41]

Growing concern for the welfare of the children made BGMEA change a former decision to dismiss all child workers from the garment sector by the end of 1994 and substitute the rapid dismissal with a phased programme aiming to ease children into more suitable activities. UNICEF-Bangladesh, invited local and international NGOs, industry representatives, officials from the Ministry of Labour, and representatives from the ILO and the US Embassy to try and formulate a plan of action which would take the best interests of these children into consideration. In 1995, more than two years after the dismissal, a 'Memorandum of Understanding' (MOU) on the elimination of underage children from the garment industry in Bangladesh was signed by the BGMEA, UNICEF, and ILO. By this time, 11,000 children under 14 years of age (out of an estimated number of 40,000-55,000 released from the factories) had been identified by UNICEF in the garment industry, of whom 80 per cent were girls.

The thrust of the MOU was a plan to verify the removal of children from the industry and to assist them to enter and remain in school through at least a basic education or until the age of 14, the legal age for employment. The problem was that there were not enough schools where the children lived to receive all those being dismissed from the garment industry. It would be necessary to set up special school facilities for approximately 10,000 children. UNICEF and local NGOs strongly felt that, provided there were certain guarantees, there was no problem with the children continuing to work within the factory until they could be accommodated in school.

The first schools were established in January 1996, three years after the dismissals took place. As of June 1997, about 400 new schoolrooms were operational and more than 8,000 children were enrolled. By that time, however, many of the child workers identified as underage had turned 14 and returned to work rather than school. It is not known how many of the identified children never made it into school or did not finish the course. In order to compensate for the lost income, those former child workers who are in school are paid approximately one-half of what the lower-paid children were paid in the garment industry. They are provided with a basic curriculum designed for their age and needs and instead to bring them literacy in three years.

The Bangladesh transition approach has proved complicated, expensive, and difficult to manage. First of all, monitoring the garment industry has necessitated establishment of a special single-industry inspectorate at very high cost, yet most concede that child workers still flow in and out of the industry surreptitiously. It has proved difficult to track children from job to school, and it is apparent that only a portion of the children now in the specially established schools were in fact the same children counted and registered for transfer. Many of those children have been lost — presumably to other jobs — and others, perhaps equally deserving, have taken their place in school. While the half-pay 'scholarship' paid to ex-garment workers in school has been helpful to many children, it has been inadequate to hold others in school. It is a sum far too high to be replicated generally in Bangladesh, and too low to attract all working children to school. That said, over 10,000 slum children are in school who were not there before, which is a social gain even if not entirely corresponding to that intended. It is open to question whether the rather elaborate and marginally efficient Bangladesh model is transferable to places and industries that do not receive the very substantial outside financial and technical resources that have been lavished on the Bangladesh child garment workers. There is also a very serious question, yet to be addressed, whether the dismissed children have gained from the transition project as much as they lost by their dismissal.

Income replacement

Although subsidizing poor children or their families with cash or in-kind income is a common approach to removing children from work and/or keeping them in school, there is amazingly little literature on the subject. For that reason this section will review in detail a unique report by the ILO and another by Save the Children Fund U.K.

The ILO has produced an overview of NGO experiences with income replacement and substitution activities as a strategy against harmful child work.[42] It was undertaken partly in response to questions raised by the Bangladesh experience. This exploratory survey of 51 organizations from 18 countries enquired into the practices, results, and opinions of programmes known to make use of one form or another of economic incentives to reduce child work and/or retain children in school. It showed that in spite of the great interest and sometimes strong belief in these programmes, much more investigation is needed before it is possible to draw broad conclusions about what kind of income replacement and substitution activities are effective, where, by whom, for whom, and to what cost. It does appear, however, that they have a potentially important role to play in at least some situations. But there are major outstanding questions about how to use them, and when <u>not</u> to try them.

Organizations participating in the ILO survey, mainly NGOs, felt that their programmes were generally effective and could be expanded. However, few had been subjected to formal, independent evaluations or impact assessments. Anker and Melkas did not find that general conclusions were possible, but they did make some "tentative generalizations". They found that information and data collection is important for programme-design, monitoring, and evaluation, especially before starting the activities. In general, different types of income replacement and substitution activities are likely to be feasible for different age groups. Community involvement is crucial in all phases of a programme's development and implementation. Also, there is a need to combine several types of activities into a comprehensive approach. One reason for this is to avoid dependency, which was often felt to be a problem. Corruption or cheating was also felt by many organizations to be a concern when providing cash or in-kind benefits or subsidies. The best way to tackle this problem, according to the responding organizations, was by close monitoring or through in-kind benefits which are not as open to corruption or cheating. Another issue is the cost and sustainability of these programmes: continuity of resources was often felt to be an obstacle, and programmes therefore tended to be of a short duration. The conclusion was that more emphasis should be given to sustainability in all phases of the programme.

Among organizations responding to the survey, the most common type of programme was in-kind payments to help increase school attendance by providing food, books, clothing or other school materials, and school fees. The purpose is to encourage children to attend school and to stay there. In-kind payments were preferred to cash payments, mainly because they were felt to be less open to misuse. While school lunch programmes are one of the most common forms of income substitution, the report emphasizes that special attention has to be paid to measures to keep children in school, so that they do not go to school only to get the meal but do not stay for the lessons, or go to school only when they do not get enough money from work, or when they are hungry. The difficulties seem to be related to the fact reported by the majority of the respondents that formal schooling by many poor families is felt as a waste of time because of the poor quality of teaching and schools, because teachers' attitudes are not encouraging, school does not provide relevant skills, and school does not make a difference regarding the child's future. This was independent confirmation of the bleak picture of public-funded schooling presented in Chapter Seven, and it raises the question of how much auxiliary economic support should be channelled to propping up poor education.

However, the survey respondents who were or had been implementing school lunch programmes were quite positive about them. Half of the respondents felt that subsidies would keep the children in school even if they and their families did not give much value to the school system. Nevertheless, many of them expressed clearly that for these programmes to be effective they need to be combined with other activities. A Pakistani NGO that was positive about the effectiveness of school lunches nevertheless pointed out that: "Free tuition will be more persuasive than free nutrition."[43]

Waiver of school fees is considered to have one important advantage over payments in kind: it must be used by the specific child in a family for whom it is intended and cannot be sold. Those respondents with experience from programmes using payments in kind and waiver of school fees seemed confident about these strategies, even if many emphasized the need to combine these activities with improvement of quality of teaching and schools. Otherwise, they pointed out, children are not likely to be retained in school. Anker and Melkas, conclude that these types of activities are likely to encourage those parents and children who value education to send their children to school. But, just as with school lunch programmes, they do not compensate the family for the opportunity costs of lost income from work because of schooling.

A way to deal with both the direct costs and the opportunity costs of schooling (lost earnings and lost economic contributions to the family) is cash grants paid either directly to children or to families to be used according to their own judgement. A Kenyan NGO in the survey gave cash stipends to children having worked part-time in salt industries. They also provided uniforms and books to the 180 children, mostly girls between 9 and 15 years of age. The child's work was thought to have contributed about 60 per cent of family income. The cash payment, about US$100, was given to the child or mother for a period of one year as a credit lending facility. According to the organization, this type of income-replacement activity could be expanded to other groups and places because, in their opinion, it creates self-reliance.

There were a few respondents who expressed arguments against payments in cash or in kind. The report cites an international NGO:

> Our experience from these programmes does not encourage us to introduce this kind of income substitution in new programmes in Africa or extend it to programmes in other regions. Providing cash or in-kind [subsidies] to selected families or children in an environment characterized by a sea of poverty is in our experience not a sustainable solution. In addition to this such programmes are: difficult to administer; not cost effective; create dependency; encourage corruption; stigmatize people; do not address the root causes of child labour.[44]

Organizations implementing apprenticeships, schoolwork combinations and 'safe work' for children were mainly positive towards their approach. Schoolwork programmes mean that children go to school in the morning, for example, and work during the afternoon. School can have flexible hours to enable children to work and include for example vocational training components in the curriculum to support the work. School can also organize the work so that it is non-hazardous and controlled. These programmes do not cause lost earnings. According to the report, apprenticeships, when not misused in order to economically exploit underage children (as in the Moroccan case described above), can provide a very positive mechanism for teaching literacy and job skills. One example is taken from the Ivory Coast, where an organization has provided technical training for adolescents in traditional craft workshops. To ensure good working conditions, an educator from the organization regularly visited the participants, their workplaces, and families. In addition, technical and pedagogical support was given to their employers. After one

317

year of apprenticeship, minimum equipment was given to the participants so that they could continue practising the occupation and make a living. The authors remark that apprenticeships, schoolwork combinations and 'safe work' are not suitable for very young children, but they may provide a relevant option for older children. Apprenticeships and schoolwork combinations correspond to what many of the survey respondents emphasized: the importance of adding vocational training components in children's education to make it more relevant and the general need to make formal schools more flexible.

The survey also asked NGOs about income-generating activities for families and communities to improve their economic situation and thus make child work less necessary. Respondents to the survey were positive about income-generating activities as part of child work programmes and several organizations indicated that they had moved to this direction in their activities as a result of evaluations and recommendations they had received. Some organizations which were against payments in cash or in kind saw income-generating activities as a better solution.

Another study, specifically on *Children and Income Generating Programmes* has been made by Gillian Peace and David Hulme for the Save the Children Fund, SCF-UK.[45] The study focused on two specific types of income-generation activities: making, selling and paid employment; and savings and credit schemes. It did not, however, look more specifically into the issue of children as income earners. But it did make a few findings that bear on the subject of children's schooling and work in relation to income-generation projects. This is an important issue because many observers insist that child work issues should be considered within an overall development framework, and some have noted that development projects often have unrecognized child work effects.

First of all, the authors found that it is difficult to find out about the actual distribution of economic impacts of income-generation programmes within the households, as impact surveys tend to only use adult respondents and the 'child's voice' is not heard. In fact, they found that children are consistently invisible in the reports, and that studies of the income-generation programme impacts aimed at household level hardly ever look at indicators of child welfare in a systematic fashion. In general, the needs and priorities of children are assumed to coincide with the household, and impacts on children are not considered separately:

> If the impacts of projects on women and children are not assessed this can have serious negative affects [sic], preventing projects from achieving economic as well as social objectives. In contexts where

women and children have some autonomy they will not cooperate and provide unpaid labour in enterprises where they do not see themselves as sharing in the benefits. Hence, the project will collapse. In contexts where women and children are powerless, then such projects may be economically viable, but that achievement will be at a high price — reinforcing the exploitation of women and children.[46]

A wide range of positive and negative effects of income-generation programmes at household level have been observed by SCF-UK and other agencies. The positive effects include: more children attending school; household members gaining technical, managerial, and marketing experience; reduced prostitution amongst women and children; increased political empowerment and protection; improved skills, including literacy; reduced levels of vagrancy for children and families; protection from the hazards of street life; and improved school enrolment for street children. Income-generation programmes have been used as tools to prevent bonded-labour families from returning to bondage after having been released, to prevent children from being sold into slavery, or ending up in servile forms of marriage or prostitution.

An example of a reasonably successful programme to help children stay in school comes from Bangladesh, where saving and credit schemes for children related to education have been tried with the Kiddy Banks in the River Project:

> Children at the SCF Children's Centres in Bangladesh were encouraged to make regular savings. Children who amassed a minimum level of savings were eligible to take a loan to buy a kid or a lamb, which is a traditional way of saving for poor people. The child would raise the kid, increasing the value of their savings. The goats (and any offspring) were sold to meet their education expenses. This scheme was self-financed, using the capital from savings, income from the sale of produce from school kitchen gardens, Child Centre registration fees and bank interest.[47]

Negative effects found by SCF and other agencies include: reduced school attendance because of work; increased work for women; increased household conflicts because of additional demands for time and resources; increased polygamy; loss of status when an enterprise fails; increased dependency because of the destruction of traditional survival mechanisms for household and communities. Chapter Three already alluded to the finding that credit and micro-enterprise projects can increase children's workload.

The authors conclude that economic interventions may be one way of working towards the all-round development of children, and their success or failure should be judged both in terms of their specific economic objectives and their broader contribution to the welfare of children. They did not find any evidence, however, that income-generation programmes have shown many sustainable impacts on poverty alleviation, on a scale commensurate with the incidence of poverty. One reason for this is that income-generation programmes do not alter the basic economic context and most programmes operate with only a minute fraction of the target population. Another reason is that these programmes operate using existing economic mechanisms which tend to concentrate wealth in the hands of a few rather than spreading wealth. The final reason, given by the authors, is that the economic context is governed by its own internal dynamics and rules which tend to force workers to accept limited returns for their labour. Thus, the changes that may be necessary to improve the income levels of poorer people, such as increases in wages, asset redistribution, access to education services, and consumer protection, often lie outside, or compete with, income-generation programme objectives.

In summary, it has not yet been proved that participation in income-generation programmes leads to a direct improvement in child health, nutrition, school attendance, and educational attainment and freedom from abuse or domestic violence. Long-term impacts are even less understood. The Save the Children Fund found that more research is needed at project level to help understand the complex factors involved and to identify appropriate indicators to show how children are affected by the work. We strongly endorse the idea that development projects attempting to raise incomes of the poor should as a matter of course evaluate their impact on children, including through child work.

Conclusion

As mentioned in previous chapters, more research is needed in order to determine negative and positive effects of child work on society in the long run, and on the relation between child work and adult unemployment. More specifically, there is also a need to find out more about how economic incentives can protect children from harmful child work. More of the ongoing programmes need to be evaluated.

This entire subject is woefully neglected by economists and researchers and the considerable potential that we feel exists in economic approaches will not be realized until the proper studies have been done. This would seem an especially appropriate challenge for the ILO and the World Bank. Tying economic interventions so closely to the export sector has been unfortunate. While various threats of sanctions have put governments under pressure to act against harmful child work, it is doubtful that these efforts could generally be said to have had any major positive effects on most working children, or even that the positive effects have so far outweighed the negative effects. A particular weakness of the trade sanction approach is that it has not sufficiently taken into consideration that the child's work in general is part of a survival strategy of impoverished families. The threat of trade sanctions may only result in the employer sacking child workers and preventing new children from being employed. The response is entirely to external pressures and not at all to internal social and economic needs. If no alternatives are available, children will look for jobs in other sectors, jobs that many times are more harmful to them than the export sector jobs they have left. Thus, 'rescuing' or 'freeing' children from their workplace does not in most cases mean freeing the children from harmful work or hunger. As a child weaver in Bangladesh puts it: "There is no freedom from this work. In order to get freedom from this work, first we will have to give freedom to our stomach."[48]

The current tendency to focus effort on the export sector alone not only simply moves the problem from one sector to another, but it invests in an approach that has little applicability outside that sector. For example, the most common form of children's work, worldwide, may be the unpaid labour of children working for their parents in their own household, on the family farm or in some other family enterprise. It is difficult to see how these children could be reached in a positive way by mechanisms designed for the export sector. These children are sometimes working under worse conditions than children working outside their families. It should be noted that children working in the urban, informal sector (so-called street children) and children working in the export sector sometimes have arrived where they are in order to escape unpaid work in the family household or business.[49]

When trade sanctions are suggested as a solution to harmful child work, an underlying assumption is that a major reason for children to work is the wish from employers to exploit cheap labour.[50] Thus, employers could be forced to comply with human rights standards through the threat of trade sanctions. This assumption may not be very applicable to the majority of working children, who work within the family. But even for those children who are employed outside the family, trade sanctions aiming at making it unprofitable for employers to exploit children, miss their goal to protect children from harmful work if they do not provide them with good alternatives to the work they are doing.

There is no doubt that children many times are exploited because of their cheap labour. But as the case of Bangladesh clearly shows, it does not always serve working children to make employers or importers part of the problem and not part of the solution. Employers must become a big part of the solution and this will require that they sometimes act creatively and audaciously, doing more than they have to. The BGMEA in Bangladesh is a realistic example of what can be done. It is obvious that it would have been much easier for the garment industry in Bangladesh to sack all the children in order to save the industry's reputation and good business instead of finding solutions that were in the best interests of the children involved:

> By removing all remaining children from the factories, the BGMEA would have been in total compliance with the 'no child labour' requirements of the Harkin Bill — UNICEF and partners would have had no basis for continuing discussions with the industry and the only group to suffer would be those children who would lose their jobs as a result.[51]

It is important that all actors contribute to eliminating harmful child work. Consumers together with trade unions, NGOs, and private business companies can all contribute to make life better for working children. The first step forward would be to start focusing on real working children rather than on an abstract notion of 'child labour'. So far, much more effort has been made to convince governments and employers that goods produced in the export sector should be freed from child labour than to free children from harmful work and to ensure they ended up better off rather than worse off. These priorities need to be reversed.

If boycotts, import bans, and 'social clauses' are to be used as weapons against harmful child work in a way that is good for the working children, they must be better planned to bring benefits rather than more harm to children. Studies are needed to understand the social, cultural, and economic background of the children, the possible alternatives, and the consequences a withdrawal from work will have for the children. If they are to be socially meaningful, measures to stop harmful child work in the export sector should also aim at having a positive effect on children working outside this sector. It is indispensable to involve the children in planning. Without it, child-friendly results might not be expectable.

A frightening scenario, when so many efforts are concentrated on removing children from the export sector, is that rich-country consumers will believe that they wear 'clean' clothes, walk on 'clean' carpets, and eat 'clean' food, assured by exporters and importers that these products are 'free of child labour'. They will then believe that the 'child labour problem' has been solved. While they live in complacent delusion that nothing more need be done, many millions of children will be working harder and more hazardously than ever — out of sight and out of mind of the rest of the world. Only by weaning 'child labour' concerns away from a fixation on the export sector, and on economic interventions to eliminate it, and by re-focusing it on all children in abusive work, will this nightmare of misguided policy be avoided. Then, truly serious work in relating economic policy to child work can begin in earnest.

Conclusion

At the outset of this book we posed the question of what policies and programmes concerning child work are in children's best interests. This question responds to the International Convention on the Rights of the Child (CRC), which suggests that the appropriateness of children's work can be assessed by the effect it has on the well-being and development of the children involved. Taking that cue from the Convention, we proposed that healthy physical, psychological, cognitive, moral, social, and emotional development constitute the most obvious and direct expression of children's best interests. Accordingly, work which impedes the well-being and development of children should be considered detrimental to their best interests; work which promotes their welfare and development generally would be consistent with them. By the same token, social interventions in child work that advance children's healthy development are in their best interests, while actions undermining children's well-being and development should be judged inimical to them. Situations injurious to children's well-being and development cannot be in their best interests, and are therefore inconsistent with child rights as defined under the CRC.

Reviewing new thinking in anthropology and developmental psychology, we reported that the best interests of children are defined differently in different contexts, with the expectations and experiences of childhood being shaped largely by the social interaction and personal attributes of individual children. Special stress was placed on the importance of approaching children's work in the context of their family and community. We also pointed out that children are not passive recipients of experience, but highly adaptable, active contributors to their own development. Their active role helps protect them against danger and stress, and facilitates their psychosocial development. They also have multiple capacities and competencies which exist in a synergistic relationship and are most effectively fostered in a variety of learning environments. Different societies present different learning opportunities and child protection strategies, with different child development outcomes. In many societies, work is one of the most important mechanisms of learning in childhood, promoting self-actualization, survival skills and family integration. These insights suggest that protective policies that are flexible, sensitive to cultural difference, respectful of children's economic and social responsibilities, based on consensus rather than coercion, and involve and empower children are more likely to have desirable developmental effects than are approaches that are imposed upon children as passive victims or beneficiaries. Examining child work issues in this light revealed many important questions that are generally neglected by more traditional perspectives.

The conceptual and practical fertility of approaching child work from a broad point of view encompassing the multiple dimensions of children's experience and development suggests that this perspective is more productive for protecting children than is the narrower 'child labour' orientation which regards work in relative isolation from the rest of a child's life and focuses almost exclusively on its dangers. It is necessary to take into consideration both the negative and positive aspects of children's work, relating it to the family and community ties around which their lives revolve. The preceding chapters have illustrated ways in which regarding children's work from a child-centred perspective redefines the issues and enriches the possibilities for protecting children. New issues are raised, old assumptions are challenged, different objectives and priorities come to the fore, more effective lines of action are implied, and the role of children in providing their own protection is greatly expanded. Thinking about the issues in new ways opens new avenues to action. Some of the long traditional interventions that tend to be recycled by a more conventional 'child labour' orientation, despite their doubtful efficacy, may provide the comfort of continuity, but they lack the fresh vitality of innovation and relevance.

Not all things traditional are necessarily outdated but, in a modern world being wrenched in new directions by rapid demographic, economic, social, and political changes, it is often necessary to challenge the conventional wisdom to thorough re-examination from the ground up. We think that the prevailing models for dealing with children's work, especially those being internationally recommended for incorporation in national policy, are long overdue for a conceptual and practical re-appraisal of their relevance, empirical support, social coherence, and practical effects on children and families. Perhaps the international discussion surrounding a possible new ILO convention against the most intolerable forms of child work provides a natural opportunity to undertake such a re-examination of the basic issues.

We note, however, that the crusading, superficial moralism that now characterizes much 'child labour' discussion and activity poses an obstacle to the open, pragmatic, and objective reconsideration the subject deserves. It may lead to rigidity of thought and action at exactly the moment when more flexibility is needed to successfully adapt child protection methods to the exigencies of a changing world. While a high level of public and interest group enthusiasm for children's rights is to be desired, an ideologically superheated atmosphere which discourages new questioning and questioners, which clings to outworn ideas and practices that should be permitted a natural death, and which discourages the birth of relevant new values, visions, and approaches is hardly in the best interests of working children. Those who are truly concerned for working children's best interests should be willing to examine all the issues as empirically and dispassionately as possible and with meaningful participation from the children involved.

The critical issues

Three major themes, differentiation, empowerment, and inclusion, constantly reappear through the preceding chapters. They are crucial concerns fundamental to all of the major child work questions we have discussed, and in each there are important problems that stand in the way of a truly child-centred approach to dealing with working children. In our view, policy and action governing children's work cannot reflect the best interests of working children until each of these theme issues has been explicitly considered and addressed. Policy-makers, programme-planners and children's advocates attempting to guarantee the rights of children according to the spirit of the Convention on the Rights of the Child need to rigorously review both national and international approaches to child work in the light of these three large and neglected issues.

Differentiation

One of the most important messages of this book is that there are so many kinds of work and working conditions, some facilitating and some hindering children's development, that it is nearly impossible to make universal judgements about either the morality of child work or its impact on children. Much current 'child labour' policy is based on unfounded generalizations about child work and child workers. As we pointed out in the Introduction, work also tends to be defined far too narrowly usually including only economic activities to match the reality of working children. In order to protect working children effectively, work must be defined broadly enough to include not only economic activities but also the essential household maintenance duties that many children perform. It must also be differentiated. The situational differences between a child factory worker and a child housekeeper are enormous, and the evidence does not suggest that factory working children are more likely to be endangered than are child house helps. Nor is it helpful to address child work issues through universal policies that do not recognize and accommodate the enormous diversity of working children, conditions, and contexts involved. Any blanket claim that child work is inherently bad and should be prohibited for pre-adolescent children is no more justifiable by the evidence than is the opposite point of view holding that work is innately good and should be encouraged for children. From the standpoint of children's best interests, national or international policies based on either of these polar suppositions would be seriously misguided. Cases have to be assessed on their own merits. Only supple and nuanced approaches that can be adapted to divergent realities have the capacity to successfully protect children's lives, rights, and development.

In the introductory chapter of this book we suggested the usefulness of differentiating working children into three main categories, pointing out that each group is characterized by unique circumstances and needs. Succeeding chapters, taken together, suggest something about the approaches that may be appropriate for each group.

- Children in work that seriously endangers their life, health or development should receive top priority attention from both government and civil society. They should be removed from detrimental work circumstances through activities that transfer them into more appropriate activities meeting their developmental needs. National laws and international conventions should unequivocally prohibit truly hazardous and oppressive work and working conditions, and they should provide viable economic and educational alternatives to detrimental child work. Civil society, families, and children themselves must be educated and organized to recognize and mobilize against intolerable work. It is especially important to search out those working children who are truly most at risk, no matter where they are and how hard they are to reach. By the same token, care must be taken to resist distracting political and economic agendas that divert attention to less endangered groups of children and away from the most needy.

- Children in work that is not inherently dangerous, but that carries some potential risk, need to be monitored by their families and communities to ensure that their work does not expose them to seriously hazardous or oppressive conditions. Most working children in at least the developing countries probably are in this category. Their work may entail a mixture of both advantages and disadvantages to them, and therefore it must be assessed from the broad perspective of its overall impact on the children involved rather than on the basis of a single element. Since public sector legislative and enforcement approaches have not generally proved effective at protecting children in working situations of this type, family and community vigilance is particularly important for preventing acceptable work from degenerating into dangerous or abusive work inappropriate for children. It is of special importance that working children themselves be equipped to participate in their own defence. Education is for these children an especially critical factor, partly through schooling and skills training and partly through broader life experience that teaches them to successfully deal with a variety of new and potentially threatening situations. Building a strong sense of initiative, efficacy, and self-esteem in children is important to their protection, as is strong family solidarity. The experience of working can, under the right circumstances, be a powerful enabling force for these children but, under the wrong conditions, it can undermine their well-being and development. While it would not be in the best interests of children in this category to restrict their freedom by prohibiting them from work that is safe for them, good policies and programmes will stimulate and support community-based oversight of their work in order to ensure that their rights are not being violated.

- Children engaged in risk-free work that is harmless or that actively promotes their development can be considered fortunate, and there is no reason for society to be unduly concerned about them or to prohibit their work. In fact, the worldwide demand from children for viable combinations of work with education suggest that child-centred policies would establish responsible work study mechanisms for children who wish to learn through both school and work. Ideally, work of the right sort might be provided as an integral part of children's normal education and training for life, becoming one of many rich opportunities for learning and self-advancement that children can find available in their community environment.

Throughout the preceding chapters, we have insisted that the principal goal of national and international policies governing children's work should be to promote and protect the physical and psychosocial development of the children involved. Policies not consistent with this objective should be replaced by policies that are. The basic issue here is the empowerment of children, for action that effectively promotes their development must provide them with the knowledge, skills, and self-confidence necessary to equip them to participate fully in their society and in shaping their own future. Empowered children are more likely to develop into citizen decision-makers as well as able income-earners, and in open societies their concern and solidarity will extend to include others beyond the circle of their immediate family and friends. But what policies and activities produce able and responsible citizens of this type?

Previous chapters have raised serious doubts about whether current 'child labour' policies that regard working children as actual or potential victims, and education policies that treat them as merely passive learners, successfully empower children of the poor. We have suggested that they often leave children more rather than less dependent and vulnerable, actually impeding vital processes that create the initiative, literacy, critical consciousness, analytic ability, social skills, and self-esteem that children require to realize their potential as fully contributing citizens. The danger is that even well-intended policies can become regressive and repressive, trapping children within the status quo of poverty and discrimination rather than providing them with viable new avenues of economic and social advancement. This is of course the very criticism most levelled at child work, but the previous chapters have revealed a sad irony; that same charge is even more applicable to the grossly inferior education facilities, discriminatory law enforcement, economic stagnation, and other forms of social neglect that current policies in many developing countries selectively impose on the poor and their children.

Policies promoting the multi-dimensional child development described in Chapter One and demanded by the Convention on the Rights of the Child would expand rather than limit the opportunities for working children. Although we reported some promising steps now being taken in that direction, such positive examples are as yet still rare, and expanding them to meet the needs of most poor children would require a level of commitment to social justice and children's development that few countries or organizations seem ready to assume. Until countries are able to establish policies and institutions that effectively empower the poor and their children, children should not be discouraged from seeking to advance themselves as best they can, developing and relying on their own skills and resilience for protection.

That said, we think that there is a limit to how much should be demanded of children's resiliency and capacity for self-protection. Should they be asked to develop resilience to gross injustice and inferior services resulting from government neglect in the same way they do to living in a low-income family and community? Even though we advocate that society should extend itself more than it now does to help children cope successfully with the realities of their work, the point to which it should stimulate coping skills and behaviour remains an open question. It would not be just to let adults avoid their child protection responsibilities simply by teaching their children to better cope with abuse and neglect. This consideration is an important reason why many people who generally favour children's participation are slow to agree that children working in difficult situations should be allowed to continue in their work. Justice demands that child empowerment and adult responsibility should be developed together.

Inclusion

Two inclusion issues appear throughout the book: one is the inclusion of children in work and the other is their participation in decisions regarding their work. We pointed to modern social science research suggesting that children develop and become empowered primarily through social inclusion, beginning in the family and subsequently in the broader community, and that often their work is a major vehicle of that inclusion. The common assertion that 'child labour' is a form of social exclusion may of course be true when children are abused in their work, but it is at odds with the evidence for children working under more benign circumstances. For many children, taking away their work role would loosen social ties that protect them in both family and community. The personal and social development of working children is accelerated by their individual and collective participation in decisions concerning their lives, and partly for that reason we argued that working children and their organizations should be important actors in framing national and international policies governing their work. We also challenged the practical and moral propriety of current practice in which economic and political elites having little experience and knowledge of child work realities unilaterally restrict the survival mechanisms of the poor without even consulting the poor families and working children that are most affected. We suggested that, in addition to being ridiculously impractical, this constitutes social exclusion of the worst sort. Policies will be neither just nor implementable until their base is socially inclusive.

General observations

In addition to the three major issues that must be faced in order to protect the best interests of working children, policy-makers, programme-planners, and children's advocates should take note of a few key observations that also emerge from the preceding chapters.

Myth dominates, and with bad effect on children

The preceding chapters have demonstrated that many of the most popular assumptions regarding child work and child workers are inconsistent with the prevailing evidence. In issue after issue it has also been shown that much of the conventional wisdom regarding how to protect children against workplace abuse is founded in myth rather than fact and that many children have suffered as a result. The blame for this rather appalling situation can be laid on a general neglect to properly investigate either child work situations or proposed interventions in terms of their impact on children. To a surprising extent, policy-makers, programme-planners, and child advocates promoting actions they assume to be good for children simply do not know what they are doing. This is unfortunately true at local, national, and international levels. The prevalence of error and ignorance is exacerbated by a tendency for groups, governments, and international organizations to decide technical issues through political processes, arriving at a mutually convenient consensus that pays scant attention to the real facts at hand. Common myths are called up to substitute for hard evidence and to justify what has been decided. Of course, those who have the greatest stake in such decisions — the poor and their working children — have little or no input into the negotiation. When such exclusion occurs, the best interests of working children are likely to be sacrificed to the narrower economic or political interests of organizations purporting to know what is best for them. Myth and social exclusion work together to produce irresponsibility.

Excluding children and their families condemns policies
and programmes to impotence

Governments, international organizations, and civil society groups such as trade unions and child advocacy NGOs may be paying a high price for excluding working children, and the poor in general, from participation in framing policies and programmes dealing with child work, education, and the implementation of child rights in general. That price is being paid in poorly informed policies that are counterproductive or cannot be implemented, in misguided programmes that are irrelevant and wasteful, and in embarrassing advocacy positions without support from those whose interests they supposedly serve. That is because they ignore the most critical resources available to them: the knowledge and initiative of those who live closest to the problems being addressed.

The preceding chapters have indicated that working children are, together with their families, already the most important social resource for protecting children from detrimental work and working conditions. Common sense would suggest that top priority should be given to assisting families and children to recognize, avoid, and combat the workplace abuse of children. Common sense does not prevail, however, for amazingly little social attention and investment is being channelled to equipping those whose action can make the biggest and most direct difference in reducing the exposure of children to detrimental work. Inexplicably, more institutional effort is being directed to legal and other means for monitoring the hiring practices of formal sector employers. This is an approach that, as we pointed out, has been singularly ineffective in reaching the vast majority of working children in agriculture, domestic service, and the informal sector who are most at risk and merit priority attention. Only a very limited number of progressive action programmes consult working children and their families about what is most needed to protect children from workplace harm. With the partial exception of Brazil, we know of no case in which working children have had substantial input into the framing of public sector policies for protecting them.

Why does this obvious departure from common sense exist? Part of the problem seems to be that political and economic elites do not trust the ability or willingness of working children and their families to understand and represent their own best interests. Grass roots groups often comment on this arrogance with considerable annoyance. Not only policy-makers and programme-planners, but sometimes even children's advocates, are so accustomed to thinking of children as victims needing outside rescue or protection that the idea of reinforcing families' or children's own defences scarcely occurs to them. Another part of the problem is that powerful interest groups sometimes fear that their own agenda would be threatened if working children and their families were allowed substantial voice and participation in the formulation of policy. Trade unions, for instance, have been particularly reluctant to admit working children's organizations into national and international 'child labour' policy discussions, fearing that such participation would tacitly undermine their historic position against all economic participation of children below the legal minimum age. Another focus of opposition comes from groups who feel that traditional adult roles and prerogatives are at stake, and who believe that protection is something adults, especially government, should do *for* children rather than *with* them. It is regrettable that the participation issue has become so ideological when it is a matter of sheer pragmatism.

Working children will have to have a voice in planning policies and programmes for their own protection if workably practical policies and programmes enjoying willing support from poor families and children are to become a widespread reality.

However, listening to, learning from, and working with children is not always easy or straightforward. As indicated in Chapter Four, care needs to be taken not to expose children to unwanted publicity, psychological distress, abuse or dismissal. It means also paying due attention to the values, attitudes, and behaviour of adults *vis-à-vis* children and developing the skills and methods for establishing trust and encouraging dialogue with children. Chapter One argued that child development research indicates that participation in defending one's own interests is likely to be a powerful means of protecting children from detrimental psychological and social effects of work. Children may well say things that adults are not happy to hear but palatability should not be the criterion of validity. Moreover, the adults who run society's institutions still have to decide which of children's views should be acted upon. It will be remembered that the CRC provides only that children's opinions be seriously considered; it recognizes that broader social perspectives sometimes must prevail. Adults do, after all, set the social and political rules within which children participate.

Healthy pluralism and international standards can be compatible

International debate about child work is influenced by the fact that 'the problem' exists primarily in one part of the world (the poor countries) while the societies and groups most determined to eliminate it tend to live in another (the rich countries). In this situation, it is almost impossible to avoid the impression that industrialized countries dominate the discussion, and that they have both defined 'child labour' and stipulated its remedies in accordance with their own interests. As was pointed out in previous chapters, rich country formulations of both problems and interventions often fit poorly with developing country realities. However, developing country perspectives that might serve as more practical alternatives have yet to be articulated with compelling force and clarity. This raises the question of what solutions more attuned to developing country characteristics might look like.

To start with, a more generally applicable approach would not impose on all children a single universal model of child development. It would support instead a more pluralistic concept of childhood which leads to the understanding that work has different meanings, and different child development effects, in different social situations. This position does not necessarily undermine the definition of children's rights through international instruments to which all countries are asked to commit themselves, such as the UN Convention on the Rights of the Child. But it does suggest that the CRC, a new ILO convention against intolerable forms of child work, and other such agreements to protect children against workplace abuse should articulate values, objectives, and principles in terms allowing each society to realize their overall intent from within its own realities. It is necessary to ensure that such agreements constitute a truly universal expression of basic human values, and that they do not merely reflect the power of rich countries to bully the rest of the world into acquiescing to their particular and often self-interested opinion on important issues of social justice and development.

International standards governing the work of children need to be seen in this light if they are to realize their protective potential. As we analyzed the United Nations Convention on the Rights of the Child while preparing the foregoing chapters, we noticed that taking the rigorously child-centred perspective it demands had the unexpected effect of throwing some aspects of the convention itself into question. In applying the CRC to a particular situation, one cannot escape asking to what degree satisfying the provisions of its various articles would serve the best interests of the child, as Article 3 insists. As mentioned in earlier chapters, for example, there is a question whether implementing all the provisions of Article 32, which deals specifically with children's work, is the best way to meet the child protection objectives which those provisions are intended to support. At least in regard to children's work, orientating policies and programmes by the spirit and purpose underlying international con-

Actions required to prevent children from engaging in work differ from those needed to protect them against abuses while working.

ventions is more beneficial for children than is adhesion to the letter when it does not fit the situation.

> *There are outstanding critical questions requiring*
> *more attention and debate*

Some fundamental strategic questions have yet to be settled in the growing debate about how and when to intervene in children's work. The most basic issue is that of purposes and objectives: What are we trying to do, and what difference in the situation are we trying to make? This is a critical question because the answers determine the selection and institutionalization of mechanisms to protect children against exploitation in the workplace, and different answers produce different results. For example, actions required to prevent children from engaging in work differ substantially from those needed to protect them against abuses while working. Other important questions concern when children should become direct objects of social care, and when they should be strengthened to defend themselves. And, on yet another issue, how much economic freedom should society be able to take from children in order to protect at least some of them from abuses, and how should that trade-off be defined? Which children should be targeted for assistance, and which ones should be left free to go their own way in the workplace? Beyond doubt, many children do suffer enormously from their work, and there is a need to reach and help them. There is in fact a growing consensus that children in especially detrimental work situations should receive top priority for attention and the allocation of resources. But is it possible to concentrate adequate effort and resources on those most urgently needing assistance if it is also necessary to intervene broadly in the work of children whose situation does not merit so much attention?

Children themselves raise the same concern; delegates of working children in the February 1997 child labour conference in Amsterdam pleaded against designating all working children as the problem, for it leads governments and other organizations to meddle unhelpfully in the activities of children who do not need or want such assistance while children who badly need help remain unattended. While agreement on this point seems to be gradually expanding, it is not yet complete, and most rich country 'child labour' concern is still riveted on the tiny minority of developing-country children who work in export industries and cannot generally be considered among the working children most at risk.

Even when the subject of priorities for action is resolved, there is still great uncertainty about what lines of activity are most appropriate and effective. In fact, controlling abuse of children's work is a very uncertain art that, as of yet, has no masters. Everyone is still in a learning mode. As the chapter on education suggested, for example, we are still unsure about how best to educate children of the poor even if we prohibit them from work and compel them by law to attend school. Even in rich countries, some educators are concerned that current schooling models may separate children so much from their real life context that they tend to emerge maladapted rather than prepared for it. How much more legitimate is this worry when dealing with the dismal quality of the only schooling available to many poor children? Why do policy-makers not take more seriously the many children from all over the world who say they learn as much (or more) at work as in school? It is high time to face up to the question of whether bad, abusive schooling, which the evidence suggests is far too common, really is better for children than is benign work. Children might be sending society a valid but discomfiting message that it resists hearing. It will take a great deal of government dedication to turn horrific schools into good ones that merit children's time and effort. Even if it is true that children's views are often myopic and that adults may have a fuller understanding of what skills are most important for success in the modern world, the fact remains that what children say stimulates or discourages their learning processes should be essential data for planning education.

To take another issue, it is broadly asserted, including by us, that child protection and development actions should address the needs of the whole child in his or her own context, but do we know very much about how to organize and deliver programmes attending to such 'holistic' needs? The sooner and more honestly that our ignorance about how best to protect and promote the development of children is recognized, the more chance there is that proper studies will be undertaken to evaluate the effects of different interventions on the children involved.

Principles of a child-centred approach to dealing with children's work

While recognizing that there is so much yet to be learned and resolved, we do believe that some valuable lessons have been learned through experience to date. Out of the material discussed at length in the preceding chapters, we have distilled some straightforward principles of action in relation to these groups which are supported by the literature and experience we have cited. If they are observed together as a whole, we feel that policy-makers, programme-planners, and children's advocates can be reasonably confident of acting in ways that will be productive and helpful for children. We state them as simply as possible.

1. Before embarking on action, gain a full understanding of why children work, the dynamics of the relationship between their work and other key aspects of their lives (especially family life and school), the nature and conditions of the work they do, and the effects of their work on their health and physical and psychosocial development. Information needs to be fully disaggregated so that it is sensitive to the different situations of real children. Assume nothing.

2. In collecting the above information, systematically listen to children and seriously consider their observations, suggestions and aspirations. Open opportunities for children to take initiatives of their own and to participate in the planning, implementation, and evaluation of actions by others on their behalf.

3. Assess the appropriateness of child work according to how it contributes to or detracts from the health, safety, and development of the children involved. Use as a reference the most updated scientific research and thinking in child development, as well as how develop-

ment and maturity are understood by the society in which the children live.

4. Evaluate all interventions in child work in terms of their outcomes on the well-being and development of the children involved, as well as on their families. Policies and programmes addressing children's work ultimately must be justified by their demonstrated benefits to children.

5. Where intervention is required, leave children with as much freedom and access to opportunity as possible. When their work is not so inherently dangerous or oppressive as to be intolerable, look for chances to make it safe and developmentally beneficial instead of abolishing it. Ensure that all children removed or excluded from unacceptable forms of work have acceptable alternatives that they can take advantage of and that will promote their physical and psychosocial development.

6. View working children in a 'holistic' perspective that considers their multiple needs and competencies, as well as the multiple (and sometimes conflicting) demands made on them by family and community. Plan even sectoral policies and programmes with this perspective in mind. Whenever possible, employ an integrated, multi-sectoral approach.

7. Connect all protective actions to child development objectives and activities, planning even short-term protective measures within the context of long-term perspectives and goals to develop the full potential of the children involved.

8. Prepare children to individually and collectively defend their own interests and rights and to act as effective partners with adults working on their behalf. At the same time, make sure that adults recognize their own child protection responsibilities.

9. Provide for the incorporation of local cultural and economic factors into all action intended to protect children against workplace abuse.

10. Focus on the *real* problems, not just those that are most visible or easiest to deal with, and place top priority for action on the most damaging forms of child work and the most endangered children.

11. **Use the power of social consensus** as far as possible, avoiding coercion unless absolutely necessary. Act in collaboration and democratic partnership with others.

Based on our review of recent literature and experience, it seems more prudent to indicate these broad principles and strategies for action than to recommend specific policy or programme models. Indeed, in view of the need to adapt methods to context, and given the paucity of reliable, effective information about the developmental outcomes of different interventions in child work, it would be precipitous at this juncture to suggest 'best practice' in terms of operational mechanisms. There is little indication that any specific legal provision or programme design is everywhere effective and practical. However, throughout the book we have mentioned strategies that we consider highly promising and in keeping with the principles outlined above. We are at the same time quite critical of certain others. It is perhaps worth touching again on some of the most fruitful lines of action.

The first and biggest problem that has to be tackled is education. In the preceding chapters, we have been very critical of education services typically offered to children of the poor, especially to working children, and we repeatedly made the point that a large part of the problem of injurious work decried by so many is the result of school-system failures. We asked how education could be made more attractive and useful to poor children in general and to working children in particular. We are especially concerned that the physically and psychologically abusive element in many schools be recognized and owned up to by the authorities, and that action be taken to eliminate such anti-child behaviour from systems in which it is endemic. Teacher training may not be by itself sufficient. Even though schools could do much to improve their performance through what already is known, there is also a need to experiment and document and disseminate successful experience that can help to make education more accessible and useful to children of the poor. Children should have schools they can love.

Education has considerable potential for protecting children from exploitative or dangerous work, but not necessarily by coercing attendance and taking children out of the labour market as is often assumed. It will play its proper role as a natural activity for all children only as it becomes more accessible, relevant, and attractive for working children. This implies creating more dynamic, interactive, and participatory school environments, as well as locating schools closer to the workplace, scheduling classes to fit work routines, and introducing school- and community-based economic incentives, whenever possible taking advantage of learning opportunities in children's everyday lives to help them develop their multiple intelligence and competencies. A major challenge for schools and community organizations is to mount 'early warning' systems to identify children who are not doing well in school and are at risk of dropping out, perhaps to end up working in dangerous or developmentally inappropriate types of work.

Given the desire and need of many children to combine school with work and the evidence that properly supervised work of the right sort can be beneficial for children, much is to be gained by creating appropriate work opportunities for children who want and need them. Ideally, these should be systematically incorporated into an educational framework, structuring children's work in such a way that it becomes a vehicle for learning and social advancement as well as income. Learning through work is integral to many informal education programmes with instruction in reading, writing, and maths typically being offered in conjunction with safe and creative work. Other programmes run properly supervised apprenticeship schemes.

Secondly, changes are needed in the way we use the law in protecting children against workplace abuses. The most fundamental shift needs to be towards a sharper and more energetic focus on the jobs and working conditions most damaging to children; what the ILO refers to as the "most intolerable forms of child labour". It makes no sense to hassle children in relatively safe work while neglecting seriously endangered children urgently needing protective assistance. Yet this is the situation now found throughout much of the world. If children are to be effectively protected, a strong sense of priorities is required, as well as a firm social commitment to eliminate the worst abuses forthwith. As we write, the ILO is in the midst of a two-year process leading to a new international convention aimed specifically at mobilizing world opinion and resources to put an end to the most hazardous and dehumanizing forms of child work, notably including the slavery-like conditions under which millions of children still labour. It goes without saying that we fully support the idea of such a convention, and hope that a clear instrument along these lines ends up being adopted and widely ratified. At the same time, we caution against the temptation to pack the new convention with universal minimum age rules and other detracting baggage that may not be in the best interests of children and which have prevented widespread ratification and application of the Minimum Age Convention (No. 138), 1973.

It also is essential that laws governing child work do not stand in isolation but are conceived and implemented to fit their social context and work harmoniously with other lines of action in a national policy. They also must be consistent with and help support healthy child development processes. We have suggested that interventions based on the minimum age criterion receive little endorsement from recent child development theories; measures better serving children's interests should be based on criteria that reflect the actual impact of work. Equally, legal interventions made without supporting social, economic, and education measures are likely to be quite devastating for children and their families. Removal of children from their jobs, when necessary, always should be accomplished through transitional measures that assure the children education and/or income alternatives that are more attractive and appropriate than the work they leave. Without wide social support, legal measures to protect children from detrimental work may risk misunderstanding and hostility from the very people they are intended to protect. Effective strategies involve high levels of grass roots mobilization and participation. Given the very limited penetration of law enforcement officials into family and other informal enterprises, community-based monitoring of children's work and working conditions may be the best and only really workable option. So far, there is not a lot of experience with this approach, so experimental programmes still are much needed.

There is a rapidly spreading belief in the potential for building working children's capacity for initiative, resilience, and self-protection. It stems from a combination of field experience, new thinking catalyzed by the Convention on the Rights of the Child and, in some cases, philosophical or religious ideologies. It also is highly consistent with modern child development theory and research as explained in Chapters One and Two. There are various ways of doing this, such as informing working children about the hazards of work, teaching them negotiating and business skills, and building self-esteem by emphasizing the positive aspects of their work. Self-representation and self-organization is seen by some as the most powerful and efficacious approach to self-protection, and it is fostered by working children's movements and other bodies. This approach has found expression in national policy dialogue in a few countries and is being introduced also into international fora. The present dialogue connected to the proposed ILO convention on intolerable forms of child work is likely to generate increased action on children's work at local and national levels throughout the world. It is our hope that this action will as far as possible reflect children's competencies and build on existing self-protection initiatives.

Priorities for further research

Throughout the book we have insisted that a child-centred orientation to children's work must be solidly empirical, basing policy and programme action on valid information about children, their needs, their situation, and the effects on them of their work and measures to regulate it. The discussion suggested a fairly large number of specific topics in which further research is needed. These topics can be put into overall perspective by grouping them into five general areas of concern which we believe deserve high priority on social science and policy research agendas.

The first and most basic area of research need is the relationship between child development and child work, as well as the developmental effects of different sorts of intervention in children's work. We find it disquieting that an activity so important to middle childhood and adolescence as work has been almost totally neglected by child development researchers. Despite the fact that huge numbers of school children spend more time in work than in school, we still know precious little about the developmental impact of their work, especially *vis-à-vis* schooling. Work is such an important element in the life of many or most children in the world that it probably rivals school as a formative context and experience during the period from middle childhood to early adolescence. There is still much to be discovered about how children under different cultural and socioeconomic conditions evolve their psychosocial competencies during the school years, and the role their work plays in that evolution. We need to learn much more about what makes work abusive for children and what social, cultural, and economic forces provoke and sustain that abuse. Attention needs to be paid not just to the identification of hazards and their physical and psychosocial impacts, however, but also to the beneficial effects of work. This will make it possible to do a better job of targeting protection of the right type to those groups of children who most need it and to know about what actions in regard to children's work create significant opportunities for child growth and development and empower children to make use of those opportunities.

Until more basic research about the nature or dynamics of the role of work in the development of a child's personality and diverse competencies is in place, it will remain difficult to say from empirical evidence what policies and lines of programme action will best promote children's overall growth and successfully protect them against work-related harm to their well-being and development.

Secondly, much more evaluative work is needed on the effects of child work interventions. We pointed out that even the most basic, traditional, and widely recommended tool against 'child labour' — a legally enforceable general minimum age for admission to work — seems never to have received a credible policy analysis that empirically weighs costs and benefits to determine its net impact on children and on society. We simply do not know if the minimum age criterion is on balance a good idea or a bad one or, more precisely, under what conditions it is likely to be either one or the other. We need to ask with an open mind what it would mean to approach child work legislation and its implementation from a child-centred perspective. All strategies, including those emerging from the particular experience of developing countries, merit careful analysis to determine their effects on children. We urge that all action options be open to serious inquiry through well-constructed evaluative studies, and we think that this is an area in which interest from the larger NGOs, the United Nations and Bretton Woods agencies, and bilateral donors can be especially useful. They, like governments, should want to know what policy and programme investments in regard to child work have the greatest positive impact on the well-being and development of children. As suggested in Chapter Four, evaluative studies of policies and programmes are best done with the full participation of affected children, for their perspective is uniquely relevant and their voice too often muted.

Thirdly, creative action research is needed on the methods and effects of working children's participation in their own protection and advancement, especially in connection with policies and programmes intended to benefit them. Article 12 of the UN Convention on the Rights of the Child, guaranteeing children a say in deliberations on issues that affect them, has faced the world with a new requirement that it does not have much experience in meeting. This situation calls for learning through trial and error and, in order to speed that learning as much as possible, it is important that all significant experimentation be conscientiously documented and evaluated. At the time of writing, a great deal of controversy is being generated around the issue of the participation of working children's own organizations in international meetings leading up to the proposed 1999 adoption of a new ILO convention on intolerable forms of child work. The CRC so clearly implies that children should indeed have the right to participate that we see no legitimate reason to exclude them. However, many important questions have yet to be answered about how the participation of children in policy deliberations should be structured and managed to provide a sense of just representation and to ensure that children are able to make their legitimate contribution. We urge that this process of generating a new international convention on a specific child rights issue be utilized as a living laboratory in which to experiment with the participation of children from local to international levels, evaluating what is tried and learning from it for use in regard to future issues.

Fourthly, more research is needed to find out how school policies and practices could better fit the needs of working children, their families, and their communities and to enable children to meet their family roles and responsibilities in ways conducive to also receiving a quality education. This entails finding out how schools could be more accessible, welcoming, safe, and accountable to all children regardless of gender, ethnic group, or socioeconomic status. It also implies learning how to equip children to deal with their present world as well as to prepare them for adulthood. Serious attention needs to be paid to children's strong demand for work-study programmes that provide both education and income, perhaps through action research exploring ways in which this might realistically be done. Those informal education programmes that have been especially successful in bringing quality education to working children should be studied to see how their methods could be adapted to more general use. And, of course, more needs to be found out about how working children can participate more meaningfully in adapting the education process to meet their needs.

Fifthly, we suggest that some of the prevailing myths about children's work be subjected to systematic analysis. We gave the example of groundbreaking ILO research that destroyed the myth that the manual dexterity of their small hands makes children uniquely essential to certain tasks, and the same studies raised serious doubts about the assertion that labour-intensive industries have to rely on children to remain competitive. Research of that creativity and scope needs to be applied to other sweeping assertions (for example, that child work perpetuates poverty, causes adult unemployment, and depresses adult wages) that have never been adequately tested, but that might reward proper investigation with more nuanced insights. There is also good reason to follow up on research begun by the ILO, UNICEF, and others into the possible role of economic incentives for retaining children in school and decreasing their involvement in at least the detrimental forms of child work.

A final word

If there is a single theme that summarizes the thrust of this book, it is the need to treat working children with respect in both attitude and action. We have shown that disrespecting children's work and its importance to them can have strong negative impact on their development, whereas approaching them with understanding and respect tends to stimulate protective resilience. Children themselves fiercely insist on being respected rather than patronized. We have pointed out that disrespect for working children in legislation and its enforcement leads them in turn to disrespect the law as unjust, and to ignore or resist it. We have explained how the humiliation many children suffer in school leads them to abandon their education in order to conserve at least a modicum of self-respect, and to many of them work may be a better alternative. We have called attention to the struggle of some working children to be heard through their own organizations and the trouble and humiliation they have experienced in being accepted as competent owners of their own minds and ideas. In some detail we have recounted how some well-intentioned but misguided reformers have disrespectfully trampled children's rights and welfare underfoot, all in the name of child protection.

If anything at all is clear from reviewing recent experience and the quickly growing literature on child work and interventions in it, it is that one can protect working children only by working *with* them and not *against* them. This can happen only in a climate of trust, and trust depends upon respect. Such respect for children should be extended to include the families and cultures which mould and support them. When transmitted consciously or unconsciously to children, respect in and of itself helps protect them by reinforcing their self-esteem and natural resilience. It also ensures that the right questions will be asked and that adequate effort will be made to fully understand the realities of children's lives before intervening in them. Those who respect children are not careless when dealing with important elements of their lives. Respect leads naturally to inviting the participation of children as deserving and trusted partners rather than patronizing them as inept clients or helpless victims. This implies graceful inclusion of working children in the research, planning, conduct, and evaluation of policies and programmes intended to assist them. Respect makes children, and their families, into willing partners rather than reluctant subjects or clients.

Therefore, our single most important conclusion is that a child-centred approach to child work invariably must begin with profound respect for working children and their rights, both as persons and as workers. In the absence of such respect even the best-intentioned attempts to protect working children are likely to fail and perhaps even injure them. But when present, this respect provides fertile soil in which everything needed to successfully protect the rights and development of working children can take root, grow, and eventually flower.

Notes

CHAPTER ONE

1. Woodhead, 1997a, p. 11; see also James and Prout, 1990
2. Burman, 1994, p. 42
3. Palmer 1983, p. 14; Collins, undated.
4. Woodhead, 1997, p. 17
5. Boyden, forthcoming
6. Bequele and Myers, 1995, pp. 6-7
7. Woodhead, 1990
8. UNICEF, 1993, p. 1
9. Woodhead, 1997a, p. 8
10. La Fontaine, 1978
11. Schildkrout, 1978
12. Rogoff, *et al.*, 1975
13. Galway, Wolff and Sturgis, 1987, p. 17
14. Collins, undated; Rogoff, *et al.*, 1975
15. Goody, 1970
16. Aziz and Maloney1985, p. 16, quoted in Blanchet 1995, p. 14
17. Rutter, Maughan, Mortimore, Ouston and Smith, 1979, cited in Collins, undated, p. 10
18. Reynolds, 1985
19. Mendoza, 1993
20. Mendoza, 1993, p. 113
21. Woodhead, 1997a, p. 7
22. Woodhead, 1997a, p. 9; see also, Le Vine, *et al.*, 1994; Rogoff, *et al.*, 1993
23. Burman 1994; Walkerdine, 1993
24. Woodhead, 1997a, p. 14
25. Super and Harkness, 1982
26. Woodhead, 1997a, p. 8
27. Woodhead, 1997a, p. 9
28. Burman, 1994, p. 183
29. Ennew, 1994
30. Burman, 1994, p. 183
31. Boyden, forthcoming
32. Johnson, Hill and Ivan-Smith, 1995
33. Dube, 1981
34. Wikan, 1989, quoted in Van Beers,1994
35. Boyden, forthcoming
36. Davenport, 1968
37. Blanchet, 1996
38. Punch, 1997
39. Robertson,1991, p. 21
40. Salazar and Alarcón Glasniovich, 1996
41. GAO, 1991
42. Morrow, 1996
43. Mussen, *et al.*, 1984
44. Schildkrout, 1978, p. 110
45. Schildkrout, 1978, pp. 109-110
46. Holland, 1992, p. 13
47. Ingham, 1996, p. 58
48. Burman, 1994, p. 35
49. Schaffer 1996; Bremner, 1994
50. Woodhead, 1997a
51. Woodhead, 1997a, p. 24
52. Richman and Bowen, 1997, p. 106
53. Garmezy, 1985; Rutter 1987; Werner and Smith, 1992
54. For example Baker, 1990; Dawes, 1992a and b; Garmezy, 1983
55. Ekblad, 1993, p. 30
56. Richman and Bowen, 1997
57. Woodhead, 1997a, p. 30
58. Richman and Bowen, 1997
59. McCallin and Fozzard,1991
60. Thompson, 1992, p. 43
61. Leyens and Mahjoub, undated
62. Thompson, 1990, p. 44
63. Gabarino, Kostelny & Dubrow, 1991
64. Punamaki, 1987
65. Thomas and Chess, 1977
66. Rutter 1981
67. Punamaki 1987; McCallin 1991; Turton, Straker and Mooza 1990; Richman and Bowen, 1997
68. Kirby and Fraser, 1997, p. 24
69. Antonovsky, 1987, cited in Ekblad, 1993
70. Ekblad, 1993, p. 30
71. Dawes, 1992a and 1992b
72. Woodhead, 1997a, p. 19
73. Turton, Straker and Mooza 1990, p. 78
74. Szanton Blanc with contributors, 1994
75. Boyden and Ennew, 1997, p. 296
76. Myers, 1992
77. Myers, 1992
78. Scheper-Hughes and Lock, 1989, p. 21
79. Woodhead, 1997a
80. Myers, 1992, pp. 169-70
81. Forastieri, 1994; Myers, 1992
82. Jemmott and Locke 1984, p. 79, quoted in Myers, 1992, p. 172
83. Zeitlin, Ghassemi and Mansour, 1990
84. Woodhead, 1997a, p. 17
85. Atkinson, 1983
86. Greenfield, 1966
87. Kohlberg, 1971
88. Silvey, 1982, p. 74
89. 21st Century Learning Initiative, 1997
90. Woodhead, 1997a, p. 9
91. 21st Century Learning Initiative, 1997
92. For example, Butterworth and Light, 1992; Rogoff and Chavajay, 1995
93. Rogoff, 1990, p. 12
94. Peacock 1992
95. Laserna, 1990

96. Pearlin and Kohn, 1966
97. Bunster and Chaney, 1985, p. 173
98. Peacock, 1992
99. 21st Century Learning Initiative, p. 7
100. Boyden, forthcoming
101. Briggs 1986, p. 1
102. Gilmore, 1990
103. Hauswald, 1989, p. 149
104. Fromm and Maccoby, 1970; Whiting and Whiting, 1975; Aptekar, 1989
105. Shonkoff, 1984
106. Cornia, 1990, p. 3
107. Cornia, 1990
108. Qvortrup, 1996, p. 65
109. Collins, undated
110. Stryker, 1997
111. Zelizer, 1985, p. 212
112. Zelizer, 1985
113. Wright, 1991
114. Elliot, 1992; Becker, 1995
115. Ekblad, 1993, p. 36
116. Palmer, 1983, p. 14; Walkerdine, 1993
117. Palmer 1983 pp. 10-11
118. Armstrong, 1994, pp. 8-9
119. Peacock, 1992
120. Woodhead, 1997a, p. 12
121. Armstrong, 1994
122. Armstrong, 1994, p. 5
123. Mead, 1954, p. 25
124. Blanchet, 1996, p. 7
125. Schildkrout, 1978, p. 17
126. Schildkrout, 1978
127. Manning, 1990
128. Ianni, 1989
129. Greenberger and Steinberg, 1986
130. Bachman, 1983

CHAPTER TWO

1. White, 1996; Cunningham and Viazzo, 1996
2. Cunningham, 1996, p. 837
3. Exceptions include Reynolds, 1985; Nieuwenhuys, 1994
4. Forastieri, 1994
5. US Department of Labor, 1995
6. US Department of Labor, 1995
7. US Department of Labor, 1995
8. International Labour Office, 1992a
9. International Labour Office, 1992b
10. Woodhead, 1997b, p.14
11. Woodhead, 1997b, p. 22
12. Woodhead, 1997b, p. 14
13. Woodhead, 1997b, p. 7
14. Woodhead, 1997b, p. 2
15. Woodhead, 1997b, p. 10
16. Woodhead, 1997, p. 25
17. Woodhead, 1997, p. 11
18. Woodhead, 1997, p. 13
19. Woodhead, 1997, p. 12
20. Woodhead, 1997, p. 26
21. Gunn and Ostos, 1992
22. Black, 1995
23. Knaul Barker and Knaul Barker, 1992
24. Salter, 1993
25. Knaul 1995, cited in Salazar & Alarcón Glasniovich, 1996
26. Salter, 1993
27. Swart, 1988
28. Oloko, 1989
29. Baker, with Panter-Brick and Todd, 1996
30. Dunn and Runyan, 1993
31. Bequele and Myers, 1995
32. Lane, 1991
33. Kohn and Schooler, 1983
34. Bequele and Myers, 1995, p. 6
35. Pollack et al., 1990
36. Palmer, 1983
37. McGuigan, 1993, cited in Forastieri, 1994
38. International Labour Office, 1992a
39. Forastieri, 1994
40. US Department of Labor, 1995
41. Mancian and Romer, 1991, cited in Forastieri, 1994
42. Dunn and Runyan, 1993
43. Forastieri, 1994
44. Forastieri, 1994
45. Forastieri, 1994
46. ILO, 1992a
47. Burra, 1986
48. Richter and Ard-am, 1995
49. Salazar and Alarcón Glasniovich, 1996
50. Bequele and Myers, 1995
51. Greenberger and Steinberg, 1986, p. 152
52. Vaillant and Vaillant, 1981, cited in Lane, 1991
53. Vaillant and Vaillant, 1968, pp. 14–38
54. Vaillant and Vaillant, 1981, pp. 1,4, cited in Lane, 1991, p. 247
55. Lane, 1991, p. 247
56. Aptekar, 1989 & 1991; Swart, 1988; Baker, with Panter-Brick and Todd, 1996
57. Aptekar, 1989, p. 435
58. Whiting and Whiting, 1975
59. Oloko, 1993, p. 480
60. Palmer, 1983
61. Forastieri, 1994
62. Wright, Kaminsky and Wittig, 1996
63. Das, Shukla and Öry, 1992
64. Mattoo, Rauf and Zutshi, 1986
65. Karmaker, 1994
66. Bequele and Myers, 1995, p. 7
67. Satyanarayana, Prasanna Krishna and Narasinga Rao, 1986
68. Szanton Blanc with contributors, 1994
69. Mansurov, 1993
70. Woodhead, 1997b, p. 23
71. Woodhead, 1997b, p. 25
72. Woodhead, 1997b, p. 23
73. Gilmore, 1990
74. Woodhead 1997b, p. 23
75. Bunster and Chaney, 1985, p. 174
76. Soy, 1996, p. 106
77. Soy, 1996, p. 106
78. Soy, 1996, p. 106

79. Soy, 1996, p. 105
80. Soy, 1996, p. 109
81. Mansurov, 1993, p. 5
82. Szanton Blanc with contributors, 1994
83. White, 1996
84. Philippine Social Science Council, 1991, cited in Szanton Blanc with contributors, 1994
85. National Institute of Urban Affairs, 1988
86. White, 1996
87. CEPAL, 1995, cited in Salazar and Alarcón Glasniovich, 1996
88. Levison, 1993, p. 16
89. Steinberg and Dornbusch, 1991
90. Steinberg and Dornbusch, 1991, quoted in Levison 1991, p. 32
91. Cariola and Cerri, 1989, cited in Schiefelbein, 1997
92. Stallones, 1992, cited by Wilk, 1993
93. Ekblad, 1993, p. 29
94. Greenberger, Steinberg and Vaux, 1981
95. Johnson, Hill and Ivan-Smith, 1995; White & Tjandraningsih, 1992; Reynolds, 1991
96. Patil, undated
97. Nieuwenhuys, 1994, p. 66
98. Ayala, 1982
99. Levison, 1993
100. Bunster and Chaney, 1985, p. 187
101. Forastieri, 1994
102. Forastieri, 1994, p. 17
103. Salazar and Alarcón Glasniovich, 1996
104. Wilk, 1993
105. Richter and Ard-am, 1995
106. SACCS, 1994, cited in US Department of Labor, 1995

CHAPTER THREE

1. Boyden, forthcoming
2. White, 1994; Badry Zalami et al., 1998
3. Greenberger and Steinberg, 1986; Pond and Searle, 1991; Hobbs and McKechnie, 1997
4. Woodhead, 1997b
5. Scheper-Hughes and Hoffman, 1997, p. 17
6. Johnson, et al., 1995
7. For example, working children statements in two international conferences: Amsterdam Child Labour Conference, February 1997; Urban Childhood Conference, Child Labour Section, Trondheim, June 1997
8. ILO, 1997, p. 3
9. International Working Group on Child Labour, 1997a
10. Oloko, 1991
11. Liebel, 1996
12. Badry Zalami et al., 1998
13. Boyden and Myers, 1995
14. Nieuwenhuys, 1994
15. Gunn and Ostos, 1992
16. Myers, 1989
17. Greenberger and Steinberg, 1986; Instituto de Estudos Especiais, 1984

18. Greenberger and Steinberg, 1986
19. Mansurov, 1993
20. White, 1996
21. Nieuwenhuys, 1996, p. 247
22. Nieuwenhuys, 1996, p. 245
23. Woodhead, 1997b; Badry Zalami et al., 1998
24. Boyden and Myers, 1995
25. Blanchet, 1996
26. International Working Group on Child Labour, 1997a; Myers, personal notes
27. Myers, personal notes; Internet report from Streetkid-L Resource Page, March 1997
28. Grootaert and Kanbur, 1995; ILO, 1995
29. ILO, 1996b
30. Nardinelli, 1990; Cunningham and Viazzo, 1996
31. General Accounting Office, 1991
32. Pond and Searle, 1991
33. General Accounting Office, 1991; Hobbs and McKechnie, 1997
34. ILO, 1995
35. Barros, et al., 1994
36. Badry Zalami et al., 1998
37. Marcus and Harper, 1996, p. 35
38. Gunn and Ostos, 1992
39. Levison, et al., 1995
40. ILO, 1995
41. Levison, et al., 1995; ILO 1997
42. Marcus and Harper, 1996
43. Boyden 1994
44. UNESCO, 1993
45. G77, undated, unpublished circular
46. Marcus and Harper, 1996, p. 24, citing Greenwood, 1996
47. Saddiqi and Patrinos, 1995; Grootaert and Kanbur, 1995
48. Grootaert and Kanbur, 1995, p. 191, citing Lloyd, 1994
49. Cunningham, 1996. On this issue see also Addison et al., 1997, Grootaert and Kanbur, 1995, Saddiqi and Patrinos, 1995
50. Grootaert and Kanbur, 1995, p. 191, citing Lloyd, 1994
51. Blanchet, 1996
52. Cunningham, 1996; Heywood, 1988; Zelitzer, 1985
53. Cunningham, 1995
54. Zelitzer, 1985
55. Andersson, 1997 (translation by Ling)
56. Zelitzer, 1985
57. Boyden, 1990

CHAPTER FOUR

1. Anon., 1996
2. Anon., 1996
3. Qvortrup, Bardy, Sgritta, and Wintersberger, 1994
4. Qvortrup, 1991
5. Salazar and Alarcón Glasniovich 1996, p. 19
6. Qvortrup, Bardy, Sgritta and Wintersberger, 1994
7. McGranahan, Scott and Richard, 1990

8. Cariola and Cerri, 1986 cited in Schiefelbein, 1997; Cariola and Cerri, 1986
9. Grootaert and Kanbur, 1994
10. Alarcón Glasniovich, 1991
11. McKechnie, Lindsay and Hobbs, 1996
12. For example, McNeil, Steinberg, Fegley and Dornbusch, 1993; Steinberg, 1993; and Santrock 1995
13. Fortes, 1938, p. 6
14. Vlassoff, 1979; Mueller, 1976
15. Cain, 1977; Caldwell, Reddy and Caldwell, 1984
16. Rodgers and Standing, 1981; White, 1982
17. Reynolds, 1991
18. Nieuwenhuys, 1994
19. Ennew and Milne, 1996
20. Ennew and Milne, 1996; Boyden and Ennew, 1997
21. Ashagrie, 1993
22. Anon., 1996; International Programme for the Elimination of Child Labour (IPEC), 1995
23. Anon., 1996; International Programme for the Elimination of Child Labour (IPEC), 1995
24. Rahman, 1986; Karmaker, 1994
25. Rahman, 1986
26. Reynolds,1986, p. 2
27. Reynolds, 1986, p. 2, also quoting Jenks, 1982, p. 11
28. For example, Muñoz and Palacios, 1980; Muñoz and Pachón, 1980; Granados Téllez, 1976
29. Campos, Raffaelli, Ude, Greco, Ruff, Rolf, Antunes, Halsey, Greco and the Street Youth Study Group, 1994
30. Kvale, 1996
31. For example, Onyango *et al.*, 1991; D'Lima Gosalia, 1992; Ghosh, 1992
32. Espinola, Glauser, Ortiz and Ortiz de Carrizos, 1987
33. Singh, Kaura and Khan, 1980
34. Gunn and Ostos, 1992
35. Mattoo, Rauf and Zutshi, 1986
36. Das, Shukla and Öry, 1992
37. Dy, 1992
38. Exceptions including, Aptekar, 1989 and 1991; Felsman, 1981; Penna Firme, Stone, Tijiboy, 1989
39. Aptekar, 1991
40. See, for example, Anon., 1996; International Programme for the Elimination of Child Labour (IPEC), 1995; Baker with Panter-Brick and Todd (1996); Reynolds 1991
41. Reynolds, 1991, p. 19
42. Punch, personal communication
43. Ennew and Milne, 1996
44. Ennew and Milne, 1996
45. McGranahan, 19890
46. Morrow and Richards, 1996
47. Ennew, 1994a
48. Reynolds, 1991; Baker, Panter-Brick and Todd, 1996; Woodhead, 1997b
49. Kvale, 1996
50. For example, Tyler, Tyler, Echeverry and Zea, 1991
51. Penna Firme, Tijiboy and Stone, 1989
52. Baker, Panter-Brick and Todd, 1996
53. Waksler, 1991, p. 6
54. Mayall, 1994
55. Reynolds, 1990, p. 161
56. Dallape, 1996
57. Tolfree, 1997, p. 15
58. Swift, 1997, p. 71
59. Tolfree, 1997, p. 16
60. Tolfree, 1997, p. 16
61. Boyden and Ennew, 1997
62. Hecht, 1995
63. Boyden and Ennew, 1997
64. Ennew, 1982 and 1985; Morrow, 1992; Swart, 1990
65. Ennew, 1982
66. Boyden and Ennew, 1997
67. Johnson, Hill and Ivan-Smith, 1995
68. Guijt, Fuglesang and Kisadha, 1994
69. Tolfree, 1997
70. Tolfree, 1997
71. Tolfree, 1997, p. 12
72. Weithorn and Scherer, 1994, citing Melton, 1991; Weithorn, 1983
73. Waksler, 1991
74. Thompson, 1992
75. Boyden and Ennew, 1997
76. Jareg, et al., 1989; Richman, 1993
77. Boyden and Ennew, 1997; Fine and Sandstrom, 1988

CHAPTER FIVE

1. Boyden, 1990 and forthcoming; White, 1996; Woodhead, 1997a
2. Grootaert and Kanbur, 1995
3. UNICEF, 1996; International Working Group on Child Labour, 1997; Marcus and Harper, 1996; Save the Children Alliance, 1997
4. UNICEF, 1996; Marcus and Harper, 1996; Save the Children Alliance, 1997; International Working Group on Child Labour, 1997
5. Save the Children-U.K., 1995
6. Bequele and Myers, 1995
7. Boyden, 1990 and forthcoming; White, 1996
8. Cunningham, 1994
9. Nardinelli, 1990; Heywood, 1988; Cunningham, 1996
10. Bequele and Myers, 1995; ILO 1996b
11. Cunningham, 1994
12. Pond and Searle, 1991; Hobbs and McKechnie, 1997
13. Bequele and Boyden, 1988; Bequele and Myers, 1995
14. Bequele and Boyden, 1988; ILO, 1996b
15. ILO, 1996b
16. ILO, 1996b
17. ILO, 1997
18. ILO, 1996b
19. ILO, 1996a
20. Bequele and Myers, 1995

21. ILO, 1996a
22. Announcement by Assefa Bequele in plenary session of the Amsterdam Child Labour Conference, February, 1997
23. Goonsekere, 1993
24. Goonsekere, 1993
25. Salazar and Glasniovich, 1996
26. Save the Children, 1997
27. International Working Group on Child Labour, 1997
28. UNICEF, 1996
29. ILO, 1997a
30. ILO, 1996c, p. 10
31. ILO, 1996c, p. 7
32. Nardinelli, 1990; Cunningham, 1996; ILO, 1995
33. ILO, 1996b; ILO, 1996a; ILO, 1995; Bequele and Myers, 1995
34. Badry Zalami et al., 1998
35. Pond and Searle, 1991; Hobbs and McKechnie, 1997
36. Derrien, 1994
37. IPEC, 1995; ILO, 1996b
38. Weiner, 1991
39. ILO, 1997
40. Bequele and Myers, 1995
41. ILO, 1996a; Bequele and Myers, 1995
42. Bequele and Myers, 1995

CHAPTER SIX

1. An-Na'im, 1994, p. 67
2. ILO-IPEC, 1995
3. UNICEF, 1997
4. Cunningham, 1994
5. Bequele and Boyden, 1988; Myers, 1991; Rialp, 1993; Boyden and Myers, 1995
6. In Children's Words, produced by UNICEF Bangladesh, 1997
7. Cunningham, 1996
8. IWGCL, 1997a
9. Personal communication and draft materials from Christopher Lowry, SKI
10. Bequele and Myers, 1995
11. For example, see Sheffield and Diejomaoh, 1972
12. Bequele and Myers, 1995
13. Blanchet, 1996
14. Boyden and Myers, 1995
15. Boyden and Myers, 1995
16. Tolfree, 1997
17. Boyden and Myers, 1995
18. ILO—IPEC, 1995
19. Bequele and Myers, 1995
20. Letter from Anagba Afi, a house-worker in Lome, Togo, published in A letter from the street, a "liaison and support bulletin for working children and shanty town children", produced by Enda Tiers Monde, Dakar Senegal, No. 15, November 1996, p. 7
21. International Working Group on Child Labour, forthcoming
22. Tolfree, 1997
23. Tolfree, 1997

24. Hart, 1992, p. 5
25. Personal communication. Report under preparation by Concerned for Working Children
26. Tolfree, 1997
27. Swift, 1997
28. UNICEF, 1997; Fyfe, undated
29. Shiela Coronel, unpublished case study material prepared in 1994 for UNICEF
30. ILO—IPEC, 1995

CHAPTER SEVEN

1. Davin, 1982; Philipps, 1912
2. MacPherson, 1982
3. Hall, 1986
4. Cunningham, 1996
5. Schiefelbein, 1997
6. Weiner, 1991
7. Cunningham, 1996; p. 46
8. International Working Group on Child Labour, 1996, p. 13
9. Marsh, Rosser and Harré, 1980
10. Fyfe, 1994; Nieuwenhuys, 1994
11. White and Tjandraningsih, 1992; Johnson, Hill and Ivan-Smith, 1995
12. UNESCO, 1993
13. Schiefelbein, 1997
14. Colbert, Garcia Mendez, and Himes, 1994; UNICEF, 1992
15. Schiefelbein, 1997
16. Schiefelbein, 1997, p. 4
17. Friedman, 1991
18. Fyfe, 1994
19. Woodhead, 1997b
20. Cho, 1995, p. 148
21. Field, 1995
22. Arita and Yamaoka, 1992, p. 12 cited in Field, 1995
23. Field, 1995, p. 59
24. Hillman, 1993
25. Burra, 1989
26. Silvey, 1982, p. 77
27. Mizen, 1991, p. 6
28. Allsebrook and Swift, 1989
29. Voice of Child Workers 11/12, October, 1991
30. International Working Group on Child Labour, 1996, pp. 16-17
31. Woodhead, 1997b, p. 18
32. Woodhead, 1997b, p. 18
33. Woodhead, 1997b, p. 20
34. Woodhead, 1997b, p. 29
35. Patil, undated; Levison, 1991; Alarcón Glasniovich, 1991
36. Schiefelbein, 1997
37. Guijt, Fuglesang and Kisadha, 1994
38. Palacios, 1981; Kanbargi, 1988
39. Woodhead, 1997b, p. 22
40. Jack Richman personal communication
41. Boyden, 1991
42. Chernet, 1995
43. Zeleke, 1995

44. Woodhead, 1997b, p. 18
45. Woodhead, 1997b, p. 20
46. Woodhead, 1997b, p. 20
47. Zeleke, 1995
48. Woodhead, 1997b, p. 20
49. Cho 1995, p. 153
50. Arita and Yamaoka 1992, p. 14, cited in Field, 1995, p. 53
51. Field, 1995, p. 53
52. Fyfe, 1994, p. 5
53. Fyfe, 1994
54. Center for Policy Studies in Education, 1993
55. UNICEF, 1997
56. International Working Group on Child Labour, 1996, p. 17
57. Personal communication and internal reports from Concerned for Working Children
58. Fyfe, 1994
59. Schiefelbein, 1997
60. Center for Policy Studies in Education, 1993
61. Burra, 1989
62. Unpublished materials provided by AXE
63. Center for Policy Studies in Education, 1993
64. Brookover, Flood, Schweitzer and Wisenbaker, 1979; Rutter, Maughan, Mortimer, Ouston and Smith, 1979, cited in Collins, undated, p. 13
65. Salazar and Alarcón Glasniovich, 1991; Schiefelbein 1997
66. Sinclair, 1990
67. Sinclair, 1990
68. Schiefelbein, 1997
69. Schiefelbein, 1997
70. Schiefelbein, 1997
71. UNESCO, 1993; International Working Group on Child Labour, 1997, p. 14

CHAPTER EIGHT

1. Cunningham, 1994
2. Anker, 1996
3. ILO, 1995, p. 11
4. Nieuwenhuys, 1994; Boyden and Myers, 1995
5. Aragão-Lagergren, 1997
6. Blanchet, 1996
7. Boyden and Myers, 1995
8. US Department of Labor, 1994
9. US Department of Labor, 1994, 1995
10. Boyden and Myers, 1995; Anti-Slavery International, 1994; International Working Group on Child Labour, 1997; US Department of Labor, 1994, 1995
11. Bissell and Sobhan, 1996
12. White, 1996, p. 835
13. US Department of Labor, 1995
14. International Working Group on Child Labour, 1997a
15. Bissell and Sobhan, 1996; Boyden and Myers, 1995
16. Boyden and Myers, 1995
17. Boyden and Myers, 1995
18. Bissell and Sobhan, 1996
19. Boyden and Myers, 1995
20. US Department of Labor, 1996, p. ii
21. Bissell and Sobhan, 1996, p. 13
22. Van Liemt, 1994, cited in LeQuesne, 1996, p. 47
23. Durai, undated
24. ICFTU, 1996
25. LeQuesne, 1996, p. 50
26. Badry Zalami *et al.*, 1998
27. Durai, undated
28. US Department of Labor, 1966
29. US Department of Labor, 1966, p. v
30. Roberts, 1996
31. Levison, 1996
32. Hilowitz, 1997
33. Kruijtbosch, 1995
34. Rugmark-buro, 1998
35. Kruijtbosch, 1995, p. 10
36. *Bread for All*, Caritas, Swiss Lenten Fund, Berne Declaration, Swissaid, IGOT
37. Foundation STEP, 1998
38. Hilowitz, 1997
39. CEPC leaflet, 1996
40. US Department of Labor, 1998
41. Boyden and Myers, 1995
42. Anker and Melkas, 1996
43. Anker and Melkas, 1996, p. 26
44. Anker and Melkas, 1996, p. 43
45. Peace and Hulme, 1993
46. Peace and Hulme, 1993, p. 17
47. Rutherford, 1993, cited in Peace and Hulme, 1993, p. 49
48. Woodhead, 1997b
49. White, 1996
50. ICFTU, 1996
51. Bissell and Sobhan, 1996, p. 8

Bibliographical References

21st Century Learning Initiative. *Schooling Alone Can Not Successfully Prepare Young People for the Economic and Social Challenges of the 21st Century*, 1997

Addison, T. *et al. Child Labour: A Preliminary View*, unpublished paper. Centre for Development Studies, University of Bath, June 1997

Agnelli, S. *Street Children, a Growing Urban Tragedy*, Report for the Independent Commission on International Humanitarian Issues, 1986

Alarcón Glasniovich, W. *Entre calles y plazas, Peru*, ADEC, ATC, IEP and UNICEF, 1991

Allsebrook, A. and Swift, A. *Broken Promise: The World of Endangered Children*, United Kingdom, Headway/Hodder and Stoughton, 1989

Alston, P. (ed.) *The Best Interests of the Child: Reconciling Culture and Human Rights*, Oxford, Clarendon Press, 1994

Anderson, M.B. *What Are We Waiting For?* New York, UNICEF, 1992

Andersson, B-E. 'Var tredje elev vantrivs i skolan', (Every third pupil is unhappy in school) in *Dagens Nyheter*, 15 June 1997, Stockholm

Anker, R. and Melkas, H. *Economic Incentives for Children and Families to Eliminate or Reduce Child Labour*, Geneva, International Labour Office (ILO), 1996

An-Na'im, A. 'Cultural transformation and normative consensus on the best interests of the child', in Alston, 1994

Anon. 'Finding out about Child Labour, guidelines for rapid assessment', draft, May, 1996

Anti-Slavery International. *World Trade and Working Children*, Briefing Notes, London, ASI, 1995

Aptekar, L. 'Characteristics of the Street Children of Colombia', in *Child Abuse & Neglect*, Vol. 13, 1989, pp. 427—437

Aptekar, L. 'Are Colombian Street Children Neglected? The Contributions of Ethnographic and Ethnohistorical Approaches to the Study of Children', *Anthropology and Education Quarterly*, Vol. 22, 1991, pp. 326—349

Aragão-Lagergren, A. *Working Children in the Informal Sector in Managua*, Uppsala University, Uppsala, Geografiska Regionstudier Nr 31, 1997

Arita, M. and Shunsuke, Y. 'Karôji Shôkôgun' (The 'Overworthy Child' Syndrome), *Asahi Journal*, Paris, Éditions de Seuil, 1992

Armstrong, A. 'School and Sadza: Custody and the Best Interests of the Child in Zimbabwe' in Alston, P. (ed.) *The Best Interests of the Child: Reconciling Culture and Human Rights*, UNICEF-ICDC, Oxford UK, Clarendon Press, 1994

Ashagrie, K. 'Statistics on Child Labour: a Brief Report', unpublished report, Geneva, INTERDEP/ILO, 1993

Ashraf, S. *On the Experience of a Major Carpet Exporter in Eliminating Child Labour While Maintaining Profitability*, New Delhi, Centre for Social Action and Research, 1996

Atkinson, C. *Making Sense of Piaget, the philosophical roots*, London, Boston, Melbourne and Henley, Routledge & Kegan Paul, 1983

Awan, S.E. and Ali Khan, A. *Child Labour in Carpet Weaving Industry in Punjab, Pakistan*, Centre for the Improvement of Working Conditions and Environment. Punjab-Pakistan, UNICEF, 1992

Ayala, V. *El Trabajo Infantil en Bogotá*, unpublished, Bogotá, Departamento Nacional de Planeacion, 1982

Azer, A. 'Modalities of the best interests principle in education', in Alston, 1994

Aziz, K.M.A. and Maloney, C. *Life Stages, Gender & fertility in Bangladesh*, Dhaka, Bangladesh, ICDDRB, 1985

Bachman, M. G. 'Premature Affluence: do High School Seniors Earn too Much?', *Economic Outlook on the USA*, 10, 1983, pp. 64—67

Badry Zalami, F. *et al. Forgotten on the Pyjama Trail, A Case Study of Young Garment Workers in Méknès (Morocco) Dismissed From Their Jobs Following Foreign Media Attention*, International Working Group on Child Labour, 1998

Baker, R. with Panter-Brick, C. and Todd, A. 'Methods Used in Research with Street Children in Nepal', in Connolly, M. and Ennew, J. (eds.), 1996

Barker Knaul, G. and Knaul Barker, F. *Three Times Exploited, Three Times Empowered: The Urban Adolescent Woman in Difficult Circumstances*, final draft report for UNICEF, urban section, New York, 1992

Barros, R., *et al. Is Poverty the Main Cause of Child Work in Urban Brazil?* Unpublished paper, IPEA/ Brazil, April 1994

Becker, S. *Carers in Britain: Research, Policy and Practice*, unpublished report, Young Carers Development Programme, Social Services Inspectorate, Skipton House, Elephant and Castle, London, May 23rd, 1995

Bequele, A. and Myers, W.E. *First Things First in Child Labour*, Geneva, International Labour Office (ILO), 1995

Bissell, S. and Sobhan, B. *Child Labour and Education Programming in the Garment Industry of Bangladesh: Experiences and Issues*, UNICEF-Dhaka, 1996

Black, M. *In the Twilight Zone*, Geneva, International Labour Office, (ILO), 1995

Blanchet, T. *Lost Innocence, Stolen Childhoods*, Dhaka, The University Press Limited, 1996

Boyden, J. Report to Rädda Barnen, Stockholm, 1992

Boyden, J. Childhood and the Policy makers; A Comparative Perspective on the Globalization of Childhood, Chapter 9, in James, A. & Prout A. (eds) *Constructing and Reconstructing Childhood; contemporary issues in the sociological study of childhood*, UK, Falmer Press, 1990

Boyden, J. 'The Relationship Between Education and Child Work', *Innocenti Occasional Papers*, Florence, Italy, UNICEF, 1994

Boyden, J. and Ennew, J. (eds.) *Children in Focus*, Stockholm, Rädda Barnen, 1997

Boyden, J. with Holden, P. *Children of the Cities*, London, New Jersey, Zed Books Ltd, 1991

Boyden, J. and Myers, W. 'Exploring alternative approaches to combating child labour: Case studies from developing countries', *Innocenti Occasional Papers*, CRS 8, UNICEF, Florence, 1995

Boyden, J. Report to Rädda Barnen, Stockholm, forthcoming

Bremner, J.G. *Infancy*, Oxford, Blackwells, 1994

Briggs, J.L. 'The Creation of Value in Canadian Inuit Society', In *Int. Soc. Sci J.*, Vol. xxxi, no. 3, 1979

Briggs, J.L. 'Playwork as a Tool in the Socialization of an Inuit Child', *Arct. Med. Res.* 49, 1990, pp. 34—38

Briggs, J.L. 'Expecting the Unexpected: Canadian Inuit Training for an experimental lifestyle', unpublished paper at the Fourth International Conference On Hunting and Gathering Societies, Ontario, Canada, 1986

Brookover, W.B., Flood, P., Schweitzer, J. and Wisenbaker, J. *School Social Systems and Student Achievement: Schools can make a difference*, New York, Praeger, 1983

Bunster, X. and Chaney, E. *Sellers and Servants: Working Woman in Lima, Peru*, New York, Praeger, 1985

Burman, E. *Deconstructing Developmental Psychology*, London, New York, Routledge, 1994

Burra, N. 'Child Labour and Education; Issues Emerging from the Experiences of Some Developing Countries of Asia', Digest 28, UNESCO-UNICEF cooperative programme, Paris, 1989

Butterworth, G. and Light, P. (eds.) *Context and Cognition*, London, Harvester Wheatsheaf, 1992

Cain, M. 'Risk and Insurance: Perspectives on Fertility and Agrarian Change in India and Bangladesh', *Population and Development Review*, Vol. 3, No. 3, 1997

Caldwell, J., Reddy, N. and Caldwell, P. 'The Determinants of Fertility Decline in Rural South India' in Dyson and Crook (eds.) *India's Demography: Essays on the Contemporary Population*, South Asian Publishers Pvt. Ltd, New Delhi, 1984

Campbell J. K. *Honour, Family and Patronage; a study of institutions and moral values in a Greek mountain community*, OUP, USA, 1964, p. 156

Campos, R. M., Raffaelli, W., Ude, M., Greco, A., Ruff, J., Rolf, C.M., Antunes, N., Halsey, D., Greco and the Street Youth Study Group 'Social Networks and Daily Activities of Street Youth in Belo Horizonte, Brazil', *Child Development*, No. 65, 1994, pp. 319—330

Cariola, L.H. and Cerri, M.L. *Trabajo infantil:¿ Mito o realidad?*, Santiago, Centre de Investigacion y Desarrollo de la Educacion, CIDE, 1986

Cariola, L.H. and Cerri, M.L. *Trabajar y estudiar, ¿Cuál es el problema?*, Santiago, CIDE, 1989

Carpet Export Promotion Council. *"Kaleen"* My Future, leaflet, New Delhi, CEPC, (undated)

Center for Policy Studies in Education *Meeting the Educational Needs of Street and Working Children,* draft submitted to the Urban Section UNICEF, New York, 1993

Cho, H. 'Children in the Examination War in South Korea: A Cultural Analysis', in Stephens, S. (ed.) *Children and the Politics of Culture,* New Jersey, United Kingdom, Princeton University Press, 1995

Colbert, V., Garcia-Mendez, E. and Himes, J. *A Proposed Latin American and Caribbean Initiative: Eradicating Child Labour and Providing Basic Education for all Children,* unpublished draft paper, Florence, 15 February 1994

Collins, A.W. *Development During Middle Childhood.* Unpublished paper, Institute of Child Development, University of Minnesota, 51 East River Road, Minnesota 55455, USA, (undated)

Cornia, G. A. 'Child Poverty and deprivation in Industrialized Countries: Recent Trends and Policy Options', *Innocenti Occasional Papers,* no. 2, Florence, Italy, UNICEF-ICDC, 1990

Cunningham, H. *Children of the Poor,* Oxford, Blackwells, 1991

Cunningham, H. 'Combating Child Labour; The British Experience' in Cunningham, H. and Viazzo, P.P., 1996

Cunningham, H. and Viazzo, P.P. 'Some Issues in the Historical Study of Child Labour' in Cunningham, H. & Viazzo, P.P. (eds.), 1996

Cunningham, H. and Viazzo, P.P. (eds.) *Child Labour in Historical Perspective 1800—1985. Case studies from Europe, Japan and Colombia,* Florence, UNICEF, 1996

Dall, F. 'Education and the United Nations Convention on the Rights of the Child: The Challenge of Implementation', *Innocenti Occasional Papers,* no. 4, Florence, UNICEF, 1993

Dallape, F. 'Urban Children: a Challenge and an Opportunity', in Connolly, M. and Ennew, J. (eds.), 1996

Das, P.K., Shukla, K.P. and Öry, F.G. *An Occupational Health Programme for Adults and Children in the Carpet Weaving Industry, Mirzapur, India: A Case study in the Informal Sector,* Great Britain, Pergamon Press Ltd, 1992

Dave, R.H., Ranaweera, A.M. and Sutton, P.J. 'Meeting the Basic Learning Needs of Out-Of-School Children: Non-formal Approaches', unpublished UNESCO paper delivered at the World Conference On Education For All, Thailand, 5th—9th March 1990

Davin, A. 'Child Labour, the Working Class Family and Domestic Ideology in 19th Century Britain' *Development and Change, 13 (4), 1981*

Dawes, A. 'Political and Moral Learning in Contexts of Political Conflict', paper prepared for the meeting: The Mental Health of Refugee Children Exposed to Violent Environments, Refugee Studies Programme, University of Oxford, 1992a

Dawes, A. 'Psychological Discourse about Political Violence and its Effects on Children', paper prepared for the meeting: The Mental Health of Refugee Children Exposed to Violent Environments, Refugee Studies Programme, University of Oxford, 1992b

Derrien, J.M. *Labour Inspection and the Adoption of a Policy on Child Labour: Training Guide,* Labour Administration Branch, document No. 35, Geneva, ILO, 1994

Dube, L. 'The Economic Roles of Children in India: Methodological Issues' in Rogers G. and Standing G., (eds.), 1981

Dunn, K.A. and Runyan, C.W. 'Deaths at Work Among Children and Adolescents', *AJDC,* 1993, pp. 1044—1047

Durai, J. and Dottridge, M. (ed.) *Helping Business to Help Stop Child Labour, Comments on How Company Codes of Conduct, 'Child Labour Free' Labels and the Social Clause Can Help Eliminate Child Labour,* No. 14 in Child Labour Series, London, Anti-Slavery International, (undated)

Dy, F.J. 'Child Labour in Hazardous Employment', in Asian Regional Seminar on Child Labour: Education and Enforcement of Legislation, Geneva, International Labour Office, 1992

D'Lima, H. and Gosalia, R. *Street Children of Bombay: a Situational Analysis,* New Delhi, National Labour Institute, 1992

Education Section, Programme Division UNICEF *Strategies to Promote Girls' Education,* New York, UNICEF, 1992

Edwards, M. 'New Approaches to Children and Development: Introduction and Overview', *Journal of International Development;* Vol. 8, No. 6, 1996, pp. 813—827

Ekblad, S. 'Urban Stress and its Effects on Children's Lifestyles and Health in Industrialized Countries', *Innocenti Occasional Papers,* UCS 6, Florence, Italy, UNICEF, 1993

Elliott, A. 'Hidden Children. A study of ex-young carers of parents with mental health problems in Leeds', unpublished report, Leeds City Council Department of Social Services, Mental Health Development Section, October, 1992

Ennew, J. *Young hustlers: Work and Childhood in Jamaica*, London, Anti-Slavery Society, 1982

Ennew, J. 'Juvenile Street Workers In Lima Peru', Report for the ODA ESCOR grant Scheme, Department of Social Anthropology, University of Cambridge, June, 1985

Ennew, J. *Street and Working Children*, London, Save the Children, 1994a

Ennew, J. 'Rapid Assessment Procedure (RAP) For The Field Of Child Labour: Psycho-Social Measurement of Hazards of Work or Working Conditions', unpublished paper, 1994b

Ennew, J. and Milne, B. 'Methods of Research with Street and Working Children: An Annotated Bibliography', unpublished report prepared for Rädda Barnen, Stockholm, 1996

Espínola, B., Glauser, B., María Ortiz, R. and Ortiz de Carrizosa, S. *En La Calle. Menores Trabajadores de la Calle en Asuncion*, Paraguay, La Imprenta El Gráfica S.R.L., 1987

Felsman, K. 'Invulnerability: on Risk, Resiliency and Adaptation in Childhood', unpublished doctoral dissertation, Harvard University, Cambridge, USA, 1981

Field, N. 'The Child as Laborer and Consumer: The Disappearance of Childhood in Contemporary Japan' in Stephens, S. (ed.) *Children and the Politics of Culture*, New Jersey, United Kingdom, Princeton University Press, 1995

Fine, G.A. and Sandstrom, K.L. *Knowing Children, Participant Observation with Minors*, Sage, 1988

Forastieri, V. *Strategies to Address Child Labour from a Health Perspective*, Geneva, International Labour Office, (ILO), 1994

Fortes, M. 'Social and Psychological Aspects of Education in Taleland', supplement to *Africa* Vol. xi, No. 4, 1938

Foundation STEP. *STEP-Info*, Vol. 1, July 1996

Fraser, M. (ed.) *Risk and Resilience in Childhood, an Ecological Perspective*, Washington D.C., NASW Press, 1997

Friedman, S. 'Education for all Girls: A Human Right, a Social Gain', New York, NGO Committee on UNICEF, Education Working Group, report of the NGO consultation, 18th—19th November 1991

Fromm, E. and Maccoby, M. *Social Character in a Mexican Village*, New Jersey, Prentice Hall, 1970

Fyfe, F. 'Educational Strategies For Street and Working Children', International Programme on the Elimination of Child Labour (IPEC), paper prepared in connection with the Conference on Street Children and Psychoactive Substances: Innovation and Cooperation, World Health Organization, Geneva, 18th—22nd April 1994

Gabarino, J., Kostelny, K. and Dubrow, N. *No Place to be a Child*, Lexington Books, New York, 1991

Galway, Wolff and Sturgis, 1987 in G. Kent, 1989

Garmezy, N. 'Stressors of Childhood' in Garmezy, N. and Rutter, M. (eds.) *Stress, Coping, and Development in Children*, New York, McGraw-Hill, 1983

General Accounting Office, United States. 'Child Labour: Characteristics of Working Children', briefing report to Congressional Requesters, United States, June 1991

Gilmore, D.D. *Manhood in the Making, Cultural concepts of masculinity'*, Yale U.P., 1990

Goonsekere, S. *Child Labour in Sri Lanka: Learning From the Past*, Geneva, ILO, 1993

Goody, E. 'Kinship Fostering in Gonja' in Mayer, P. (ed.) *Socialization, the Approach from Social Anthropology (A.S.A. 8)*, London, Tavistock Publications, 1970

Gouveia A. *Youth Employment and Schooling in Brazil*, University of Sao Paolo FFLCH-Dept. of Social Sciences, (undated)

Grandos Téllez, M.F. *Gamines*, Bogotá, Editorial Temis Ltda, 1976

Greenberger, E., Steinberg, L. and Vaux, A. 'Adolescents who Work: Health and Behavioural Consequences of Job Stress', *Developmental Psychology*, 17, 1981

Greenberger, E. and Steinberg, L. *When Teenagers Work*, New York, Basic Books, Inc., Publishers, 1986

Greenfield, P.M. 'On Culture and Conservation' in Bruner, J.S., Oliver, R.R. and Greenfield, P.M. (eds.) *Studies in Cognitive Growth*, John Wiley, New York, 1996

Greenwood, S. *Daughters for Sale, Child Prostitution in Thailand: A Preliminary Analysis of 'Selling' Daughters into Prostitution*, unpublished BA dissertation, Anthropology Dept., Brunel University, London, 1996

Grootaert, C. and Kanbur, R. 'Child labour: An economic perspective', *International Labour Review*, Vol. 134, No. 6, 1995, pp.187—203

Grootaert, C. and Kanbur, R. 'Child Labour: A Review', background paper for the 1995 World Development Report on Labour, 1994

Guijt, I., Fuglesang, A. and Kisadha,Y. (eds.) *It is the Young Trees that Make a Forest Thick*. A report on Redd Barna learning experience with Participatory Rural Appraisal, Kampala, IIED, London and Redd Barna, Norway, 1994

Gunn, S. and Ostos, A. 'Dilemmas in Tackling Child Labour: the Case of Scavenger Children in the Philippines', *International Labour Review*, Vol. 131, No. 6, 1992, pp. 629—646

Hall, T. 'Education, Schooling and Participation' in Midgley, J. *et al. Community Participation, Social Development and the State*, London, Methuen, 1986

Hansson, G. *Social Clauses and International Trade*, London & Canberra, Croom Helm, New York, St. Martin's Press, 1983

Hart, R. Children's Participation: From Tokenism to Citizenship, *Innocenti Essays*, no. 4, UNICEF International Child Development Centre, Florence, Italy, 1992

Hecht, T. 'At Home in the Street. Street Children of Recife, Brazil' unpublished draft paper, Claremont, USA, 1995

Heywood, C. *Childhood in Nineteenth-Century France*, Cambridge, UK, Cambridge University Press, 1988

Hillman, M. (ed.) *Children, Transport and the Quality of Life*, London, Policy Studies Institute, 1993

Hillman, M., Adams, J. and Whitelegg, J. *One False Move... A Study of Children's Independent Mobility*, London, Policy Studies Institute, 1991

Hilowitz, J. *Labelling Child Labour Products. A Preliminary Study*, Geneva, ILO, 1997

Hobbs, S. and McKechnie, J. *Child Employment in Britain: A Social and Psychological Analysis*, Edinburgh, The Stationery Office, 1997

Holland, P. *What is a Child? Popular images of childhood*, London, Virago Press, 1992

Ianni, F.A.J. *The Search for Structure: A Report on American Youth Today*, New York, Free Press, 1989

Ingham, J. *Psychological Anthropology Reconsidered*, Cambridge, UK, Cambridge University Press, 1996

Instituto de Estudos Especiais da Pontifica Universidade Católica de São Paulo, *Mitos e Dilemas do Trabalho do Adôlescente*: Programas de Geração de Renda, São Paulo, Puc, 1994

International Programme for the Elimination of Child Labour (IPEC). 'Finding out about Child Labour (Quickly), a manual on how to do situation analysis on child labour using rapid assessment', unpublished draft, Geneva, International Labour Office, March, 1995

International Labour Office. *Towards Action Against Child Labour in Zimbabwe*, Geneva, International Labour Office (ILO), Interdepartmental Project on the Elimination of Child Labour, 1992a

International Labour Office. *Child Labour in Tanzania*, Geneva, International Labour Office, (ILO), Interdepartmental Project on the Elimination of Child Labour, 1992b

International Labour Office 'Child labour', paper prepared for the Committee on Employment and Social Policy of the Governing Body, GB.264/ESP/1, Geneva, ILO, November 1995

International Labour Office 'Child labour: What is to be done?', Document for discussion at the informal tripartite meeting at the ministerial level, Geneva, ILO, 12 June 1996a.

International Labour Office *Child Labour: Targeting the Intolerable*, Geneva, ILO, 1996b

International Labour Office. 'Combating the Most Intolerable Forms of Child Labour: A Global Challenge', background document prepared for the Amsterdam Child Labour Conference, 26th—27th February 1997, Geneva, ILO, 1997

International Labour Office, *Second Item on the Agenda: Date, Place and Agenda of the 86th (1998) Session of the International Labour Conference*, paper prepared for the Governing Body, Geneva, ILO, March 1996c

International Working Group on Child Labour. 'Preliminary Report: First International Meeting of Working Children', 29th November—9th December 1996, Kundapur India, 1996

International Working Group on Child Labour. 'Have We Asked the Children?', Discussion paper, February 1997

International Confederation of Free Trade Unions. *Breaking Down the Wall of Silence: How to combat child labour*, Brussels, ICFTU, 1985

International Confederation of Free Trade Unions. Campaign Document, Brussels, ICFTU, June 1994

International Confederation of Free Trade Unions. *'No Time to Play, Child Workers in the Global Economy'*, report prepared by Eileen Cadman, Brussels, ICFTU, 1996

Jahoda, G. and Lewis, I. (eds.) *Acquiring Culture: Cross Cultural Studies in Child Development'*, London, New York, Croom Helm, 1988

James, A. *Childhood Identities, Self and Social Relationships in the Experience of the Child*, Edinburgh University Press, 1993

James, A. and Prout, A. 'Hierarchy, Boundary and Agency: toward a theoretical perspective on childhood', *Sociological Studies of Children* 7, 1995, pp. 77—99

Jareg *et al.* 'Some Guidelines to Listening and Talking with Children who are Psychologically Distressed', unpublished paper, Oslo, Redd Barna, 1989

Jemmott, J.B. and Lock, S.E., 'Psychosocial Factors, Immunological Mediation, and Human Susceptibility to Infectious Diseases: How Much Do We Know?' *Psychological Bulletin*, Vol. 95, no. 1, 1984, pp. 78—104

Jenks, C. 'Introduction', in Jenks, C. (ed.) *The Sociology of Childhood; Essential Readings*, London, Batsford Academic and Educational Ltd, 1982

Johnson, V. *'Introduction: Starting a dialogue on children's participation'*, PLA Notes 25, IIED, London, February 1996

Johnson, H., Hill, J. and Ivan-Smith, E. *Listening to Smaller Voices; Children in an Environment of Change*, London, Action Aid, 1995

Kanbargi, R. 'Child Labour in India: The Carpet Industry of Varanasi' in Bequele, A. and Boyden, J. (eds.) *Combatting Child Labour*, ILO, Geneva, 1988

Kanbargi, R. and Kulkarni, P. 'Child Labour, Schooling and Fertility in Rural Karnataka, South India', mimeo, Bangalore, Population Research Centre, Institute for Social and Economic Change, (undated)

Karmaker, R. *et al.* 'Child Workers in Informal Sector, A Dhaka City Scenario', unpublished paper, 1994

Kirby, L.D. and Frazer, M. 'Risk and Resilience in Childhood' in Fraser, M. (ed.), 1997, pp. 34—49.

Kitzinger, S. *Ourselves as Mothers; the universal experience of motherhood*, London and New York, Doubleday, 1992

Knaul Barker, F. 'Young Workers, Street Life and Gender: The Effect of Education and Work Experience on Earnings in Colombia', PhD. Thesis, Cambridge Mass., Harvard University, 1995

Kohlberg, L. 'From Is To Ought' in Mischel, T. (ed.) *Cognitive Development and Epistemology*, New York., Academic press, 1971

Kohn, M. L. and Schooler, C. *Work and Personality: An Inquiry into the Impact of Social Stratification*, Norwood, N.J., Ablex, 1983

Kruijtbosch, M. *Rugmark — A Brief Resumé of Concept to Reality for Visual Guarantee of Carpets Made Without Child Labour*, New Delhi, South Asian Coalition on Child Servitude, 1995

Kvale, S. *InterViews; an Introduction to Qualitative Research Interviewing*, Thousand Oaks, London, New Delhi Sage Publications, 1996

La Fontaine, J. *Initiation Ritual and Secret Knowledge across the World*, London, Pelican, 1985

La Fontaine, J. S. (ed.) *Introduction to, Sex & Age as Principles of Social Differentiation*, London, Academic Press, 1978

Landes, W. and Solomon, L. 'Compulsory schooling legislation: an economic analysis of law and social change in the nineteenth century', *Journal of Economic History*, 1972

Lane, R. *The Market Experience*, Cambridge, UK, Cambridge University Press, 1991

Laserna, C. 'Lessons in Milking and Math' in Ross, J. and Bergam, V. (eds.) *Through the Looking Glass: Children and Health Promotion Ottawa*, Canadian Public Health Association, 1990

LeQuesne, C. *Reforming World Trade — The Social and Environmental Priorities*, Oxford, Oxfam Publications, 1996

LeVine, R.A., LeVine, S., Liedermann, P.H., Brazelton, T.B., Dixon, S., Richman, A. and Keffer, C.H. *Child Care and Culture: Lessons from Africa*, Cambridge, UK, Cambridge University Press, 1994

Levison, D. 'Children's Labour Force Activity and Schooling in Brazil', unpublished dissertation submitted in partial fulfilment of the requirements or the degree of Doctor of Philosophy in the University of Michigan, 1991

Levison, D. 'Child work and schooling in Brazil's cities: lessons from survey data', mimeo, Center for Population Analysis and Policy, University of Minesota, Minneapolis, USA, 1993

Levison, D., *et al.* 'Is Child Labour Really Necessary in India's Carpet Industry?', Labour market paper no. 15, Geneva, ILO, 1996

Leyens, J. and Mahjoub, A. 'The Psycho-Social Effect of War on Children and Adolescents', mimeo of the Catholic University of Louvain-la-Neuve, Belgium, (undated)

Liebel, M. 'What do working children want?', in *Envio, Managua, Nicaragua, Universidad Centro-Americana*, Vol. 15, No. 175—76, February—March 1996

Lloyd, C. B. *Investing in the Next Generation: The Implication of High Fertility at the Level of the family*, Research Division Working Paper no. 63, New York, The Population Council, 1994

Mancian, M. and Romer, C.J. (eds.) '*Accidents in Childhood and Early Adolescence: the Role of Research*', Geneva World Health Organization (WHO) and INSERM, 1991

Manning, W. Parenting Employed Teenagers, *Youth and Society*, Vol. 22, No. 2, December, 1990, pp. 184—200

Mansurov, V. *Child Work in Russia*, Geneva, ILO, INTERDEP/CL/1993/1,1993

Marcus, R., and Harper, C. *Small Hands, Children in the Working World*. Save the Children, Working Paper 16, London, 1996

Marsh, P., Rosser, E. and Harre, R. *The Rules of Disorder*, London, Routledge and Kegan Paul, 1980

Mattoo, G. M., Rauf, A. and Zutshi, M. L. 'Health Status of School Age Children Employed in Carpet Weaving in Ganderbal Block', *British Journal of Industrial Medicine*, 43, 1986, pp. 698—701

Mayall, B. 'Introduction' in Mayall, B. (ed.) *Children's Childhoods: Observed and Experienced*, London, Washington, The Falmer Press, 1994

McGranahan, D. *Improvement of Information on the Conditions of Children*, United Nations Institute for Social Development, Geneva, 1980

McGranahan, D., Scott, W. and Richard, C. '*Qualitative Indicators of Development*', United Nations Institute for Social Development, Discussion paper 15, Geneva, November 1990

McGuigan, M.M. 'Exposure of Working Children to toxic Substances, its medical control', lecture presented at the Regional Experts' unpublished paper given to Pre-Congress Workshop on Child Labour in Africa: Safety, Health and Psychosocial Development, Dakar, Senegal, 4th—5th December, 1993

McKechnie, J. *et al. Still Forgotten: Child Employment in Dumfries and Galloway*, Glasgow, Scottish Low Pay Unit, 1994

McKechnie, J., Lindsay, S. and Hobbs, S. 'Child employment: a Neglected Topic?', *The Psychologist*, May 1996

Mead, M. *Coming of Age in Samoa*. Melbourne, London, Baltimore, Pelican Books, 1954

Melton, G.B. 'Socialization in the Global economy: Respect for the Dignity of Children', *American Psychologist*, 46, 1991, pp. 66—71

Mendoza, I. *Trabajo Infantil Rural en el Peru: la Agricultura de Esparragos en la Costa Norte (en Valle de Viru)*, Geneva, ILO, INTERDEP/CL/1993/2, 1993

Mizen, P. 'Learning the Hard Way: The Extent and Significance of Child Working in Britain', *British Journal of Education and Work*, Vol. 5, No.1, 1991, pp. 5—17

Montgomery, H. 'Public Vice and Private Virtue: Child prostitution in Pattaya, Thailand', unpublished PhD thesis, Dept. Social Anthropology, University of Cambridge, UK, 1996

Morrow, V. 'Rethinking Childhood Dependency: Children's Contributions to the Domestic Economy', in Smith, D. and Hetherington, K. (eds.) *The Sociological Review*, Vol. 44, No.1, February 1996, published for Keele University, Blackwell Publishers

Morrow, V. and Richards, M. 'The Ethics of Social Research with Children: an overview', *Children and Society*, Vol. 10, 1996, pp. 91—105

Mortimer, J. and Finch, M. 'The Effects of Part-time Work on Adolescent Self-concept and Achievement', in Borman, K. and Reisman, I. (eds.), *Becoming a Worker*, Norwood, New Jersey, Ablex, 1987

Mueller, E. 'The Economic Value of Children in Peasant Agriculture' in Rider, G. (ed.), *Population and Development: The Search for Selective Interventions*, London and Baltimore, published for Resources for the Future by John Hopkins University Press, 1976

Muñoz, C., Pachón, X.C. *Gamines Testimonios*. Bogotá, Colombia, Carlos Valencia Editores, 1980

Mussen, P., Conger, J. and Kagan, J. *Child Development and Personality*, New York, Harper and Row, 1984

Myers, W.E. *Characteristics Of Some Urban Working Children: A Comparison Of Four Surveys From South America*, Geneva, International Labour Review, 1989

Myers, W.E. (ed.) *Protecting Working Children*, London, ZED Books, 1991

Myers, R. *The Twelve Who Survive*, London, USA, Canada, Routledge, 1992

Nag, M., White, B. and Peet, R. 'An Anthropological Approach to the Study of the Economic Value of

Children in Java and Nepal', *Current Anthropology*, Vol. 19, No. 2, 1978, pp. 293—306

Nardinelli, C. *Child Labour and the Industrial Revolution*, Bloomington, University of Indiana Press, 1990

National Institute of Urban Affairs (NIUA). 'Dimension of Urban Poverty: a Situational Analysis' research Studies Series no. 25, New Delhi, 1980

Nieuwenhuys, O. 'The Paradox of Child Labour and Anthropology', *Annual Review of Anthropology*, Vol. 25, 1996, pp. 237—51

Nieuwenhuys, O. *Children's Lifeworlds, Gender, Welfare and Labour in the Developing World*, Routledge, London, 1994

Nunes, T., Dias Schliemann, A. and William Carraher, D. *Street Mathematics and School Mathematics*, Cambridge, UK, Cambridge University Press, 1993

Oloko, B.A. 'Children's work in urban Nigeria' in Myers, W.E., *Protecting Working Children*, London, Zed Books

Onyango, P., Orwa, A.A., Ayako, J.B., Ojwang and Kariuki, P.W. *Research on Street Children in Kenya*, Nairobi, ANPPCAN, May, 1991

Palacios, M. 'Child Labour in Colombia', paper presented at Child Labour Workshop, Institute of Development Studies, University of Sussex, Brighton, 1981

Palmer, O.J. *The Psychological Assessment of Children*, second edition, New York, Chichester, Brisbane, Toronto, Singapore, John Wiley and Sons Inc., 1983

Patil, B. 'The Working children of Bangalore City', unpublished report, Bangalore, Indian Institute of Management, (undated)

Peace, G. and Hulme D. 'Children and Income Generating Programmes', London, Save the Children Overseas Department Working Paper No. 6, SCF, 1993

Peacock, A. 'Access to Science Learning for Children in Rural Africa', unpublished paper presented at the World Conference on Research and Practice in Children's Rights, University of Essex, Colchester, September 8th—11th, 1992

Peltzer, K. 'Children as Commercial Farm Labourers and Prostitutes in Africa' in Child Labour in Africa Proceedings of the First International Workshop on Child Abuse in Africa, Enugu, Nigeria, 27th April — 2nd May, 1986

Penna Firme, T., Stone, V.I. and Tijiboy, J.A. 'The generation and observation of evaluation indicators of the psychosocial development of participants in programmes for street children', in Myers, W.E. (ed.) 1989

Philipps. 'The School as a means of Social Betterment' in Whitehouse, J.H. (ed.) *The Problems of Boy Life*, London, King, 1912, pp. 206—27

Pollack, S.H., Landrigan, P.J. and Mallino, D.L. 'Child Labour in 1990: Prevalence and Health Hazards' *Annu. Rev. Public Health*, 11, 1990, pp. 359—75

Pond, C. and Searle, A. 'The Hidden Army: Children at Work in the 1990s', London, Low Pay Unit Pamphlet, No. 55, (undated)

PSCC Philippine Social Science Council. 'Situation Analysis for the Metro Manila cities, Olongapo and Davao', report prepared by A. Torres for the Urban Child Project, UNICEF International Child Development Centre, Florence and UNICEF, Manila, 1991

Punamaki, R. Psychological Stress of Palestinian Mothers and their Children in Conditions of Political Violence, *the Quaterly Newsletter of the Laboratory of Comparative Human Cognition*, 9, 1987, pp. 116—119

Punch, S. 'Involving children in Research: Using a Variety of Research Methods in Rural Bolivia', draft paper presented at INTRAC Workshop: Involving Children in Research for Programme Planning and Policy Development, Ruskin College, Oxford, July 1997

Qvortrup, J. 'Childhood in a Post-Industrial World', *Development, Journal of SID*, Vol. 1, 1996

Qvortrup, J., Bardy, M., Sgritta, G. and Wintersberger, H. (eds.) *Childhood Matters*, Aldershot, Avebury, 1994

Rahman, M. 'Hazardous Child Labour in Bangladesh, Dhaka', unpublished study for Department of Labour Government of Bangladesh, 1996

Reynolds, P. 'Through the Looking Glass. Participant Observation with Children in Southern Africa', unpublished paper delivered at a Workshop on the Ethnography of Childhood, King's College, Cambridge, UK, July 1986

Reynolds, P. 'Children in Zimbabwe. Rights and Power in Relation to Work', *Anthropology Today*, Vol. 1, No. 3, June 1985, p. 17

Reynolds, P. *Dance Civet Cat: Child Labour in the Zambezi Valley*, London, Athens, Zimbabwe, Zed Books Ltd, Baobab Books, Ohio University Press, 1991

Richman, J.M. and Bowen, L.G.'School Failure: An Ecological Interactional-Developmental Perspective' in Fraser, M.W. (ed.) 1997, pp. 95—116

Richman, N. *Communicating with Children: Helping children in Distress,* London, Save the Children Fund (UK), 1993

Richter, K. and Ard-am, O. *Child Labour in Thailand's Fishing Industry,* Salaya, Nakhon Pathom, Thailand: Institute for Population and Social Research, Mahidol University, 1995

Roberts, L. Sporting Goods Industry Position Paper, SGI, London, 1996

Robertson, A.F. *Beyond the family: The Social Organization of Human Reproduction,* Polity Press, 1991

Rodgers, G. and Standing, G. (eds.) *Child Work, Poverty and Underdevelopment,* Geneva, International Labour Office, 1981

Rogoff, B. *Apprenticeship in thinking,* New York, Oxford University Press, 1990

Rogoff, B.S., Pirrotta,S., Fox, N. and White, S. 'Age Assignment of Roles and Responsibilities in Children; A cross-cultural survey', *Human Development (18),* 1975

Rogoff, B. and Chavajay, P. 'What's Become of Research on the Cultural Basis of Cognitive Development?', *American Psychologist,* Vol. 50, No. 10, 1995 pp. 859—877

Rosenzweig, M. and Evenson, R. 'Fertility, Schooling, and the Economic Contribution of Children in Rural India: An Econometric Analysis', *Econometrica,* Vol. 45, No. 5, 1977

Rugmark-buro Information Update, RMF, Göttingen, 1998

Rutter, M. 'Psychosocial Resilience and Protective Mechanisms', *American Journal of Orthopsychiatry,* 57, 1987, pp. 316—30

Rutter, M. 'Pathways from Childhood to Adult Life', *J.Child Psychiat.,* Vol. 30, No.1, 1989, pp. 23-51

Rutter, M., Mortimore, P., Ouston, J. and Smith, A. *Fifteen Thousand Hours: Secondary schools and their effects on children,* Harvard University Press, Cambridge, Mass., 1979

Salazar 'Child Labour in Bogotá's Quarries and Brickyards' in Bequele, A. and Boyden, J. (eds.) *Combating Child Labour,* Geneva, ILO, 1988

Salazar, M.C. and Alarcón Glasniovich, W. 'Better

Schools: Less Child Work. Child Work and Education in Brazil, Colombia, Ecuador, Guatemala and Peru', *Innocenti Essays,* No.7, Florence, UNICEF, 1996

Salter, W. 'The Forgotten Children: Child Labour in Domestic Service', unpublished report, Geneva, ILO, 1993

Satyanarayana, K., Prasanna Krishna, T. and Narasinga Roa, B.S. 'Effect of Early Childhood Under Nutrition and Child Labour on Growth and Adult Nutritional Status of Rural Indian Boys Around Hyderabad', *Human Nutrition: Clinical Nutrition,* 40c, 1986, pp. 131—39

Save the Children. *Towards a Children's Agenda: New Challenges for Social Development,* London, Save the Children, 1995

Schaffer, H.R. *Making Decisions about Children: Psychological Questions and Answers,* Oxford, Blackwells, 1990

Schaffer, H.R. *Social Development,* Oxford, Blackwells, 1996

Sheffield, J. and Diejomaoh, V. *Non-formal Education in African Development,* New York, African-American Institute, 1972

Scheper-Hughes, N. and Hoffman, D. 'Street kids', *Worldview,* Vol. 10, No. 1, Winter 1996—97

Scheper-Hughes, N. and Lock, M. 'The mindful body: A prolegomenon to future work in medical anthropology', *Medical Anthropology Quarterly,* Vol. 3, No. 1, 1989, pp. 6—41

Schiefelbein, E. 'School-Related Economic Incentives In Latin America: Reducing Drop-Out and Repetition and Combating Child Labour', *Innocenti Occasional Papers,* CRS 12, Florence, Italy, UNICEF, 1997

Schildkrout, E. 'Roles of children in urban Kano', in La Fontaine, J.S. (ed.), *Sex and Age as Principles of Social Differentiation,* London, Academic Press, 1978

Shonkoff, J.P. 'The Biological Substrate and Physical Health in Middle Childhood' in W.A. Collins. (ed.) *Development During Middle Childhood: The Years from Six to Twelve,* Washington D.C., National Academy of Sciences Press, 1984

Schubert, C. 'Non-Formal Education For Working and Street Children: UNICEF Experiences and Observations in Asia', in Asian Regional Seminar on Child Labour: Education and Enforcement of Legislation, Geneva, International Labour Office, 1992

Siddiq, F. and Patrinos, H. *Child Labour: Issues, Causes and Interventions,* Human Resources

Development and Operations Policy, Working Paper, Washington D.C., World Bank, June 1995

Silvey, J. 'Education', in MacPherson, S., Social Policy in the Third World, UK, Wheatsheaf Books Ltd, 1982

Sinclair, M. 'Education and Training for Out-Of-School Afghan Refugee Youth and Adults', Convergence, Vol. XXIII, No. 3, 1990, pp. 49—56

Singh, M., Kaura, V.D. and Khan, S.A. Working Children in Bombay - a Study, New Delhi, National Institute of Public Cooperation and Child Development, 1980

Soy, M. 'Helping Out: Children's Labour Participation in Chinese Take-away Businesses in Britain', in Brannen, J. and O'Brien, M. (eds.) Children in Families: Research and Policy, London and Washington, Falmer Press, 1996

Stafford, C. The Roads of Chinese Childhood, Cambridge, UK, Cambridge University Press, 1995

Stallones. 'Fatal Farm injuries among Children in Colorado Farms 1980—88' Paper presented at the Third International Symposium: Issues in Health, Safety and Agriculture', Saskatoon, Canada, May 10th—15th 1992

Steinberg, L. Adolescence, third edition, New York, McGraw-Hill, 1993

Steinberg, L., Greenberger, E., Jacobi, M. and Garduque, L. 'Early Work Experience: a Partial Antidote for Adolescent Egocentrism', Journal of Youth and Adolescence, Vol. 10, No. 2, 1981, pp. 141—157

Steinberg, L., Greenberger, E., Vaux, A. and Ruggiero, M. 'Early Work Experience Effects on Adolescent Occupational Socialization', Youth and Society, 12, 1981, pp. 403—22

Steinberg, L. Greenberger, E., Guarduque, L., Ruggiero, M. and Vaux, A.'Effects of Working on Adolescent Development', Developmental Psychology, No. 18, 1982

Steinberg, L., Fegley, S. and Dornbusch, S.M. 'Negative Impact of Part-time Work on Adolescent Adjustment: Evidence from a Longitudinal Study', Developmental Psychology, 29, 2, 1993, pp. 171—180

Stern, D. 'School-Based Enterprise and the Quality of Work Experience. A study of High School Students', Youth and Society, Vol. 15, No. 4, June 1984, pp. 401—27

Stryker, J. 'The Age of Innocence Isn't What It Once Was', in The New York Times, Sunday, July 13, 1997

Super, C.M. and Harkness, S. 'The Developmental Niche: A Conceptualization of the Interface of Child and Culture', International Journal of Behavioural Development, 9, 1986, pp. 545—69

Super, C. M. and Harkness, S. 'Cultural Perspectives on Child Development' in Wagner, D. and Stevenson, H. (eds.) Cultural Perspectives on Child Development, W.H. Freeman, 1992

Swart, J. 'An Anthropological Study of Street Children in Hillbrow, Johannesburg, with special reference to their moral values', M.A Dissertation in Anthropology, University of South Africa, 1988

Swift, A. Children for Social Change: Education for Citizenship of Street and Working Children in Brazil, Nottingham, UK, Educational Heretics Press, 1997

Szanton Blanc, C. with contributors. Urban Children in Distress, Switzerland, Australia, Belgium, France, Germany, UK, India, Japan, Malaysia, Russia, Singapore, USA, Gordon and Breach, 1994

Taçon, P. 'My Child', unpublished report for UNICEF, New York, April, 1981.

Theis, J. 'Children and Participatory Appraisals: Experiences from Vietnam', PLA Notes25, London, IIED, 1996

Thompson, R.A. 'Developmental changes in Research Risk and Benefit: A Changing Calculus of Concerns' in Stanley, B. and Sieber, B. (eds.) Social Research on Children and Adolescents California, UK, New Delhi Sage Publications Inc., 1993, pp. 31—64

Tolfree, D. Draft Report to Rädda Barnen, 1997

Turton, R., Straker, G. and Moosa, F. 'The experiences of violence in the lives of township youth in "unrest" and "normal" conditions', South African Journal of Psychology, Vol. 21, No. 2, 1991

Tyler, F.B., Tyler, S.L., Echeverry, J.J. and Zea, M.C. 'Making it on the Streets in Bogotá: A Psychosocial Study of Street Youth', Genetic, Social & General Psychology,Vol. 117, No. 4, 1991, pp. 395—417

US Department of Labor. Bureau of International Labor Affairs. By the Sweat & Toil of Children, Vol. I, The Use of Child Labor in American Imports, Washington. D.C., 1994

US Department of Labor. Bureau of International Labor Affairs. By the Sweat & Toil of Children, Vol. II, The Use of Child Labor in US Agricultural Imports & Forced and Bonded Labor, Washington D.C., 1995

US Department of Labor. The Apparel Industry and Codes of Conduct: A Solution to the International Child Labor Problem?, Washington D.C., 1996

US Department of Labor. Bureau of International Labor Affairs. *By the Sweat & Toil of Children, Vol. IV, Consumer Labels and Child Labor*, Washington. D.C., 1998

UNESCO. World Education Report, Paris, UNESCO, 1993

UNICEF. *Los niños de las Américas Santa Fé de Bogotá*, UNICEF, 1992

UNICEF. *The State of the World's Children*, Oxford University Press, 1997

UNICEF. 'Towards a comprehensive strategy for the development of the young child', an Inter-agency Policy Review, New York, unpublished, UNICEF, Education Cluster, March, 1993

Vaillant G. and Vaillant, C. 'Natural History of Male Psychological Health: Work as a Predictor of Positive Mental Health', *American Journal of Psychiatry*, 138:1, 1981, pp. 433—40

Van Beers, H. 'In Search of the Girl', InDra occasional paper no. 2, Amsterdam, University of Amsterdam, 1994

Vlassof, M. 'Labour Demand and Economic Utility: A Case Study in Rural India', *Population Studies*, Vol. 33, No.3, 1979, pp. 415—28

Vygotsky, L.S. *Mind in Society: The Development of Higher Psychological Processes*, Cambridge, Mass, Harvard University Press, 1978

Waksler, F.C. *Studying the Social Worlds of Children: Sociological Readings*, London, Falmer Press, 1991

Walkerdine, V. 'Developmental Psychology and the Child-centred pedagogy: the insertion of Piaget's theory into primary school practice' in Heurigies, J. et al. (eds.) *Changing the Subject*, London, Methuen, 1984

Walkerdine, V. 'Beyond Developmentalism?', *Theory and Psychology*, 3, 1993, pp. 451—70

Weiner, M. *The Child and the State in India: Child Labour and Education Policy in Comparative Perspective*, Delhi, Oxford University Press, 1991

Weithorn, L.A.'Children's Capacities to decide about Participation in Research', IRB: A Review of Human Subjects' Research 5(4), 1983

Weithorn, L. A. and Scherer, D. G. 'Children's Involvement in Research Participation Decisions: Psychological Considerations' in Grodin, M.A. and Glantz, L.H (eds.) *Children as Research Subjects: Science, Ethics and Law*, Oxford, Oxford University Press, 1994

Werner and Smith *Vulnerable but Invincible. A longitudinal study of resilient children and youth*, New York, Cambridge University Press, 1992

White, B. 'The Economic Importance of Children in a Javanese Village', mimeo, 1974

White, B. and Tjandraningsih, I. 'Rural Children in the Industrialization Process: Child and Youth labour in "Traditional" and "Modern" Industries in West Java, Indonesia', unpublished, ISS, The Hague and Akatiga Foundation, Bandung, 1992

White, B. (ed.) (1982) 'Child Workers', in *Development and Change, A Special Edition*, Vol.13, No. 3, October 1982, London, SAGE Publications

White, B. *Children, Work and 'Child Labour': Changing Responses to the Employment of Children*, The Hague, Netherlands, Institute of Social Studies, 1994

White, B. 'Globalization and the Child Labour Problem', *Journal of International Development*, Vol. 8, No. 6, 1996, pp. 829—39

Whiting, J.M.W. and Child, I.L. *Child Training and Personality: A Cross-Cultural Study*, New Haven, Yale University Press, 1953

Whiting, B.B. and Whiting, J.W.M. *Children of Six Cultures: a psycho-cultural analysis*, Cambridge, Mass., Harvard University Press, 1975

WHO, report of a study group. 'Children at Work: Special Health Risks', World Health Organization Technical Report Series 756, Geneva, World Health Organization, 1987

Wikan, U. 'The Situation of the Girl Child In Bhutan', final report to UNICEF, Butan, unpublished report, 1989

Wilk, V. (1993) 'Health Hazards to Children in Agriculture', *American Journal of Industrial Medicine*, 24, 1993, pp. 283—90

Woodhead 'Is there a Place for Work in Child Development, unpublished draft report for Rädda Barnen, Centre for Human Development and Learning, The Open University, United Kingdom, September, 1997a

Woodhead, M. 'Psychological and Cultural Construction of Children's Needs', Chapter 3, James A., Prout, A. (eds.) *Constructing and Reconstructing Childhood*, Falmer Press, 1990

Woodhead, M. 'Children's Perceptions of their Working Lives' draft summary report, for Rädda Barnen, Centre for Human Development and Learning, The Open University, United Kingdom April/May 1997b

Wright, R. 'The Hidden Cost of Child Labour', *Family Circle*, 3.12.91, pp. 83—136

Wright, J.D, Kaminsky, D. and Witting, M. 'Health and Social Conditions of Street Children in Honduras' in *The Experience of Project Alternatives, 1996, pp. 279—83*, reprinted from the *American Journal Diseases of Children*, March 1993, vol.147

Zeitlin, M., Ghassemi, H. and Mansour, M. *Positive Deviance in Child Nutrition, with Emphasis on Psychosocial and Behavioural Aspects and Implications for Development*, Tokyo, The United Nations University, 1990

Zeleke, B. 'Corporal Punishment and its Impacts in Addis Ketema Comp. Sec. School', unpublished draft paper, Addis Ababa, 1995

Zelizer, V.A. *Pricing the Priceless Child*, New York, Basic Books Inc., 1985